Praise for *The Conservative Party after Brexit*

'Written by one of Britain's most respected experts on British politics, this timely book clearly explains the rapidly unfolding crises and political drama of Brexit and its impact on the Conservatives since 2016. Bale writes with wonderful flair and panache, and skilfully provides a highly absorbing and engaging account of recent momentous events.'

Peter Dorey, Professor of British Politics, Cardiff University

'Tim Bale provides a masterly account of the twists and turns in the fortunes of the Conservative party since the Brexit Referendum. For anyone who wants to understand the desperate position in which the party now finds itself this book is an essential guide.'

Andrew Gamble, Chair in Politics, University of Sheffield

'*The Conservative Party After Brexit* is a rare combination: gripping and erudite. A triumph of objectivity and pace.'

Garry Gibbon, Political Editor, Channel 4 News

'A fascinating book with so much detail on why the political explosions and implosions of the past few years have happened, and what they'll mean for politics in years to come. It's essential reading to understand where the Conservative party is today.'

Isabel Hardman, author, Assistant Editor of the Spectator, and presenter of the BBC's *Week in Westminster*

'Tim Bale has written a careful, immaculately constructed, balanced and convincing account of what happens when a governing party ceases to remember what it most believes in.'

Andrew Marr, LBC presenter and Political Editor of the New Statesman

'An extraordinary account of an astonishing period. It's only seeing it committed to print that rams home to me what a privilege it's been to be in the thick of it and trying to make sense of it. Tim brings an admirable clarity to an incredible sequence of events.'

Chris Mason, BBC Political Editor

'One of the most acute, witty, and historically-informed observers of British politics, bringing a fierce historian's eye to the present-tense.'

Rory Stewart, author and co-presenter of *The Rest is Politics* podcast

'Brilliantly captures a governing party struggling with the historic decision to leave the EU and its many epic consequences…a dream book for those who relish a gripping narrative combined with illuminating analysis.'

Steve Richards, author and presenter of the BBC's *Week in Westminster* and the *Rock & Roll Politics* podcast

'Tim Bale's gripping book perfectly captures the facts, the drama and the mood of the "Brexit wars" that set the Conservative Party on its current reckless and self-destructive path. Some of it I read through my fingers like a horror story, but I couldn't put it down!'

Amber Rudd, former Conservative Secretary of State

The Conservative Party after Brexit

THE CONSERVATIVE PARTY AFTER BREXIT

Turmoil and Transformation

Tim Bale

polity

First published in 2023 by Polity Press

Polity Press
65 Bridge Street
Cambridge CB2 1UR, UK

Polity Press
111 River Street
Hoboken, NJ 07030, USA

ISBN-13: 978-1-5095-4601-5

A catalogue record for this book is available from the British Library.

Library of Congress Control Number: 2022948488

Typeset in 11.5 on 14pt Adobe Garamond
by Fakenham Prepress Solutions, Fakenham, Norfolk NR21 8NL
Printed and bound in Great Britain by CPI Group (UK) Ltd, Croydon

The publisher has used its best endeavours to ensure that the URLs for external websites referred to in this book are correct and active at the time of going to press. However, the publisher has no responsibility for the websites and can make no guarantee that a site will remain live or that the content is or will remain appropriate.

Every effort has been made to trace all copyright holders, but if any have been overlooked the publisher will be pleased to include any necessary credits in any subsequent reprint or edition.

For further information on Polity, visit our website:
politybooks.com

Contents

Those who know how to win are much more numerous than those who know how to make proper use of their victories.
Polybius, *Histories*, Book 10, Ch. 31

Acknowledgements

So many people have contributed – most of them unwittingly – to this book that it's clearly impossible to name them all. Most obviously, that includes the journalists, the bloggers, the tweeters, and the politicians whose words I've read or listened to, sometimes in person, sometimes 'by remote', whether on Zoom or in the media, be it legacy or social (especially Twitter). The same goes to all those academics, pollsters, and think tankers whose work on policy and politics has provided both food for thought and fascinating data. Without those people, there would be no book, so I owe them a huge debt of gratitude which, I know, can't really be compensated for by a fleeting appearance in the notes or the text. As for institutions, as well as my own university, Queen Mary University of London (QMUL), and its Mile End Institute, I would like to thank the ESRC initiative UK in a Changing Europe, and in particular its Director, Anand Menon, firstly, for creating the invaluable repository of first-hand interviews that is the Brexit Witness Archive and, secondly, for letting me disappear off to write this book. I wouldn't have been able to do that, however, without the incredibly generous funding provided by the Leverhulme Trust, which kindly awarded me a Major Research Fellowship that gave me the time, space, and resources to put it together. I'd also like to acknowledge the ESRC for funding the Party Members Project, research from which (conducted by me, Paul Webb, and Monica Poletti, with the help of YouGov) features in the pages of this book. Thanks go, too, to Palgrave Macmillan for permission to draw, in several places, on material from *The British General Election of 2019*. As usual, this book's publisher, Polity (especially Louise Knight and Inès Boxman, and also the two readers they persuaded to review the manuscript), have been absolutely brilliant. The same goes for my copy-editor, Justin Dyer. Then, of course, there are the various colleagues, collaborators, and co-authors who have had to put up with me not only banging on about the Tories (and, in some cases, whining pathetically about being selected as an 'impact case study' for the Research Excellence Framework [REF]) but also occasionally delaying other things I've committed to in order to progress this particular project. In addition to everyone (not just academics but our wonderful professional services staff) at QMUL's School of Politics and International Relations, people who spring most immediately to mind in this context (with red-faced apologies to anyone I've missed) include Paul Webb, Cristóbal Rovira Kaltwasser, Rob Ford, Will Jennings, Paula Surridge, Anand Menon (yes, him again), Alan Wager, Phil Cowley, Karl Pike, Matthew Barnfield, Patrick Diamond, Lee Jones, Sophie Harman, James Dunkerley, James Strong, Kim Hutchings, David Williams, Matthew Hilton, Sofia Cusano, and my always inspirational friend (and Twitter threadmeister) Rob Saunders. The person who has had most to put up with and has also done most to help me out, however, is, as per, my wife Jackie. I dedicate this book to her, as well as – not for the first (nor, I hope, the last) time – to Javi, Bel, and Jack.

1

Going with the flow

10 p.m. on *Thursday, 12 December 2019: time for the exit poll to drop. To no-one's great surprise, it forecast a convincing overall majority and another term in office for the Conservative Party. The Prime Minister was understandably delighted. So many people had wondered whether he could ever really do it. But George Osborne had always backed himself to win and, when the time came, win big.*

So now for that reshuffle. Never an easy task, of course. But at least he no longer had to worry about what do with Boris. Having bet the house on Leave and lost, Johnson may have been the darling of the grassroots, but, as Osborne had long calculated, that hardly mattered given how many of his parliamentary colleagues had been determined to ensure that a man they regarded as both a total shit and a complete joke didn't make it into the final two. His ambitions thus dashed, the would-be 'World King' had decided not to stand again at the general election but had opted instead to step away from politics in order, as 'friends' told journalists, to 'make money and have some fun'.

Theresa May, of course, had done no such thing. Having joined Osborne in the run-off phase of the autumn 2019 leadership contest only to crumble (just as he guessed she would) when exposed to a few weeks of intense campaign scrutiny, she'd opted to continue with a proverbial life of public service in the House of Commons. But if May was harbouring any hopes that she would be allowed to enjoy a record tenth year as Home Secretary, she was about to be deeply disappointed. True, thought Osborne, she was bound to make herself awkward on the backbenches now and then. But that would be a price worth paying just to see her face when he called her in to Number Ten tomorrow to give her the news. Whether he'd do it brutally – perhaps even tell her she ought to get to know the party better before bundling her out of the back door – or instead twist the knife by sarcastically laying it on thick, he hadn't quite decided.

In any case, he had more than enough to do before then. First thing tomorrow he'd take a few calls from his fellow EU heads of government. Some of them, he knew, had been surprised when they'd heard he was calling a snap general election in mid-December – until, that is, he'd explained that he, of all people, wasn't going to make the same mistake as Gordon Brown had made back in 2007 when he'd hesitated and so blown the best chance he'd had of winning his own mandate. Besides, David Cameron, now looking forward to his seat in the Lords (somewhere to pop into for lunch after a morning of lucrative lobbying or between speaking trips abroad), had been incredibly supportive of the idea: 'Yes, it'll be cold and damp on the doorstep,' he'd said. 'But it'll all be over by Christmas – and then you can chillax at Chequers over the New Year.'

And that was exactly what Osborne was going to do. It wasn't as if the Opposition was going to trouble him much over the next few weeks – or months, or even years. Sure, Labour's MPs had been canny enough not to try to overthrow Corbyn mid-term – better, they'd reckoned, to let him lose so badly that even the party's deluded members would wake up to the fact that he'd have to go. But the veteran left-winger's reluctant resignation, announced soon after it became obvious that he'd presided over a catastrophic defeat, would now be followed by a lengthy leadership contest and an even longer period of navel-gazing, if not full-blown civil war.

That should leave Osborne plenty of time to carry on implementing what he still rather enjoyed calling his 'long-term economic plan' – even if it involved little more than keeping tax, spending, and borrowing as low as possible, all the while chucking a few prestige infrastructure projects at the North, persuading the Chinese to keep investing, and encouraging EU citizens to keep coming to the UK to do the jobs Brits either wouldn't or couldn't do.

The only question for the PM now was would he fight the 2025 election or instead hand over to one of his protégés (Matt Hancock perhaps?) before going to the Lords himself, taking up a few lucrative directorships, doing a spot of journalism, and generally becoming one of the great and the good – you know, editing a newspaper, one or two part-time roles in the City, chairing the Board of Trustees at the British Museum, that sort of thing...

*

This is a book, of course, about what *has* happened and is happening still, not about what might have been. Yet, however much we might like to emphasize underlying structures and institutions, we nevertheless need to acknowledge the part played by chance, contingency, and human agency. Take the result of the June 2016 referendum on the UK's membership of the European Union.[1] To hear some talk, it was somehow inevitable. In reality, however, it was far from a foregone conclusion – as Dominic Cummings, one of the architects of Leave's victory, has often stressed.[2] Indeed, given how narrow Leave's margin of victory was, any number of things might have made a difference, most obviously Boris Johnson, Michael Gove, and Cummings himself not deciding to campaign to quit the EU, or else Jeremy Corbyn deciding to put the full weight of the Labour Party behind Remain. Had either, or certainly both, of those things happened, then we might well have lived through, and still be living in, the parallel universe sketched above.

The EU referendum is also a reminder of the fact that the really big splits in the Conservative Party's long history (and well before political scientists began to talk about 'personalization' and 'presidentialization' in parliamentary democracies) have always seen fights over an issue conflated with competition for the crown – or, at the very least, competition for a place in 'the court' of whoever wears (or aspires to wear) it.[3] For today's Tories, no less than for Edmund Burke, 'men not measures' are what matter, although now, quite rightly, women matter too. As a result, arguments over what passes for high principle always take on an additional edge by being bound up with high (and therefore also low) politics – all the more so because Britain's highly stratified class, educational, and media systems mean that the characters involved have often been playing the same game with the same people for what can seem like forever.[4] In any case, and as I have argued elsewhere, all politics inevitably involves not just ideas, interests, and institutions, but also individuals.[5]

I'm also increasingly persuaded that those individuals, and therefore parties as a whole, are as much tactical and reactive as they are strategic and proactive – actors, in other words, with incredibly short time horizons, who (to quote Cummings again) are 'dominated by what's going to appear on TV tonight, what's going to appear in the papers tomorrow' and so 'generally optimise for focus on the political media's immediate concerns and signalling to in-group factions'.[6] Winning elections does, of course, matter to Tories – particularly to Tory MPs worried about hanging on to their seats. But for many of those at the very top of the party an awful lot of their time and energy is devoted to the next *leadership* election rather than the next *general* election. Hence, as we shall see, the endless briefing against each other, the continual (highly partial) leaks from Cabinet meetings, the (often ghost-written) op-eds and speeches intended to signal to, and to curry favour with, firstly, the sometimes bewildering array of internal groups that now seem to loom so large in the life of the parliamentary Conservative Party and, secondly, 'the party in the media'. The latter consists of the editors, commentators, and journalists from the *Telegraph* and the *Mail*, as well as the *Sun*, the *Express*, and the *Spectator*, who, while they play no formal role, are, in reality, every bit as integral to the Tory milieu as those who do, even though their product (at least in its print form) now reaches fewer ordinary members of the public than ever it used to – and even though they now compete, co-exist, and cross over with those who work for websites like ConservativeHome and Guido Fawkes and right-wing think tanks/pressure groups like Policy Exchange, the Centre for Policy Studies, the Adam Smith Institute, the Institute for Economic Affairs, and the Taxpayers' Alliance, as well as the rather more centrist Onward and Bright Blue.[7]

While, then, it is perfectly possible and often very useful to pull apart contemporary politics thematically and structurally – something I myself have done in other books – I have quite deliberately chosen here to go with (and only occasionally to interrupt) the flow, to present an analytical narrative that captures (but also, I hope, cuts through and makes sense of) the 'blooming, buzzing confusion' of political life as it is actually experienced by politicians and parties, as well as by those broadcasters and newspapers and news websites who cover them but who, because they help decide who and what matters, are inevitably players too.[8] I've also tried hard to reflect the fact that political life seems to have accelerated in recent years owing to the rise of social media, especially Twitter and group-chat messaging services like WhatsApp.[9]

Accordingly, Chapter 2 begins with the extraordinarily dramatic Tory leadership contest triggered by David Cameron's decision, the morning after the night before, to step down as Prime Minister. It then looks at the all-too-brief honeymoon enjoyed by the victor of that contest, Theresa May, during which she committed the country to a harder Brexit than many had anticipated (or thought wise) before calling an early election that she had initially insisted wouldn't take place. Chapter 3 analyses that election. Where did it all go so wrong? And what were the consequences for a party that, right up until the last minute, was confidently expecting to be returned with an overall majority, not scrambling to ensure it could carry on as a minority government in a hung parliament? Chapter 4 explores May's titanic struggle (for once, the adjective is truly apposite) to secure parliamentary support for an orderly withdrawal from the European Union between the summer of 2017 and the summer of 2019. What did that struggle do to the Conservative Party's ideological balance and integrity (in both the organizational and the moral sense of that word), not just at Westminster but also at the grassroots?

Chapter 5 analyses the second leadership race staged by the party in the aftermath of its disastrous showing at the European Parliament elections – a race which this time involved a contest in the country and not just in the Commons. Boris Johnson may have been one of the few British politicians to be routinely referred to by his first name (even if, in fact, his first name was actually Alexander), but was he really bound to win? And, if so, why? What was the problem to which he seemed (if not to all his parliamentary colleagues or, indeed, their grassroots members) to provide such an obvious solution? Chapter 6 covers the crucial period between Johnson becoming Tory Party leader and the Conservatives securing a 'stonking' Commons majority at the 2019 general election. Was it all down to the Prime Minister and his mantra-cum-promise to 'Get Brexit Done'? Or might there have been rather more to it than that?

Chapters 7 and 8 explore how the Conservatives coped with the challenges posed by Covid-19 and the need to complete the Brexit transition over the course of 2020 and 2021. What tensions did the handling of the pandemic trigger in a party traditionally reluctant to spend money and often very dismissive of the so-called nanny state? And how much were those tensions – exacerbated by individual ambition as much as by ideology and material interests – responsible for the UK experiencing one of the worst death tolls in any advanced democracy?

Chapter 9 looks at how things began to go badly wrong for the party and for Boris Johnson in the autumn of 2021. Chapters 10 and 11 then bring the story to a close with his reluctant resignation and Rishi Sunak's eventual victory in the bitter contest to replace him as Prime Minister. Where exactly is, and *what* exactly is, the Conservative Party after Brexit? Has it, over the course of six years of turmoil and with no little irony, effectively transformed itself – not always intentionally but rather as the by-product of both internal and external electoral competition – from a mainstream centre-right outfit into an ersatz version of the populist radical right insurgency that the referendum was supposed to help see off? And if so, does the Tories' new leader, chosen only after the spectacular implosion of the woman who had defeated him just a few weeks earlier, stand any chance, or even have any intention, of changing course? Or is this, at least for a while, 'the new normal'?

2

May in her pomp
(July 2016–April 2017)

David Cameron had been Prime Minister for six years and, while he may not have been planning to fight the next election, he'd assumed he'd be doing the job for a while yet. At 8.10 a.m. on 24 June 2016, however, he found himself facing the world's media (and, a little further off, crowding around the security gates that separate Downing Street from Whitehall, the public) to announce his resignation.

During the referendum campaign Cameron had maintained the fiction that he would stay on if Remain were defeated: to have done anything else, he reasoned, might well have seen the Leave vote swollen by people who had no particular beef with the EU but would have found the opportunity of removing a sitting Tory Prime Minister simply too good a chance to pass up. But it is clear that Cameron himself, and most of those closest to him, knew that, should he lose, he would have to go – not least because, had he not stepped down of his own accord, he would have been 'hounded out' by Tory Brexiteers at Westminster and their cheerleaders in the media.[1] Even grassroots Conservatives, normally slower than the party's MPs to lose faith in their leaders, agreed he had to go. Some 59 per cent of the Tory rank and file were telling YouGov, which was now able to conduct surveys of party members as well as voters, that Cameron was right to resign (with only 36 per cent demurring), in spite of the fact that an impressive 87 per cent of them thought he had done well as party leader – including as many as 86 per cent of the 63 per cent of rank-and-file members who had ignored his recommendation and voted Leave.[2] In any case, having been through such a bruising battle, during which he had nailed his colours firmly to the mast only to see them unceremoniously torn to shreds by colleagues he'd once considered friends, Cameron was in no mood now to help them out of the mess they'd created: as he reportedly put it to his inner circle that morning, 'Why should I do all the hard shit for someone else, just to hand it over to them on a plate?'[3]

Gone and soon forgotten: The Camerons head for the door.
Source: Daniel Leal-Olivas / Alamy.

Johnson and Leadsom implode – and May takes the crown

Quite how hard that shit would turn out to be was not immediately apparent, although the expressions on the faces of Boris Johnson and Michael Gove as they faced the media the morning after the night before gave them, in the words of the *Financial Times*'s Janan Ganesh, 'the haunted look of jokers at an auction whose playfully exorbitant bid for a vase had just been accepted with a chilling smash of the gavel'.[4] The immediate shock to sterling and the stock market was bad enough, although cushioned somewhat by some well-targeted reassurance from Bank of England Governor Mark Carney. But the real question was how whoever took over from Cameron could negotiate a deal that would simultaneously satisfy Leavers, mollify Remainers, and prove acceptable to the European Union.

As it turned out, the options for doing just that were significantly narrowed even before the result of what would turn out to be a particularly dramatic Tory leadership contest was announced. The politician charged with making a start on Brexit by Cameron (who, while obliged to stay on in Downing Street until the end of the leadership contest, was careful to keep out of the race) was Cabinet Office Minister Oliver Letwin. He decided, reasonably enough, that the best way to proceed was to find out straight away what sort of arrangement with Brussels the likely runners and riders wanted. Not surprisingly, perhaps, Michael Gove – speaking (it seemed at the time anyway) both for himself and for Boris Johnson – made it clear that he intended 'to negotiate as complete a system of free trade with the EU as [was] compatible with (a) the UK exercising control over migration, and (b) the UK being in total control of its own legal system so that the ECJ [European Court of Justice] has no jurisdiction in this country'. Significantly, Theresa May (who, incidentally, Letwin noticed, seemed to be working much harder on her leadership campaign than were her rivals) intimated that she wanted pretty much the same thing.[5] In short, while they may not have been able to articulate it even to themselves, the Conservative politicians most likely to succeed Cameron had effectively already decided that the UK would commit to a 'hard Brexit': it would be leaving not only the EU but the single market and the customs union, too.

For the moment, however, exactly how the leadership contenders planned to leave the EU was less important than the fact that all those who declared they would stand publicly pledged to respect the result of the referendum, whether, like May (and Secretary of State for Work and Pensions Stephen Crabb), they had supported Remain or, like Johnson and Gove (and Energy Minister Andrea Leadsom and former Defence Secretary Liam Fox), they were well-known Leavers. That did not, of course, mean that the stance they had previously taken, and indeed their conduct during the referendum campaign, counted for nothing. Indeed, it was initially assumed – especially, of course, in the Brexit-supporting print media – that the party was somehow duty bound to pick a Leave campaigner. And since the first post-referendum poll produced could be interpreted as giving Boris Johnson the lead over other Tory politicians, that assumption swiftly led to him being seen as the favourite, at least among voters.

Yet even a cursory examination of the numbers hinted at a rush to judgement. For one thing, some 37 per cent of those questioned about their preferred leader answered 'Don't know'. For another, although May, in second place, registered just 13 per cent support, support for Johnson at 28 per cent was not exactly overwhelming. Moreover, when the survey asked respondents who they'd pick if the two went head-to-head, the outcome was 50.4 per cent Johnson vs 49.6 per cent May – hardly a rout.[6] Even more worrying, perhaps, for the supposed frontrunner was a larger YouGov poll which came out a few days later. It found that, while the two were effectively (though not very impressively) tied on just under 20 per cent, May led Johnson by 31 to 24 among those currently intending to vote Tory.[7]

Most alarming for Johnson, however, was YouGov's survey of Conservative Party members, conducted over the same period. These, after all, were the people (older, whiter, and more comfortably off than most voters, as well as more likely to be male and to live in the South of England) who, it was presumed, would eventually decide who would take over from Cameron – once, that was, MPs had reduced the field to a shortlist of two via a series of votes in which the last-placed candidate would drop out until only the final pair were left to face the rank and file.[8] Far from being the frontrunner, and in spite of the fact that nearly two-thirds of Tory members had voted Leave, Johnson trailed May by 27 to 36 percentage points and, even more starkly, by 38 to 55 when members were asked to imagine a run-off between the two. Helpfully, the survey also provided a clue as to why that might be the case by asking members about the strengths they associated with the contenders. Predictably enough, Johnson won hands down when it came to 'Best media performer' (62:13) and 'Understands what it takes to win elections' (48:21). But May outperformed him as the 'Strongest leader' (44:29) and on the qualities required to actually run the country, namely 'Most prepared to take tough decisions' (46:18) and 'Most able at handling a crisis' (49:18). Indeed, she was also judged 'Best at negotiating a new relationship with the EU' (32:22). Finally, May easily beat Johnson on 'Best at uniting the Conservative Party' (46:16) – a stunning reversal of the figures a membership survey had produced back in the New Year, when Johnson had the edge over May on that particular question by 42 to 17 percentage points.[9]

This was crucial. Study after study suggests that the ability to hold one's party together is, or at least has been historically, the number one criterion employed by British parties faced with having to pick a new leader. And, given how unbelievably divisive the referendum had turned out to be, it is scarcely surprising that many Tories were especially desperate to find someone who they thought stood a chance of healing the wounds rather than rubbing even more salt into them. Allied to this, as a persuasive piece of academic research on the 2016 contest points out, members knew they would be choosing not only their party leader but also the country's Prime Minister. As a result, competence may well have been seen as more important than electability, especially given the assumption (hardly an unreasonable one) that a steady hand on the tiller would anyway help to persuade the public to return the party to power in an election which, after all, was not scheduled to take place for another three-and-a-half years.[10] Johnson, given his charisma and media experience, might well have backed himself to perform better than May in the membership hustings, but he would still have been battling against the perception that what the party needed was a serious politician for serious times.

Of course, these were the views of grassroots Conservatives, none of whom would be able to vote in the contest until the party's MPs had had their say. But were those MPs really thinking so very differently to the rank and file? Arguably, the fact that the parliamentary stage of the 2016 leadership election turned into something approaching a soap opera, or even, some would say, a tragicomedy, has fed the myth that it was only the supposed treachery of Michael Gove that prevented Boris Johnson winning the Tory leadership three years earlier than proved to be the case.[11] Obviously, we should not minimize the significance of Gove's decision to declare himself a candidate just a few days after promising to manage Johnson's campaign in return for being made Chancellor of the Exchequer. Clearly, it put paid to both men's chances. Johnson's first reaction on getting the news was to declare 'It's over' but he reluctantly agreed to meet with members of his team before quitting. At the meeting everyone agreed to stick by him if he wanted to carry on but he was told that his support among MPs had collapsed from nearly one hundred the night before to fewer than forty that morning. If he pulled out now, no-one would ever know for sure how well or how badly he would have done; so, if and when he stood in the future, he wouldn't need to explain away such a poor performance. It was also pointed out that, in order to justify his sudden decision to stand in his own right, Gove would have no alternative but to spend his entire campaign repeating why, in his view, Johnson was unfit to be Prime Minister. After consulting privately with his then wife for a few minutes, Johnson chose not to stand – at least this time around.[12] And, while Gove's 'coup' (prompted, it seems, by a mix of latent ambition and genuine, last-minute doubts about Johnson's fitness for office) saw him enter the contest proper, it turned so many of his colleagues against him that he was able to win over only around one in seven of them when he was knocked out in the second round of voting.[13] However, this should not blind us to the basic truth that Johnson's decision not to carry on in the contest was less the product of shock (although shock, it appears, may have played a part) than it was of his team crunching the numbers and coming to the conclusion that there was no realistic path to victory when it came either to his Commons colleagues or to the party in the country.

This, in turn, is not to take anything away from the skill with which those around Theresa May conducted her campaign, most obviously her former Home Office advisers Fiona Hill and Nick Timothy and her campaign manager Chris Grayling, as well as Damian Green,

Stephen Parkinson, Will Tanner, JoJo Penn, Lizzie Loudon, and Gavin Williamson – the latter now remembered as a clownish Defence and Education Secretary but then best known as Cameron's Parliamentary Private Secretary and, as such, someone who knew the parliamentary party inside out. May pitched herself as the ultimate safe pair of hands and a 'reluctant Remainer' (albeit one who, in private, had wept when she'd realized Leave had won) now absolutely committed to delivering Brexit.[14] And she made full use of the organizational, networking, and rhetorical talents of her team in order to overcome her lack of easy familiarity with colleagues and journalists alike. As well as meeting MPs (although resisting the temptation, unlike Johnson, to guarantee them jobs), she (or rather Nick Timothy, who drafted her speech) even managed at her campaign launch to turn what some saw as her lack of social skills to her advantage, claiming,

I know I'm not a showy politician. I don't tour the television studios. I don't gossip about people over lunch. I don't go drinking in Parliament's bars. I don't often wear my heart on my sleeve. I just get on with the job in front of me.

Such an approach, especially in the wake of the Gove/Johnson psycho-drama, was bound to strike a chord with Paul Dacre, still at that point the Editor of the Brexit-supporting *Mail*, one of the most influential titles in Conservative circles. And the very next day, its editorial – 'A Party in Flames and Why It Must be Theresa for Leader' – delivered in spades, claiming that of all the candidates 'only Mrs May has the right qualities, the stature and the experience to unite both her party and the country'.[15] Surveyed again by YouGov over the following three days, grassroots members appeared to agree – even if Boris Johnson, who declared for Leadsom, did not: 54 per cent of them backed May against 20 per cent for Leadsom, with Gove on just 9 per cent, not that far ahead of Crabb and Fox (who were shortly to fall by the wayside after the first round of parliamentary voting on 5 July) on 5 per cent each. In the survey's notional head-to-heads, May had the beating of Leadsom by 63 to 31 and Gove by 72 to 21 (with only 32 per cent of members now saying they felt positive towards him compared to the 68 per cent who'd said so before he brought down Boris Johnson).[16]

Quite how many MPs had these numbers in mind when they voted in the first round, we cannot be sure. But it is hard to believe that they did so with no thought whatsoever as to the likely result of the membership vote. The parliamentary stage, overseen by the 1922 Committee (effectively the governing body of the party in the Commons, elected by backbenchers), proceeds by way of a secret ballot. However, many Conservative MPs publicly declare their support for one or other of the candidates and, if that candidate is subsequently knocked out, then declare who they will be backing instead – declarations which are reported on by the media and often helpfully collated (by way of running totals) by websites like ConservativeHome and Guido Fawkes. By doing so they may be hoping to encourage colleagues to row in behind their choice for leader, which is why endorsements from high-profile MPs are so eagerly sought (sometimes with the offer of a job in a future frontbench team) and also so loudly trumpeted by candidates' campaign teams. Or MPs may simply have calculated (with the help of membership polling that has swiftly established a good reputation for accuracy) which way they think the wind is blowing – at which point they jump on the bandwagon before it rolls off into the distance, very likely in the hope (in some cases the forlorn hope) of boosting their chances of preferment under what they assume will be the next dispensation.

As well as YouGov's surveys showing that, going into the first round of parliamentary voting, May seemed to have established a clear lead among the membership, ConHome could, on the morning of the vote, list 124 MPs who were supporting her (compared to 39 for Leadsom, 26 for Gove, 22 for Crabb, and 7 for Fox). It was therefore hardly surprising that the Home Secretary emerged later that day as the clear winner with 165 votes, followed by Leadsom on 66 and Gove on 48. Fox, coming in last on 16 votes, was officially eliminated, while Crabb, although quite a long way above him on 34 votes, decided to withdraw of his own accord – which (at least from the party's point of view) was probably a good thing given that, less than a fortnight later, he was forced to resign from his post as Secretary of State for Work and Pensions after being implicated in a 'sexting' scandal. Both men immediately endorsed May, who went on to increase her vote in the second round two days later to 199 (with 183 public endorsements by colleagues) against second-placed Andrea Leadsom on 84 (and 50 public endorsements).

That second round saw the elimination of Michael Gove, who, with the support of 46 of his colleagues, had actually managed to lose two votes (owing partly, perhaps, to some of his votes in the first round coming from May supporters hoping to knock Leadsom out of the contest and partly to his team's overly aggressive attempts to dissuade colleagues from plumping for Leadsom).[17] But if anyone had assumed that his departure from the stage marked the end of the melodrama, if not the contest itself, then they were very much mistaken, as the role of anti-hero passed from the Minister of Justice to the Minister of State for Energy. Andrea Leadsom, already facing criticism over her apparent reluctance to release her personal tax records and over her supposedly misleading CV, gave an interview to the *Times*'s ace interviewer, Rachel Sylvester, in which she implied that, because, unlike Theresa May, she had children, she had a more 'tangible stake' in the country's future. Cue a public pile-on which included some sharp criticism from Tory MPs supporting May and which, by the end of a torrid weekend, persuaded Leadsom (who had only entered the contest after a mix-up had seen Johnson, when still a candidate, fail to honour a promise to publicly name her in his putative 'top three') to withdraw her candidacy on 11 July.[18] As a result, a contest that had been due to drag on until the second week of September was all over in just seventeen days. Accordingly, Theresa May, who formally took over from Cameron on 13 July, became Britain's fifty-fourth Prime Minister – the ninth Conservative leader to take on the job (and the fourth to do so before winning a general election) since 1945.

Brexit means 'hard Brexit'

Once again, however, we would do well to tear our eyes away from the twists and turns that led to this faintly anticlimactic denouement in order to gain a more fundamental understanding of the balance of forces inside the party as May assumed the leadership – a balance that would go on to have major implications over the course of her premiership. And we are helped by an academic study which painstakingly worked out who voted for which candidate in the second and final parliamentary ballot on 7 July and then used statistical techniques to isolate what really drove support for each of them.[19] Those techniques tell us, for instance, that although May won the support of seven out of ten female Tory MPs, that

No contest: May enters Number Ten as Leadsom drops out.
Source: 10 Downing Street.

wasn't statistically significant. Likewise, whether an MP was privately educated and/or attended Oxford or Cambridge made no difference to whom they voted for.

In fact, the thing that most distinguished those MPs who supported May from those who did not was – not surprisingly perhaps – which side they were on in the referendum a fortnight previously. An estimated 73 per cent of May's vote came from MPs who had backed Remain and only 23 per cent from those who backed Leave, with the rest coming from MPs who did not declare either way. Leadsom, on the other hand, drew an estimated 87 per cent of her supporters from the Leave camp and just 8 per cent from Remainers, while the figures for Gove were 72 and 28 per cent respectively.

Putting it the other way round, May won the support of 91 per cent of Tory MPs who voted Remain (a group, one should recall, who were in the majority at the time even if most of them quickly reinvented themselves as more or less enthusiastic Brexiteers) as opposed to just 35 per cent of those who backed Leave. Leadsom's supporters, on the other hand, made up nearly half of those 'Spartan' Tory Brexiteers who would go on to vote against the third and final iteration of Theresa May's Withdrawal Agreement at the end of March 2019 – among them MPs like Steve Baker, Bill Cash, Bernard Jenkin, Owen Paterson, John Redwood, and Theresa Villiers, who were never happier than when sharing their thoughts with journalists. In other words, while May, with the support of 60 per cent of her MPs, had won a parliamentary mandate that exceeded that given to all of her predecessors since 1965, those colleagues ranged against her were a highly motivated, vocal, and reasonably coherent bunch. Unless they could somehow be reconciled, the Conservative Party's new leader was perhaps more vulnerable than she looked.[20]

One obvious way that May could reassure, if not necessarily reconcile, the 65 per cent of Leave-supporting MPs who chose not to vote for her was to signal her intention to respect what Brexiteers were already dubbing 'the will of the people'. And one way of doing that, after dismissing fully thirteen of those who had sat in (or at least attended) Cameron's Cabinet, was to appoint prominent Leave campaigners to her own.[21] Michael Gove may have been beyond the pale: historically, defeated Tory leadership contenders were normally offered a job (one reason, it is often thought, that some MPs with little hope of winning nevertheless decide to put themselves forward); but what was widely seen (by many Leavers now, as well as Remainers) as the Justice Secretary's serial disloyalty made him, for the moment at least, *persona non grata*. Boris Johnson, on the other hand, was rewarded – much to his surprise and to considerable consternation in the civil service – for his disloyalty (albeit to David Cameron) with one of the so-called great offices of state, the Foreign and Commonwealth Office. That said, he would not be responsible for negotiating Brexit: that job (at least nominally) was given to another prominent Leaver, David Davis, who would head up the newly created Department for Exiting the European Union (DExEU). Liam Fox was also brought back in from the Cameroon cold and made Secretary of State for International Trade – another portfolio with a direct bearing on Brexit, albeit more potential than actual since no deals with third countries could be firmly negotiated until the UK's formal withdrawal from the EU. And while May's erstwhile opponent in the membership stage of the leadership contest, Andrea Leadsom, was kept at arm's length from Brexit, she was at least brought into the

Cabinet, even if only as Secretary of State for Environment, Food and Rural Affairs. Room around the Cabinet table was also found not just for May's campaign manager, Chris Grayling, who swapped his post as Leader of the House of Commons for the Transport brief, but also for fellow Brexiteer Priti Patel, who – perhaps rather incongruously, given her scepticism about overseas aid spending – was promoted to Secretary of State for International Development, helping to increase the number of Cabinet members educated at state schools and meaning that, of the twenty-two ministers who had attended Cameron's last Cabinet, only thirteen kept their place at the table (and only four of them the same job).

Sceptics, of course, could point to the fact that, although May had unceremoniously (and perhaps unwisely) sacked George Osborne (who had apparently, if inexplicably, thought she might just keep him on), the majority of seats around the Cabinet table continued to be occupied by MPs who had backed Remain.[22] Philip Hammond at the Treasury and Amber Rudd at the Home Office were most often singled out in this respect, since May could defend appointing lower-profile Remainers like Justine Greening (Education), Damian Green (Work and Pensions), and Jeremy Hunt (kept at Health) on the grounds that she needed identifiably centrist, 'One Nation' Tories to signal to the public that she was serious about tackling what she had labelled in her first statement outside Downing Street as Prime Minister the 'burning injustices' that continued to disfigure twenty-first-century Britain. Brexiteers, though, were prepared, at least initially, to give their new leader the benefit of the doubt – helped, perhaps, by May's decision to appoint fervent Brexiteers like her former Home Office advisers Nick Timothy (Fiona Hill, also back, supported Remain) and Stephen Parkinson (who led Vote Leave's ground operation) as close confidants.

Arguably, in her rush to carry out what was not just a replacement of key personnel but effectively something akin to regime change in Number Ten and in Cabinet, May did herself few favours by apparently leaving many of the decisions on the lower ranks of the frontbench (i.e. junior ministers and Parliamentary Private Secretaries) to her advisers and to Gavin Williamson – decisions which, not least because of the manner in which they were delivered, left too many disappointed people on the backbenches who were subsequently disinclined to support her in her hour (indeed, hours) of need.[23] Just as damagingly, perhaps, there was also an extent to which even those Tory MPs who weren't left off the frontbench – up to and including those appointed to the Cabinet itself – nevertheless felt left out since, as May's Transport Secretary, Chris Grayling, later put it, 'Nick and Fi had a kind of wall of steel around Theresa.'[24]

This notwithstanding, Leadsom and other Leave supporters in Cabinet were encouraged to suspend judgement by May's seemingly uncompromising rhetoric. During the leadership campaign May (or rather Nick Timothy) had coined the tautology 'Brexit means Brexit' in order to emphasize that, as she put it, 'There must be no attempts to remain inside the EU, no attempts to rejoin it through the back door, and no second referendum.' It was, she went on, 'the duty of the Government and of Parliament to make sure' that the public's 'verdict' was implemented.[25] But that was little more than a holding position: it bought time (not least for the civil service, which was rather banking on the leadership contest carrying on over the summer so that it could implement May's machinery-of-government changes and work up some detailed options).[26] Something more definite was needed, however, if she were to retain the confidence of her Brexit-ultras on the backbenches.

The obvious time and place to prove her bona fides was the party's annual conference, due to be held in Birmingham at the beginning of October. Rather than wait until the Wednesday, when she would be delivering the usual closing speech, May's team – keen that she be seen to take control as this was the first time the whole party was meeting since she'd taken over (and done so without the legitimacy conferred either by a general election or by a full-blown leadership contest) – decided that she would give an keynote address on the opening Sunday, too. Inevitably (though, in the event, rather more definitively than they had intended), it offered her the opportunity to communicate to the party and to the country where she stood on Brexit.[27]

First of all, May calmed nerves (and supposedly guaranteed that the UK would not take part in the 2019 European Parliament elections) by pledging to trigger Article 50 (giving Brussels two years' notice of the UK's withdrawal from the EU) no later than the end of March, even if – as it turned out – her insistence that the government could do this without a parliamentary vote would later be contradicted by the UK Supreme Court. Secondly, she announced the introduction of a so-called Great Repeal Bill, which, although intended to create certainty by putting existing EU law onto the statute book, would, once passed, end the direct effect of any subsequent European Law. Thirdly, and in some ways most importantly (given her advisers' desire that she be seen to be responding to the profound demand for change and reconnection they believed had driven Leave's victory), she stressed that, like all 'independent, sovereign countries', the UK would be setting its own rules on immigration; she also stressed that 'Global Britain' would be aiming to negotiate a trade deal with the European Union – all without returning to the jurisdiction of the European Court of Justice.[28]

To anyone who knew anything about the EU, as well as to the EU itself, this represented – without saying it explicitly (Remainers, May's team reasoned, were not yet quite ready to hear it out loud) – a commitment to a 'hard Brexit'. Not surprisingly, then, the speech appeared to go down well in the conference hall. However, it blindsided both the other member states (who had blithely assumed that leaving on that basis was economically so damaging that no sane British Prime Minister would advocate it) and May's colleagues – including Leavers like Davis, Fox, and Johnson, whom May was determined to keep out of the loop, whatever their impressive-sounding job titles.[29] The shock they felt was all the greater because neither Cabinet ministers nor top civil servants had been fully consulted or briefed. Indeed, had they been given the chance, some of them would have advised against narrowing the country's options so severely before the government had agreed on the kind of Brexit it wanted.

May's newly appointed Chancellor, the former Foreign Secretary Philip Hammond, was among those who were most alarmed. In common with his Treasury civil servants, he recognized that the UK would have to leave the EU but hoped that Leave's deliberate failure to define the terms on which it should do so meant that any economic damage that would result could be minimized by staying as close to the EU as possible. A hard Brexit, on the other hand, could turn out to be, as he later put it, 'an economic catastrophe'. Moreover, having had no input into the speech and sight only of a small part of it, he had, as he later recalled, 'no idea that she was going to describe Brexit in the hardest possible terms'. Accordingly, as he sat looking up at May with the rest of the audience in the hall,

I was absolutely horrified by what I was hearing. All I remember thinking was, 'There will be a television camera that will be on your face. If you move a muscle, it will be the story on the front page of every newspaper tomorrow.' I remember I wasn't even really listening to her. ... I just remember focusing my entire energy on maintaining a rictus half-smile, and trying not to show any reaction at all, and then get out of the room without speaking to any journalists. I was completely and utterly horrified by what I felt was almost a coup: a definition of Brexit without any proper Cabinet consultation at all. ...

I left ... and had to go immediately by car to a helicopter landing site just outside Birmingham, to be flown to Heathrow to catch a plane to the US because the IMF [International Monetary Fund] annual meetings were coincidental with the party conference. When I arrived in Washington, it was to discover that the pound was in free-fall, on the back of the Prime Minister's speech and the markets' reaction to it. I then had to get out on the TV in Washington, to try to reinterpret the Prime Minister's speech for the markets in a way that would try to stop the slide in sterling. We had what looked like a genuine sterling crisis on our hands in the couple of days immediately after the speech. It was a disaster on all fronts, a total unmitigated disaster that scarred her Prime Ministership and should have sealed Nick Timothy's fate, but I think she only realised later how badly that had constrained her ability to deliver any kind of practical Brexit at all.

That said, he continued, because, as a long-serving Home Secretary who'd never taken much interest in economics, May tended to see things 'through the prism of immigration and security',

I'm not even sure that she understood, as she was delivering that speech, how extreme the words coming out of her mouth really were. I think if she'd understood, if she realised that she was lining up people like me and metaphorically kicking us in the groin, I don't think she would have done it.[30]

For many Remainers, however, it was May's second, closing speech at the conference – again heavily influenced by Nick Timothy's ideas – that really added insult to injury, although, in her defence, one might argue that some, at least, were positively looking to take offence.[31] Essentially a more fully developed version of the credo that May had outlined outside

Downing Street before stepping through the door as Prime Minister, the speech was intended to present her as a change-maker and a different kind of Conservative from her immediate predecessor – one happy to acknowledge 'the good that government can do'. Claiming that she had 'a plan to tackle the unfairness and injustice that divides us' that was 'rooted in the centre ground' and would mean 'government stepping up, righting wrongs, challenging vested interests', she promised she would 'stand up for the weak and stand up to the strong' and put the power of government 'squarely at the service of ordinary working-class people', even if that meant intervening in the economy and criticizing business in ways that were bound to spook fans of the free market (and, indeed, the markets themselves).

Yet these weren't the words that caused most controversy. First up, there was a warning – supposedly directed at unscrupulous international business people but perhaps inevitably interpreted more widely in the light of Brexit as an attack on the 48 per cent who had voted Remain – that 'if you believe you're a citizen of the world, you're a citizen of nowhere. You don't understand what the very word "citizenship" means.' And that was closely followed by a dig at politicians and commentators who supposedly found 'the fact that more than seventeen million voters decided to leave the European Union simply bewildering' and (now addressing those voters directly) apparently found 'your patriotism distasteful, your concerns about immigration parochial, your views about crime illiberal, your attachment to your job security inconvenient'.

To those already sensitized by the tactics employed by Vote Leave, this was straight out of the populist playbook, pitting the supposedly common-sense people against what was framed as an unrepresentative, uncaring, cosmopolitan, and liberal elite – and making plain that the Prime Minister and her party were on the side of the former against the latter. Moreover, it came on top of an unexpectedly hardline speech by the new Home Secretary, Amber Rudd, who, in her concern (or at least the concern of her advisers) to prove she was going to be as tough on immigration as her predecessor, garnished her announcement of some surprisingly draconian new measures with a promise that they would help 'ensure people coming here are filling gaps in the labour market, not taking jobs British people could do'. Quite how she failed to spot just how incendiary those words (reminiscent as they were of a familiar far-right refrain) would sound to those already worried about the nativist turn in British politics remains something of a mystery.[32]

The referendum had divided the country, but May's move, rather than helping to heal the divide, argued her critics, only served to polarize it still further. It was more than simply a refusal even to contemplate the idea that, faced with the evident determination of the EU-27 to negotiate as a bloc, it might be better for a government with a small majority to try to achieve some kind of bipartisan (or even tripartisan) consensus on Brexit.[33] Whether on purpose or accidentally, the new Prime Minister and her advisers seemed to be seizing opportunistically (but in some ways wholly rationally) on the way Brexit had ripped apart Labour's already fraying electoral coalition. Labour's younger, better educated, and more socially liberal voters, many of them living in cities, had generally voted Remain, while its older, less well-educated, more socially conservative voters, many of them living in smaller, sometimes post-industrial towns in the Midlands and northern England, had backed Leave. If the gap that had opened up between the two groups could be turned into a permanent gulf – one that would see Leave and Remain rapidly harden into lasting and profound political identities and animosities – then there was the serious prospect of catalysing or at least accelerating a major electoral realignment.[34] David Cameron and George Osborne had focused, especially in the early years of opposition, on arresting the Tories' diminishing appeal to middle-class social liberals.[35] Theresa May's mix of austerity-ending centrism and authoritarian, nationalist (shading into nativist) populism (although never explicitly acknowledged as such, nor defined in such highfalutin terms, either by May herself or by Nick Timothy) would instead encourage working- and lower middle-class voters – particularly those in middle or old age who had never attended university – to come over to the Conservative Party in greater numbers than had ever been dreamed possible by 'the modernizers' of the early 2000s (not least one Theresa May, who had warned in 2002 against the Tories becoming 'the nasty party').

But while the electoral potential of this strategy may have been apparent to some, most of those in Number Ten and most Conservative MPs assumed – especially after May, on more than one occasion, had ruled out going to the country – that it would be some time before they would be fighting an election.[36] True, it may have been tempting to take immediate advantage of the chaotic state of the Labour Party, whose ongoing civil war had only worsened when Remain's defeat in the referendum had triggered mass resignations from the Shadow Cabinet and then (after Jeremy Corbyn failed to stand down after an overwhelming vote of no confidence in him by his own MPs) a second leadership contest saw grassroots members re-elect him with an increased majority. The moment, however, appeared to have passed and, besides, there was the rather more pressing need to be seen to be getting on with Brexit.

This was especially the case after the High Court, in early November, ruled that, contrary to May's insistence, the government could not trigger Article 50 without a parliamentary vote. The judgment provoked a near-hysterical reaction among Brexiteers, including the *Mail*'s notorious 'ENEMIES OF THE PEOPLE' front-page screamer – an attack on the judiciary penned by its Political Editor, James Slack (soon to become Theresa May's official spokesman), that saw Justice Secretary Liz Truss take far longer to issue the requisite statement upholding judicial independence than the Bar Council and the Law Society would have liked.[37] In the view of many Leave-supporting Tories, 'Remoaners' (a soubriquet that was by then beginning to stick) were bent on delaying the UK's withdrawal from the EU, or even preventing it altogether, by introducing what they saw as an unwarranted degree of potentially never-ending legislative interference in what should have been the prerogative of an executive rightly committed to implementing 'the will of the people'.[38] There was little, though, that said executive (already, incidentally, torn by infighting between the more cautious Treasury and Business ministers and the more gung-ho approach to Brexit adopted by the government's Leavers) could practically do – apart, that is, from appealing the decision to the Supreme Court, only to have its justices confirm in mid-January that a parliamentary vote would indeed be necessary. Still, the government needed to demonstrate before Christmas the strength of feeling on the question – at least on the Tory side. In the end this was done via a Commons motion that pledged Article 50 would be triggered by the end of March 2017, albeit accompanied by a promise (made in order to placate not just Labour but also those Tory Remainers worried about the malign influence of the European Research Group [ERG] chaired by Brexit-ultra Steve Baker) that the government would publish its 'plan for Brexit' before then.[39]

Although intended to be both more and less than that, in the sense of providing an idea of what May and her team wanted Britain to look like after leaving the EU while simultaneously avoiding giving away the detail of their negotiating positions, the Prime Minister's speech at Lancaster House on 17 January 2017 effectively confirmed that the UK would be pursuing a hard Brexit.[40] May made it clear that the country would be leaving both the single market and the customs union, at least (and this was a concession to Chancellor Philip Hammond) as its membership of the latter was currently configured. Moreover, although she claimed that she was 'sure a positive agreement can be reached', May declared (fatefully, some would say) that she was 'equally clear that no deal for Britain is better than a bad deal for Britain'. The aim of the speech (drafted by Nick Timothy and Director of Strategy Chris Wilkins with most Cabinet ministers allowed only last-minute suggestions and with any hope of robust internal critique from officials having disappeared with the high-profile resignation of the UK's 'man in Brussels', Ivan Rogers) may have been to provide a degree of clarity to the EU-27 and to impress upon the party the inevitability of the UK's complete rather than semi-detachment. But its lasting effect was to whet rather than satisfy the appetites of the most zealous Brexiteers.[41] Initially, walking away from the table was seen by most of them as a useful, even indispensable, negotiating technique. From then on, however, departing the EU without any deal whatsoever (which they took to labelling 'leaving on WTO [World Trade Organization] terms') began to be talked about by some of them as a viable, maybe even superior, alternative to a deal – especially when any agreement realistically on offer from the EU could never hope to give them everything they wanted.[42]

Not for the first time, the immediate reaction of the party in the media was instructive. As ever, the *Mail* led the pack: its 18 January front page on Lancaster House, written once again by James Slack, contained a cartoon Theresa May, hands on hips and holding a Thatcher-style handbag, standing in defiant pose on a chalk cliff, the EU flag underfoot and the Union Jack fluttering in the breeze on a flagpole behind her, accompanied by a headline 'STEEL OF THE NEW IRON LADY' and a subhead reading 'On the momentous day Theresa May said Britain WILL quit the single market, she put Cameron's feeble negotiations to shame with an ultimatum to Brussels: We'll walk away from a bad deal – and make EU pay.' The *Telegraph* went with 'May's bold terms for Brexit' and '"No deal is better than a bad deal"'. But in some ways, the most surprising front page of them all belonged to the normally rather more measured *Times*: 'May to EU: give us fair deal or you'll be crushed'.

Quite how one soon-to-be former member state (albeit a big one with an economy to match) would 'crush' a bloc of twenty-seven, all of whom were now more than ever determined not to give any quarter in the upcoming negotiations, was never convincingly explained. However, the fact that the newspapers which were most popular with the Conservative Party's rank and file were prepared not just to countenance the possibility of No Deal but also to celebrate it was important. In its survey of the Tory grassroots back in early July YouGov had asked party members to choose between three options.[43] The results made it clear that, on balance, May was going with the grain when she'd declared that free movement would have to end. On UK–EU trade, however, there had been precious little enthusiasm for what some Brexit-ultras, when they weren't using the 'WTO rules' formula, would come to characterize as a 'clean break'. Admittedly, only 33 per cent of members in the summer thought the next Prime Minister should 'try to negotiate a free trade deal with the rest of the European Union, even if it means allowing EU citizens the right to live and work in Britain', while 57 per cent thought they should 'try to negotiate a free trade deal … but only if it can be done *without* allowing EU citizens the right to live and work in Britain'. However, a mere 4 per cent of members (irrespective of whether they were intending to vote for Leadsom or for May, and with hardly any difference between Leavers and Remainers) thought the next PM 'should not negotiate any sort of free trade deal with the rest of the EU'. If grassroots members were to change their minds, then the advocates of No Deal in the parliamentary party, high-profile as some of them were (or were soon to become), were presumably going to need some help from their journalistic allies.

Snap! The road to an early election

Interestingly, the July 2016 YouGov survey of Conservative Party members had also solicited their views on calling an early general election later in the year. The results were pretty conclusive. Once Boris Johnson was out of the race, what limited enthusiasm for the idea the firm had recorded a week or so earlier had all but evaporated: just 14 per cent were in favour while 80 per cent said no. This was not entirely surprising: after all, the average of the five surveys of voters that had been taken in the days since Brexit may have had Labour on just 30 per cent and the Lib Dems on 8 per cent, but the Tories themselves were only on 35 per cent, with UKIP on 14 per cent. Obviously, the hope, both at the grassroots and among MPs, was that their new leader would provide the party with something of a boost; but it would need to be pretty sustained and substantial before a contest became a serious possibility. In fact the early signs were encouraging: in July 2016, a week after May took over, YouGov put the party on over 40 per cent for the first time since early the previous December. But they were not stupendous: Labour may have begun to dip now and then below 30 per cent by the autumn, but the Lib Dems were often making it into double figures while UKIP, for all the trouble it was having finding someone to fill Nigel Farage's shoes after he quit as leader in the summer, was normally managing to avoid dropping below the 10 per cent mark. Little wonder that May herself saw no reason to resile from her assurances that there would be no early election.

Among some of her key advisers and colleagues, however, opinions were beginning to shift – or, in some cases, harden. Nick Timothy, for one, had always wanted to keep the option of an early election open, believing May could and should win a mandate of her own – not least because the last contest had been fought on a manifesto that was some way off expressing the more interventionist and more communitarian Conservatism that he was keen to see her promote. Moreover, that manifesto was also becoming a more immediate, real-world constraint – as proven by the increasingly personal, indeed poisonous, rows he and Chancellor Philip Hammond were having over the latter's refusal to sanction spending without making cuts elsewhere.[44] Ironically, Hammond himself was also coming round to the idea of going to the country early, albeit for different reasons. He had become convinced, after talking to businesses up and down the land, that the economy would need some kind of transition period, ideally lasting two years, following the UK's formal departure from the EU. That, however, would mean, as he later put it, 'going into an election in 2020 having promised to deliver Brexit, with Brexit still not fully delivered' – something that was bound to prove 'bloody difficult'.[45] But since his relationship with Theresa May had deteriorated within weeks of his being appointed (largely as it became apparent that, urged on by her advisers, he was not accorded anything like the influence or even the courtesy granted to his predecessors at the Treasury), he first shared his thoughts with David Davis, the Brexit Secretary, whom both he and May found more congenial than they found each other.[46] As Hammond recalled,

> I spent a lot of time and effort seeking to persuade David of the case for a transition and then of the logic that, if we wanted to be able to have a transition, we had to have a general election in 2017 off the back of the Prime Minister's bow wave of popularity and secure a five-year mandate. That would then mean that we effectively had five years in which to deliver Brexit, with a proper transition and a bit of time and space to think about the whole thing, ideally delivering the final coup de grâce, the big flag-waving Brexit moment, in the run-up to what would then have been the 2022 general election. It would work economically and it would work politically.[47]

Davis could see the logic. And it was reinforced by his concern that the EU-27, knowing that an election would have to be held only a year on from the point at which the UK had committed to leave the European Union, might try to use the tight timetable as a means of exerting additional pressure on him in negotiations. All of this was shared with the PM when they went to see her together in her flat above Number Ten in February 2017.

Ultimately, however, what seems to have eventually persuaded May to risk (and she did see it as a risk) calling an election sooner rather than later was the parliamentary arithmetic back home.[48] To some ministers, getting a bigger majority would 'allow her to see off the extreme Brexit nutters'.[49] However, it was the Remainers who, for Number Ten, were the real concern. True, the government had been able to pass its European Union Bill. But it had not been entirely plain sailing. In the Lords, where there was no Conservative majority, peers had inflicted two defeats on the government, passing amendments (later overturned in the Commons) on citizens' rights and giving parliament the opportunity to vote on (and therefore veto) whatever Withdrawal Agreement the government finally came up with. Meanwhile, later on in the Commons, the government had only avoided defeat on a Labour amendment mandating parliamentary approval of any EU–UK deal by promising up to twenty Remain-supporting backbenchers (who'd sent former ministers Nicky Morgan, Dominic Grieve, and Alistair Burt to Number Ten to negotiate on their behalf) that, prior to ratification, the Commons would be given 'a meaningful vote' on a motion covering both the Withdrawal Agreement and the future relationship with the EU. Even then it had faced a rebellion from a group of seven MPs which (as well as the veteran Europhile Ken Clarke) included the former frontbenchers Anna Soubry (who during the debate accused her Brexit-backing colleagues of 'willy waving') and Claire Perry (who confessed, 'I feel sometimes that I am sitting with colleagues who are like *jihadis* in their support for a hard Brexit').[50] Several other MPs abstained, including Morgan, who did not believe that the government's promise guaranteed that parliament could prevent it taking the UK out of the EU without a deal. And George Osborne, soon to shock everyone by leaving the Commons to edit the *Evening Standard*, refused to cancel a prior engagement in order to turn up and vote.

Little wonder, then, especially as it became clear that the putative 'Great Repeal Bill' would need to be accompanied by additional pieces of legislation lest it become completely unmanageable, that an election – one which looked set to increase the government's Commons majority and (via the Salisbury convention) stymie opposition in the Lords – looked like an increasingly attractive proposition, particularly to a Prime Minister who, if the going got tough, would then be able to claim the legitimacy of a supposedly personal mandate from the public.[51] The fact that, in mid-March, Theresa May had to insist on her Chancellor U-turning on his budget announcement that he would be raising National Insurance contributions for the self-employed after it hit a brick wall of backbench resistance only made it more tempting still. So did the fact that, even if May (very much a tribal Tory, for all that she claimed to be a different kind of Conservative) had been more inclined to explore cross-party cooperation than she was, the idea of reaching out to a 'Leader of the Opposition who is a Kremlin-hugging terrorist cheerleader, who later turns out to be an anti-Semite as well, who has been against his country in every dispute' (to quote one of her advisers), was anathema.[52] Clearly also a consideration was the Tories' by-election victory, three weeks previously, in Copeland (a constituency held by Labour since 1935), making May the first Prime Minister since Margaret Thatcher in 1982 to snatch a seat from an opposition party.

That said, the party's internal polling, overseen by Chris Wilkins and run and analysed by James Johnson, provided no explicit rationale for going early. But nor did it suggest that doing so would be a bad idea. In fact, it found not only that the party had consolidated support among what it labelled 'Traditional Conservatives' (older, relatively well-off Leave voters), but also that, in contrast to Labour, it was doing reasonably well among 'Working Class Strugglers' (less well-off, less well-educated Leave voters). All this, concluded Wilkins and Johnson in a written summary delivered to a stock-taking 'awayday' at Chequers in mid-February, meant the Tories had 'a unique opportunity to move forward and gain ground' as well as 'to address a deep discontent with and mistrust in the political class' displayed in the referendum, 'which was a vote for a fundamental change to how the country works as well as a vote to leave the EU'. That said, 'focusing on new groups of voters available to us – not so much Middle England as Working Class England – more resolutely than before' would mean 'clearly demonstrating that we are the "change candidate"'. It also meant, however, having regard for the feelings of what Wilkins and Johnson called 'Conservative Leaners' (younger, well-educated, and more socially liberal, many of whom had voted Remain).[53]

All this suited Nick Timothy's (and, by implication, Theresa May's) agenda: it was with the first two groups in mind that Timothy and Wilkins had put together the government's *Plan for Britain*, released (to a rather disappointing media reception, it has to be said) in mid-March, while the need to keep the Leaners onside was partly what drove the optimistic rhetoric around an outward-looking 'Global Britain'. However, at no point did Wilkins and Johnson's work anticipate a Tory landslide. Indeed, the working assumption of most of those involved in the decision to go to the country was apparently a majority – albeit a substantially improved majority – of around fifty to sixty seats.[54]

In the third week of March, a few days after the bill allowing the government to trigger Article 50 received royal assent, May, together with her husband Philip, met with her top advisers (Timothy and Wilkins, together with Fiona Hill and JoJo Penn) in her Downing Street flat for what was her first truly serious discussion about an early election. Polling did not loom that large in the conversation, but all those there were aware that it looked pretty favourable: although an average of the polls published so far that month still put UKIP and the Lib Dems on 10 per cent, the all-important lead over Labour, with the Tories on 44 per cent and Corbyn's party languishing on 27 per cent, was overwhelming. So, May's advisers argued, were the reasons (outlined above) why she should go for it, especially if (as some of them hoped) the election could be called on the day that Article 50 was officially invoked and timed to coincide with local elections on 4 May.[55]

The PM, however, was still not wholly convinced, her main concern (and that of her husband, whose political advice she valued highly) being how she could justify going back on her repeated assurances that there would be no early election.[56] She did, however, commit to thinking about it further and began to consult one or two other trusted confidants. Stephen Gilbert, a veteran of Conservative Campaign Headquarters (CCHQ), was one of them. He believed, on balance, that it was the right call, with a couple of caveats. Firstly, the party machine might find it a big ask since, not for the first time, it had been allowed to run down after the last election in the expectation (perfectly reasonable given the repeated denials from Downing Street) that it would only need to gear up again for a contest in 2020. Secondly, Gilbert could see no realistic alternative to re-hiring Lynton Crosby to manage the party's campaign – a recommendation that May, for all the success he'd enjoyed with David Cameron in 2015, was not entirely comfortable with.

Yet as March turned into April, the Prime Minister, while never entirely confident she was making the right decision and in spite of internal polling (the gist of which somehow leaked to journalists) which suggested seats might well be lost to the Lib Dems, was increasingly inclined to go for it.[57] She was not subjected to any pressure to do so by the Whips' Office, but she was certainly made aware by its Chief, Gavin Williamson, among others, that many of her MPs (although not so much the newbies in more marginal seats) were urging her to go to the country, believing, on the basis of what now looked like a very comfortable double-digit lead over Labour, she would win a landslide.[58] Moreover, Williamson, when asked by May for his own views, didn't try to put her off, reminding her of how high she was riding in the polls.[59]

Certainly, former Tory leader William (now Lord) Hague was speaking for many of his ex-colleagues in the Commons when he made the case for an early general election in an op-ed for the *Telegraph* in the first week of March – even if (although this was largely ignored when the rest of the media excitedly echoed his views) he imagined that, because it would take legislation to get around the fact that 'Labour turkeys [were] unlikely to vote for a very early and particularly juicy Christmas', the PM wouldn't be able to secure one until 2018.[60]

For all that, when May left with her husband for a walking holiday in Wales in the second week of April, she hadn't quite decided to press 'go'. And while she was away, Gilbert had commissioned some 'benchmark' polling from Crosby's firm CTF which really should have given Number Ten some serious pause for thought.[61] The summary produced for Gilbert on 12 April began by stating 'there is clearly a lot of risk involved with going for an early election', even if it went on to discuss how that risk might best be mitigated. Voters, the research made clear, weren't at all convinced there needed to be an election – indeed, as soon as respondents had been presented with likely arguments for and against holding one, support for doing so dropped precipitately, with likely Tory voters actually the most opposed to the idea. Getting on for 60 per cent of respondents thought that (a) the Tories 'should focus on delivering the policies they promised in their [2015] manifesto not having another election'; (b) 'having an election now would simply waste a couple of months of the two years Britain had to secure a deal with the EU'; and (c) 'Britain already faces enough uncertainty with nobody knowing what Brexit deal we can secure. There is no need to add additional uncertainty by having an election.' These arguments resonated far more than what were recommended (and eventually used) as the most persuasive arguments for going early: just 16 per cent of voters, for instance, agreed that 'Theresa May only has a small majority in Parliament at the minute and this means that she can be held hostage by small groups of MPs pursuing their own agendas – so she should call an election and get a larger majority which would provide strong and stable government,' while a mere 9 per cent of voters agreed that 'Theresa May should call an early election because if she won the election with a bigger majority this would give her a stronger hand in negotiations with the EU.'

Just as worryingly, CTF also warned Gilbert (and therefore May) that 'Fifteen per cent of the current Conservative vote is soft' and that a similar proportion of current Conservative voters 'say that their vote is *against* another party rather than a vote *for* the Conservatives – with almost three quarters (70 per cent) of this vote being a vote against the Labour Party … creating a risk of voters leaving the Conservatives for Labour over the course of a campaign'. Moreover, around a quarter of voters, they estimated, were likely to change their mind, four in ten of whom would switch (if they switched) to Labour, two in ten of whom would switch to the Lib Dems, and only one in ten of whom would switch to the Tories. And then there was the question of expectations: some 56 per cent of respondents expected a Conservative majority government, along with 20 per cent who thought a Conservative-led coalition more likely; the figures for Labour were just 6 and 8 per cent respectively. This huge gap, CTF cautioned, 'creates the potential for voters to use their vote to secure a good local member in the belief that the national outcome is locked in'.

True, the memo prepared for Gilbert also noted that there was 'a strong preference for a Conservative Government, a strong preference for Theresa May to be Prime Minister, and no real desire for change'. And the Tory leader was massively better rated than her Labour counterpart. Among those who said they were sure to vote, some 41 per cent were concerned that Jeremy Corbyn was 'weak/ineffective/lacking party support' compared to just 8 per cent who though May was 'weak/illegitimate [because she hadn't won an election]/inexperienced'. Among the same group of 'definite voters' Corbyn's net favourability rating was an incredible minus 40 per cent, with Labour's at minus 32 per cent. Admittedly, May's rating, at plus 24 per cent, was hardly stratospheric, but it was the best of any politician tested and was considerably better than the Conservative Party's, which stood at just 2 per cent. Even so, anyone reading CTF's memo, especially anyone who bothered to look at the accompanying graphics detailing the results of their survey work, might well have thought twice about going to the country even at that late stage.

Not, however, it seems, Theresa May. Having all but made up her mind in Wales, she consulted the Party Chairman, Patrick McLoughlin. He was not, it must be said, too enthusiastic, telling her the party was 'not ready'; yet he also assured her that 'CCHQ would just get on with it' if she had made up her mind to call an election.[62] Had McLoughlin been rather less dutiful and rather more forthcoming (for instance, about the way the party's field, targeting, and digital operations had been allowed, as usual, to wind down in order to save money), he might have given May further cause to doubt she was making the right decision. But since he did not, and since there was no attempt made to go back to the membership – the 'poor bloody infantry', the 'boots on the ground' – to see if they were still as sceptical about an early election as they had been back in the summer, the die was cast. Whether, by then, the contest she was about to call really deserved to be called a 'snap' election, however, is debatable. May's humming and hawing, combined with both the need to ensure there would be sufficient time to pass a bill through parliament should Labour object and a desire to avoid polling day falling in the school holidays, meant that the campaign would run for seven long weeks – still not much time to get properly ready, yet more than enough time for something to go wrong.

Hubris to nemesis
(April–June 2017)

Such was the secrecy that surrounded May's decision to call a general election for 8 June that, when, on the morning of 18 April, she stepped out into Downing Street to announce it, she not only caught opposition politicians and political journalists by surprise, she did the same to the Conservative Party – from the grassroots all the way up to the front-bench. Not all of those gathered around the Cabinet table as she finally let all of them into the secret were thrilled at the prospect. Boris Johnson, for one, looked far from happy and (after she'd informed him in advance) had apparently even tried to talk her out of it. But if that was the case, many concluded, it was less because he had some unique inkling of what was to follow and more because he assumed, like most of his colleagues, that May was set to win a convincing majority, cementing her position as Prime Minister for another five years, by which time his opportunity to have another crack at the leadership might well have passed.[1] Certainly, most Conservative MPs considered it a bold but clever move – 'risky but logical', as one Cabinet minister later put it – and those who didn't (mainly those who had only just won their seats in 2015 and were banking on May's repeated assurances that she wouldn't go early to give them time to fully benefit from any 'incumbency effect') generally kept their misgivings private.[2] Any doubts were assuaged, if not entirely swept aside, firstly, by polling which put the Tories' lead over Labour well into double figures and, secondly, by the local elections held on 4 May, which saw them gain 563 seats and take control of 11 councils.

Those MPs who looked more carefully at those results, however, were a little less confident. The BBC's projected national share of the vote was reassuring in the sense that it showed Labour on 27 per cent, but also slightly worrying in that the Conservative share, at 38 per cent, fell somewhat short of what the party was registering in opinion polls. Had those MPs known what was going on at CCHQ in Matthew Parker

Street, just round the corner from the Palace of Westminster, they would have been even more concerned: no-one there was quite sure who was really in charge and there were profound differences of opinion over the strategy and the messaging the party should be pursuing.

Pulling in different directions: disagreements on strategy and messaging

Those disagreements arguably went all the way back to the stock-taking 'away day' held at Chequers in February. May's regular advisers, although far from agreed at that point on holding an early election, were convinced that, when it came, it should be fought on a manifesto emphasizing the more interventionist, reforming Conservatism articulated in May's early speeches and what became the *Plan for Britain*: Brexit, yes, but as a means to an end, namely (to quote what they had drafted as May's election opener) 'a country that works for everyone, not just the privileged few'.[3] Lynton Crosby, who was invited to Chequers (along with business partner Mark Fulbrook) not to discuss the next election but simply to talk about how the last one had been won, was unpersuaded and, although the discussions were amicable enough, said so.[4] It wasn't, however, until a couple of days before the election was called that Crosby (in Fiji on a long-planned family holiday) and his other business partner, Mark Textor (whose firm CTF had by then agreed to help run the campaign, with CCHQ's Stephen Gilbert acting as its Director), set down on paper – not least for May herself – what they believed needed to be done.[5]

Crosby and Textor, building not just on the polling CTF had already supplied but also on two new focus groups, were at pains to stress that while 'A good campaign could deliver an increased majority for the Conservatives ... there is also a clear risk that the party could end up with fewer seats than it has currently if the campaign is not framed in the correct way.' Nor did it take much reading between the lines to detect their concerns about the way May's advisers wanted to play and manage the election and what, given the risks involved and the Tories' relative strengths and weaknesses, Crosby and Textor thought was necessary. For one thing, 'the campaign director, with a direct line to the leader, not through any filter, must run the campaign' according to an agreed strategy and a plan that, for all that tactics could and should be adjusted according to ongoing opinion research, must be stuck to – failure to ensure this 'will result in bad strategic decisions being made under pressure, or even worse, no decisions being made with the senior team engaged in constant discussion over the right course'. For another, given that voters didn't want an early election, and that calling one would potentially contribute to the 'instability and uncertainty' they wanted to end,

> The Conservatives must show how in the long-term holding an election now will actually reduce uncertainty and is a way of getting on with Brexit. This is not an election about changing social policy, or changing the way the economy works as that will come from implementing Brexit. Rather, this election is about securing the best leadership to make Brexit work and see the UK through the uncertainty that lies ahead.
>
> The message 'a Britain that works for everyone and not just the privileged few' … will not help the Conservative vote for three reasons. Firstly it implies change when voters don't want any more change, they want stability and continuity. Secondly it is one of the least influential phrases and descriptors of people's voting intention – it just doesn't move votes. Thirdly it is associated by voters with the Labour Party rather than the Conservatives so if it becomes more salient and therefore has more of an impact on people's voting intention it will actually boost Labour's vote.

This, they reasoned, together with the risks they had identified in their earlier memo (namely the lack of any real appetite for an election, the number of 'soft voters' who could easily change their minds, and the widespread belief that the Tories would win easily), meant the following: putting May front and centre and stressing that she had no alternative but to call the election in the national interest so as to deliver Brexit and 'secure long term stability and economic security'; emphasizing the narrowness of her current majority and playing down the idea that the election would be a cake-walk; recognizing that it was 'not about change but continuity'; and 'understanding that this is not an "ordinary election" where a focus on policies, manifesto and what the Tory party might do are the central element'.

What resulted, however, was precisely the uneasy and ultimately unsuccessful compromise that CTF had counselled against. While

Gilbert retained his nominal role as Campaign Director, in practice lines of authority in CCHQ ended up being badly blurred between him, 'the Chiefs' (Nick Timothy and Fiona Hill), and 'the Australians' (Crosby and Textor).[6] May's team (principally in this respect Nick Timothy and the MP and Cabinet Office Minister Ben Gummer) put together what was essentially their dream 'change' manifesto – one chock-full of big new policies. Meanwhile, May (who seems to have regarded her role as doing what she was told, however unhappy that made her) toured the country in what up until then ranked as one of the most presidential election campaigns the country had ever seen, with the Tories' leaflets and even their shiny blue battlebus showcasing the Prime Minister rather than her party.[7] It was no small irony that, while she was being sold to the electorate as every inch a leader, behind the scenes May seemed unable, unwilling even, to operate as such. She was passive rather than active – done to rather than doing. According to someone centrally involved, not only did she not really seem to know what she wanted to do politically (in marked contrast, they noted, to both David Cameron and Boris Johnson), 'she didn't [even] want to come into CCHQ every day. … She only asked two questions in thirty days of campaigning.' And, instead of getting a grip and knocking a few heads together, she (as the journalist Tim Shipman put it) 'never chose between the competing campaign visions or forced the policy wonks, spin doctors and strategists to develop an integrated campaign'.[8]

Just as damagingly, it quickly became obvious that May was utterly miscast in the quasi-presidential role she'd agreed, however reluctantly, to play in public – a role that Crosby and Textor might not have insisted she take on in the first place had they been personally acquainted with her and therefore as familiar with her limitations as those who knew her well were. There was nothing unusual in the party limiting her television appearances or keeping her out of head-to-head debates (a decision made, incidentally, by those who *did* know her limitations rather than by 'the Australians'). After all, incumbents with big leads often shy away from such events, knowing they have more to lose than to gain from them and opting instead for stage-managed photo-ops where they recite well-rehearsed lines against a backdrop provided by carefully corralled party members holding up placards. But when she did take part in broadcast events and press conferences, May was seemingly unable to think on her feet or (although here it is worth considering the possibility that she was judged more harshly than a man might have been) to emotionally connect with the public.[9] She could handle set-piece speeches and claimed to enjoy door-knocking, but that was about it. As someone centrally involved in the campaign put it, although 'she was a decent person', 'She was scared. … She literally needed notes to say "It's great to be here in Slough again."… She was one of the most nervous people I've ever met.'

Policy and presentational problems

Two examples of May's difficulties stand out and were perhaps the most damaging to the party's campaign. The first has become somewhat legendary since it flowed from what, in hindsight, turned out to be the disastrous decision to include in the manifesto a plan to reform the funding of social care that, because it eschewed a cap on the costs paid by the recipient, was immediately (and devastatingly) labelled by opponents 'the dementia tax'. By no means everybody involved in the manifesto process had been thrilled with the policy in the first place: when tested (although in rather more abstract terms) in focus groups by Crosby and Textor, it had participants scratching their heads, and Fiona Hill felt so sure it would bomb that she tried on several occasions to get it removed. May, however, had backed Nick Timothy and Ben Gummer, and was therefore as dismayed as they were when Tory MPs and canvassers reported from the proverbial 'doorstep' that it had gone down like the proverbial cup of cold sick – so much so that she was eventually persuaded to execute a U-turn by announcing that the government would indeed cap the amount anyone would be obliged to pay for care. However, in her frustration with journalists asking awkward follow-ups, she then made a bad situation worse by claiming 'Nothing has changed', thereby seeming to treat voters as fools and coming over as anything but 'strong and stable' – the tagline for her campaign.[10]

The second example also took on a life of its own, and was possibly just as damaging. May had refused to take part in head-to-head debates – a refusal that inevitably drew accusations that she was running away both from them and from public scrutiny, as well as being a gift for Labour (which was taking every opportunity the campaign offered to get its left-wing populist leader out on the stump in front of adoring fans). However, she did agree to answer questions in front of a live studio audience less than a week away from polling day. Confronted with an NHS nurse complaining about her low pay, May informed her that 'there isn't a magic money tree that we can shake that suddenly provides for everything that people want' – a remark that not only appeared condescending and lacking in empathy but also appeared strikingly at odds with her promise that, with the Conservative Party under new management and parking itself on the supposed centre ground of British politics, there would be an end to austerity.

May, and by extension the Conservative campaign, also had a problem when it came to Brexit. While clearly a potential trump card with many of the Leave voters the party was hoping to win over from Labour, it was also something of a double-edged sword. Emphasizing it, as Crosby and Textor felt had to be done (especially after May, angered by a leak of her private meeting with the Head of the European Commission, Jean-Claude Junker, publicly accused Europeans of threatening Britain and trying to affect the result of the election), risked alienating what Number Ten's private polling operation had some months previously labelled 'Conservative Leaners' – younger, better educated and more socially liberal, and largely Remain-voting.[11] Meanwhile, May's understandable reluctance at that stage to flesh out the government's negotiating position in any detail meant she was forced to fall back on vague platitudes – Brexit means Brexit being only the most notorious – which did nothing, along with her wooden delivery and often rather awkward demeanour, to counter her growing reputation as 'the Maybot'. And because Labour, by joining the Tories in voting to trigger Article 50, was formally committed to the UK's withdrawal from the EU, the absence of a concrete plan that might have highlighted the differences between government and opposition made it harder than it might otherwise have been to persuade 'Labour leavers' that she, rather than Corbyn, would deliver precisely the kind of Brexit they wanted.

Brexit and the dementia tax weren't the only problems with the Conservatives' offer. The manifesto might have made only cursory mention of issues that its authors regarded as relatively unimportant, at least in the view of those ministers whose brief they fell under.[12] But its authors had nevertheless rejected calls to come up with a manifesto that did little more than offer a direction of travel. Instead Timothy and Gummer had come up with a document that, in their view, would answer the needs of a country crying out for change and signal a shift away from a Conservatism all-too-easily caricatured, in the words of the powerfully written introduction, as a commitment to 'untrammelled free markets' and 'the cult of selfish individualism' towards a more communitarian, Burkean approach that recognized 'the good that government can do'.[13] They were also intent on restoring trust in government and providing the party with a mandate that would simultaneously give civil servants clear running orders and discourage the House of Lords from attempting to override what they assumed would be a healthy Tory majority in the Commons. As a result, the document was packed with policies that, as one of those heavily involved in the campaign later pointed out, were (like the dementia tax) taken all the more seriously by voters because of the widely shared belief (at least at the start of campaign) that the Tories were going to win easily and were therefore actually going to be able to do not just what they were saying they wanted to do but all they'd ever wanted to do. The sheer range of policies also meant that there was plenty for other parties (and enterprising journalists) to take a pot shot at.

One such policy was the continuation of an existing commitment to a free vote on hunting with dogs, which, not for the first time, had apparently originated, at least in part, in the hope that the country's highly committed horse and hound community might consequently go out canvassing for the Conservatives, thereby helping to make up the difference between a Tory membership of, at most, 150,000 and a Labour membership of just under 520,000. Already attracting some negative attention on social media, the issue really caught fire (and probably did change some minds, especially among those who until then had been prepared to believe that May was a different kind of Tory) when the Prime Minister, answering questions at a campaign event, confirmed that she was personally in favour of hunting.[14]

Probably even more serious in terms of the damage done – partly because the compensatory measures involved were less arresting than the decisions themselves, and partly because the issues in question were squarely in Labour territory – were the party's pledges to remove the entitlement to free school lunches for all primary school children (albeit replacing free lunches with free breakfasts), to abandon the so-called 'triple lock' on pensions, and to means test the winter fuel allowance for pensioners. Whether, however, their inclusion in the manifesto – and indeed the content of the latter more generally – can necessarily be blamed on the process, as some aggrieved Tory ministers suggested after the event, is more of a moot point. In the Conservative Party, anyway, manifestos are always put together by a small, tight-knit group operating under conditions of secrecy, with ministers individually signing off on 'their sections' (for which their suggestions are, after all, just suggestions) and only seeing the whole thing very late in the day when little more than minor changes are usually practicable. And while, to echo another commonly heard complaint, it was, at an estimated 30,000 words or so, one of the longest the party has produced, it is worth recalling that so was the document that helped procure a surprise victory for another Tory Prime Minister who had been installed after a dramatic leadership contest and was now seeking a mandate of their own; indeed, in 1992 John Major won what is still the highest number of votes for any party ever recorded at a British general election.[15]

This is not to deny that the lack of a joined-up approach to the campaign at the very top – one that occasionally bordered on the positively dysfunctional – was a problem. Quite why, for instance, the party, having costed its manifesto, was reluctant to reveal those costings, even make a virtue of them, as it often had before and would do again, remains something of a mystery. It does seem clear, however, that its failure to press home an attack on the gaping holes in the exercise Labour claimed to have carried out on its own document originated with the Chiefs' determination, firstly, not to follow the Osborne playbook and, secondly, to sideline certain ministers – most obviously (indeed, almost painfully so) the Chancellor, Philip Hammond.[16] Perhaps if the party had been able to rely on its other traditional strength – its commitment to protecting and promoting national security – this decision to fight with one hand effectively tied behind its back on the economy might not have been so debilitating. But two terrorist attacks (one in Manchester and one in London) during the campaign undermined its reputation on that score too. Internal polling suggested support among voters who were particularly worried about immigration began to soften.[17] Meanwhile, Labour, desperate to distract from reminders of its leader's distinctly underwhelming record on such matters, was quick, particularly after the second attack, to point to the cuts to police numbers made under Theresa May when she was Home Secretary.

Organizational shortcomings

That Labour's response proved so effective, preventing, as it did, the Conservatives from getting back onto the front foot after the battering they had already received over the dementia tax, exposed another of the problems at CCHQ, namely the way it had allowed its digital operation to fall behind Labour's in the two years since the last election. Although it managed to tempt back the two men who had been in charge in 2015, Craig Elder and Tom Edmonds, they were hampered by a lack of preparation, by how long it sometimes took to get sign-off from higher-ups, and (though this was a more familiar problem) by the fact that Conservative Party activists were both thinner on the ground and (perhaps because they were older) less adept than their Labour counterparts at sharing content, let alone actually organically creating it. As a result, while the party could, with the partial exception of George Osborne's *Evening Standard*, count on friendly newspapers doing what they normally did, namely praising the Tories to the skies while laying into Labour at every opportunity, social media was a whole other ballgame – one that, according to detailed analyses (showing, for example, that Labour's Facebook likes increased by 75 per cent in comparison to only 10 per cent for the Tories despite CCHQ blowing 70 per cent of its digital spend on the platform), they pretty comprehensively lost.[18]

This wasn't, it should be stressed, down to any lack of money. True, Labour's two leadership elections in two years had been something of a cash bonanza for Corbyn's party, allowing it occasionally to outspend the Tories. However, after May took over from Cameron, and especially once she announced she was going to the country, the cash came pouring in. Indeed, in the first six months of 2017, the Conservative Party received nearly three times as much money in donations (£27 million) as Labour and nearly ten times as much as the Lib Dems; and in the six weeks prior to polling day, it took in twice as much (£12.5 million) as it had done under David Cameron in 2015; corporate donations to the party, meanwhile, were a third up on 2010 (when they had been higher than they were in 2015). Whether that was an endorsement of Theresa May or more fear of Jeremy Corbyn's brand of Labour politics, however, is impossible to know. What we do know, though, is that it is one thing to have the money and another to be able to spend it quickly enough, whether it be on staffing or on advertising (much of which, especially in the digital realm, is now done at the national level to support local candidates), to make a significant difference to a campaign.[19]

Even had that not been the case, the Tories would still have been left facing some severe organizational shortcomings. The lack of boots on the ground was always going to be a problem – one to which some of the solutions employed last time round, most obviously the 'Road Trip' bussing of young 'Team 2015' volunteers around the country (which had gone on to generate one scandal after another), were no longer available. Academic survey research made it obvious that Conservative members fell far behind their Labour counterparts in terms of what they did for their party during the election, being less than half as likely to do something as undemanding as displaying an election poster in their window, as well as being more reluctant to canvass voters – and even less keen to do anything to boost their party's efforts in the digital realm.[20] Some of this may have had to do with complacency in the face of what looked like an overwhelming poll lead at the start of the campaign. But it may also have been due to a degree of disappointment (extending in some cases to acrimony) at the way CCHQ, pleading lack of time, severely limited local associations' choice of candidates – not that it led, incidentally, to significantly more women, for instance, being adopted: the figure was 26 per cent in 2015 rising to 29 per cent in 2017, producing a parliamentary party which was 21 per cent female, compared to Labour's 44 per cent. Moreover, many of those volunteers who were still willing to knock on doors anyway found themselves (even on election day itself) directed to contact voters who had absolutely no intention of voting Conservative, their lists having been compiled not from local canvassing records (which they had not really had time to update) but instead from 'big data' guesses about which households in their area looked like good prospects.[21]

That data, together with polling, also helped inform changes to the party's list of target seats. Overseen by CCHQ veteran Stephen Gilbert, who nominally directed the Tory campaign, at least until Lynton Crosby could make it to the UK, the list (based initially on Labour Leave seats that had a reasonably sized 2015 UKIP vote) started out identifying thirty-plus 'attack seats' – a number which shifted up and then down as the campaign progressed – most of which were visited (to no great purpose, it turned out) by Theresa May.[22] Given the eventual result, the exercise proved fairly futile in the immediate sense, although, arguably, not entirely fruitless in the long term since many of the Labour seats identified by the Tories as targets in 2017 eventually fell to them in 2019. It should also be noted that a separate targeting exercise run by the Scottish Conservatives, relying heavily on the insights of data analyst James Kanagasooriam, proved far more successful, helping them to an additional 324,000 votes, thereby doubling their vote share and taking them from just one seat to thirteen seats on a distinctly unionist platform that helped consolidate their support among those who rejected independence. Wales proved less fertile territory, although even here there were some encouraging signs: mirroring the situation across the border in England, the party lost seats but its vote share was its highest for a century, helped by a collapse in support for UKIP.

That things weren't working out as well as everybody had first hoped was no secret to anyone working in CCHQ. True, only a select few at the top were privy to CTF's tracking polling in the marginals, which, even as early as late April, was suggesting that the overall swing to the Tories recorded in most public polling was unlikely to result in as many gains as people thought since, to quote from an accompanying memo, 'A clear trend can be seen to exist whereby incumbent Conservative MPs are underperforming the party's national vote share, while Labour MPs (and Liberal Democrat challengers) are overperforming their parties' national position.'[23] But even so, morale flagged as the campaign wore on (not helped by an unseasonable flu bug that ran through CCHQ), with Theresa May, on the rare occasions that she appeared before the serried ranks of staffers, apparently as hopeless at whipping up enthusiasm among them as she was among voters.

In fact, morale might have been even lower had the party's later polling, modelled by Jim Messina, been more widely distributed as the campaign entered the final days – indeed, as election day approached, those privy to it were well aware that a hung parliament was a distinct possibility. Yet so, too, was an increased majority of almost sixty.[24] Earlier, Messina and Textor had ridiculed a worrying YouGov poll which used a new technique (multilevel regression and poststratification: MRP for short) to extrapolate results from a large national sample to predict results in individual seats. This confidence had not entirely evaporated, helping to persuade people to stick to the strategy even when May was misfiring as the campaign's figurehead. In any case, only a handful of people in CCHQ (outside the leader and her team, who were made aware of it) had seen Textor's very alarming final estimate of vote share showing the Tories and Labour at nearly level pegging on forty-something per cent. Which was why, when the exit poll dropped at ten o'clock, suggesting that the Conservatives were on course not for a majority but simply to become the largest party in a hung parliament, the shock was as great for the vast majority watching in Matthew Parker Street as it was in the rest of the country.

Post-mortem: the election result analysed

When all the votes were counted, the Conservative Party had gained 20 seats but lost 33, reducing its total to just 317.[25] It had increased its vote share by getting on for 6 percentage points – one of the biggest rises in support ever recorded by an incumbent government that had won the previous election. It had also managed (partly, perhaps, by pouring resources into them and partly by playing on their electorate's antipathy to Jeremy Corbyn) to hold on to 23 of the 27 seats it had snatched from the Lib Dems in 2015, as well as capturing 12 seats from the Scottish National Party (SNP). However, Labour's share of the vote had risen nationally by nearly 10 percentage points – the biggest increase achieved by any party since the 1945 election. Given the relative standing of the two parties when May had called the election, the fact that the gap between them on polling day was just 2.5 percentage points (Labour on 40 per cent and the Tories on 42.5 per cent), it is difficult to believe that the poor campaign she fought had nothing to do with the outcome. The proportion of voters (nearly one in five) who changed their minds over the course of the campaign may not have been particularly high, but what was unusual was that one of the two big parties (Labour) seems to have won more than half of them (as well as more than half of those who were originally undecided), while the other (the Conservatives) converted only around a fifth.

How much this was driven by or reflected in the ratings of the two party leaders is debatable. But what is inarguable is that one fared so much better than the other: YouGov polling at the end of April suggested May had a lead over Corbyn of 30 percentage points, yet by the end of the campaign that had dropped to 11 points; by the same token, May's favourability rating fell from +17 in late April to -5 by the start of June, while Corbyn's rose from a truly awful -52 to a relatively neutral -2. The Conservative Party's lead on competence also fell to just 3 percentage points over the course of the campaign. According to YouGov, it was also the case that whereas the average age at which people were more likely to vote Tory than Labour stood at 34 at the start of the campaign, it reached 47 by the end of it, which suggests a severe loss of support among people in their thirties and forties – perhaps because they were most likely to be households with children still at school and therefore more attuned to Labour's anti-austerity appeals, as well as more aware than most that May's much-trumpeted desire to do something for the 'just about managing' had resulted in few if any concrete measures in the half a year she had been in Number Ten. More generally, polls suggested that, after seven years of spending restraint, voters were now more worried about the state of public services than they were about the public finances.

Further analysis of the result revealed that the Tories performed particularly well (even if they didn't always win them) in seats with more homeowners, fewer ethnic minorities, and fewer people with qualifications, with a 22 point lead over Labour among people with GCSEs or less and a 17 point deficit to Labour when it came to university graduates. Support for Labour from the UK's ethnic minority voters was, once again, overwhelming, whereas the Conservatives led among white voters by 6 percentage points; the party's ethnic minority candidates also fared on average worse (by some 3.6 percentage points) than their white counterparts. More generally, Tory candidates who were defending their seats for the first time didn't in the end underperform in the way CCHQ had initially feared, although any incumbency effect turned out to be relatively small once the demographics of the seat they were defending were taken into account. Across the country as a whole the Tories' support among working-class voters improved markedly (up 12 percentage points among social grades C2DE on 2015, giving them a 7 point lead over Labour among the proverbially crucial C2, skilled manual workers). And while the Conservative Party's support among younger people declined, its support among older people was even more rock-solid than it had been in 2015, winning it the votes of an estimated 69 per cent of those 70 and over and 58 per cent of those aged between 60 and 69. Many (though not, of course, all) of these demographic differences were, it seems, ultimately driven by voters' views on Brexit.

The Conservatives did better in seats where the local economy seemed to be faring worst, suggesting that significant numbers of so-called 'left-behind' voters were now more concerned with issues like immigration and leaving the EU than punishing the incumbent government for austerity and/or their stagnant or even falling standard of living. In this respect, the Tories were clearly helped by the collapse of the UKIP vote, winning well over half of it while Labour only won a fifth. Partly (but only partly) because of that, there was a clear correlation between how well the party performed in a particular constituency and how heavily that constituency was estimated to have voted for Brexit: where the Leave vote was under 45 per cent, the Conservative vote actually dropped by just under 2 percentage points relative to 2015; where it was over 60 per cent, however, the party's support had risen by just over 10 points. The problem was that in all too many cases, even that impressive improvement in the Tory vote share wasn't quite sufficient yet to overcome fairly large Labour majorities, whether or not (as in the North East but not, unfortunately, in the Midlands or Yorkshire/Humber) there was a regional swing to the Conservatives. In the 18 Labour seats which, in 2019, sent their first Conservative MPs to Westminster since at least 1945, the Tory vote share in 2017 rose on average by 14 percentage points, but Labour's also rose by 7 points. In part, this was because Labour won considerably more support than the Tories among Remain supporters. But it was mainly because a fair few 'Labour Leavers', who – as 'identity conservatives' – may initially have been tempted to vote Tory, decided, in 2017 anyway, to prioritize their domestic concerns (such as strains on healthcare and education and, especially in the wake of the terrorist attacks, cuts to policing) over their desire to quit the EU and opted, for now at least, to stick with their traditional choice.[26]

This reflected, firstly, the fact that Labour at that point was not widely seen as wanting to block Brexit and, secondly, a finding from post-vote polling which found that while Brexit was seen as the single most important issue facing the country (albeit by a plurality of just under 30 per cent of voters), it dropped down to third place behind the NHS and the cost of living when people were asked to say what was most important for 'me and my family'. Surveys also suggested that, in contrast to the 2016 referendum, when a fair few habitual non-voters were persuaded to go the ballot box (and to vote for Brexit), on 8 June 2017 around a million more Remain than Leave supporters turned out to vote.

Ultimately, of course, the fact that Theresa May lost her majority also owed something to the UK's first past the post electoral system failing to manufacture a majority government on the basis of a small lead held by one of the two largest parties over the other – something that until recently it could normally be relied on to do. That system, at least in 2017, was far from biased against the Conservatives. Indeed, their vote was so efficiently distributed that it more than compensated for the advantage accruing to Labour from the fact that many of its constituencies had smaller populations. Had the two parties finished on level pegging, for instance, the Tories would have won 12 more seats than their main rival, and as it was they won 48.9 per cent of Commons seats for their 42.5 per cent of the vote. But these days there are more small parties (the Scottish Nationalists being the best example) whose geographically concentrated strength outweighs the disadvantages they would otherwise face under first past the post. And there are also far fewer marginal seats than there once were: even though the total of 89 that were fought over in 2017 was an increase on the record low of 74 contested in 2015, it still represented a significantly lower number than the 149 in play back in 1970. As a consequence, any result falling between a 3 percentage point lead for the Tories and a 7 point lead for Labour would likely have resulted in a hung parliament. Having beaten Labour by just 2.5 points, however, that was precisely the scenario in which May would now have to operate.

4

A bad hand played badly
(June 2017–May 2019)

There were moments in the hours and days that followed the release of the exit poll when Theresa May was barely able to hold it together. Indeed, when, just after learning of its findings, she phoned her Chief of Staff, Nick Timothy, 'She was sobbing ... like a child who wanted to be told everything was just fine.'[1] But although resignation had briefly crossed her mind, by the next morning she had somehow convinced herself, firstly, that others (not least Lynton Crosby) were to blame for the defeat and, secondly, that she could, and should, remain Prime Minister, even if she couldn't yet be certain that no-one was intending to try to replace her.[2] In fact, there was never any determined effort to persuade May to stand down. For a start, in the words of one of her advisers, 'There was a tacit understanding all round that she wasn't going to lead the party into another general election. But there was also an understanding that most of the party ... wanted to get Brexit done and changing leaders and having more uncertainty put that at risk.' It also helped that her Cabinet colleagues, like most people, had been expecting a fairly comfortable Conservative victory. Consequently, none of them were remotely prepared for a challenge or, given the uncertainty into which defeat had plunged the party and the country, even appeared really to want the job.[3] As a result, May, occasionally still tearful but increasingly determined to get on with it, moved rapidly, firstly, to secure a deal with the Democratic Unionist Party (DUP) to keep her in Downing Street (details to be negotiated by her then ultra-loyal Chief Whip, Gavin Williamson) and, secondly, to reappoint her 'big beast' Secretaries of State: Boris Johnson (who was regarded as the biggest threat) at the Foreign Office; David Davis (who would have stood against him if he had decided to try to replace May) at the Department for Exiting the European Union (DExEU); Amber Rudd at the Home Office; and Philip Hammond at the Treasury.

May tries to steady the ship

May also brought in, for ballast, her old friend Damian Green as a de facto deputy in whom she could trust. Then, so as to signal her bona fides to Brexiteers, she brought Michael Gove back into Cabinet as Environment Secretary and appointed arch-Eurosceptics Steve Baker and Anne-Marie Trevelyan to junior roles, space having been freed up by nine frontbenchers losing their seats at the election – not that their promotion was necessarily enough to assuage all their concerns, especially about her supposedly pro-EU advisers. May decided almost immediately that she would have to dispense with her long-time loyal lieutenants Nick Timothy and Fiona Hill (both of whom were blamed – fairly or unfairly – for the election débâcle and for the way a number of ministers had been treated prior to and during the campaign). And she also decided very early on that Timothy's successor as her Downing Street Chief of Staff should be Gavin Barwell, who had extensive experience in the voluntary, professional, and parliamentary party and who she might well have promoted into Cabinet had he not been one of the frontbenchers who lost their seats. But while Barwell was well liked and well respected right across the party, and had both the intelligence and the people skills required to steady the ship and repair relations with the parliamentary party, there was no disguising the fact that, unlike Timothy, he was a Remainer.

That was not, however, true of all those around her. While JoJo Penn stayed on as May's Deputy Chief of Staff, so, as her Political Secretary, did Vote Leave's Stephen Parkinson. Moreover, the vacancy that opened up with the departure of May's Director of Strategy and Chief Speechwriter, Chris Wilkins (who had decided to go after apparently being passed over for promotion), was filled, as Director of Communications, by Robbie Gibb, a former BBC news and current affairs producer and, very usefully, an avowed Brexiteer. Meanwhile, James Marshall replaced John Godfrey as the Director of the Policy Unit, Godfrey having decided, along with another key member of May's staff, Will Tanner, that her small majority and her focus on Brexit would probably leave little room for other policy ambitions – a hunch that was borne out a few weeks later when the Queen's Speech outlined a domestic programme that bore only the slightest resemblance to the party's ambitious election manifesto.[4] That tight parliamentary arithmetic also led May to appoint Nikki da Costa to oversee legislative affairs.

The deal with the DUP may have taken a little longer than originally envisaged but it looked, initially anyway, to have been achieved at relatively little political cost. The financial gain for Northern Ireland (£1 billion of additional spending over two years) inevitably occasioned a fair degree of criticism. However, the DUP, much to the relief of politicians in Westminster and Whitehall, declined Williamson's offer of a full-blown coalition in favour of a confidence-and-supply agreement. And, beyond confirming that the government would not now mess with the triple lock on pensions and winter fuel allowances, it made no policy demands. In return, the government, which emphasized that it would maintain its impartiality on Northern Ireland, believed it had secured the support of the DUP on budgetary matters, on the Queen's Speech, on confidence motions, on national security measures, and on 'legislation pertaining to the United Kingdom's exit from the European Union'.

Securing the support of the DUP was one thing. Securing the support of Conservative MPs for the woman who had blown their party's majority and cost some of their friends and colleagues their seats was another. May hadn't helped matters by the tin-eared address she'd made outside Downing Street on Friday, 9 June, the day after the election – one which, in its desperation to demonstrate she would be getting on with the job, failed to communicate much, if anything, by way of an apology. By Monday, 12 June, however, things were very different. After a difficult Cabinet meeting during which ministers (in a manner which made it painfully obvious how much her authority had been eroded by the election result) vented their feelings about the previous set-up in Number Ten, May addressed her MPs at a packed meeting of the 1922 Committee (helpfully backed by its Chairman, Graham Brady) with just the right combination of contrition, humility, and determination.[5] Barwell's appointment was welcomed by all those present, as was his concerted attempt over the coming months to rebuild relations between Number Ten and the parliamentary party through weekly lunches with assorted groups of backbenchers.

But just as things seemed to be looking up, May found herself criticized, even condemned, for failing to appear immediately at the scene of the terrible fire that destroyed Grenfell Tower in North Kensington, an error she compounded by choosing (in marked contrast with Jeremy Corbyn) only to meet emergency services staff rather than the survivors and the families of the seventy-two people who had perished. It was, as May herself later admitted, a bad mistake, and one that she did her best to atone for in due course (albeit more in private than in public).[6] Moreover, especially in the wake of a hastily arranged 'car-crash' interview with the BBC's Emily Maitlis, it reinforced the impression formed during the election campaign of a leader who lacked the common touch and the emotional intelligence that most politicians need if they are to rise to the top. But if it left MPs – particularly those who had decided not to try to replace her as leader in the immediate aftermath of the election – wondering whether they'd done the right thing in sticking by her, there were few signs that their local party members were ready for a change of leader. Surveyed by academics at the end of June and beginning of July, some 71 per cent of the Tory rank and file said they thought she should stay as leader, with only 21 per cent saying she should stand down and let someone else take over – this despite the fact that, when asked to rate her performance during the general election on a scale of zero ('extremely disappointing') to ten ('excellent'), eight out of ten of them scored her somewhere between zero and four.[7] Fortunately, grassroots Tories appeared to be broadly supportive of the deal with the DUP, being in no mood for a second general election – something that less than a fifth of them wanted to see happen were that deal not to work out.

As well as providing a useful reminder that 'members' and 'activists' are by no means interchangeable terms (some 42 per cent of the former admitted they had spent no time whatsoever helping out the party during the election, a figure which rose to 58 per cent when they were asked about the average month outside elections), the survey also asked the Conservative rank and file for their views on Brexit. What came over most clearly was their overwhelming antipathy to the idea of a second referendum, with some 71 per cent saying another vote should definitely not be held compared to just 7 per cent who thought one should. It was also clear that eight out of ten (58 per cent 'definitely' plus 25 per cent 'more yes than no') saw the referendum as meaning that EU citizens should not be accorded any preferential treatment as far as immigration to the UK was concerned. Interestingly, there was slightly less certainty with regard to two options – single market and customs union membership – that May had already appeared to have ruled out, with, in both cases, just under 50 per cent saying the country should definitely depart from both and around 20 per cent saying they were more in favour of departing than staying. Still, that indicated basic support for the hard Brexit the PM had set a course for in her 2016 party conference speech, meaning that there was little pressure – outside as well as inside parliament – for the kind of reset or recalibration that some of her colleagues, worried at the time that any softening of her position would have led to her immediate defenestration, believed in hindsight might have been worth a try.[8]

Quite what such a move might have entailed – beyond, perhaps, actually spelling out to some of the zealots on her own side of the House the hard choices and trade-offs Brexit was bound to involve – is difficult to gauge, although it is highly doubtful that any pivot on her part could have involved 'reaching across the aisle' in the Commons. May remained convinced that Leave had won the EU referendum in large part because of public concern about immigration, therefore ruling out continued membership of the single market – which many Labour MPs favoured but which would have entailed the continuation of uncontrolled entry by EU citizens. As one of her frustrated Cabinet colleagues, Chancellor Philip Hammond, later observed, 'the Prime Minister was obsessed by migration, as were a sizeable chunk of the Tory Party'.[9] There were narrower partisan factors at play too – seeking support from Jeremy Corbyn's Labour was anathema to a lifelong, deeply tribal Conservative like May, and would have prompted an immediate revolt from hardline Tory backbenchers, particularly those in the Eurosceptic European Research Group (ERG) who were already worried they might 'lose Brexit' altogether. Just as crucial, there was a genuine fear (from the Cabinet all the way down to the backbenches) that the instability triggered by any such uprising might spin out of control and somehow end up with Jeremy Corbyn moving into Downing Street.

As if that weren't enough, it was obvious as summer moved towards autumn that those Cabinet ministers most associated with Vote Leave – particularly those who, while they might not have been prepared to strike back in June, still harboured leadership ambitions – had no intention of allowing May to soften the government's position. Boris Johnson, in part because he was genuinely concerned about that possibility, in part because he wanted to maintain his visibility, had, with the help of Vote Leave's Dominic Cummings, been working up a typically boosterish speech on Brexit but had been asked not to give it by Downing Street while legislation affecting some of the technical details of withdrawal was going through the Commons. In mid-September, however, apparently worried he was being eclipsed in the eyes of the membership by Brexit-ultras like Jacob Rees-Mogg, Johnson decided to turn it into 4,000-word article for his old bosses at the *Telegraph* (who, as ever, were more than happy to feature it in their front-page splash), only informing Number Ten that it was about to be published once it was too late for them to request any changes. Her authority too shot to enable her to sack or even openly criticize her Foreign Secretary, May, acting on Barwell's advice, instead invited him, along with Michael Gove, to contribute to the drafting of a big speech on Brexit she was due to give in Florence the following week. Cabinet was also allowed to discuss the text in advance of her delivering the speech, which – in markedly friendly tones but without going into much detail on the precise nature of the future relationship – basically confirmed that the government wanted as close a trading relationship with the EU as it was possible to have while remaining outside the single market, the customs union, and the jurisdiction of the European Court of Justice; it also made vaguely reassuring noises on citizens' rights and contributions to the EU budget, and signalled the need for some kind of transition period following the UK's departure.

To the understandable fury of some inside Number Ten, as well as a fair few of his Cabinet colleagues, this did not prove sufficient to prevent Johnson, keen as ever to maintain his position as the darling of the Conservative Party conference, from making another intervention on Europe in another Brussels-bashing newspaper (the *Sun*) on the Saturday before delegates gathered in Manchester. The interview itself (headlined 'BREXY BEAST Boris Johnson reveals his four Brexit "red lines" for Theresa May') may have been sanctioned by Downing Street, but its content, cutting, as it did, across much of the carefully crafted message May had delivered in Italy a week or so before, most definitely wasn't.[10] Once again, however, a severely weakened Prime Minister could do nothing to rein in her ambitious rival. For his part, the Foreign Secretary not only refused to accept that there were very real obstacles standing in the way of the clean break with Brussels that he was demanding; he also seemed to regard rules as something that applied to other people, not to him – up to and including collective Cabinet responsibility.[11]

With Johnson treating delegates gathered in the main hall to a typically upbeat, nationalistic speech that ranged, ominously, far beyond his Foreign Affairs brief, while Rees-Mogg told members during one of his many appearances at fringe meetings that they should have more say in the party's direction, a lot was riding on May's closing speech. Sadly for her, it was a disaster. As she attempted to pull the focus away from Brexit and highlight pledges on housing, health, and student finance, she was handed a P45 by a prankster ('Boris asked me to give you this'), after which she began to fight a losing battle with a sore throat and a persistent cough just as assorted letters began to disappear one by one from the slogan *Building a country that works for everyone* glued (none too securely, it turned out) to the backdrop behind her. Had Grant Shapps (a former minister and Party Chairman whom May had declined to bring back on to the frontbench when she replaced Cameron) not launched a half-arsed attempt – one ruthlessly, even gleefully, exposed by the Whips' Office – to gather support for some sort of coup against her in the immediate aftermath, then the dismay felt by many Tory MPs at her performance in Manchester may have built into something more threatening. As it was, she appeared fairly safe – for now.

Post-mortem as catharsis – and some home improvements

In fact, in another respect, albeit one less evident to most of those covering the event for the media, the conference was something of a success. The disastrous election result had left many Tory MPs, candidates, and grassroots activists feeling let down by the leadership and CCHQ. They needed an opportunity to express their frustrations lest they fester over the summer only to burst out when politics proper returned in the autumn. As well as providing an early post-mortem, the review into the election defeat that Theresa May and Patrick McLoughlin commissioned from the veteran former Cabinet minister (and former Party Chairman) Sir Eric Pickles also afforded an opportunity for catharsis.[12]

Pickles, who had stood down from parliament in 2017 after over three decades as an MP and council leader, was pretty much the perfect choice:

as one of those involved put it, not only was he 'masterful in the way he handled everything and everybody', but he

> was seen to be an honest broker – not particularly a Theresa May ally, not particularly associated with people who were against her. He allowed that process to take place and facilitated it in a way that people felt they were venting and it was being heard. That was clearly important. Had that not happened we would have imploded.

Just as importantly, they stressed, Pickles agreed that there was no point in trying to 'find victims to nail to the cross'. After all,

> We were in crisis at that stage. ... We'd had a couple of sacrifices – Theresa's two chiefs of staff had fallen on their swords and gone – [but] ultimately if you were going to hold anybody accountable it would have been the Prime Minister. She called the election and ... she lost the election. ... At the time we were not ready for a leadership contest and the party had to try and pick up the pieces.

Inviting submissions and testimony from right across the country, Sir Eric – assisted by Graham Brady, Chairman of the 1922 Committee; Patrick McLoughlin, Party Chairman; Sir Mick Davis, the party's new CEO; Rob Semple, the Chairman of the voluntary party's National Convention; and MP Nus Ghani – managed to put together his Review in time for Manchester, by which time, as one of those involved in its production confirmed, it had

> allowed for a whole range of people to vent, for people engaged in the process to do a little bit of penance, and for Pickles to get up and present a report which laid no blame anywhere other than to say that, going forward, these are the sort of things that we should be concentrating on. And it did the trick because we moved on quite smartly after the report was presented.

Many of the Review's 126 recommendations were already seen as common sense. But just as importantly, they, along with its underlying message, reinforced the rationale for reforms that were then underway at CCHQ – namely, as one of those involved put it, 'that you can't go into a general election without proper preparation, and that means that you have to have a proper campaign machine, effective activists on the ground, people [who] have to be trained and know what to do'. Chief amongst the architects of reform was the Party's Treasurer, Sir Mick Davis. A successful businessman and generous party donor, Davis, in the wake of the election defeat, had composed a no-punches-pulled memo to Theresa May outlining what had to done – and done urgently. It recommended a radical restructuring of CCHQ. The party needed not just a Chairman but a full-time, permanent, professional (as opposed to political) CEO. It had to expand its donor base to reduce reliance on a few high-net-worth individuals. It needed to plan for a major expansion of organizational capacity and to present a better proposition to potential donors – one that should include a pledge to revamp field campaigning, digital comms, data capture, membership recruitment and retention, fundraising, business engagement, and support for incumbents in marginal seats. Never again should the Conservative Party do what it had done after the general election in 2015, namely bank the win and wind down the organization on the assumption that the machine could simply be fired up for an election in five years' time.

If Party Chairman Patrick McLoughlin had concerns about some of the suggestions, in particular the creation of the CEO role, which might cut across his own, he did not try to talk Theresa May out of them or, indeed, out of accepting Sir Mick's offer to take on the new CEO role himself. As a result, internal changes came thick and fast. The most immediate was the decision to move forward with an existing plan, implemented by the Director of Campaigning, CCHQ stalwart (and future CEO) Darren Mott, to hire at least seventy (rising to a hundred) campaign managers. They would be placed in marginal and target seats, funded mainly by CCHQ but also, where possible, from local associations, very few of which nowadays contribute much money to CCHQ itself despite their often possessing substantial financial resources.

In contrast to the agents of old (nearly 300 of whom, for example, were employed by the party back in the early 1970s), many of these campaign managers were young, politically passionate recent graduates whose largely untested skills and suitability would be measured by assessing their performance at the 2018 local elections – one reason why a fair few were posted to London in the first instance, particularly in vulnerable boroughs like Barnet, which the Tories were desperate to hold and in which lay highly marginal parliamentary seats such as Chipping Barnet (2017 maj. 353), Finchley and Golders Green (2017 maj. 1,657), and Hendon (2017 maj. 1,072). But whether the new hires were placed in seats the Conservatives were defending or intending to target, the hope was that, especially once they gained experience and were given proper training, they might be able to offset the advantage a larger and more active membership supposedly gave Labour – particularly if a combination of canvassing and data purchased by CCHQ allowed them to better identify potential Tory voters.

This contrast between the Tory and Labour grassroots may not have bothered everyone at the top of the Conservative Party but CCHQ had clearly begun to take it seriously.[13] It was not just the difference in raw numbers: the massive expansion of Labour's dues-paying membership meant that, for the first time in years, there was a realistic prospect of the Conservatives being outspent by their main rival. Labour's revival also played into wider Conservative concerns about its own support base, which was increasingly 'pale, male and stale', with relatively few women, people from ethnic minorities, and employees in the public sector. Such an unrepresentative bunch might find it more and more difficult to engage directly with potential voters, both during and outside election campaigns, and digitally as well as 'on the doorstep'. The 2017 election had only served to confirm that, in the words of one CCHQ insider, the Tories had fallen 'light years behind Labour' on social media since 2015. Accordingly, CCHQ strengthened its marketing and its membership sections, and accelerated progress towards a single, centrally administered membership system in order to improve recruitment and retention by providing an improved membership experience. It also set itself an ambitious goal of boosting membership from around 150,000 to between 275,000 and 300,000 by October 2019, although this target was later scaled back to 200,000 and was never in fact reached, at least under May.

The 2017 election had also revealed major problems with the Conservative Party's data collection and analytics – problems that, as noted earlier, had seen canvassing teams all over the country sent to households they were told were Tory prospects but turned out to be either immune to the party's charms or actively hostile. Lack of good-quality information on, and analysis of, potential and actual Conservative voters was also hamstringing the party's attempts to improve communications and targeting. The proposed solution was not only to spend more on all this but also to bring more of it back in-house, ramping up the capacity to interpret data gathered on the doorstep and through the purchase of commercially available databases and then to put it to use improving voter communication. After all, as an internal CCHQ briefing noted, 'Data is a valuable asset, but without it converted into actionable insight, and then acted upon, it is merely an expensive one.' CCHQ also wanted a year-round increase in resources going to Tory MPs in marginals to assist them in developing localized business and media campaigns to help them better leverage the electoral benefits that often accrue to incumbents.[14]

The party looked, as well, to beef up the Conservative Research Department (CRD) to improve not only its rebuttal and attack operation but also its policy capacity – something which always tends to suffer when the party goes into government. A start was made on this by hiring Adam Memon, the 26-year-old Economic Adviser to the Chief Secretary to the Treasury, to be the new CRD Director – the youngest person, and first British Asian, to occupy the post. More important, though, was his grip on matters financial, since it was widely felt that the party had failed to effectively land an attack on Labour's economic policies in the 2017 campaign, even if that failure ultimately had more to do with campaign strategy than research capacity. Under Memon, the CRD's staffing complement, in single figures when he arrived, doubled – and included people with more real-world economics experience; the department also did its best to maintain the gender balance it had achieved by the 2017 election. By the time Memon moved on in the summer of 2019 to become Special Adviser to the new Chancellor, Sajid Javid, CRD had gone from being, in the words of one involved in revamping it, 'a bit of a shell to being a machine that could fight an election' – a task made easier by the occasional leaks it received of Labour's economic policies.

None of CCHQ's changes came cheap, notwithstanding the fact that political commitment often enables parties to hire staff on lower salaries than they could command elsewhere. The party's annual conference was now netting around £2 million every year, substantial but nowhere near enough to finance the rebuilding and retooling envisaged. Nor was there much scope for savings, even if some staff were let go. Hence the ambition to achieve a 50 per cent increase in revenue, in part by expanding membership of the tiered 'donor clubs' for well-heeled supporters but also by trying to increase smaller donations (solicited, for example, through direct mailshots) so as to decrease the party's reliance on a few very dedicated and very rich supporters. Initially, there was some reluctance on the part of both newly approached and established donors unimpressed by the 2017 campaign to part with their money. That reluctance, interestingly, continued longer among some strong advocates of Brexit (who refused to give until the latter was delivered or on the grounds that the government wasn't Leave enough) than among former Remainers, who had accepted the result of the referendum and whose main goal now was preventing Jeremy Corbyn from getting into Downing Street. Conversations with potential donors now featured a fully costed, detailed business plan which stressed, in the words of Sir Mick Davis (still a significant donor himself), that they were being presented with 'an investment proposition rather than a donation proposition'. This more business-like approach, combined with greater fear of a Corbyn-led Labour Party in Downing Street, helped ensure the ambitious fundraising target was met. This achievement was all the more impressive given donors' concerns about the Tories' increasingly obvious internal divisions in Cabinet and parliament.

Before those began to open up in earnest, however, the Cabinet met, without civil servants present, to consider a detailed analysis of what had gone wrong for the party prepared by May's pollster James Johnson, working with Tom Lubbock at CCHQ, and based primarily on British Election Study (BES) surveys conducted before and immediately after the election. It began by telling some hard truths about just how old the Tory electorate had become and, most importantly, about how much of the surprise result was actually down to 'perceptions of Conservative performance on domestic issues like public services – the NHS, … tuition fees, schools, public spending, austerity … and the real influence that had on voters' views of the Conservative Party'.[15] The furore over the manifesto was important, Johnson noted, but only in the context of voters' deeper concerns about successive Conservative governments since 2010 presiding over declining public services. Conservative attacks on Corbyn in 2017 hadn't cut through for all sorts of reasons: they seemed too shrill; people didn't trust the media that was carrying the attack message; they cared less about personality than promises on public services and Brexit; and Labour didn't look like winning anyway – which (interestingly in hindsight), while 'it wasn't important for swing voters, … *was* important for those longer term Labour voters who didn't like Corbyn [and] who felt they could vote for him without it costing anything'. The Tories' commitment to Brexit, James Johnson argued (to the chagrin of less Eurosceptic ministers), had, overall, turned out to be a net benefit: it encouraged Leave voters to plump for the Tories, while those who did not vote Conservative were discouraged less by their dislike of Brexit than by their fear that a Conservative government would revert to type on austerity.

James Johnson's analysis segmented voters into groups that the government could use to produce electorally attractive policies over the next few years. One group, the Traditional Conservatives, would carry on supporting the party regardless. Conversely, the Labour Left – relatively young, university-educated, and Remain-voting – were pretty much unreachable. Labour's Working Class – inner-city, low-paid or unwaged, and Leave voting – would be hard to reach but weren't altogether a lost cause because of Brexit. Then there were Urban Middle-Class Defectors – not yet middle-aged, often living in southern England, Remain-supporting but needing reassurance on public services. New Conservative Supporters were older, working-class Leave voters for whom Brexit really mattered. And finally there were Conservative Considerers – a volatile group who tended to be working class, to live in the North and the Midlands, a little bit more female and somewhat Leave – voters the party hadn't quite persuaded in 2017, in the main because they were more concerned with domestic issues and had doubts about whether the Tories were really interested in looking out for them. This was the group, James Johnson argued, that should be uppermost in ministers' minds when making policy, although this was not necessarily a message some of the more socially liberal, sometimes Remain-supporting, fiscally conservative politicians around the Cabinet table wanted to hear. To them it felt like doubling down on the failed 2017 strategy.

Their misgivings, however, had relatively little impact on policy choices. For one thing, it was clear from the June Queen's Speech that

Brexit was going to leave room for little else. For another, May's team had all but made up their minds (supported not just by survey evidence but also by post-election feedback from MPs) that more needed to be spent on schools and the health service in particular – a decision that had already led to an early announcement of an extra £1.3 billion for schools by Education Secretary Justine Greening and which was eventually to lead (albeit just before May's eventual departure two years later) to the 'Long-term Plan' for the NHS, the latter winning support from Brexiteers who otherwise might have bridled at the cost to the taxpayer but were happy to sell any increase in health spending as Britain's 'Brexit dividend' and fulfilment of the promise plastered on the side of Vote Leave's battlebus back in 2016.[16]

Rebellion and reshuffle

Given May's misfortune in Manchester, the post-conference political cycle actually began relatively well, with the government moving quickly towards agreement on how much the UK would pay into Brussels' coffers upon leaving the EU with few of the feared fireworks from backbench Brexiteers. The Budget in November also provoked little complaint, except perhaps from May herself, who, since she was too weak now even to pretend she might sack him, could do little to persuade Chancellor Philip Hammond, always a fiscal hawk, to be more generous.

It wasn't long, however, before some of the problems that were going to give the Prime Minister and her party recurring headaches over the next two years became apparent. May's decision to move top civil servant (and the UK's main negotiator with the EU-27) Olly Robbins out of his job as Permanent Secretary at DExEU and into the Cabinet Office – a move intended to resolve the apparent tension between him and David Davis – backfired, since it effectively drained the Brexit Secretary of authority. Over time, Davis, who had loyally backed the Prime Minister in the immediate aftermath of the election, became increasingly detached from Downing Street, likely hastening his eventual departure from government in the summer of 2018. Another factor was May's belief that, in order to uphold the Good Friday/Belfast Agreement and prevent a hard border on the island of Ireland, but at the same time not treat Northern Ireland any differently from Great Britain, the whole of the UK would have to remain in a close economic relationship with the EU until more permanent arrangements could be forged.

When the EU-27 agreed at the end of December 2017 to see its talks with the UK proceed to the second phase, the precise nature of this so-called 'backstop' and that relationship was not yet set in stone. However, Brexiteers on the Tory backbenches (who now included Priti Patel, sacked from the Cabinet in late November for being less than forthcoming about meetings she'd held on a private trip to Israel) were already beginning to worry. After all, wasn't the whole point of Brexit to break free from the EU's orbit? And they were not the only ones who were anxious. In another development with long-term implications, eleven 'Europhile' Tory MPs (Dominic Grieve, Heidi Allen, Ken Clarke, Jonathan Djanogly, Stephen Hammond, Oliver Heald, Nicky Morgan, Bob Neill, Antoinette Sandbach, Anna Soubry, and Sarah Wollaston) voted with the Opposition to secure an amendment to the EU (Withdrawal) Bill tabled by Grieve (the former Attorney General) which obliged the government to provide a 'meaningful vote' in the Commons on any Withdrawal Agreement with the EU in the form of an amendable bill.

That rebellion might arguably have been prevented had May's first (and, in that job at least, highly rated) Chief Whip, Gavin Williamson, not been promoted to Secretary of State for Defence to replace Michael Fallon, who had resigned at the beginning of November amidst allegations of sexual harassment as #MeToo finally caught up with Westminster. But Williamson may well have been promoted soon anyway in the Cabinet reshuffle that May undertook in January 2018, a few weeks after she had been obliged to demand the resignation of her old friend and de facto deputy Damian Green, who was judged, following another #MeToo scandal, to have breached the ministerial code of conduct.

The reshuffle itself proved to be a messy affair, with Jeremy Hunt refusing to move from Health and Justine Greening resigning rather than leave her Education brief.[17] That said, none of this was overly worrying for Tory Brexiteers – Greening, after all, was seen as a 'Remainer' and they were able to celebrate the promotion to a junior role at DExEU of the ERG's Suella Braverman – although the promotion of the emollient former Minister for Europe, David Lidington, to replace Damian Green did raise some eyebrows. Otherwise, much to the frustration of some in the middle ranks and the backbenches who believed their turn had come, there were no big moves, although one or two of the lesser promotions were later to give cause for concern, most obviously the appointment of Karen Bradley as Secretary of State for Northern Ireland. Bradley, who was later to confess to a journalist that before her promotion she 'didn't understand things like when elections are fought, for example, in Northern Ireland – people who are nationalists don't vote for unionist parties and vice versa', was perhaps not the ideal choice to manage relations with a divided region at the centre of growing Brexit disputes.[18]

Meanwhile, closer to home, Patrick McLoughlin was finally granted his wish to stand down as Party Chairman and was succeeded by the former Immigration Minister, Brandon Lewis, with James Cleverly becoming Deputy Chairman. Lewis was a reliable media performer and, as an Essex boy (albeit a privately educated one), very much not an identikit, plummy-voiced Tory. He had an impressive record as a campaigner, having wrested control of Brentwood council from the Lib Dems in the early 2000s before going on to take the parliamentary seat of Great Yarmouth from Labour in 2010 on a swing of nearly 9 per cent and holding it (against both Labour and UKIP) with an increased majority ever since.

Fortunately, Lewis and Sir Mick Davis immediately struck up a good personal relationship, the party's new Chairman agreeing with its CEO that, while CCHQ would still want to bring in hired guns like Lynton Crosby at election time, it nevertheless needed to create in-house capacity and, by being better organized all-round, drive up membership and membership activity. Both took some early encouragement from the party's performance at the May 2018 local elections. True, its fortunes may have been boosted by the Prime Minister's firm handling of the nerve agent attack in Salisbury back in March, her response having garnered widespread praise – at least in part because it contrasted so markedly with Jeremy Corbyn's initial reluctance to join with the government and the country's allies in laying the blame squarely on the Putin regime in Moscow. On the other hand, the locals had been held just days after Amber Rudd had been forced out of the Home Office over what became known as the 'Windrush Scandal' – the revelation that the UK had, as a result of the 'hostile environment' regime established by May when she was Home Secretary, wrongly tried to deport (and in a few cases *had* deported) a number of elderly people of Afro-Caribbean and Asian origin.[19] As the results from the locals came in, it became clear that the Tories had been unable to prevent the loss of Trafford in Greater Manchester or to stop the Lib Dems retaking the heavily Remain-voting London borough of Richmond. However, they had held on to their 'flagship' London boroughs of Kensington and Chelsea, Wandsworth, and Westminster, and regained control of Barnet while also winning control in places like Basildon and Peterborough. There were early signs, too, that, with the collapse of UKIP, some of the Leave voters who had held back from voting Conservative at the general election the year before were now coming on board. The potential for Tory gains in Leave England was underscored by Labour's losses in Nuneaton, Derby, and Bedworth, and its failure to win councils like North East Lincolnshire (which contains Grimsby) and Walsall in the West Midlands, as well as by a swing to the Tories in Sunderland.

To those in the Cabinet who saw Brexit as a genuine opportunity, as opposed to colleagues like Philip Hammond who saw it primarily in terms of minimizing risk, these results only served to strengthen their belief that playing hardball with the EU-27 would pay dividends, electoral and otherwise. And with the promotion of Sajid Javid, who had replaced Rudd as Home Secretary, and Gavin Williamson, the new Defence Secretary (each of whom embraced Brexit with the zeal of a convert having more or less reluctantly backed Remain in the referendum), they were now even better represented on crucial Cabinet committees. Moreover, they were evidently supported by a substantial number of their parliamentary colleagues, sixty-two of whom signed an open letter towards the end of February insisting that there be no post-Brexit transition/implementation period during which time the UK might be prevented from pursuing 'full regulatory autonomy' and its own trade deals – something Boris Johnson was known to be arguing for in Cabinet. Partly as a consequence, the tone of May's Mansion House speech in early March, in which, among other things, she confirmed that the UK would be seeking an enhanced Free Trade Agreement, was slightly less conciliatory towards the EU-27 than initially intended; it also failed, not for the first or last time, to fully confront Brexit-ultras in the Conservative Party with the hard choices and trade-offs that they continued to deny existed.

Chequers chucked

The months that followed saw May attempting to persuade those reluctant colleagues to accept her 'New Customs Partnership', aimed at avoiding both a hard border between Northern Ireland and the Republic and one running down the Irish Sea, rather than their proposed 'Maximum Facilitation' approach. The arguments were conducted not just in Cabinet and its subcommittees but in informal caucuses of Cabinet ministers, with Boris Johnson, for example, getting likeminded colleagues to meet at the Foreign Office to discuss their objections to the PM's plans, among them Liam Fox, Michael Gove, Andrea Leadsom, Esther McVey, and David Davis, who had already made up his mind to resign unless he could somehow persuade the Cabinet, at a meeting they were due to have at Chequers, to go with ideas he was outlining in a White Paper that Number Ten wouldn't allow him to release.[20] The argument also spilled over into the media, all too often through authorized and unauthorized briefings by both sides, with groups on the backbenches joining battle in the pages of newspapers via interviews and open letters.

It was hardly surprising, then, that the Chequers 'away day' called by May to secure Cabinet agreement for her 'Faciliated Customs Arrangement' (which would supposedly avoid a border on the island of Ireland and allow the UK to negotiate its own trade deals with third countries, albeit at the cost of continuing alignment, via a 'common rulebook', with EU regulations) was billed as a showdown by journalists. Neither was it surprising that David Davis (along with his junior minister, the Brexit-ultra Steve Baker) announced he would be resigning the next day – or, indeed, that Johnson, in spite of indicating his assent to May's plan at the meeting itself, swiftly followed him, both because he saw the FCA as essentially Brexit in name only (BRINO) and because he feared that not to do so would place him at a disadvantage when May eventually stepped down and a leadership contest ensued. At the very least, this, as his Cabinet colleague, fellow Leaver, and future supporter Andrea Leadsom later declared, was 'the moment when the desire of some Brexiteers to see Brexit done became an ambition to destabilise the government and get rid of Theresa and do it themselves'.[21]

Chequers, July 2018: May fails to convince.
Source: 10 Downing Street.

Whether the public, who couldn't possibly be expected to get their heads around the details of the Chequers plan, would have responded more positively to it had May managed to secure the support of Brexiteers like Davis and Johnson is ultimately impossible to know for sure, although that was certainly the view in Downing Street.[22] What we do know, however, is that any hopes the government may have had on that score were rapidly extinguished in the wake of their resignations and the withering fire the plan subsequently received from their allies on the backbenches and in the media, with survey evidence attesting not just to opposition to the plan itself among Leave and Conservative voters but also to a more general loss of faith on their behalf – both in the government's handling of Brexit and in the Prime Minister in particular.[23] Remarks made by the American President Donald Trump during his visit to the UK in the week after Chequers, to the effect, firstly, that the plan agreed there would 'probably kill' a trade deal with the US and, secondly, that Boris Johnson 'would make a great Prime Minister', only made things more difficult for May. Little wonder, perhaps, that Number Ten, having decided that it had no alternative but to press ahead with its Customs and Trade Bills in the Commons, thought it politic to accept blatantly hostile amendments to the Customs Bill proposed by the ERG that ran completely counter to the Chequers plan and, in the case of the Trade Bill, to dismiss accusations of dirty tricks by the Whips in order to see off Opposition amendments backed by a dozen 'Europhile' Conservative MPs.

If it were possible, however, worse was to come. With Steve Baker back in charge, the ERG, who believed '"The British Establishment" ... had seized their opportunity and persuaded a now weakened Prime Minister to change tack and effectively override the result of the Referendum,' wasted little time in presenting what they claimed was a workable alternative to Chequers on Northern Ireland.[24] And Boris Johnson, keen to make it clear that his imminent divorce (occasioned by his relationship with Carrie Symonds, former Head of Communications at CCHQ) wasn't about to deter him from realizing his leadership ambitions, took to the pages of the *Mail on Sunday* to declare (with his characteristic gift for arguably distasteful but assuredly headline-grabbing overstatement) that Chequers was

a humiliation. We look like a seven-stone weakling being comically bent out of shape by a 500 lb gorilla. ... We have opened ourselves to perpetual political blackmail. We have wrapped a suicide vest around the British constitution – and handed the detonator to Michel Barnier.[25]

A week later Johnson was back where he really belonged, as the *Telegraph*'s star columnist, bigging up the ERG's alternative as if he'd actually read it, laying into the Irish backstop on his own account, and generally dumping all over May's plan: 'The whole thing', he raged, 'is a constitutional abomination, and if Chequers were adopted it would mean that for the first time since 1066 our leaders were deliberately acquiescing in foreign rule.'[26] This was hyperbole, obviously, and arguably only a step or two away from Tony Hancock's 'Does Magna Carta mean nothing to you? Did she die in vain?' But Nigel Farage was now declaring that May 'doesn't believe in Brexit, she doesn't believe in Britain', and announcing that he would be 'restarting the Brexit campaign' alongside Leave Means

Leave, the cross-party pressure group which was already raising large amounts of money and was eventually to help give birth to the Brexit Party.[27] Consequently, such highly coloured rhetoric from the blond pretender to May's throne must have seemed wholly justified – especially to Tories desperate to prevent the emergence of some sort of UKIP 2.0. What was less expected, perhaps, was the fact that David Davis (whom May's team had initially tried to dissuade from resigning by offering him Johnson's job as Foreign Secretary and normally felt they could rely on to do the decent thing) agreed to appear side-by-side with Farage at a Leave Means Leave rally in Bolton ten days before delegates gathered in Birmingham for the start of the 2018 Conservative Party conference.

In Birmingham itself, things got off to a sticky start. May was booed at one fringe meeting when she referred to her proposals for a deal with the EU-27 – a deal which anyway had been brutally rejected by the European Council meeting in Salzburg just a few days previously. Worse, she then had to put up with king-over-the-water Boris Johnson being greeted like some kind of rock star by his adoring fans as he turned up to deliver a barnstorming 'Chuck Chequers' address to a jam-packed auditorium.[28] Fortunately, however, she was able to pull off a surprise of her own in her closing speech, not only sashaying on stage to the strains of Abba's 'Dancing Queen' but also painting an uplifting picture (albeit one not properly cleared in advance with a furious Philip Hammond) of an 'end of austerity' Britain that would finally build the houses it needed and get the health service it deserved.[29] Brexit naturally got a mention, but with less stress on the details and more on the need for party unity on the issue. And in a thinly veiled rebuke to Johnson and the 'Chuck Chequers' crowd (one that included hundreds of delegates wearing badges to that effect), she noted that, while it was 'no surprise that we have had a range of different views expressed this week ... it is my job as Prime Minister to do what I believe to be in the national interest'.

But it was too little too late for many Leavers, now convinced that they weren't going to get the hardest of hard Brexits they wanted out of this particular Prime Minister. May's angry reaction to her humiliation at Salzburg – in a Downing Street statement on 21 September, she reminded the EU that 'I have always said no deal is better than a bad deal' – had bought her one or two cheers from government loyalists but that was about it.[30] True, a few weeks into August, the government had

Dancing Queen, not Conference Darling: October 2018.
Source: Xinhua / Alamy.

issued guidelines on how the UK would handle a No-Deal departure. But its announcement looked a lot more like an effort to placate the ERG than a serious attempt to prepare for an outcome which May's Chancellor, Philip Hammond (who, according to her Chief of Staff, always 'viewed Brexit as an exercise in damage limitation'), was known to be determined to prevent.[31] Indeed, Hammond made it pretty obvious in any case that he was loath to spend even more public money than the millions (possibly billions) the government had already spent on what he thought were 'ludicrous gestures' designed to pretend to the EU-27 and to Brexiteers that departure without a deal was a serious option for the government, as opposed to something forced on it by failure.[32] So while May's conference speech won her some praise – especially when compared with her disastrous effort the year before – it did not put Johnson and the ERG back in their respective boxes for long. Certainly, hostile language used about her by critics remained as intense (and, sometimes, deeply unpleasant) as ever, with one anonymous MP telling the *Sunday Times*, 'The moment is coming when the knife gets heated, stuck in her front and twisted. She'll be dead soon.'[33] The best that could be said of May's speech, then, and of Hammond's post-conference austerity-busting Budget in October, was that it bought her some time.

In some ways – and this, after all, was what exercised Brexit-ultras – the UK and the EU-27 were by that stage not so very far apart. The future relationship would be signalled in a Political Declaration, while a legally binding treaty – a Withdrawal Agreement – would set out the financial settlement, arrangements for citizens, and arrangements to avoid a hard border in Ireland. And while the latter proved too tricky to resolve by the time the European Council met again in mid-October, a compromise on it was eventually reached a month later – one facilitated by the EU-27 conceding (thanks to lobbying by the Irish government) to May's demand that, rather than Northern Ireland being treated differently to the rest of the UK, the whole of the UK would effectively remain in the customs union until a permanent solution could be found. Neither side was getting exactly what it wanted, but, as May told Tory MPs at a meeting of the 1922 on 24 October, while rumours swirled that the number of letters to its Chairman demanding a vote of confidence was getting close to the forty-eight (i.e. 15 per cent of the parliamentary party) required, this was the best, indeed the only, deal on the table.[34]

Sadly for the Prime Minister, however, it turned out to be a case of déjà vu (or at least Chequers) all over again. The morning after the Cabinet (in many cases reluctantly) had signed off on the draft agreement, complete with Irish backstop, Dominic Raab, the man who had replaced David Davis as Brexit Secretary, took to Twitter, doubtless with one eye on the next leadership contest, to tender his resignation – a move that some in Downing Street believed he'd pretty much planned from the moment he'd taken the job.[35] Raab was followed by Number Ten's Director of Legislative Affairs, Nikki da Costa, along with the Work and Pensions Minister, Esther McVey, and the junior minister at DExEU (and prominent ERG member), Suella Braverman. Michael Gove, however, was persuaded to stay, not least because he didn't want to be seen as the man who had helped assassinate not one but two Tory Prime Ministers. Had that not been the case, his departure might well have brought the house of cards crashing down there and then. However, by no means all of those Cabinet colleagues who, like him, decided to stick with May held out much hope that she could·get the deal through parliament or that she could survive her failure to do so, with Foreign Secretary Jeremy Hunt, for instance, telling her so in no uncertain terms.[36]

May hangs on – but cannot win

While the departures reflected real differences in principle over Brexit, they were also symptomatic of an accelerating decline in deference among Tory MPs – one exacerbated perhaps by social media giving a chance to shine even to those who in earlier times would have struggled to make a splash in their local newspaper. In the words of one of her advisers, Brexit had, for some of them, gone 'beyond logic' and become 'near religious'. Suitably emboldened, and convinced that the Withdrawal Agreement (which they had read and most of their colleagues apparently hadn't) was 'Brexit in name only' because the backstop could supposedly see the UK trapped in the customs union forever, the hardcore Eurosceptics of the ERG piled in when, on 15 November, May came to the Commons to defend the deal Cabinet (minus those who had left the sinking ship) had just approved.[37] Once they were done savaging said deal in the chamber and agitating for the dismissal of May's advisers, the ERG's leading figures, like Jacob Rees-Mogg, Steve Baker, and Mark Francois, quickly moved on to discuss when and how best to force her out of Number Ten via a vote of no confidence in her as Conservative Party leader.

As for their intended victim, all she could do was to press on with her attempt to persuade as many of their colleagues as possible to support the deal she'd done with the EU-27, all the while knowing that, as she wrote letters to MPs and toured the country to promote it, members of her own Cabinet were far from confident that it would (or even should) pass. These included ministers like Michael Gove, Penny Mordaunt, Liam Fox, and Chris Grayling, who, together with its founder, Andrea Leadsom, made up what was known as 'The Pizza Club' – as they were more than happy to tell any journalist who would listen.[38] May might not, then, have felt too sorry for Michael Gove, who, with four of the five days the government had allotted to debate the Withdrawal Agreement in the Commons already under its belt, was sent out on to the media on the morning of 10 December to confirm that the 'meaningful vote' on it would be going ahead, only to discover a few hours later that Number Ten had decided to delay holding it after a warning from the Whips' Office that around a hundred MPs intended to vote against.

On the one hand, that may have been a mistake: pulling the vote only encouraged the Prime Minister's opponents to pretend that the EU-27 could be persuaded to make some sort of bankable concession on the Irish backstop – an illusion that was soon shattered at the December European Council. On the other, however, it prompted the plotters to overreach themselves: the day after the postponement was announced, Graham Brady informed Number Ten that he had received the forty-eight letters required to trigger a vote of confidence in her leadership. Cannily, May got him to agree to hold the vote the very next day (12 December), thereby denying those moving against her the chance to build up the momentum they were hoping for. The comprehensive whipping operation by the ERG (run, ironically, out of the office of Iain Duncan Smith, removed as Tory leader by the same procedure in 2003) managed, in the main, only to mobilize those MPs determined to vote down May's deal; the majority who were still prepared to support it were, at that point anyway, unwilling to pull the trigger.[39] After all, opinion research suggested that getting rid of the PM would not be a magic bullet, especially when it was far from obvious, at least at that stage, that a successor genuinely capable of uniting the party and winning an election could be found and crowned in short order – and certainly not in time to afford said successor the time needed to negotiate and ratify a deal with the EU-27 by 29 March and therefore to avoid a humiliating extension to Article 50.[40] As a result, May beat off the challenge by 200 votes to (a nonetheless wounding) 117 – although not before formally conceding, with voting already underway, that she would not lead the party into the next general election. Most of her parliamentary colleagues had long hoped, even assumed, that that would be the case, of course. Now it was confirmed, however, those intending to fight the next leadership election – Johnson, of course, but also Cabinet members like Javid and Hunt, for instance – would, more than ever, be thinking just as much about how best to position themselves for that contest (one that would hinge on the votes of a highly Eurosceptic grassroots membership as well as their Westminster colleagues) as doing what might be best for the country as a whole.[41]

As it was, any hopes on Downing Street's part that the PM's victory in the confidence vote might provide a boost to her authority were swiftly dashed. A survey of party members and voters released just after the New Year bank holiday made for bleak reading, revealing as it did that May had not only failed to convince voters – including Conservative voters – that her Brexit deal was a good one, but she had also failed to persuade her own rank and file.[42] Some 72 per cent of grassroots Tory members, and 68 per cent of current Tory voters, had voted Leave in 2016. And those members were still preoccupied by Brexit: while 60 per cent of voters as a whole ranked Brexit as the most important issue facing the country, that figure rose to 68 per cent among Tory voters and a whopping 75 per cent among Tory members. Nor had the latter changed their minds on the merits of leaving the EU. Some 79 per cent of Conservative Party members thought voters had made the right decision in the 2016 referendum – a proportion that rose to a full 97 per cent of those who had voted Leave two years previously.

But what was really striking in the findings was how little support there was at the Tory grassroots for May's deal. Conservative Party members, like most voters, thought that the government had made a mess of negotiating Brexit: 68 per cent of the Tory rank and file (and 78 per cent of Leave-voting members) gave their government a poor grade. And their dissatisfaction extended to the Withdrawal Agreement itself. Some 49 per cent of voters overall said they opposed May's deal, with only 23 per cent saying they supported it. True, among those intending to vote Conservative, things looked a little more optimistic: 46 per cent in favour, 38 per cent against. But among card-carrying members of the Conservative Party, opposition to the deal outweighed support by a margin of 59 points to 38. Furthermore, a majority of them (53 per cent) thought May's deal did not respect the result of the referendum, rising to a super-majority of 67 per cent among members who had voted Leave in 2016.

Even more worrying for the government, the Tory rank and file were convinced that No Deal – a prospect that May herself had helped to legitimize, after all – was better than the deal the PM was offering. Respondents were asked what their first preference would be in a three-way referendum where the options were (a) remaining in the EU, (b) leaving with the proposed deal, or (c) leaving without a deal. Among voters as a whole, some 42 per cent of them plumped for Remain, with 13 per cent going for the PM's deal, 25 per cent for No Deal. The respective figures for Tory voters, however, were very different: 23 per cent Remain; 27 per cent Deal; and 43 per cent No Deal. Among Tory members, support for No Deal was even higher: 57 per cent said leaving without a deal would be their first preference compared to just 23 per cent whose first preference was the current deal and only 15 per cent saying Remain. Members' strong dislike of the PM's deal also emerged when asked about binary choices. Asked to choose between May's deal or No Deal, only 29 per cent of Tory members said they would vote for the Prime Minister's deal, compared to 64 per cent who would vote to leave without a deal.

Certainly, an overwhelming majority of the Conservative rank and file – presumably following the lead of celebrity ultras like Jacob Rees-Mogg and, of course, Boris Johnson – were convinced that the Irish backstop was a bad idea: only 11 per cent thought it made sense and should be part of the deal; some 23 per cent thought it was a price worth paying to get a deal; but 40 per cent thought it was a reason in itself to reject a deal – and, added to that, 21 per cent considered it irrelevant because May's deal was a bad one anyway. Tory members – like Tory voters – were also utterly unconvinced that a No-Deal Brexit would cause serious disruption: some 72 per cent of voters who were intending to support the Conservatives thought the warnings were 'exaggerated or invented' – a figure that rose to an eye-watering 76 per cent among Tory members. Meanwhile, members were convinced by a margin of 64 points to 19 that leaving without a deal would have a *positive* effect on Britain's economy in the medium to long term. And asked how they would feel if the UK were to leave on the basis of May's deal, some 23 per cent of members said they would feel 'betrayed' and 10 per cent 'angry', with a further 22 per cent confessing they'd be 'disappointed'.

Admittedly, many Tory rank-and-file members doubted there was anyone else who could have done better than May: leaving aside the 15 per cent who thought 'She's got a good Brexit deal', some 43 per cent agreed that 'She's got a poor Brexit deal, but any other leader would have done just as badly'. Nevertheless, that left 37 per cent who thought that 'She's got a poor Brexit deal, and an alternative leader would have got a better deal.' Moreover, that substantial minority probably contributed to the equally substantial minority of members (44 per cent) who thought that, should parliament vote to reject her deal, May should resign as leader and PM. And if May took any comfort from the fact that half (exactly 50 per cent) of the Conservative rank and file thought she should stay in the job regardless, she would have been alarmed at the fact that only 51 per cent of her party's own members thought she was doing well as Prime Minister, while 48 per cent thought she was doing badly.

A survey of MPs conducted for the think tank UK in a Changing Europe just before Christmas and released a week after the membership survey suggested May's MPs were similarly unimpressed. Nearly half (47 per cent) of Tory MPs thought the government had done a bad job of handling Brexit, with just 37 per cent thinking it had done well. Moreover, more than half (55 per cent) of them claimed there were viable solutions to the Irish border question short of the backstop, and that the difficulties implicit in finding a solution were being exaggerated. Conservative MPs also remained bullish about the prospects for trade with countries outside the EU after Brexit: 70 per cent were optimistic that the UK would be able to quickly sign deals with major powers such as China and the US, compared with just 12 per cent who were pessimistic. Some 85 per cent of Tory MPs also thought that these trade deals would at the very least compensate for loss of EU trade, and 58 per cent thought new trade deals would *more* than compensate for any lost EU trade. Most importantly, 80 per cent of Conservative MPs, many of whom prized the regulatory autonomy they believed Brexit would bring about above all else, felt customs union membership would not honour the referendum result. Conservative MPs were also particularly sceptical that a No-Deal outcome would involve the kind of economic disruption forecast by some commentators.[43]

As those MPs returned to Westminster after the break, then, the ERG now knew for sure that they, and not the Prime Minister, had both the grassroots and many of their colleagues on their side. Just as importantly, it was now obvious that they cared far more about getting the Brexit they wanted than they did about party unity – or, indeed, about the broader constitutional stability of the UK. And the chances of May being able to deliver further last-minute concessions that might have secured extra votes in the Commons were vanishingly small. As a result, the government's Chief Whip, Julian Smith (who had been hitting the phones hard over Christmas), was effectively powerless, caught once again between his personal desire to see some kind of compromise with the EU-27 and his certainty that anything his boss could negotiate would fail to satisfy the parliamentary party.[44] Indeed, in the absence of any movement on the part of the DUP (which would have freed Tory MPs from the worry that it might pull the plug on the confidence-and-supply arrangement and so precipitate an early election), he and his team were reduced, like Dickens's Mr Micawber, simply to hoping something would turn up.

It didn't. The government may have tried to begin the New Year on an optimistic note and to remind target voters that politics wasn't all about Brexit, announcing on 7 January the new (and by recent standards generous) ten-year funding plan for the NHS. But it was fooling no-one: the headlines a day or two later were all about its failure to prevent the Commons supporting an amendment tabled by the pro-European Conservative backbencher (and former Attorney General) Dominic Grieve which obliged the government to table its alternative approach swiftly should May's Withdrawal Agreement be rejected in the upcoming Meaningful Vote. That defeat – occasioned, to the fury of Number Ten, by the Speaker, John Bercow, allowing the amendment to be debated in the first place – was wounding enough. But the defeat in the Meaningful Vote itself was utterly brutal, both in terms of the historic overall margin involved (432–202) and in terms of the sheer number of Tory MPs (118) who, organized by the ERG's unofficial whipping operation ('the Buddies'), rebelled against their own Prime Minister.[45] The Whips, it turned out, had been unable to persuade more than two-thirds of their backbench colleagues to support the government – and unless that changed any time soon, there was very little hope of persuading more 'Labour Leave' MPs (only three of whom, out of an estimated twenty, had supported the government) to risk their careers by helping May get her deal through.

The circle that the Prime Minister now had to square – and the impossibility of so doing – is perhaps best captured by Anthony Seldon, one of the most astute chroniclers of the ups and downs of the occupants of Ten Downing Street over the years:

> She needed to convince MPs of mutually contradictory outcomes from their actions: for the Labour MPs, that voting against her would result in the UK

leaving the EU without a deal, and for Conservative and DUP MPs, that voting against her would result in no Brexit at all. If May looked too far from victory then Labour MPs would not expend their political capital to vote with the government, but in order to gain credibility by acquiring a significant portion of those 110 Brexiteer Tory votes, she would have to harden her stance considerably. To make matters worse, any concessions made in favour of Labour risked scaring away the ERG and DUP, and vice versa.[46]

Despite the Opposition tabling a motion of no confidence in her government (one that was defeated 317–306), May's initial response was to let Cabinet ministers David Lidington and Michael Gove and her Chief of Staff, Gavin Barwell, begin exploratory talks with Labour. Many of their colleagues (including Chief Whip Julian Smith) were extremely reluctant to hold them, however. And, anyway, they quickly ran up against Labour's insistence that the only thing that would lead it to vote for the deal was the offer of a second referendum – something that it knew full well was anathema to May (who rejected the idea of a second referendum again and again when privately pressed to consider it by a handful of Tory MPs).[47] At the same time, May also brought together MPs on both sides of the parliamentary party over lunch at Chequers to see if they could agree a way forward. Sadly, all that eventually emerged from that initiative were two fantasy Brexit solutions – the so-called Malthouse compromise and Brady amendment – neither of which ever stood the slightest chance of being accepted by the EU-27.[48]

Despite that, May agreed (partly on the grounds that it might at least offer a way of bringing the ERG on board and partly because it would hopefully prevent pro-European Tories voting for amendments tabled by Dominic Grieve and by Labour's Yvette Cooper) to throw the government's weight behind the Brady amendment. This was a mistake in the view of some in the Cabinet since it was so obviously a 'unicorn' yet encouraged the hardliners to continue thinking that they could get what they wanted, notwithstanding the fact that parliament (with the help of some pro-European Tories) had also expressed (by 318–310 votes) its opposition to leaving without a deal. In any case, relations with the ERG soon soured again, helping to ensure that the second Meaningful Vote would now be held in March rather than February. The delay meant that it would be incredibly difficult to secure the UK's departure by 29 March, as noted by Remainers Amber Rudd, Greg Clark, and David Gauke in a jointly authored op-ed in the *Mail* in which they bemoaned the fact that 'too many of our parliamentary colleagues appear complacent about the consequences of leaving the EU without a deal'.[49] The already febrile atmosphere at Westminster was only made more so by the decision of three centrist Tory MPs – Anna Soubry, Sarah Wollaston, and Heidi Allen, all of whom had grown fed up of what one of them called 'the right-wing, the hard-line anti-EU awkward squad' – to leave the Conservative Party in order to join eight former Labour MPs in 'The Independent Group' (TIG).

May was understandably devastated at the news of their defection, and this may have contributed to her increasing tendency to rely on the advice of a smaller and smaller circle of advisers rather than fellow politicians, even those who could normally be relied on to be supportive.[50] But it was actually getting out of Downing Street and meeting community groups in Northern Ireland in early February that made her more convinced than ever that ditching the backstop and/or ending up with No Deal must be avoided at all costs – with the result that she was now focused on trying to persuade the EU-27 to agree to a backstop that, because it would be time-limited and contain some kind of escape clause, might just about pass muster with Brexit-ultras and even perhaps the DUP.[51] This took her up to Leave-voting Grimsby to make a speech practically begging the EU to do so.[52] She then dispatched Attorney General Geoffrey Cox to Brussels to see if he could do any better. He couldn't and was unwilling to furnish a legal opinion confirming that the additional text that the EU-27 had agreed to attach to the deal provided a cast-iron guarantee that the UK couldn't be 'trapped' in the backstop. As a result, the government was unable to persuade any of the big-name Brexiteers apart from David Davis (who by then had lost interest in standing for the leadership) into supporting it on the second Meaningful Vote on 12 March. Consequently, that vote was lost by another huge, albeit slightly smaller, margin (391–242).

Humiliation was immediately piled on humiliation when the government was then defeated on a motion (passed by 321 to 278 votes) to block a No-Deal departure from the EU. Not only that, but it felt unable – to the private fury of some of its ministers – to take any disciplinary action against the dozen or so frontbenchers (including four

Cabinet members) who'd refused to toe the party line. Nor – unsurprisingly – did it prove possible the day after to take action against the eight cabinet ministers who opposed the government's motion to extend Article 50 and delay the UK's departure. With some Cabinet discussions dissolving into shouting matches routinely leaked to the press, collective responsibility had now completely collapsed.[53] It was also more obvious than ever that parliament would not sanction leaving without a deal, meaning that it was no longer an outcome that could be used either to gain concessions from the EU-27 or to persuade MPs who were afraid of 'crashing out' to vote for May's policy as the least worst option. Little wonder perhaps that, behind the scenes, and without May's knowledge, discussions had already begun at CCHQ about how it could fight an early election, albeit one that nobody there or in Number Ten really wanted.

Denied, for the moment, a third Meaningful Vote by Speaker Bercow (who thereby cemented his position as a hate figure on the Conservative benches), May had run out of options and, on 20 March, requested a three-month extension to Article 50 from the EU-27. Furious and frustrated in equal measure, she made what many in her team would later concede was an unwise decision to deliver a Downing Street address to the nation in which she attempted, in populist language largely drafted by Robbie Gibb, to put herself on the side of the people versus the politicians.[54] Voters, she claimed, were 'tired of the infighting, tired of the political games and the arcane procedural rows, tired of MPs talking about nothing else but Brexit when [people] have real concerns about our children's schools, our National Health Service, and knife crime'. Parliament, she claimed, had done 'everything possible to avoid making a choice'.[55]

Endgame

The speech, conceived in frustration and delivered in the heat of the moment, went down badly on all sides but especially among Conservative MPs, prompting the Whips to meet with the PM privately to tell her that she should go – a position apparently supported by eleven Cabinet ministers asked for their opinion by the *Sunday Times*.[56] It contributed, too, to the Commons (just a few days after hundreds of thousands marched through central London to demand a 'People's Vote' for a second EU referendum, leading, they hoped, to a different result) approving a plan to stage a series of 'indicative votes' in parliament at the end of March – the first of two unsuccessful attempts to break the logjam in that way. May and her advisers had little or no expectation that those votes would produce an option capable of commanding sufficient support on the Tory benches for it to be politically viable. But she did hope that the frustration which followed the votes' failure might at last persuade the House to approve her deal, which she now put to what was effectively a third Meaningful Vote.

In a further last-ditch effort to drum up support, May agreed to resign once her deal was passed (as recommended by, among others, Iain Duncan Smith). That move was sufficient to bring one or two celebrity ultras and leadership hopefuls like Rees-Mogg and Johnson back on board. But, partly because she refused to name a date when she made her dramatic announcement at a highly charged meeting of the 1922, it proved insufficient to win the support of ERG hardliners, some of whom she'd invited over to Chequers that weekend in one last, desperate attempt to bring them round.[57] Yet, although recalcitrant Conservative MPs were apparently promised promotions and additional government investment in their constituencies, May would not, could not, promise either the soft Brexit concessions or second referendum pledge that might have attracted significant support from the Labour benches.[58] Without either the DUP (now convinced that whoever succeeded her would ditch the backstop) or the so-called 'Spartans' (the least malleable members of the ERG, who were now sure that they would soon be able to replace May with a 'real' Brexiteer), May was still nowhere near the critical mass needed to convince the minority of pro-Brexit Labour MPs that their support could be decisive.[59] Her deal was rejected for a third and final time by a 344 to 286 margin.

Since the Commons, offered a second set of indicative votes, could not agree on a different deal, May had no alternative but to ask the EU-27 for an additional extension to the Article 50 period. Her request was granted: the UK now had until 31 October or else the first day of the month in which a Withdrawal Agreement could be passed through parliament. In the hope that this might be possible, although with little expectation of success, the Cabinet had already authorized cross-party talks to that end, one big incentive being the possibility (however remote) that they might lead to a Withdrawal Act passing before 22 May, thereby freeing the UK from its obligation otherwise to hold European Parliament elections that – given the decline in the Conservative Party's poll ratings – looked likely to prove disastrous.

Meanwhile, the Commons had narrowly passed the 'Cooper–Letwin' Act (the work of Labour's Yvette Cooper and the Tories' Oliver Letwin), which had not only ensured that parliament rather than government had the final say on the length of any extension but also signalled once again that it would not allow the UK to leave without a Withdrawal Agreement. The ERG and grassroots members, who now appeared to be even more overwhelmingly behind a No-Deal departure, were predictably furious at the situation.[60] Many ministers were too, although none, perhaps, as angry as Gavin Williamson was about to be when he was summarily sacked as Defence Secretary after being fingered for leaking from a meeting not of Cabinet (that, after all, had become absolutely endemic so couldn't be punished) but the National Security Council.[61] Williamson's tragicomic threat to whip up 'the world's biggest shitshow' should May let him go was never really realized. But his dismissal did lead to him linking up earlier than he otherwise might have done with Boris Johnson. As a result, the latter's 2019 leadership campaign hit the ground running – a far cry from the disorganization that had characterized his tilt two years previously.

The official start of that leadership campaign, however, was still weeks away. And, as much as it was already preoccupying Tory MPs, it was far from the only thing they had on their minds. The Brexit Party, now led by veteran UKIP leader Nigel Farage, formally launched on 12 April – a couple of days after the EU-27 agreed the latest Article 50 extension. Focus groups conducted for Number Ten on the Thursday before and the Monday after suggested it had made an immediate impact.[62] Ten days later (by which time it was polling well into the teens while the Tories had dropped well below 30 per cent), some seventy Conservative association chairmen signed a motion of no confidence in Theresa May. This prompted the Executive of the 1922 Committee (which had recently been persuaded by two former chairmen that, contrary to popular belief, there was no obstacle to them calling another vote of confidence in addition to the one held in December) to ask her to clarify her position, not least by naming a date for her departure.[63] She refused once again to commit, occupied as she was with the last-gasp attempt to construct a cross-party Brexit deal with Labour. The resulting talks, which had begun in early April, limped on until mid-May, although it quickly became obvious that there was little real prospect that they would succeed. Labour wanted a softer Brexit than the Conservative side could deliver, while the Conservative side wanted a harder Brexit than the Labour side could support. Moreover, with May's days clearly numbered, the Conservative team lacked the authority to sell any compromise to their own side, while many on the Labour team feared that enabling a 'Tory Brexit' could split their party.[64]

In the middle of those cross-party talks, the Conservatives had gone down to a bad defeat in local elections on 2 May, losing 1,330 councillors. Understandably, Tory MPs were beginning to panic. Within a fortnight, the Executive of the 1922 was trooping in to see May, emerging from what was a tense encounter to say that a timetable for the leadership election would be agreed as soon as the second reading of May's reheated Withdrawal Agreement legislation, scheduled for the first week of June,

It all ends in tears: Theresa May resigns, May 2019.
Source: 10 Downing Street.

had taken place – irrespective of whether it passed or was voted down. It was now obvious that the Prime Minister was on her way out – and made even more so when Andrea Leadsom resigned from the Cabinet, unable as she was to support the Withdrawal Agreement being put to the vote for fear that if passed it would facilitate a second referendum, and having one eye on the forthcoming leadership contest (for which she and her supporters had, by that time, been preparing for over a year).[65] Other Tory leadership hopefuls were already gearing up in anticipation of an imminent vacancy; some indeed had been doing little else for weeks, even months. Having suffered the indignity of two colleagues – Rory Stewart and Boris Johnson – announcing they would be standing in the contest to replace her before she'd even formally announced she was leaving, May struggled to maintain her composure as she finally declared she was going in a speech outside Number Ten on 24 May, the day after voting took place for the European Parliament. From 7 June onwards she would stay on in a caretaker capacity until her successor was chosen. The race, as they say, was on.

Over before it began
(June–July 2019)

By late May 2019, the Conservative Party was on the edge of a nervous breakdown. The results of the European Parliament elections, announced on 26 May, were even worse than many Tories had feared. Not only had they finished fifth behind the Green Party on just 8.8 percentage points – their worst ever result in a nationwide election since the introduction of full-franchise democracy in 1928 – but the top spot had gone to Nigel Farage's Brexit Party, which, despite having been in business just a few short months, had captured 30.5 per cent of the vote. According to the pollsters Lord Ashcroft and YouGov, around two-thirds of those who had voted Tory in 2017 had deserted, with the vast majority switching to the Brexit Party, which had also picked up nearly 70 per cent of 2017 UKIP voters.[1]

At the grassroots, the mood was toxic. According to one veteran agent – a Leaver like most members – his charges had been growing more and more disillusioned with May's leadership:

> She started with great goodwill. … That turned into mild irritation … and then very quickly to despair. … The nadir for us was when we announced we would be holding European elections. That was the point where everyone on my wing of the party just gave up and thought, 'This can't go on.'

Membership, he noted, had been slipping for a year or so: 'There was no rush of angry emails, more an atrophy of people not renewing or stopping being active.' As a result, 'it was a case of trying to hold the ship steady … and dealing with wave after wave of anger and disappointment as various deadlines to Leave just came and went', while the few domestic policy achievements the government managed to chalk up were 'just marginalized in the cacophony of Brexit'. Unsurprisingly, therefore, at the Europeans,

There was no activism. There was no campaign apart from the mailshot. The message from our members was, 'If you ask us to do anything, you'll be told where to go.' I turned a blind eye to many, many members campaigning for the Brexit Party.[2]

All this was borne out when, a few days after the results were announced, YouGov released a survey of party members suggesting that a mere one in five (19 per cent) of grassroots Tories had backed their own party at the elections, while more than three times that number (59 per cent) voted for the Brexit Party and one in ten hadn't bothered to turn out at all.[3] It was, perhaps, more of a shock than a surprise, then, when, a few days after that, Tory MPs woke up to find that their candidate at the Peterborough by-election had been beaten into third place by a Brexit Party opponent who finished just 683 votes behind Labour's newest MP. Clearly, they desperately needed to find someone who could extricate them from the hole they had dug for themselves over the last three years, and there was no time to waste.

A tweak to the rules

The basics of the system used to elect a Tory leader were by now familiar: there would be a two-stage process, the first involving a series of exhaustive ballots among the party's MPs, with the last-placed candidate dropping out after each successive round until just two of their colleagues were left to go forward to the final ballot of grassroots party members. But what fewer people were aware of was the ability of the party to flex the rules when it saw fit, normally via a process of consultation between the Party Board and the body that really ran the contest: the Executive of the 1922 Committee, which represented Tory members of parliament at Westminster.

Almost as soon as it became clear in the summer of 2019 that Prime Minister Theresa May was about to resign, that body was coming under severe pressure. Both colleagues and the party in the media were demanding that something be done to reduce the number of candidates eligible to stand in the parliamentary ballot – not so much because they wanted to limit the choice to their favoured runners and riders but because to allow too many of them into the race would inevitably elongate a process which, they felt, simply had to produce a winner before parliament broke for the summer recess. The obvious way to ensure that was for MPs to converge on just one candidate, obviating the need for the second stage of the process, as had happened in 2005. However, there was a near-unanimous consensus among MPs that there must be no repeat of the 2016 contest, when the last-minute withdrawal of the runner-up in the parliamentary stage meant that the wider membership was denied the chance to have its say – an outcome which had not only left rank-and-file Tories disappointed but had also lumbered the party with a leader who, as it found to its cost at the 2017 general election, turned out to be a hopeless campaigner.

The need nevertheless to render the 2019 contest more manageable was all the more urgent as media speculation about who might stand suggested the roster of candidates could easily run into double figures. Some of those mentioned ruled themselves out fairly quickly, the best example being Secretary of State for Work and Pensions (and former Home Secretary) Amber Rudd, who made it clear after a few days that she would instead be doing her best to ensure that those who *were* going to run took into account the views of more centrist, less Europhobic Tories like herself. Others, including some of those whose public flirting with the idea of standing for the leadership stretched the credulity of commentators and colleagues alike (MPs like self-styled 'hard man of Brexit' Steve Baker and the cerebral Treasury Minister Jesse Norman), took a little longer. The same was true of the well-respected and well-liked Graham Brady, whose announcement that he was considering running obliged him (even though in the end he decided against it) to step down temporarily from his position as Chairman of the 1922 Committee, handing the organization of the parliamentary stage to vice-chairs Cheryl Gillan and Charles Walker.

It was they who declared (after consulting the Party Board) that the membership stage would be completed in four short weeks, thereby allowing the new leader (and therefore the country's new Prime Minister) to be announced in the last full week of July. It was also they who informed their colleagues of two new rules. Firstly, as announced publicly on 4 June, the threshold for nominations would change: instead of simply a proposer and a seconder, anyone wishing to enter the parliamentary stage of the contest would now need eight MPs to support their nomination. Secondly, rather than only the last-placed candidate being eliminated after each round of parliamentary voting, candidates who wished to proceed to the next round would have to secure support from at least 17 out of 313 Tory MPs in the first round and 33 in the second round.

There was little or no complaint about the change, even though it led in short order to the withdrawal of three MPs (junior Brexit Minister James Cleverly, Housing Minister Kit Malthouse, and Sam Gyimah, the pro-European former Universities Minister) – presumably because they were unable to muster sufficient nominations and/or pledges of support. Nevertheless, some ten Conservative MPs were able to enter the first round of the contest held on Thursday, 13 June, with further rounds of voting scheduled for 18, 19, and 20 June – a process which would take place in a Committee Room in the House of Commons with MPs lining up over the course of two or three hours to deposit in one of two black metal ballot boxes the slips of paper issued to them on entering.

Before voting, candidates traditionally try their best to build momentum. This they do by collecting endorsements from colleagues willing to declare their support publicly. Indeed, only two days after May officially announced her resignation, nearly four in ten Tory MPs had expressed their support for one candidate or other, a figure that less than a week later had risen to encompass over half of the 313 members of the parliamentary Conservative Party.[4] Sometimes those endorsements are the product of friendship. Sometimes they are down to ideological affinity: even though most candidates are known quantities in this respect, they nevertheless waste no time in using mainstream and (increasingly) social media to set out their stalls on the issues of the day, in this case primarily on Brexit and tax and spend; they also take private meetings with individual colleagues to reassure them that they are for or against particular policies. Those meetings are also used, predictably enough, to discuss – albeit often in oblique terms – jobs the candidate might be able to offer a prospective supporter in the event that they emerge victorious.

Naturally, their chances of doing so – and their putative appeal, both to the 'selectorate' (initially, fellow MPs and, thereafter, rank-and-file members) and to the electorate (ordinary voters up and down the country) – weigh very heavily, too. So does the likelihood that they will be able to unite the party around them once the contest has taken place. Indeed, as decades of research on the question has shown, the desire for party unity may well take precedence over ideological, electoral, and competence considerations, although clearly they are to some extent linked.[5] Too radical a leader, for instance, might alienate sections of the party as well as the electorate and, as the saying goes (despite the absence of systematic research being done to confirm it), 'divided parties don't win elections'. Nor (generally) do parties led by a politician seen as even less competent than their main rival for the premiership.

Nowadays, of course, those voting in the contest are able to do more than simply hazard a guess as to the popularity of those hoping to pick up their support. This has been true for decades when it comes to voters in general, and in 2019 there were eight surveys (most commissioned by newspapers) which tested the appeal of likely and then actual candidates. There were also one or two private polls leaked to the media, including a survey of marginal seats conducted by Lynton Crosby's CTF. Having helped run three general election campaigns for the Tories and as a fan of Johnson's, Crosby was doubtless happy to find the *Telegraph* reporting the results under the headline 'Only Boris can fight off Farage', especially given that the Peterborough by-election held the day before showed the Brexit Party splitting the centre-right vote, thereby allowing Labour to hang on to the seat.[6]

Since the second decade of the new millennium, however, it has been possible to gauge the opinion not just of the electorate but also of the selectorate. As well as YouGov, the partisan website ConservativeHome, in addition to providing (along with the rather edgier Guido Fawkes) running totals of which MP has backed which candidate, has also taken to regularly surveying its readers as to who is up and who is down in their estimation. Added to that are the changing odds produced by betting companies. Although this is presumably a metric driven by the millions of pounds' worth of bets placed rather than any particular ability to read the political runes among the companies involved, these are figures which newspapers and news websites find hard to resist publishing. In 2019, for instance, the *Sun* was giving out Betfair's odds (Johnson on 8/5, and rivals Dominic Raab, Jeremy Hunt, and Michael Gove on 4/1, 11/1, and 14/1 respectively) a few hours *before* May formally announced she was going. The odds from various different companies continued to appear throughout the contest, although after the first round of voting Johnson's shortened so much that they turned negative while those of his rivals lengthened considerably, in some cases to prices that would have tempted only someone with far more money than sense.

As a result of all this, and in combination with soundings taken in their local associations, Conservative MPs, in some ways irrespective of their preferred outcome from an ideological, electoral, competence, or party unity perspective, had a pretty good idea of which candidate it might be best to attach themselves to should they be seeking preferment and/or approval from the grassroots.

The bookies' favourite

YouGov was early into the field with a survey of party members commissioned by the *Times* and then written up with additional detail on its own website.[7] Boris Johnson had spent most of his time since resigning as Foreign Secretary a year previously burnishing his Brexiteer credentials through his (£250,000 p.a.) column in the *Telegraph* and his star appearances at the party's annual conference. And it appeared to have worked. His support, of 39 per cent, was exactly three times that (13 per cent) of his nearest rival, Dominic Raab – another Cabinet minister who had resigned over Brexit. In addition, when YouGov presented members with a series of head-to-head challenges, Johnson beat them all hands down, with Raab once again his closest challenger (albeit closer this time on 41 to his 59 per cent). YouGov also asked about each of the candidates on seven characteristics: whether they would be a good leader; how likeable they were; their ability to win an election; whether they shared a respondent's political outlook; whether they were up to the job; whether they were a strong leader; and if they were competent. 'Boris' (routinely referred to by his first name in so much of the media) won on every measure, scoring anything from 61 to 77 per cent.

Perhaps not coincidentally, Johnson made it clear he would be running the very same day (namely 17 May) – a full week before the Prime Minister confirmed she would be stepping down at the beginning of June. He was also able to point to several opinion polls in the weeks that followed which showed that, although he was far from universally popular among voters, he was the only one of the candidates on offer to win the support of more (although not much more) than a fifth of them.

Johnson was not alone, however, in being able to point to a membership survey released in early January that had provided a very clear steer as to where members stood ideologically. For one thing, they were convinced Brexiteers – possibly even more ERG than the ERG. For another, while not perhaps as pro-market and anti-state as often assumed, they were hardliners on social issues, particularly crime, with over three-quarters believing in stiffer sentences for lawbreakers and over half even willing to back the death penalty.[8]

Equipped with this information and, of course, their own familiarity both with their local party members and with their colleagues at Westminster, any ambitious MP was in a good position to know, even before the first vote in the parliamentary stage of the contest, who was likely to finish top. Accordingly, it was no surprise that one of the first to publicly declare his support for Johnson (in the popular Tory-supporting tabloid the *Sun*) was the recently sacked Gavin Williamson. This was important because Williamson was famous for knowing the parliamentary party inside out and even for (as the phrase goes) 'knowing where the bodies are buried'. He was therefore in a position to be able not just to mount an efficient canvassing operation but also to persuade otherwise reluctant colleagues to jump on the bandwagon before it passed them by.

Williamson was soon joined by other famously ambitious colleagues, with Chief Secretary Liz Truss, who had been rumoured to be thinking of standing herself, becoming the first Cabinet minister to endorse Johnson – something she did on 2 June in a gushing op-ed ('WHY I'M BACKING BORIS, BRITAIN'S FREEDOM FIGHTER') for the best-selling Tory-supporting *Mail on Sunday* – a newspaper, incidentally, read by around a fifth of grassroots Conservative Party members. And Truss was quickly followed by a trio of equally ambitious young colleagues, Rishi Sunak, Robert Jenrick, and Oliver Dowden, writing an equally gushing joint op-ed for the *Times* (likewise read by around a fifth of Tory members) entitled 'The Tories are in deep peril. Only Boris Johnson can save us'. It may, of course, have been completely coincidental that, following Johnson's victory, all three were promoted straight into the Cabinet, along with the high-profile chair of the ERG, Jacob Rees-Mogg, the very first MP to come out publicly for Johnson but who had never held a frontbench role before in the nine years he had been in the House.

There they joined Truss, who was promoted to International Trade Secretary, and Williamson, brought back into the Cabinet as Secretary of State for Education. Also brought back – and as Home Secretary no less – was Priti Patel, another former Cabinet minister who had, like Williamson, been embarrassingly fired by May and who had, like Truss, been considering a run herself before deciding instead to declare for Johnson.

The enthusiastic backing of so-called (and doubtless self-styled) 'rising stars' undoubtedly helped to indicate to potential waverers which way the wind was blowing. But Johnson had other resources at his disposal as well, not least the support of the favourite newspaper of the Tory grassroots (around a third of whom read it), the *Telegraph* – often seen as the 'house journal' of the parliamentary Conservative Party. While not offering him an explicit early endorsement, the paper for which he was (both before he became and after he resigned as May's Foreign Secretary) its highest-paid star columnist, nailed its colours pretty clearly to the mast, its editorial on 27 May declaring that

> The Tories need to elect as their new leader someone who can connect immediately with the country. Facing the imminent prospect of an election against the twin threats posed by Nigel Farage and Jeremy Corbyn …, he or she will not have the luxury of easing themselves into the post. Their impact will have to be instant.

Writing on the same day – the day after the disastrous European Parliament elections were announced – and with the title of his column ('The message of these results is clear. If we go on like this, we will be dismissed') positioned, along with his photo, above the *Telegraph*'s distinctive masthead, Johnson made his pitch for leader. This was followed the next day (28 May) by an editorial ramming home his point: 'For the party of government to secure less than 10 per cent of the popular vote in a national election', it thundered, 'is more than extraordinary; it is epochal. … After nearly 200 years as the most successful political movement in the world, the next two months will determine whether they have a future or sink into oblivion.' It concluded that 'There is only one clear route to survival and that is for the Conservatives to be unequivocally the party of Leave.' Simply 'promising to tweak the Withdrawal Agreement here or there is not going to work; nor is further equivocation over leaving without a deal'. Nigel Farage and his Brexit Party posed an existential threat to the Conservatives. 'The Tories', the *Telegraph* declared, 'need to find a way to embrace both him and the phenomenon he has unleashed or they are doomed.'

Not all the newspapers, even the Tory-supporting titles, made it quite so obvious who they believed was the only candidate – and of course the only Brexiteer – who could pull the party out of its nose-dive. But even those that reminded readers of Johnson's patchy track record and 'colourful' personal life did so mainly to emphasize that MPs who had previously expressed reservations about him on both scores were now coming round to the idea that there was no alternative but to elect him as their leader. However, perhaps the *ne plus ultra* of the Realpolitik rationale for backing Johnson (albeit produced when his triumph was all but assured going into the final day of the contest's parliamentary stage on 20 June) was the leader penned by former Chancellor of the Exchequer George Osborne. Osborne had become Editor of the *Evening Standard* after his own political career had been effectively destroyed by Johnson, making his endorsement all the more telling. On the back of an interview that Johnson had given the *Standard* – the first, note, that he had granted to a daily newspaper throughout the entire campaign and which generated its front-page screamer 'Bojo: I've got mojo to unite Britain' – Osborne suggested the frontrunner probably stood the best chance of uniting the party and 'might just get Britain feeling good about itself again'. Most importantly (and, it has to be said, most cynically), he continued, 'Ask yourself which of these potential Prime Ministers is most likely to persuade the Conservative Party to vote for a repackaged version of the existing deal?' and immediately supplied the answer: 'The one with the greatest credibility with hard Brexiteers.' It was even possible that Johnson (who, Osborne noted, was just as aware as his rivals that parliament would block a No-Deal exit, the threat of which he was nevertheless claiming would help ensure the UK left the EU on 31 October) could sell his party a second referendum. After all, he would do anything to get into Number Ten and stay there once he'd made it – and, as Osborne rather mischievously put it, 'Opportunism knocks'.

The also-rans

None of this is to say, of course, that the other candidates got no media attention. Some of them even managed 'human interest' interviews accompanied by shots of them with their families, or at least their spouses, perhaps the most cringeworthy example of the genre being the *Mail*'s meeting with Jeremy Hunt and his wife in which they revealed their pet names for each other.[9] The other candidates also produced campaign videos and social media content (@ReadyForRaab anyone?) and provided op-eds to newspapers (including the *Telegraph* itself) in which, as they did at their launches and during television debates and in several hustings with colleagues and with journalists, they set out their stalls and attempted (not always with great success) to distinguish themselves from each other.

Esther McVey, the first candidate to officially declare she was running and also the first to be eliminated, attempted to portray herself as the hardest of hard Brexiteers: in her book, there would be no room in government for Remainers and the UK should end talks and leave on 31 October without a deal unless the EU begged it to come back to the negotiating table. She also pitched herself as an advocate of what she called 'Blue-Collar Conservatism' – apparently exemplified both by tax cuts and by significantly increased spending on schools. Those who turned up at her launch found themselves being addressed from a lectern adorned with a large photo of the iconic Tory leader Margaret Thatcher. But while it may be tempting to poke fun at politics-as-tribute-act, Johnson's rather more successful evocation of Winston Churchill proves it can work a treat. And at least it got McVey noticed, albeit briefly. After all, another candidate who failed to make it past the first round, Mark Harper, struggled badly in this respect, having made so little mark on the public consciousness in the five years since he'd resigned as Immigration Minister that, as Marina Hyde, one of the country's sharpest satirical columnists, put it, he 'might as well have been living in witness protection'.[10]

Joining Harper and McVey in the bottom three was Andrea Leadsom, who had chosen to stand again despite pulling out of the 2017 leadership contest. Possibly, she was hoping that her last-minute resignation from the Cabinet just two days before May announced her own departure would revive her support among Brexit-ultras. It didn't – and nor did her claim that, as well as being particularly in touch with young people because of her children (yes, really; them again) and so alive to the importance they placed on the environment, she had a 'three-point plan for Brexit'. This consisted of being prepared to leave without a deal on 31 October but also bypassing the European Commission and talking to EU-27 heads of government in order to get a new agreement that would make doing so unnecessary. As she quickly found, however, none of this mattered: some of her fellow Brexiteers still felt let down by her decision to pull out two years previously; others thought she should have resigned from May's Cabinet far earlier; virtually all of them had moved on.[11]

Another candidate, Health Secretary Matt Hancock, did manage to make it through the first round but decided to withdraw anyway, realizing that his attempt to portray himself as a pro-business, 'next generation' candidate (he was only 40) would not be enough to overcome two insuperable obstacles. The first was his reputation as both a Remainer and a protégé of George Osborne. The second was his willingness to concede (unlike most of the candidates) that leaving without a deal was an empty threat given parliament's obvious determination to block such an outcome – an outburst of truth-telling that did not (predictably enough, given his obvious desire to stay in government) prevent him endorsing Johnson a few days later, apparently in the deluded belief that he might be appointed Chancellor of the Exchquer.[12]

The only other candidate who, like Hancock (and, incidentally, the Chancellor of the Exchequer, Philip Hammond), was willing to acknowledge that No Deal was effectively impossible unless the government chose to undermine democracy by ignoring parliament was Rory Stewart, the Secretary of State for International Development. Stewart made a virtue of conducting his campaign outside Westminster, offering to meet members of the public in a series of filmed encounters rapidly uploaded to social media, where they gained a relatively wide audience. He was also the only candidate who explicitly ruled out serving under Johnson should the latter become Prime Minister – both as a matter of policy and, it seemed, on the issue of trust.

Stewart actually progressed one round further (into the third ballot) than the candidate who many had expected to do rather better than he eventually did, and who in some senses was his polar opposite, Dominic

Raab. For Raab it was who decided to pitch himself as the ultimate hard Brexiteer, having resigned from May's government after just four months as her Brexit Secretary, citing his opposition to her version of the Withdrawal Agreement with the EU. Not only did he insist on the feasibility (and maybe even the desirability) of a No-Deal departure from the EU, he also insisted that government could, if necessary, achieve it by proroguing (i.e. suspending) parliament. Moreover, he refused to back down when challenged on the issue by most (though not all – Johnson stayed out of the fray) of his rivals, with Home Secretary Sajid Javid telling him during the first live television debate (which took place on 16 June between rounds one and two), 'You do not deliver democracy by trashing democracy. We are not selecting a dictator,' and Environment Secretary Michael Gove assuring viewers, 'I will defend our democracy. You cannot take Britain out of the EU against the will of parliament.'

As well as upping the ante on Brexit, Raab had burnished his Thatcherite credentials by proposing to cut the basic rate of income tax by a penny every year for the next five years, although quite how he proposed to finance the policy was never clear. Certainly, the money wasn't going to come from the budget for maintaining law and order, which was his other main focus, with much talk of the stiffer sentences that, as we have seen, so appealed to the grassroots. Whether that was particularly wise, however, is debatable since another of his rivals was the current Home Secretary, Sajid Javid, whose promise to recruit an additional 20,000 police officers and therefore ensure that (to coin the crushingly predictable cliché) there were more 'bobbies on the beat' may have carried rather more weight. Somewhat more refreshing, perhaps, was Javid's rejection of Theresa May's repeated insistence that net migration be reduced 'from the hundreds to the tens of thousands' and his bouncing his fellow contenders during the second televised debate (on 18 June between rounds two and three) into pledging an inquiry into Tory Islamophobia. Away from the studio, Javid also made the argument that putting him, with his Pakistani heritage, into the run-off with Johnson would help demonstrate to the country how much the party had changed. Apart from that, however, Javid, too, based his appeal on promising tax cuts and taking the country out of the EU by 31 October with or without a deal. Yet quite how he would achieve this in the face of parliament's evident opposition, and why he was somehow the candidate who could best unite the party and the country (his other big pitch), was never really explained.

Environment Secretary Michael Gove, since he had helped lead the Leave campaign during the EU referendum, was under less compulsion to play the hard Brexiteer than Javid, who had (albeit reluctantly and because he assumed it would win) backed Remain back in 2016. Indeed, Gove even went so far as to admit that leaving without a deal, especially without adequate preparation, was best avoided if there was any prospect of a renegotiated agreement with the EU-27, even hinting that he might be prepared as Prime Minister to countenance an extension beyond 31 October. But his honesty in this regard (and in regard to his having snorted cocaine when working as a journalist) put him at a huge disadvantage, negating much of the low-profile preparations he and his friends had been conducting for another crack at the leadership while May was still PM.[13] So did the fact that, notwithstanding his reputation as a minister with real achievements under his belt and as one of the party's best parliamentary and media performers, a fair few Tory MPs had simply never forgiven him for scuppering Johnson's chances in the 2017 leadership campaign. Equally unhelpful was the fact (attested to in opinion poll after opinion poll) that he was unpopular with the public. Arguably, too, Gove's pitch to colleagues – that whoever they picked as Prime Minister actually needed to be able to deliver rather than simply talk tough on Brexit – only served to remind them quite how bruising the second stage of the contest might turn out to be should it end up reprising the 'psychodrama' (the word was regularly used) between him and Johnson. Except for the latter's most determined opponents, the prospect of the frontrunner having to face the man sometimes referred to by his friends and foes alike as 'the polite assassin' during the sixteen (yes, sixteen) public hustings the party had planned for the second stage of the contest was anything but appetizing.

Concerns among Tory MPs that, by putting Gove into the final two, they risked reopening the scarcely healed wounds of June 2016 and exposing the frontrunner to arguably his most effective (and certainly most forensic) critic probably boosted Foreign Secretary Jeremy Hunt's chances of finishing as runner-up. And, as someone who had backed Remain back in 2016, it was a boost he badly needed – particularly after he opined, early on in the contest, that leaving the EU without a deal, albeit a strategy he claimed he was willing to countenance, could be 'political suicide'. His main point, in fact, was that the government could not go into a general election until it had resolved Brexit – something he claimed that, as an entrepreneur who had made millions by doing deals before going into politics, he was particularly well suited to deliver, in part by putting together a new negotiating team that would include not only Scottish and Welsh Tories but also the ERG and the DUP. He also argued that his business background meant he understood what the post-Brexit economy and electorate needed, namely a big housebuilding programme, a reduction in student debt, and, as his signature policy, slashing corporation tax from 19 per cent to just 12.5 per cent.

Bowing to the inevitable: the contest plays out

But for all the efforts of his rivals to gain a hearing, it was Johnson who managed to pick up the plurality of the media's coverage during the first stage of the leadership contest – and this in spite of his pursuing, on the advice of those around him, what some wags labelled a 'submarine' strategy. This involved him refusing to appear at the first televised candidates' debate, granting hardly any interviews with journalists, and, even at his launch event, severely restricting the number of questions they were allowed to ask him. Indeed, notwithstanding the criticism that his avoidance of scrutiny drew from his rivals, his team even managed to make a virtue of his being backward in coming forward: firstly, by using the time he might otherwise have spent preparing for interviews and debates to instead meet fellow MPs for reassuring one-to-ones, and, secondly, to argue that his reluctance to seek the limelight portended a new, more serious, more focused, more disciplined Boris than the Boris so many of those colleagues worried was not really up to running the country, even if he was a great campaigner.

That said, whether in his limited media appearances or in those face-to-face meetings, Johnson was quick to remind his colleagues of his record as an election-winner and the fact that he, of all the candidates on offer, had the charisma needed to take on and beat both Corbyn and Farage. Seeing off the latter, he stressed, did not allow for half-measures. Indeed, almost as soon as Theresa May had finished praising the virtues of compromise in her resignation speech in Downing Street, Johnson, who was speaking at a paid corporate gig in Switzerland, emphasized that whoever took over could 'do things differently', and (while he didn't go quite as far as former Tory leader Iain Duncan Smith, who argued, 'We must now become the Brexit Party') he insisted that the UK must 'leave the EU on October 31, deal or no deal'. He then went on to float the possible negotiating ploy of withholding the tens of billions Britain owed the EU as a so-called 'divorce payment'. Nor did he completely rule out proroguing parliament as a means of leaving without a deal. Indeed, his declaration to MPs that he was 'strongly not attracted' to the idea merely served to signal that, as far as he was concerned, the measure was not necessarily off the table. That tactical ambiguity, along with his main message – that the threat posed to the party was 'existential' and that, to quote him, 'I am the person to put the Brexit baby to bed. Unleash me on Corbyn' – was a powerful combination, especially when supercharged with promises both to raise the threshold at which people begin to pay the higher rate of income tax and, in a nod to 'One Nation Conservatism', to significantly raise spending to meet increasing concern among voters (and therefore Tory MPs) about underfunding in education, health, and policing.

That these promises were potentially contradictory, even economically illiterate, seemed to matter little. Johnson (in common, it should be said, with most of his fellow candidates) paid little or no attention to several public calls by Chancellor Philip Hammond for the contenders not to sacrifice the government's hard-won reputation for 'balancing the books' on the altar of eye-catching but unfunded spending pledges and tax cuts. Johnson also achieved the considerable feat not only of avoiding a meeting with US President Donald Trump, who was visiting London and had earlier been fulsome in his praise, but also of actually persuading him to keep quiet on whom he wanted to win the leadership. Equally in his favour, Johnson managed to ensure that the popular leader of the Scottish Tories, Ruth Davidson, with whom he had enjoyed a fairly rocky relationship in the past and who gave her backing to Sajid Javid, refrained from attacking him head-on – possibly helping to avoid some of her colleagues kickstarting a plan (apparently codenamed 'Operation Arse') to persuade their English counterparts to vote against Johnson lest, in becoming PM, he tempt even more Scots to support Independence. His chances of picking up votes beyond the ranks of hardline Brexiteers may also have been boosted by the decision of the ERG not to 'frighten off' pro-Europeans by officially endorsing him after they'd decided to back him over Dominic Raab – once, that was, they'd extracted a promise from him that 'we will leave the European Union on the 31st of October, come hell or high water'.[14]

The morning of the second round of parliamentary voting saw the release of a YouGov survey of the Tory grassroots, the results of which only served to confirm to MPs the strength of Johnson's appeal to the folk who would make the final decision once they had whittled the field down to just two candidates.[15] In one of many stand-out, even breath-taking, findings, some 63 per cent of members claimed they wanted Brexit to take place even if it meant Scotland leaving the UK, with only 29 per cent rejecting that outcome, and with similar figures produced when the question involved Northern Ireland and when it involved 'significant damage to the UK economy'. Most incredible of all, however, was the fact that while a bare majority (51 vs 39 per cent) did not think Brexit worth a Jeremy Corbyn government, some 56 per cent (vs 34 per cent) said they would prefer to see the destruction of the Conservative Party rather than forgo leaving the EU.

Presumably, of course, members did not regard that last outcome as very likely since, for them, Brexit and electoral success were closely corre-lated, with 52 per cent believing that leaving with a deal (and 44 per cent saying the same for leaving *without* a deal) would win the Tories the next election, while a stunning 51 per cent believed that failing to leave at all would so damage the party that it would never lead a government again. Not unreasonably, given the results of the European Parliament elections, a greater proportion of members saw the Brexit Party as a bigger threat than Labour, while (perhaps paradoxically, perhaps not) getting on for half of them (46 vs 40 per cent) said they would be happy for Nigel Farage to become Conservative Party leader. Fortunately for Johnson, however, he was regarded as a much better prospect – and compared not just to Farage but also to his more immediate rivals. Johnson (whose emphasis on Brexit, like that of the other candidates, was surely the right one given only 28 per cent of ordinary members were more interested in hearing about their domestic policies than their views on Brexit) was clearly in first place when it came to who would make a good leader, with 77 per cent agreeing that he would and only 19 per cent disagreeing.

Figures for other candidates finishing in the top five came in as follows: Raab, 68–21; Javid, 61–30; Hunt, 56–37; and Gove 50–45. Moreover, the clear preference of members (83 vs 14 per cent) was for a leader 'who backed Leave at the EU referendum, backs Brexit and would be willing to leave the EU without a deal' – boxes which Johnson would very soon be the only candidate left in the race able to tick.

The results of the various rounds of voting are displayed in Table 1. Prior to the first round, the best-placed candidates were said to have received declarations of support from colleagues as follows: Johnson, 86; Gove, 33; Raab, 24; Hunt, 34; and Javid, 19. All of them received more votes than declarations but Johnson had clearly done far better in this respect. More importantly, he was way ahead of his nearest competitors, winning more votes than the next three candidates put together. That led his 'allies' (namely his campaign team speaking off the record) to make an only half-serious attempt to suggest that the rest of the field might want to drop out on the grounds that fighting on would be 'an indulgence' – an invitation taken up only by Matt Hancock (who, like McVey and, later on, Leadsom, backed Johnson). That said, as soon as the results were declared, speculation began that Johnson might somehow 'lend' votes to Jeremy Hunt so as to ensure he faced an easy run-off in the membership stage against someone who could be conveniently (and, of course, damagingly) labelled as the 'continuity May' and 'Remainer' candidate.

In the second round, however, although Johnson (having skipped the first televised debate, in which Rory Stewart emerged as the standout performer) added only an extra 12 votes to his tally out of the 50 on offer, it seems unlikely that any that were 'loaned' went to Hunt, who added only 3 to his. If such 'tactical voting' did occur (easily done, not least when some MPs were casting multiple proxy votes for absent colleagues), then it seems more likely that it helped Sajid Javid (up 10 to 33) or Rory Stewart (who almost doubled his tally from 19 to 37) – the aim, presumably, being to achieve the elimination of Dominic Raab, whose hard line on Brexit endeared him to the membership even as (along with his rather dour personality and very dry economic views) it alienated some of his more pragmatic Westminster colleagues. If that was indeed the plan, then it worked: Raab, who had clearly been regarded as a serious prospect at the very start of the contest, was out of the race.

Table 1. The 2019 leadership contest: parliamentary stage

Candidate	First ballot: 13 June		Second ballot: 18 June (preceded by first TV debate, 16 June, from which Johnson absented himself)		Third ballot: 19 June (preceded by second TV debate, 18 June)		Fourth ballot: 20 June		Fifth (and final) ballot: 20 June	
	Votes	%	Votes	%	Votes	%	Votes	%	Votes	%
Boris Johnson	**114**	**36.4**	**126**	**40.3**	**143**	**45.7**	**157**	**50.2**	**160**	**51.1**
Jeremy Hunt	**43**	**13.7**	**46**	**14.7**	**54**	**17.3**	**59**	**18.8**	**77**	**24.6**
Michael Gove	37	11.8	41	13.1	51	16.3	61	19.5	75	24.0
Sajid Javid	23	7.3	33	10.5	38	12.1	34	10.9	Eliminated	
Rory Stewart	19	6.1	37	11.8	27	8.6	Eliminated			
Dominic Raab	27	8.6	30	9.6	Eliminated					
Matt Hancock	20	6.4	Withdrew							
Andrea Leadsom	11	3.5	Eliminated							
Mark Harper	10	3.2	Eliminated							
Esther McVey	9	2.9	Eliminated							

The third round was preceded by the rather fractious second televised debate, which was carried by the BBC and pulled in 5.7 million viewers at its peak, compared to the first, carried by Channel Four, watched by, at most, 1.5 million. There was no clear winner, except in the sense that Johnson survived the ordeal, in spite of a few sticky moments over (a) his caricaturing of Muslim women wearing the veil as looking like bank robbers or letterboxes; (b) his careless talk as Foreign Secretary that many believed had helped Iran justify the continued detention of a British-Iranian woman, Nazanin Zaghari-Ratcliffe; and (c), although it wasn't picked up on as much as it might have been, his insistence that the UK leaving the EU on 31 October was 'eminently feasible' rather than something that (in contrast to the other hard Brexiteers in the studio) he would explicitly 'guarantee'. The real loser in that second debate, however, was Rory Stewart, who, by his own admission, put in a relatively 'lacklustre' performance. Nor, it turned out, did he do himself any favours by sending very similar (supposedly copied and pasted) texts to a range of MPs asking for their support in the wee small hours. Few believed, however, that any of that could account for Stewart actually shedding 10 votes in round three, preferring instead to see it as evidence that what Johnson's operation had once given it had subsequently taken away – this despite the fact that the 14 vote increase in Johnson's vote could just as easily be explained by many of those who had previously voted for Leadsom and Raab moving over to him.

While disputed by Johnson's supporters (who pointed out that 'lending' votes was a risky business and militated against the sense of momentum their man wanted to maintain), speculation about recourse to the so-called 'dark arts' inevitably continued into the fourth and fifth rounds, which took place in the morning and afternoon of 20 June. If votes were 'loaned', however, in order to get Javid into the final ballot instead of Michael Gove, then they proved insufficient – although they may, of course, have helped ensure that Gove was accompanied by Jeremy Hunt.

At that point, Johnson's campaign team faced a real dilemma. Clearly it was in their man's interest to see Gove finish behind Hunt, so the temptation to lend the latter some votes (particularly when there were 90 votes cast by proxy) must have been strong. On the other hand, Johnson badly wanted to claim he had the support of the majority (even if, in truth, it was only a bare majority) of his Westminster colleagues. As an out-and-out Brexiteer, some of Javid's 34 votes would presumably come his way. And there had been a big effort to get MPs associated with the cause – notably David Davis ('he gave me the absolute assurance I was looking for'), Dominic Raab and Liz Truss ('no ifs, no buts'), and the ERG's Mark Francois ('come hell or high water') – to go into the media to reassure waverers that Johnson would indeed deliver the UK from the EU on 31 October. But the fact that Johnson only put on three additional votes when four of Javid's erstwhile supporters had publicly declared they were backing him before the last ballot did little to scotch the accusations of 'skulduggery', especially when Gove lost out to Hunt by just two votes.

In the end, though, the rumours counted for far less than the fact that Johnson could indeed claim the support of over half the parliamentary party, that the prospect of a 'psychodrama' in the membership stage of the contest could be put to bed, and that he would go into that second and final stage with over twice as much support as his opponent. That said, his leadership team were taking no chances. Johnson agreed to only one televised debate with Hunt – ITV's on 9 July – plus one that was streamed from the offices of the *Sun* in association with Talk Radio, both ultimately owned by Rupert Murdoch. Both Sky and the BBC were unable to persuade him to take part in events that they had planned – much to the chagrin of Hunt, who took to the *Times* to chastise the frontrunner in no uncertain terms.[16] His reluctant opponent, however, remained resolute – even more so, perhaps, because the Sky News debate Hunt was trying to goad him into attending would have taken place just days after the *Guardian*, following a tip-off that came with audio-tapes, reported that Johnson and his girlfriend, Carrie Symonds, had had such a furious row that their neighbours had called the police.[17]

Johnson could not, however, completely escape since the day after the reported row he, along with Hunt, was scheduled to appear at the first of the sixteen hustings that took place in front of party members between 22 June and 17 July. Nevertheless, when Iain Dale, the author and journalist who hosted ten of those events, repeatedly pressed him on the issue (bravely, since it was clear from their jeers and cheers that the majority of the audience didn't want him to), Johnson managed to bluster his way through without giving any account of himself or even properly addressing the question of whether it was legitimate to consider 'character' when picking a Prime Minister.[18] Still, a YouGov survey of members conducted a few days later suggested that the incident had done little to affect Johnson's grassroots popularity, with some three-quarters of respondents favouring him over Hunt. Polls of Conservative voters by Opinium indicated that he was rather less popular among

Talking past each other? Hunt and Johnson debate, July 2019.
Source: Matt Frost / ITV / Shutterstock.

them than he was among members but that (once the one in five or so 'don't knows' were eliminated) Johnson was still favoured over Hunt by a convincing 60 to 40 margin.

Anecdotally, the hustings may possibly have eroded Johnson's support among members, which would go some way to explaining why, after YouGov's survey of members that was published in the *Times* on 6 July put Johnson on 76 per cent to Hunt's 24 per cent, his eventual winning margin when the results were announced on 23 July was actually slightly lower.[19] But, doubtless due in part to the fact that 90 per cent of members reckoned Johnson was prepared to take the UK out of the EU without a deal (compared to just 27 per cent for Hunt) and only 13 per cent thought the UK would still be in the EU on 31 October if Johnson were PM (compared to 72 per cent for Hunt), it was nevertheless overwhelming. After just over 139,000 (or an impressive 87 per cent) of the party's grassroots members turned out to vote, Johnson beat Hunt by a two-thirds/one-third margin (66 vs 34 per cent) to be elected Tory leader. He took over as Prime Minister the very next day.

During the contest, May had refused to be drawn on whom she was supporting and focused instead on trying to deliver on some of her domestic agenda, most of which had been either overshadowed or simply squeezed out by Brexit. And on moving towards legislating for net-zero carbon emissions and the introduction of a Domestic Abuse Bill, she made important progress.[20] However, any hope that she might persuade Chancellor Philip Hammond to approve significant new funding for schools – something that Number Ten's opinion research showed was a top priority for 'Conservative considerers' – quickly foundered on his understandable reluctance to approve a multi-year, multi-million package at the behest of a Prime Minister who had already announced her resignation.[21] This notwithstanding, May was given a standing ovation at her last Cabinet meeting and was greeted with loud cheers from Tory MPs in the House of Commons the day after – a mixture perhaps of genuine admiration, understandable pity, nauseating hypocrisy, and sheer bloody relief. As for May herself, she was (if only in private) apparently distraught at being succeeded by a man she considered 'morally unfit to be Prime Minister'.[22]

Brexit achieved; Boris rampant
(July–December 2019)

Speaking as Boris Johnson readied himself to move into Downing Street, John Major, who served as Tory leader and Prime Minister between 1990 and 1997, declared that Theresa May's successor 'must choose whether to be the spokesman for an ultra-Brexit faction or the servant of the nation he leads. He cannot be both and the choice he makes will define his premiership from the moment of its birth.'[1] To that faction, of course, this was a false choice: to deliver Brexit was to honour the by now proverbial will of the people. Whether or not he really believed this (or indeed anything), Johnson knew – and, just as importantly for a politician so dependent on the counsel of others, those advising him knew – that achieving Britain's withdrawal from the European Union as quickly as possible was an absolute necessity. Failure risked what was the Conservative Party's ultimate nightmare: Nigel Farage and some of his friends making it into parliament and, even worse, the election of a socialist Labour government under Jeremy Corbyn.

Rewarding loyalty and readying for an election

A vote in the Commons that had taken place the week before Johnson took over as Prime Minister served as a powerful reminder of just how difficult things were and might well become. Seventeen Tory MPs had backed amendments to a bill that, by obliging the government to report to the Commons in the absence of an Executive being in place in Northern Ireland, was intended to prevent it proroguing parliament in an attempt to force through a No-Deal Brexit. Four Cabinet ministers had abstained, and two of them, Chancellor of the Exchequer Philip Hammond and Justice Secretary David Gauke, had made it plain that they could not serve under Johnson since it would mean committing to the possibility of that outcome.

World King at last: Johnson enters Number Ten, July 2019.
Source: 10 Downing Street.

Not all their anti-No-Deal colleagues, however, were so prepared to take a stand. Amber Rudd, for instance, announced that she could live with the threat of a No-Deal Brexit since she apparently bought the argument that it provided much-needed leverage in negotiations with the EU-27. As a result, she was one of the few high-profile Remainers to be given a prominent post (in her case, Work and Pensions Secretary) in Johnson's first Cabinet – one which, although it can be said to have put more of a premium on support for him during the leadership contest than which side its members were on back in 2016, saw three of the four most senior jobs going to Tories strongly associated with Vote Leave. Priti Patel, notwithstanding her departure in disgrace from May's government, went to the Home Office, Dominic Raab to the Foreign Office, and Michael Gove to the Cabinet Office. Even Sajid Javid, whom Johnson appointed Chancellor, had been very much a 'reluctant Remainer' back in 2016. And in any case, in common with other ambitious ministers such as Liz Truss (International Trade), Matt Hancock (Health and Social Care), and (another politician summarily sacked by May) Gavin Williamson (Education), Javid had since embraced Brexit with the zeal of a convert.

Having ditched seventeen of May's ministerial colleagues in what the *Sun* had dubbed 'The Night of the Blonde Knives', Johnson also found room around the table for arch-Brexiteers Andrea Leadsom (Business) and Theresa Villiers (Environment, Food and Rural Affairs). However, with the signal exception of Jacob Rees-Mogg (who became Leader of the House), no space could be found for luminaries of the European Research Group like Steve Baker – which may well have had something to do with Dominic Cummings, who was reported to have referred to the ERG as a 'narcissist delusional subset' and a 'metastasizing tumour' that needed to be 'excised'. Although Eddie Lister (a veteran from Johnson's days as London Mayor) was officially Chief of Staff, Cummings had been named 'Chief Adviser', arriving in Downing Street along with fellow stalwarts of the Vote Leave campaign Lee Cain (made Director of Communications) and Robert Oxley (appointed Press Secretary). Advice on who should be made a minister also came from another Brexiteer, Munira Mirza (a former Revolutionary Communist who had worked for Johnson at City Hall and whom he had appointed Director of the Number Ten Policy Unit), as well as from Johnson's choice as Chief Whip, Mark Spencer – another MP who had swiftly switched from Remain to Leave after the referendum. All backed Johnson's decision – an unusual one given that runners-up in leadership contests tend to be kept on board for the sake of party unity – not to retain the services of Jeremy Hunt after he refused an obvious (and presumably intentionally provocative) demotion from Foreign to Defence Secretary.

According to a Twitter thread posted by erstwhile Cameroon and (since 1 April) erstwhile Conservative MP Nick Boles, all this meant that

> The hard right has taken over the Conservative Party. Thatcherites, libertarians and No Deal Brexiters control it top to bottom. Liberal One Nation Conservatives have been ruthlessly culled. Only a few neutered captives are being kept on as window dressing. The takeover that started in local constituency parties is now complete. The Brexit Party has won the war without electing a single MP. Boris Johnson isn't our new Prime Minister; Nigel Farage is.[2]

This was hyperbole, perhaps – not least because, although Johnson's short victory speech on 23 July predictably saw him pledge (just as he had in his typically optimistic, 'can-do' final column for the *Telegraph* the day before) to 'get Brexit done' by 31 October, it also confirmed, yet again, that this was only one of three aims, the second being to 'unite the country' and the third to defeat Jeremy Corbyn.[3] Moreover, his first speech as Prime Minister in Downing Street majored on a series of supposedly 'One Nation' pledges to increase spending on policing, on the NHS, and on schools. All of these (along with Brexit, of course) featured heavily in a veritable blizzard of Facebook ads designed to punch home and perfect the party's messages – so much so, in fact, that it made it even harder for nervous Tory MPs to believe the assurances Johnson had given them at a meeting of the 1922 Committee the previous evening that an early election was not on the cards.[4] Still, even those dreading the prospect were heartened by his bravura performance at the despatch box in his first outing as Prime Minister, even if his insistence that the UK would leave the EU, deal or no deal, by the Halloween deadline left the pound plummeting to its lowest level in three years. The Tories' grassroots supporters seemed happy too: a readers' poll of 1,300 party members by ConservativeHome suggested that some 58 per cent now expected their party to win an overall majority – up from just 29 per cent when the question was asked back in June. The upbeat mood was no doubt further boosted by the first of a series of announcements, trailed by the Prime Minister and amplified by Communities Secretary Robert Jenrick, of hundreds of millions of pounds that would be made available to local authorities through the so-called 'Towns Fund' – one that very persuasive academic research later argued had been allocated according to political-electoral rather than economic logic.[5]

But it wasn't just Tory MPs and the party's rank and file who responded positively to the change at the top. Polls published in the week after Johnson took over from May suggested the Conservatives had experienced a bounce of between 3 and 10 percentage points, some of it, very encouragingly, coming from what looked like a consolidation of the Leave vote as Conservative supporters who had 'defected' to the Brexit Party began to return to the fold while (equally encouragingly) the Remain vote continued to split itself between Labour and the Lib Dems. That said, there was no room for complacency: no-one in Downing Street or across the road in parliament or in CCHQ could guarantee that Leave voters in the Midlands and the North would prove more inclined than they had been in 2017 to desert Labour. Nor could they discount the possibility that the party's hardened Brexit position might cost it seats to the seemingly resurgent Liberal Democrats – especially after they won (on a 12 per cent swing) a by-election in Brecon and Radnorshire triggered by a recall petition and held just a week after Johnson had replaced Theresa May. Scotland, too, continued to be a worry, with the Prime Minister, on a visit to the country in late July, obliged to sneak out of the back entrance to Bute House (the official residence of First Minister Nicola Sturgeon) so as to avoid a hostile crowd.

Indeed, a deeper dive into UK-wide polling also gave grounds for caution. In its July 2019 Political Monitor, for instance, Ipsos MORI reported that 'Johnson's net satisfaction rating (-7) compares unfavourably to the first monthly rating achieved by Theresa May (+35), Gordon Brown (+16) and John Major (+15).' In fact, it continued, his 'first ratings as a new party leader are actually most similar to Jeremy Corbyn's, who received a score of 33 per cent satisfied, 36 per cent dissatisfied in September 2015'. Just as worryingly, it noted that '75 per cent are dissatisfied with how the Johnson government is running the country compared to 18 per cent that are satisfied. This net satisfaction rating of -57 is the worst starting rating held by any government assuming office in the 40 years of the Ipsos MORI Political Monitor series …, the closest being John Major's (-31) in December of 1990.' And, on Brexit, the pollster reported that '74 per cent think it is unlikely that the "UK and the EU will have agreed the terms of the UK's departure from the European Union in time for the UK to leave by October 31st".'

As far as some Tory MPs were concerned, these low expectations weren't necessarily such a bad thing: if the deadline were somehow hit, then hitting it could be spun as all the more remarkable. Alternatively, if, as seemed more likely given the arithmetic, it were missed, then the backlash might not be quite as bad as some imagined, especially if the government could argue it had done everything in its power to leave on time. Doing just that was also seen by Downing Street as vital to persuading the EU-27 to reopen the Withdrawal Agreement it had negotiated with Theresa May. Change needed to come on Northern Ireland, since the backstop would prevent Britain pursuing an independent trade policy, and on the commitment to the UK remaining in some kind of alignment on regulation and standards, which, for many Brexiteers, would likewise defeat the whole point of Brexit. It was therefore seen as essential that, should the EU fail to budge, then Johnson, unlike May, be seen as willing to leave without a deal – Brexit 'by any means necessary', as Dominic Cummings put it (Malcolm X-style) in early meetings with departmental special advisers.

The fact that at those same meetings Cummings insisted that those advisers would ultimately be responsible to him, plus the fact that so many of them had worked for ministers in the May government, prompted some in the Westminster bubble to complain of a 'jihad on SpAds'.[6] But the latter were hardly the most significant staff appointments made by Johnson and his inner circle in the early days of his premiership. Far more critical was the decision to hire the campaign strategists who would take the party into the next election. Isaac Levido and Michael Brooks had worked on Conservative campaigns before as colleagues of Lynton Crosby, but, just as importantly, both had earlier that year been crucial components in the team that had pulled off a surprise third term for the Australian Liberal Party. To those who remembered the difficulties of the disastrous 2017 Tory campaign, the choice of two Crosby protégés to run things in 2019 may have looked somewhat perverse. But that, in the view of the two men themselves anyway, was to overlook a couple of the main reasons things had gone wrong two years previously: namely the failure both to establish who was actually in charge from the outset and to persuade voters that a general election was really necessary.

On the first point, things were clarified from the get-go. As Levido himself put it, 'We came to a very clear mutual agreement' that he would be 'in charge of the campaign – building it and executing it ... all the way through, ... hiring and firing. ... At the end of the day the only one who could overrule my decisions would be the Prime Minister. So effectively, I answered to the PM.'[7] That did not, of course, mean that – at least until an election proper was called – Cummings was absent from discussions. Nor did it prevent other members of the Vote Leave team coming on board in the run-up to the campaign itself. However, people like Hanbury's Paul Stephenson, as well as some of the consultancy's data analytics team, were brought in not because they were 'friends of Dom' but because they had valuable expertise and experience (in Stephenson's case, for example, attack and rebuttal). This also applied, in spades, to the choice of the team that would augment the party's in-house digital capacity, particularly on the creative side, with CCHQ hiring New Zealand firm Topham Guerin, which had delivered a widely praised online campaign for the Australian Liberal Party back in May.

The second point – the need to convince voters of the need for an election – was every bit as important. As Levido put it, 'The fundamental thing was voters in 2017 did not see a burning need for an election and so we had to firmly establish that in voters' minds.' It was essential, he continued, that, in any election that did take place, the Tories would be able to tell voters that

> This was a last resort. There was no other choice. ... We are having this election because Parliament is broken. The only way we're going to be able to get this issue, whether you voted Leave or Remain, off the table so we can move on as a country is with a strong majority government that is going to be able to deliver that.

Something else was vital too. Achieving the UK's withdrawal from the EU (ideally with a deal but, if necessary, without one) may have been important in and of itself to the Conservatives. But the party's campaign team were convinced that, for many of those whose support they were hoping to win, Brexit was more a means to an end than an end in itself. As a result, the coming campaign would need to focus not just on getting Brexit done, but on what the government would deliver on popular public services once it was achieved. And since, as Australian politician John Howard memorably put it, 'You can't fatten the pig on market day,' this meant a seemingly endless series of million (and often billion) pound announcements of new funding for towns, health, crime and policing, and schools. These were what the Chancellor, Sajid Javid, labelled 'the people's priorities' in an op-ed for the *Telegraph* that teed up a one-year Spending Review in which, by revising the government's existing fiscal rules, he was able to announce £11.7 billion for new day-to-day spending over the next year, along with £1.7 billion on infrastructure.[8] As Dominic Cummings, doing his best Donald Trump impression, told SpAds in late August, 'There will be billions and billions and billions of pounds. ... It's going to be the most beautiful spending round you've ever seen. It's going to be beautiful.'[9] All this – especially the renewed emphasis on law and order typified by a prime ministerial op-ed for the *Mail on Sunday* trailing new money and measures under the headline 'Left wingers will howl. But it's time to make criminals afraid – not the public' – was very much in keeping with a widely covered report stressing voters' hunger for 'security' rather than 'freedom' produced by the centre-right think tank Onward, run (ironically enough) by Theresa May's former policy adviser, Will Tanner.[10] Whether those now in charge in Number Ten and CCHQ, who were well aware that social and cultural values mattered as much as the economy to their target voters, really needed to be reminded of that hunger is debatable, although being seen to be in tune with the zeitgeist rarely does a party any harm.

Punishing dissent and proroguing parliament

Unleashing a torrent of spending announcements over the summer reinforced the impression that May's replacement by Johnson represented not just a change of leader but also a thoroughgoing change of regime. Of course, May, too, had declared 'the end of austerity', but this time it was essential that message was not drowned out by Brexit. Unfortunately, however, the latter was already shaping up to dominate the headlines as autumn approached. Those Tory MPs determined to avoid a No-Deal exit wasted no time in publicly warning their new leader that his so-called 'red lines' would make agreement with the EU-27 difficult if not impossible, provoking a calculatedly furious reaction from Number Ten, which went as far as to brief journalists that Philip Hammond had, while Chancellor, undermined his government's negotiation strategy and its No-Deal preparations so as to prevent the UK ever leaving the European Union.[11] Not that the party in the media (the *Mail, Telegraph, Express,* and *Sun*) needed much encouragement. Indeed, some were already accusing Hammond and his colleagues (soon to be routinely referred to, after one of its most prominent members, as 'the Gaukeward squad') of preferring to risk a Labour government under Jeremy Corbyn if that was what it took to stop Brexit. If there were any justice, then this surely meant that – to borrow the title of a ferocious (but, it turned out, prescient) op-ed penned in mid-August by the *Telegraph's* Deputy Editor, Allister Heath – 'Tory arch-Remainers will soon find they have no place left in their party.'

The reaction of the paper's erstwhile star columnist, Boris Johnson, was, if anything, even more pointed. Taking part in what proved to be a short-lived gimmick – a 'People's PMQs [Prime Minister's Questions]' on Facebook Live – he declared that 'there's a terrible kind of collaboration, as it were, going on between people who think they can block Brexit in parliament and our European friends'. The follow-up – an uncompromising letter from him to Hammond et al. shown to the *Mail on Sunday* – was, however, overshadowed by the leak to the *Sunday Times* on 18 August of the government's planning for No Deal.[12] Codenamed Operation Yellowhammer, the dossier made for alarming reading, suggesting as it did a country inadequately prepared for the severe supply shortages and disruption that would likely result. It also poisoned the atmosphere still further: notwithstanding Michael Gove's rather unconvincing assertion that it was an old document, its contents strengthened the case of those MPs (some of them Tory) determined to prevent No Deal; hence the attempt on the part of Downing Street to suggest that 'a former minister' had leaked the dossier so as to undermine the new dispensation – a claim furiously denied by Hammond and others.

The next weekend produced another alarming leak. The government, it seemed, was intending to prorogue parliament from the beginning of September to the middle of October, having been assured of the move's legality and boosted by front-page misreporting of a controversial poll that purported to show public support for it.[13] Its justification revolved around the need to prepare a new Queen's Speech – an argument to which few gave any credence given that prorogations for that purpose normally lasted a matter of days, not weeks. Critics pointed instead to the government's desire to curtail the time available to MPs who wished to prevent it taking the UK out of the EU without a deal – not necessarily because No Deal was the outcome Johnson wanted but because (as the Prime Minister pointed out to his Cabinet) it would, by convincing the EU-27 that it could not rely on parliament to 'frustrate' Brexit, persuade European governments to make Britain a better offer. And, reasoned Cummings, it would also be a useful, indeed crucial, reminder to voters, be they 'Labour leavers' or erstwhile Tories who'd 'defected' to the Brexit Party, that Johnson was doing all in his power to get Brexit done but was being prevented from doing so by a 'Remainer

Parliament'. Presumably that was what helped change the mind of all those current Cabinet ministers who had condemned prorogation as 'trashing democracy' during the leadership election just a few months previously.[14]

The impression that the PM meant business was to be further reinforced by a decision – briefed not for the first (or last) time to James Forsyth, the well-connected columnist for the *Spectator*, the *Sun*, and the *Times* – that Johnson was planning (to the discomfort, if not the horror, of some of his Cabinet colleagues as well as many backbenchers) to remove the whip from Conservative No-Deal rebels in the event that they backed moves to legislate against that outcome in the few days left before prorogation. Johnson himself played the 'these are friends of mine and believe me I take absolutely no joy in any of it' card in an appearance on ITV's flagship *Peston* show after said legislation (labelled by Downing Street 'the surrender bill' and then 'the surrender act') was passed a few days later, triggering the expulsion of twenty-one Tory rebels (including a number of former Cabinet ministers like Philip Hammond, David Gauke, Greg Clarke, and Justine Greening, as well as Churchill's grandson, Nicholas Soames, and the 2019 leadership candidate Rory Stewart). However, it was pretty clear from media reports (for instance, the account of a highly charged phone call between Cummings and one of the rebels written by the *Mail*'s Jack Doyle, who went on to become Downing Street's Director of Communications in 2020) that what even some Tories regarded as the brutality of the decision was very much part of the plan.[15] Indeed, the high-profile, often harsh, criticism it received – not least from former Tory leaders William Hague (who called it 'the most egregious and counter-productive act of self-harm committed by the party leadership that I can recall in my lifetime') and John Major (who urged Johnson to 'reinstate those members of parliament you have expelled because, without them … we will cease to be a broad-based national party, and be seen as a mean-minded sect') – was all grist to the mill. The same was probably true of the resignations from the government a few days later of Amber Rudd, who had been one of the few 'moderates' willing to give Johnson the benefit of the doubt on Brexit, and (more woundingly perhaps) his younger brother Jo.

Any doubts that MPs had about the expulsions, however, were somewhat assuaged by a ConservativeHome readers' poll of party members which found that only one in ten disagreed with the decision to withdraw the whip. Meanwhile, on prorogation itself, although a plurality of the British electorate, as measured by various surveys, appeared to take a dim view of it, the vast majority of those who did so were Remain voters. Nor did it seem to make much impact on vote intentions, which were still moving in the right direction for the Tories. Supporters who had 'defected' to the Brexit Party seemed to be returning home, while Johnson's ratings on electorally important criteria like 'strong' and 'decisive' were already on the rise.[16] That said, he was starting from a low base: his ratings had been none too impressive to start with and, just as they had when he had been elected leader a few weeks previously, at least half of respondents still thought he was 'dishonest' and 'untrustworthy'.[17]

Whether the justices serving on the UK's Supreme Court thought the same, we can only speculate. All we know for sure is that on 24 September they ruled unanimously that the government's prorogation of parliament was unlawful and void. In so doing, they essentially confirmed the decision of Scotland's highest court announced two weeks previously – a decision which Downing Street had clearly attempted to politicize, firstly by anonymous briefing and then by sending out Cabinet minister Kwasi Kwarteng into a TV studio to suggest, in rather mealy-mouthed fashion, that

> The extent to which lawyers and judges are interfering in politics is something that concerns many people. I'm not saying this, but many people are saying that the judges are biased ... many Leave voters, many people up and down the country, are beginning to question the partiality of the judges.

Predictably, the party in the media had suggested the same, with the *Mail* producing a faint echo of its infamous 'Enemies of the People' front-page splash by producing pen portraits of the supposedly Europhile Scottish justices who had 'ruined Boris Johnson's week'.[18]

Presumably in the hope that, now that the Supreme Court had ruled the same way, they could avoid further embarrassment to Minister of Justice Robert Buckland and Attorney General Geoffrey Cox (both serving lawyers), government Whips asked Tory MPs not to sound off in similar fashion this time – not entirely successfully, it turned out:

that well-known legal sage Steve Baker apparently thought it 'odd' that a lower court's earlier, more favourable judgment on prorogation had been overruled by more senior judges, while Leader of the House Jacob Rees-Mogg even talked in Cabinet of a 'constitutional coup'.[19] The party in the media was no less outraged, with the *Sun* leading the charge: the Supreme Court, its next-day leader column screamed, had 'done the bidding' of 'braying Remainers' and

> Boris, victim of yesterday's staggering legal coup, has to respect this court and its supposed impartiality. But in one unprecedented act of constitutional vandalism 11 judges became an unelected political entity, granting themselves immense power to overrule our Government and Queen.

Whether the paper was speaking for its readers is hard to know for sure, but it was certainly reflecting the views of Conservative and Leave voters: a snap poll by YouGov suggested that, overall, people agreed with the Supreme Court by 49 to 30 per cent, but the figures for Tory voters and Leavers were 22–56 and 22–57 respectively.[20] This was music to the ears of Number Ten and, in a largely successful attempt both to distract from its court defeat and to blame parliament for delaying Brexit, Johnson and his colleagues went all-in during the Commons debate which followed its resumption. With all the courtroom theatricality at his command, Geoffrey Cox slammed the government's opponents for their lack of 'moral guts' and claimed that, absent an election, parliament was 'dead' and had 'no moral right to sit'. Johnson then doubled down, enraging Opposition MPs by referring (fifteen times) to legislation which prevented the UK leaving without a deal by obliging him to ask for an extension from the EU-27 as the 'surrender act' or 'surrender bill'. Even worse, he accused Labour's Paula Sherriff of 'humbug' when she begged him not to use the kind of language that had foreshadowed the murder of her friend and parliamentary colleague Jo Cox. 'The best way', Johnson continued, 'to ensure that every parliamentarian is properly safe, and we dial down the current anxiety in this country, is to get Brexit done.'

Johnson later admitted, when he met colleagues at a 'political Cabinet' (i.e. one with no civil servants present) a couple of days later, that he regretted his use of the word 'humbug', albeit claiming at the same time that he had been misunderstood. But he also assured them that focus groups were showing the term 'surrender act'/'surrender bill' (which he went on to use sixteen times in an appearance on *Marr*, the BBC's flagship Sunday politics show) was cutting through. They were also delighted to hear that Brexit-backing donors were now very much back in the fold and helping the party to build up a considerable election war-chest. Perhaps even more extraordinarily, Johnson's senior staff then helped the ever-friendly *Mail on Sunday* concoct a cock-and-bull story smearing those MPs who had been instrumental in the legislation:

> Downing Street has launched a major investigation into alleged links between foreign governments and the MPs behind the 'Surrender Act' which could force Boris Johnson to delay Brexit, *The Mail on Sunday* can reveal. Sources said No 10 took the unprecedented action after officials received intelligence that the MPs, including former Cabinet Minister Oliver Letwin, had received help drafting the bill from members of the French Government and the European Union. ... Last night, a senior No 10 source said: 'The Government is working on extensive investigations into Dominic Grieve, Oliver Letwin and Hilary Benn and their involvement with foreign powers and the funding of their activities. Governments have proper rules for drafting legislation, but nobody knows what organisations are pulling these strings. We will demand the disclosure of all details of their personal communications with other states. The drafting of primary legislation in collusion with foreign powers must be fully investigated.'[21]

All this tough talk, however, was combined with – and effectively disguised – a softening of the government's negotiating position. From mid-September onwards, and in Johnson's speech to the Conservative Party conference, it became clear that he would accept some kind of compromise on Northern Ireland. Meanwhile, sympathetic journalists were being briefed that, although the government supposedly remained committed to the 'do or die' 31 October deadline, a delay forced upon it by parliament wouldn't necessarily prove fatal to its chances of winning an election. Polling soon added weight to this impression: YouGov found that 73 per cent of those intending to vote Conservative said it wouldn't be Johnson's fault if the UK failed to leave at Halloween and (significantly) 78 per cent of Brexit Party voters (many of whom the Tories hoped to persuade to come over to them) said the same; and ComRes found that more people (83 per cent) would blame 'Parliament generally', the European Commission (63 per cent), and 'Remain-supporting MPs' (70 per cent) than would blame Boris Johnson (56 per cent).[22]

Election victory, however, would also depend, as Campaign Director Isaac Levido stressed, on the Conservative Party persuading the public that it was prepared to spend, spend, spend on their priorities – an emphasis that was clearly causing some friction with the Chancellor. Sajid Javid, after all, was very much a fiscal hawk, concerned that the Tories preserve their hard-won reputation for balancing the books. He had also been angered by Cummings' decision at the end of August to dismiss his media SpAd, Sonia Kahn, for supposedly leaking damaging material to No-Deal rebels, especially after she was theatrically escorted from the building, for no good reason, by armed police. Nor was Javid best pleased to read in the newspapers that Johnson and Cummings preferred to deal with his more biddable junior, the Cabinet's young Chief Secretary to the Treasury, Rishi Sunak.

Disappointing the DUP to seal the Brexit deal

If there were tensions, however, they were not allowed to spoil the optics at conference, that year held in Manchester's Central Convention Complex hung with banners bearing the slogan 'Get Brexit Done: Invest in Our NHS, Schools and Police'. It began with big announcements of additional funding for hospital building and a planned hike in the minimum wage, before moving on to law and order, with Justice Minister Robert Buckland announcing tougher sentences for violent and sexual offences and Home Secretary Priti Patel, in a speech heavily trailed by the ever-helpful *Daily Express*, promising to spend millions on stun guns for the police, beating up on 'the north London metropolitan liberal elite', and telling criminals, 'We're coming after you.'[23]

Johnson's speech was, of course, the highlight for the delegates, but, even though he was among friends, it had not been a particularly easy week for the Prime Minister since much of the coverage of the conference had been taken up with stories that he had enjoyed an inappropriate relationship with an American businesswoman, Jennifer Arcuri, when he was Mayor of London and that he had groped female journalists when he was Editor of the *Spectator*. He and his team were also well aware of eve-of-conference polling by Ipsos MORI which suggested 81 per cent of the public were dissatisfied with how the government was running the country, 55 per cent with the job Johnson was doing as Prime Minister, and 53 per cent with how he was handling Brexit – the only consolation being that Labour's and Corbyn's ratings were even worse and that those who intended to vote Tory were far more impressed with him than were respondents as a whole.[24] Still, Johnson's speech did not disappoint. While suggesting he was indeed open to some kind of compromise with the EU-27 on Northern Ireland, he recommitted to the 31 October deadline and laid into parliament for trying to prevent or delay the UK's departure. He also, of course, set about Corbyn, warning that a Labour government would trash the economy and usher in more referendums: one in Scotland and a second referendum on Brexit. Overall, the message was 'Get Brexit done' (with the phrase, or slight variants of it, used eleven times during the speech) so that the government could start spending on voters' bread-and-butter priorities.

The government's messaging was not, however, always quite so clear – especially on the question of how and whether it could reach a deal with the EU-27. Dominic Cummings, for one, was keen to give the impression that it was still do or die, that the UK would walk away, and that it could find a way round 'the Surrender Act' – so much so that he allowed the *Spectator*'s James Forsyth to publish verbatim a long message laying out his views, albeit without explicitly naming him as the source. However, that, plus the briefing out of what many considered a highly tendentious account of a phone call between the Prime Minister and German Chancellor Angela Merkel, proved too much for some of Johnson's colleagues, the majority of whom were still hoping for a deal, with one confiding to journalists that Cummings had been told, when ministers met at Downing Street that week, 'Cabinet will set the strategy, not unelected officials. … We are not a Cabinet of sock puppets and nodding dogs.'[25] A significant number of Conservative MPs were also concerned enough about the prospect of going into an election with some sort of No-Deal manifesto to talk to journalists about it and to back a delegation, made up of four of their colleagues, going to Number Ten to seek reassurances from the PM that a deal was still very much the preferred outcome – only to find, once it had told journalists that it had received those assurances, that a 'Senior Downing Street Source' was suggesting that it had 'over-interpreted the meeting' and that No Deal was still a distinct possibility.

Yet a couple of days later there came the announcement that a one-to-one meeting between Johnson and Irish Taoiseach Leo Varadkar had come up with the makings of a deal which both sides could live with (albeit one that looked likely to do even more damage to the UK economy than May's). May's 'backstop' was to be replaced by a 'protocol' that would see Northern Ireland remain aligned to single market rules on goods, agriculture, and VAT. It would be in UK customs territory, but there would be checks on goods going from Britain to Northern Ireland. The arrangement would remain in place unless and until the Northern Ireland Assembly were to vote to end it. And the UK would therefore be able to pursue an independent trade policy, while the Political Declaration on the future relationship between the UK and the EU would now talk about 'an ambitious trading relationship on goods on the basis of a Free Trade Agreement' rather than one that was 'as close as possible'.[26]

It was this last aspect (along with the fact that there was nothing to stop the UK, if it wanted to, leaving without any kind of Free Trade Agreement once the one-year transition period expired) that was crucial for Brexit-ultras on the Tory benches. And it was the reason why Johnson had reason to hope that they would come on board – in spite of the distinct possibility that the new deal (because it effectively placed a customs border down the Irish Sea) would be rejected by Northern Ireland's DUP. Given that there were twenty-eight so-called 'Spartans' (ERG members who had voted against May's Withdrawal Agreement), nearly all of whom seemed suddenly willing to cast aside their supposedly cast-iron commitment to their unionist allies, and only ten DUP MPs, this was a sensible trade-off – both arithmetically and in terms of Tory Party unity. There was also a very good chance that nearly all the twenty-one MPs who had lost the Conservative whip would vote for the deal. Throw in those Labour MPs keen to do so too and that made for the majority that May had signally failed to construct.

An Irish Sea border, of course, was hardly ideal – and had been rejected on Unionist grounds by Theresa May, who back in February 2018 had insisted that 'No UK Prime Minister could ever agree to it.' But, as both confidential security briefings and more public assessments made clear, the risk to peace in Northern Ireland of anything resembling an east–west land border on the island of Ireland made the alternative practically unthinkable. Besides, as report after report – and the government's own planning documents – made clear, leaving without a deal would be disruptive and economically damaging in both the long and short term. It would also make coming to a trade agreement, as well as forging a political, diplomatic, and security relationship with the EU-27, so much more difficult. And in any case, deep down, most of those around the Prime Minister knew that parliament would almost certainly be able to prevent it ever happening, raising the unthinkable possibility that Brexit itself might never be delivered. They were also convinced, along with the Tory campaign team, that it would be far easier to win an election with a deal than without one.

Johnson's task was made much easier by the former ultras now entitled to attend Cabinet immediately rowing in behind, with Jacob Rees-Mogg writing a particularly supportive op-ed ('My plea to Brexiteers – you must trust Boris') in the *Sunday Telegraph*. And there was clearly a concerted move on the part of the party in the media to do the same: the *Sun on Sunday*, for instance, ran a leader column headlined 'Boris Johnson has stunned the Brexit-denying Remoaners by getting the UK close to a deal'. True enough, perhaps, but what he could not do was persuade parliament, when it met for an extraordinary Saturday sitting on 19 October, to reject an amendment by the Tory MP Oliver Letwin which effectively prevented a vote on the new deal until Johnson had complied with the so-called 'Surrender Act' and requested an extension to Article 50. This Johnson duly did, albeit making it clear that he was doing so under duress by refusing to sign the letter and attaching another missive explaining why he didn't want one. If this arguably puerile display of petulance was designed as a 'dead cat' – an issue that would generate controversy sufficient to distract people from something rather more problematic – then it worked reasonably well: Johnson received little or no criticism, least of all from the Tory- and Brexit-supporting print media, for missing his supposedly 'do or die' deadline. Moreover, the ERG's 'Spartans' were now firmly in his tent, after some of their high-profile members were wooed personally by the PM and once they'd met collectively to confirm their approval of the new deal.[27]

All this – plus polling which indicated that the public (including, very importantly, Leave voters) were significantly keener on Johnson's deal than May's – was enough, a few days later, on 22 October, to see the Withdrawal Agreement Bill given a majority at second reading of 30.[28] Sadly for Johnson, however, his triumph lasted barely fifteen minutes. MPs swiftly rejected (by 322 votes to 308) the government's programme motion on the grounds that, in attempting to pass the bill in time to meet the 31 October deadline, it clearly left them insufficient time to properly scrutinize its detailed provisions – concerns interpreted, of course, by the party in the media as nothing more than a transparent attempt to disguise Labour's desire to wreck Brexit.[29] The government, which now wanted an election, as was made patently obvious by its Queen's Speech a week or so previously – more a manifesto than a literal legislative programme – was left with two choices.[30]

Some advisers and Cabinet ministers (Gove, Smith, and Morgan, for instance) feared a repetition of Theresa May's ill-fated attempt to boost her majority before doing a deal with the EU and so wanted to allocate more time to the bill in order to pass it before going to the country. Others, including the 'Vote Leave crowd' of staffers led by Dominic Cummings and the majority of Cabinet ministers, were concerned that Opposition MPs might exploit a revised timetable to try to sabotage or materially alter the Withdrawal Agreement. In any case, they believed that going to the country having passed the bill into law risked removing the main reason why Leave-supporting Labour voters might be persuaded to switch to the Tories, especially if Labour were somehow able to ditch Corbyn in the meantime. Holding an election would also mean the cancellation of Sajid Javid's Budget on 6 November – not necessarily a bad thing, firstly, in view of the rather pessimistic take on the nation's finances on the part of some experts and, secondly, because it would allow the party to trumpet its spending pledges once again without having to show precisely how it proposed to pay for them since the Office for Budget Responsibility would not now be required to issue its assessment.[31]

Perhaps not surprisingly, especially in view of the fact that polling was beginning to show the Conservatives moving from the low to the high 30s and Labour dropping into the mid- to low 20s, Johnson went with the second approach and announced that he would be 'pausing' the bill.

Then, once his acceptance of the EU's offer of an extension until 31 January effectively removed the prospect of an imminent No-Deal exit (and therefore Labour's justification for blocking an election), he was able to get around the Fixed-term Parliaments Act and, on 29 October, call a contest for 12 December – being aided in this by the Liberal Democrats and the SNP, both of which hoped to win additional seats and maybe even prevent Brexit.

Preparing for battle

The majority of the former Conservatives in the Commons voted for an election, with the rest abstaining. Philip Hammond was one of the abstainers but had already by then forfeited any chance of standing as a Tory candidate – in spite of a decision by his association a few weeks previously to readopt him. The same went for David Gauke, who had earlier survived a no-confidence motion debated by his local membership. They were joined in not having the whip restored to them by Guto Bebb, Justine Greening, Dominic Grieve, Oliver Letwin, Anne Milton, Antoinette Sandbach, and former leadership contender Rory Stewart, as well as, of course, another former Chancellor (and indeed another former leadership contender), Ken Clarke. Ten former Tory MPs had the whip restored, although, in the event, a number of them decided not to stand. Sadly, we shall never know which of the rebels it was who told a journalist that 'The party is now led by a narrow sect who wouldn't be out of place in a Muppet version of *The Handmaid's Tale*.'[32]

In fact, the rebels weren't the only Tory MPs who decided not to stand again following the calling of the general election. Indeed, there were 32 Conservative retirees – on a par with the 38 who'd departed voluntarily in 2015 and the 35 who'd stepped down in 2010, but considerably more than the mere 12 who'd stood down in 2017. This suggested that two years of infighting may have taken their toll, not least because a fair few MPs decided to call it a day rather earlier than might have been expected. For example, as one study noted:

Overall, 19 women MPs stood down, which is roughly proportionate to the representation of women in the House, but the nine Conservative (or former Conservative) women MPs who retired were noticeably younger and had spent less time on average in the House than either retiring Conservative men or retiring Labour MPs. The average age of Conservative (and former Conservative) women MPs was 53 and they had spent on average only 10 years in the Commons. These women could have been prominent in politics for another decade or so.[33]

This might have been due to the hostility (and sometimes downright intimidation) experienced by all too many female MPs. But it might also have had something to do with the fact that the Conservative Party they joined – David Cameron's supposedly moderate, relatively internationalist, and socially liberal Conservative Party – had morphed into something less in tune with their values; this, after all, was the case for relatively young men like Nick Boles, Jo Johnson, and Rory Stewart, the latter having already announced he was leaving the Commons in order to stand for the London Mayoralty as an independent.

Whatever, the consequence was a scramble among wannabe MPs for some plum safe seats, along, of course, with those target seats that, in spite of CCHQ encouraging them to select early, still had vacancies. The resulting rush to recruit inevitably threw up one or two controversies, both locally and nationally. Indeed, it prompted the resignation of one of the vice-chairs of the 1922 Committee, Charles Walker, from the Party Board, apparently after a row with Party Co-Chairman Ben Elliot and Johnson adviser Dougie Smith over the centralization of the process and the supposed sidelining of the other Co-Chairman, the MP James Cleverly. But (possibly because the outcome of the election was so much more favourable; possibly because associations in target seats often did their best to pick candidates with local connections, however tenuous) CCHQ ultimately faced nowhere near as much criticism as it had done in 2017.[34]

Nor, fortunately, did staffers in Matthew Parker Street need to seriously entertain the prospect of having to stand down candidates as part of an electoral pact with the Brexit Party – an arrangement which no less a figure than US President Donald Trump opined would create 'an unstoppable force'. When tested by YouGov in early September, the idea clearly appealed not just to Brexit Party supporters (by a 70- to 17-point margin) but also to Conservative voters (by a lesser but still impressive 60–23 margin). But when included in ConservativeHome's readers' survey of party members the following month, the reaction was far less favourable: true, just over half (51 per cent) supported it, but opposition (at 42 per cent) was significant – and probably increased as Farage's outfit fell in the polls, thereby lowering its value as a potential ally.

This did not, of course, prevent Farage, from late summer onwards, from snatching every opportunity to suggest that the Tories could not win unless Johnson came to some kind of arrangement with him – particularly in Labour Leave seats in the North and the Midlands, which, according to him anyway, the Tories stood no chance of taking.[35] The response from Number Ten, however, was consistently unequivocal – to the point where one source suggested in mid-September that Farage was not 'a fit and proper person' to be allowed anywhere near government. And when, at the end of that month, the Brexit Party took out a two-page ad in the *Sunday Telegraph* to press the case for a pact, Johnson, knowing full well that polling suggested support for the Brexit Party was continuing to soften, was crystal-clear when he spoke to the BBC's Andrew Marr that same morning: 'We don't do deals with other parties.' Both Farage and his deputy, Richard Tice, were supposedly sounded out about some kind of preferment from the government (a peerage here or a safe Tory seat there) in return for them 'calling off the dogs'. But it seems highly unlikely, if there really was such an approach, that it was sanctioned (or even known about) by the Conservative Party leadership.[36] And once the deal with the EU-27 was done and the election called, Tory Brexit-ultras and their favourite newspapers left their audience in no doubt where they stood: if anyone was going to stand down candidates, then it would be Farage, not Johnson. As Iain Duncan Smith (whose own seat, it is worth recalling, looked increasingly vulnerable to Labour) wrote in the *Telegraph*,

> The Brexit Party has helped enormously to focus the minds of politicians and it led the charge during the Euro elections to deliver Brexit. Yet sadly it could now inadvertently throw it all away. … Ironically, as disarray in the Remain camp breaks out, there is now the threat of the same happening among Leave supporters if the Brexit Party puts candidates up against Conservatives in this election.
>
> Such a move, I believe, will damage the cause which we all support and weaken Boris Johnson's ability to deliver Brexit. The harsh reality is that the

Conservative Party is the Brexit party, for only the Conservative Party has the capacity to deliver Brexit after this election.[37]

The *Sun*'s leader on 2 November was even more forthright:

> Voters tempted by the Brexit Party now need to face some harsh realities:
>
> Nigel Farage will not be Prime Minister. Nor is he remotely likely to hold the balance of power.
>
> There is no longer a route to the No Deal Brexit he wants. Nor any prospect of Boris Johnson caving to his demands for a pact, destroying the Tories' unity. And it is patently untrue to say Boris's deal is not Brexit. The Tory ERG simply wouldn't back it if so. ...
>
> In a few constituencies Farage's party could hurt Labour more than the Tories. Overall it is FAR more likely to prevent Boris winning the majority which is vital to delivering Brexit and without which it is lost. ...
>
> Farage's legacy won't just be that his vanity wrecked his life's work. That a party he founded with only one aim, a real Brexit, became the very instrument of the project's destruction.
>
> He will be remembered as the right-wing maverick who handed anti-Semitic, anti-Western Marxists an unprecedented chance to plunder the world's fifth-largest economy. The Sun admires Farage.
>
> His pressure brought about the referendum AND a better deal. But he could now be the author of a double national catastrophe.
>
> He and his voters should think again.

These words dovetailed nicely with the attack line sent out by the Tories to their MPs and candidates: 'A vote for the Brexit Party lets Corbyn in by the back door.' Not to be put off, however, Farage persisted with his claim that the Conservatives had tried to buy him off with 'baubles' and with his promise to stand candidates in every constituency unless Johnson committed to No Deal.[38] Tory Brexiteers and the party in the media remained resolute – and unimpressed: the *Telegraph*, for instance, reported that

> Nigel Farage risks becoming the 'man who threw away Brexit', the most senior Tory Eurosceptic backbencher has warned, as the Brexit Party leader prepares to unveil his 600 election candidates. In a blistering attack on Mr Farage,

Steve Baker, the chairman of the European Research Group (ERG), accused him of 'setting out' to create a 'weak and indecisive' hung Parliament.[39]

Meanwhile, another high-profile Tory Brexiteer, Jacob Rees-Mogg, speaking to LBC radio, insisted that the government's deal represented 'complete Brexit' and suggested Farage should now 'retire from the field', since 'it would be a great shame if he carries on fighting after he has already won to snatch defeat from the jaws of victory'. Meanwhile, although the election campaign had yet to be formally launched, CCHQ was already pumping out an even more direct message via Facebook ads targeted at people living in seats in the North and the Midlands which the party hoped to win from Labour: residents in one Welsh border constituency, for instance, were told that 'It only takes 2,618 people to switch their vote in Alyn & Deeside to elect a Conservative MP that will back Boris to get Brexit done. A vote for anyone else, including the Brexit Party, will just create a hung parliament with more delay, confusion and indecision.'

The Conservatives began the campaign with double-digit polling leads and Johnson strongly preferred over Corbyn. But after what happened in 2017, they were taking nothing for granted and leaving nothing to chance. They had overhauled their party machine, built up a war chest, and (in marked contrast to Labour) knew exactly what their campaign would be about and, just as importantly, exactly who would be running it. They also had a pretty good idea of where they stood their best chance of winning seats. Their list of targets included not only familiar marginals but also Labour-held constituencies (labelled the 'Red Wall' by electoral strategist James Kanagasooriam) where the demographics, just not the history, meant they were vulnerable to a Tory challenge, especially if that challenge focused on the social and cultural values held by what the think tank Onward had labelled 'Workington man'.[40] The party's campaign team were also determined to do everything they could to avoid producing a manifesto that would court controversy and create hostages to fortune. It had decided, too, to avoid 2017-style attacks on Corbyn that were so over the top that they risked proving counterproductive. Finally, it knew it had a leader who, for all his faults, was seen as likeable and authentic by many (if not all) target voters and was capable (most of the time anyway) of sticking to a message without boring them to death.

Winning big: the 2019 election

Johnson kicked off the campaign proper in Birmingham on 6 November with a speech criticizing a parliament 'as incapable of digestive function as an anaconda that has swallowed a tapir' and promising to end the deadlock over Brexit, which was 'like a bendy bus jackknifed on a yellow box junction ... blocking traffic in every direction'. Labour, with all its 'dither and delay', was in no position to do this, he argued, but nor was the Brexit Party. Indeed, Farage and co., he claimed, reminded him of 'candle-sellers at the dawn of the age of the electric light bulb, or the makers of typewriters on beholding their first laptop computer. They have a terrible sense that they are about to lose their market. Because this deal delivers everything that I campaigned for.' The mantra, of course, was 'Get Brexit Done', with the Withdrawal Agreement promoted as 'oven-ready' and a string of campaign trail events and social media posts featuring Johnson brandishing 'oven-ready' food such as pies, biscuits, bagels, and doughnuts.

Unsurprisingly, perhaps, in view of Johnson's relentless yet entertaining messaging, support for the Brexit Party began to wane, prompting Farage to announce on 11 November that he was standing down candidates in Conservative-held seats – a move presumably based more on his desire to save face than on electoral logic: a split Leave vote in Labour-held Tory targets, after all, was more likely to help Labour incumbents than Tory challengers. It was nevertheless helpful to the Conservatives since it allowed CCHQ to focus on those target seats. It also sent yet another signal to Leave voters that, realistically, the Tories were the only game in town, and it dashed Lib Dem hopes of picking up Conservative-held seats as a result of the Brexit Party siphoning off Leave voters.

Not everything, of course, was going the Tories' way. On the eve of Johnson launching their campaign, Jacob Rees-Mogg was forced to apologize for a spectacularly ill-judged remark on Grenfell Tower, after which he duly (and very wisely) disappeared from view for the rest of the campaign.[41] Johnson was criticized for being slow to visit places in the North and the Midlands that were hit by floods in mid-November. Meanwhile, the release of official statistics revealed the worst accident and emergency waiting times on record – potentially damaging since polling released the same day suggested that, while Labour Leave voters rated Brexit as the most important issue *for the country*, they saw the NHS as the most important issue *for their own families*.[42] And Labour, of course, was doing all it could to portray itself once again as the party of the NHS, promising to spend huge amounts to put things right. Yet such promises inevitably had a downside, helping CCHQ, in the first week of the campaign, to argue that the Opposition was apparently planning to spend a staggering £1.2 trillion. What CCHQ did not do, however, much to the despair of the Labour campaign, was to attack particular initiatives, reasoning that to do so would (as it had done in 2017) merely amplify them. Instead, the Conservative campaign chose to emphasize its own pledges of extra cash for policing, green energy, flood protection, free childcare, town high streets, and the NHS. True, the sums offered were generally lower and more tightly targeted than Labour's. Nor did they, as was repeatedly stressed, break the Chancellor's much-vaunted 'fiscal rules'. But they nevertheless reinforced the 'your priorities' message that the party had been pushing ever since the start of Johnson's premiership – one reiterated at the annual conference of the Confederation of British Industry (CBI) when Johnson informed delegates that a previously promised corporation tax cut was no longer affordable since the money was needed for public services.

Johnson carried that same message into the televised leaders' debates. In 2017, May's decision not to take part in a direct confrontation with her opponents had badly damaged her campaign, making her look weak and evasive when she was running as 'strong and stable'. But in 2019, Conservative strategists, believing that Johnson was a good enough TV performer and that Corbyn was now hopelessly unpopular, decided that agreeing to debates would be less risky than avoiding them. They also hoped they could minimize the risk, firstly, by bringing over from the US Brett O'Donnell, an experienced Republican operative who had coached George W. Bush and Mitt Romney for presidential debates and, secondly, by staging full dress rehearsals, with Michael Gove cast as Corbyn. True, Johnson's claim in the first debate on 19 November that truthfulness mattered in this election drew mocking laughter from the audience, and for several hours during and after the debate there was much (one could argue, helpfully distracting) handwringing over the decision by CCHQ's social media team to change the Conservatives' Twitter profile to resemble a non-partisan fact-checking service. But a snap YouGov poll in its aftermath suggested a 'bore draw', with 51 per cent declaring Johnson the winner and 49 per cent Corbyn.

A couple of days later, Johnson was given a predictably rough ride when he joined the Labour, Lib Dem, and SNP leaders for a BBC *Question Time* special from Sheffield but stuck doggedly to his party's main attack lines, in particular ridiculing Corbyn's Brexit neutrality pledge. Johnson's second head-to-head clash with Corbyn, which took place on the final Friday night of the campaign, was as underwhelming and as predictable as the first, the Labour leader turning every question into an opportunity to talk about austerity and the NHS while Johnson tried to work 'Get Brexit Done' into every response and emphasized that his party, too, would invest heavily in public services. Snap polling by YouGov once again had viewers declaring the whole thing a frustrating dead heat – in short, then, another hazard negotiated by the frontrunner, another opportunity missed by his opponent.[43]

But if the debates passed off with little incident, there was always the possibility that, when it came to the Conservative manifesto, 2019 could see a repeat of 2017. Indeed, the fear that it might do so haunted all those involved in its preparation – principally think tanker and opinion researcher Rachel Wolf, Number Ten policy chief Munira Mirza, and think tanker and journalist Robert Colvile. As such, it was extensively 'red-teamed' and 'bomb-proofed' (not least by journalist-turned-Number Ten adviser Ross Kempsell) before it was finally launched by Johnson in a deliberately low-key Sunday evening event on 24 November. Out went the tax cuts for higher earners and the promise to ponder a return to fox hunting, which cast the Conservatives as the party of the rich, while May's ambitious root-and-branch reform of social care was replaced by an ambition to build 'cross-party consensus' on the issue. In came headline-grabbing offers whose specificity in some ways masked their relative modesty: nurses hired, hospitals built (or at least renovated), and more police on streets which (thanks to a new fund) would have their potholes filled in. Commentators – some disappointed, some reassured – duly declared it a somewhat dull, essentially 'safety-first' document, allowing CCHQ, along with Conservative candidates up and down the country, to breathe a huge sigh of relief.

Manifestos, of course, are still seen as a must for parties fighting general elections in the UK, and so can't be sidestepped. Media appearances, however, can be avoided, however high-profile. When Corbyn suffered a brutal interrogation at the hands of the BBC's veteran broadcaster Andrew Neil, his only consolation was that Johnson was bound to get the same treatment when he was grilled a few days later. But it never happened: despite Neil's best efforts, Johnson refused to take part in the programme – yet another example, claimed critics who recalled the leadership contest and the Prime Minister's repeated failure to turn up to the Commons Liaison Committee, of a tendency to swerve any situation likely to involve sustained cross-examination.

Nigel Farage, desperate as he was to raise his party's flagging profile, could afford no such luxury, however, and accepted Neil's invitation when it came. Awkwardly, YouGov's much-anticipated MRP (multilevel regression and poststratification) analysis, published on 27 November, not only gave his Brexit Party little or no chance of winning a seat but also suggested that the presence of its candidates was, if anything, likely to help Labour more than the Conservatives.[44] And then, a week later, four of Farage's own MEPs (including the sister of Cabinet minister Jacob Rees-Mogg), all of whom had been elected to the European Parliament just a few months earlier, resigned and urged voters to back the Conservatives instead, claiming a vote for their (now former) party posed a risk to Brexit.[45] This was a message that Dominic Cummings, who had willingly handed Levido and co. control of the Tory campaign, had already hammered home in his only public intervention during the election – a blogpost published on his personal website which sent what he called a 'bat signal' to Leave voters to warn them that 'Brexit was in danger' and that a vote for the Brexit Party 'is effectively a vote for Corbyn-Sturgeon', as well as to remind them that Johnson's opponents 'will do anything to stop YOU, normal voters, taking back control of THEM'.[46] Needless to say, Farage's interview with Neil, which inevitably explored the conundrum in question, probably helped Johnson more than it did him.

YouGov's model had given the Tories a 68-seat majority, projecting major gains in Leave-leaning Labour constituencies, with double-digit swings away from Labour in seats that the party had held for generations. Nevertheless, the Conservative campaign team were still concerned (worried would be too strong a word) about public and internal polling that showed the NHS was garnering increasing public attention, thereby potentially boosting Labour support in the run-up to polling day. Their response was to try to lock in socially conservative Leave voters with more red meat on immigration, crime, and national security (particularly in the wake of the London Bridge terrorist attack on 29 November, which they swiftly blamed on Labour's early-release policy) while also reiterating the promises of cash for the NHS and schools. Fortunately, US President Donald Trump, who arrived in London on 3 December for a two-day NATO summit, did the Tories a favour in his opening press conference by averring that the US, contrary to Labour's claims, had no interest in the NHS, declaring 'we wouldn't want it if you handed it to us on a silver platter'.[47] Just as helpfully, given Trump's unpopularity with British voters, he did not insist on his meetings with Johnson in Downing Street and at the NATO summit itself being caught on camera – and even cancelled his end-of-summit press conference to fly home early.

Having overcome that obstacle, and growing more confident that their polling lead would deliver a comfortable majority, the campaign team began the week determined to hammer home their 'Get Brexit Done' message. At the start of a whirlwind tour of five 'Red Wall' seats on Monday, 9 December, Johnson posed with a glistening cod in Grimsby's fish market before returning in his stump speech to Brexit in tones shot through with the populism that had helped win the 2016 referendum:

> The Labour Party has let you down most of all. Under Jeremy Corbyn, they promised to honour the result of the referendum, before voting against Brexit every chance they had. They won their seats on a false prospectus and then stuck two fingers up to the public. Now they are proposing another referendum, this time rigging the result by extending the franchise to two million EU citizens. It's been the Great Betrayal, orchestrated from Islington by politicians who sneer at your values and ignore your votes.
>
> You voted to leave the EU because you wanted to stop sending the EU money we could spend at home, to end uncontrolled and unlimited immigration from the EU, to take back control from an unelected elite in Brussels, and to force politicians in Westminster to listen to you, not just London and the southeast.[48]

That same day, Home Secretary Priti Patel burnished the Conservatives' law-and-order credentials in an article for the *Telegraph*, claiming

Labour's concerns about stop-and-search powers would result in fewer seizures of weapons. She then reeled off alarming statistics provided by the Conservative Research Department about the additional violent crimes that would allegedly result – an 'extra killing a week' in the words of the *Sun*.[49] Like Johnson, Patel was careful to stress the binary choice facing voters 'between a functioning Conservative majority which will turbocharge the recruitment of 20,000 additional police officers and increase sentences for serious and violent criminals. Or a Labour–SNP coalition who support automatic release of those convicted of terrorist offences.' She then trotted out another CCHQ campaign line – focused on combating any complacency among Conservative-leaning voters: 'Make no mistake, a hung Parliament with Corbyn in Downing Street supported by Nicola Sturgeon is a real possibility. I've been to every region of the country in the last few weeks speaking to voters and I can promise you that this election is very close.' Patel wasn't alone in sounding this warning. The next day's edition of the *Telegraph* miraculously got hold of 'a Tory Party memo ... dated 7 December' supposedly warning Campaign Director Isaac Levido that 'Jeremy Corbyn is much closer to becoming prime minister . . . than many voters realise.'[50]

For all that, the start of the campaign's final week didn't go entirely smoothly for the Conservatives or for Johnson, who, confronted by a reporter asking him to look at damaging photos of a four-year-old boy forced to lie on the floor on a pile of coats owing to a shortage of space in an A&E department, snatched the reporter's phone and slipped it into his own coat pocket, generating a video clip viewed on social media over 3.5 million times before the day was out. This was worrying: a YouGov poll released in the final week showed health had drawn level with Brexit as the main issue for voters – a marked contrast with the start of the campaign, when Brexit enjoyed a 28 point lead.[51] And although CCHQ had an answer for those voters – that getting Brexit done would allow them to devote more time and money to the NHS – it was well aware that the issue was inevitably one that played better for Labour.

That said, the start of the week wasn't all bad news for the Conservatives, since it marked the release of a widely praised and much-watched YouTube ad based on the film *Love Actually*.[52] Moreover, by beginning with a shot of a (mixed-race) couple sitting on their sofa watching another Conservative advert, it may have contributed to the 3.5 million views clocked up by that earlier ad too, although those numbers were also boosted by the small fortune spent by CCHQ to get it onto the top banner of YouTube's homepage.[53] That, however, was not characteristic of the Tories' strategy, which tended towards purchasing a large number of relatively low-budget, often below-the-radar ads on a variety of platforms.[54] The Conservative campaign team could also congratulate themselves on the success of Johnson's trip to a JCB factory in Uttoxeter owned by the Conservative peer and arch-Brexiteer Anthony Bamford. It produced one of the iconic images of the campaign – that of the Prime Minister driving one of the firm's machines, its bulldozer bucket bearing the slogan 'Get Brexit Done', through a wall of Styrofoam bricks on which was stamped one word: 'Gridlock'.[55]

Johnson was not, however, quite out of the woods yet. On the final day of campaigning, CCHQ had him delivering milk before dawn broke in West Yorkshire. Unfortunately, his minders were unable to prevent him being approached as he loaded crates on to the van by ITV's *Good Morning Britain*, at which point Johnson took refuge in a walk-in fridge with his staff, one of whom (Vote Leave veteran Rob Oxley) uttered an expletive in front of the millions watching at home. Still, although the incident generated myriad reports of the Prime Minister 'hiding in a fridge' to escape media scrutiny, the inevitable hashtag #fridgegate, and a viral video clip which rapidly racked up hundreds of thousands of views, it also effectively crowded out coverage of other party leaders, including (most usefully for the Tories) Nigel Farage.

As the campaign closed, internal CCHQ analysis pointed to a national swing of around 2.5 points from Labour and a firming up of the Tory vote in target seats sufficient, according to its MRP model, to deliver upwards of 360 seats, a substantial majority. In the end, the party gained just under 50 seats on a vote share of 43.6 per cent – the highest achieved by either party since Thatcher won in 1979 with 43.9 per cent of the vote. That represented a lead over Labour of 11.4 points – almost the same as Thatcher managed in 1987, albeit not quite as huge as the 14.8 point lead she had achieved four years previously. Still, with 365 seats, the Tories ended up with an overall Commons majority of 80. The exit poll on election day itself had produced projections that slightly overestimated that number – but only just. And even if it wasn't quite enough to be called a landslide (being in double rather than triple figures), it nonetheless represented, as Johnson put it at his count in Uxbridge and South Ruislip, 'a powerful new mandate. To get Brexit done! And not just to get Brexit done but to unite this country and to take it forward and to focus on the priorities of the British people, above all on the NHS.' The size of the win was also confirmation – if confirmation were needed – that the Tories' decision to ditch May in favour of Johnson was, electorally speaking anyway, by far the most effective switch of leaders ever made by a British political party.[56]

The results explained

Later that morning, Johnson gave the first of two victory speeches to overjoyed staffers in CCHQ. Not only had they, the Prime Minister told them, 'routed the doubters and confounded the gloomsters' by securing 'a huge great stonking mandate' to get Brexit done and fulfil 'the will of the British people', they had also helped ensure that the Conservative Party now represented every part of the country. As such it was in a great position to deliver its 'one nation agenda' of 'fantastic public services' and

'A huge great stonking mandate': December 2019.
Source: Phil Gates / Alamy.

'unleashing Britain's potential'. The One Nation theme ('We're going to unite and level up') was also prominent in the later, rather more sober, address to the nation delivered on the steps of Number Ten. Johnson promised his government would 'repay the trust' of those voters who had switched to the Conservatives and would seek to build a friendly relationship with the EU, with London and Brussels treating each other as 'sovereign equals'. 'Let the healing,' he declared, 'begin.' Keen, however, to rub salt into Labour's wounds, he then travelled up to Tony Blair's old seat of Sedgefield, now Conservative-held for the first time since 1931, and had his spinners brief the media that he had 'called in senior civil servants … and announced that the whole government had to shift its focus to improving the lives of the working-class voters in the north of England who backed Brexit and switched to the Tories'.

There is no doubt from post-election analysis of the results, both at an individual and a constituency level, that this switch was an important reason why the Conservatives won such a handsome victory – or that it had a lot to do with their promise to 'Get Brexit Done'. The Conservatives were now as popular with voters in the Midlands (though not, as yet, in the North) as they were in their southern England heartlands, while Remain-voting London had emerged as their weakest region. As Tory MP Neil O'Brien noted (albeit making the starkest possible comparisons for rhetorical effect),

> Since 1997 we've gone from having from three per cent to 34 per cent of seats in the North East. From 13 per cent to 43 per cent of seats in the North West. From 13 per cent to 48 per cent in Yorkshire. From nought per cent to 35 per cent of seats in Wales. And from 24 per cent to 75 per cent of seats in the West Midlands.
>
> Our new intake are 30 per cent of the parliamentary party. And their seats are different. In 2001, we had just no seats in the 30 per cent most deprived constituencies in England. In 2010, we had 24. Now it is 49 of those seats. In 2001, we had just 14 seats in the most deprived half of England. Now we have 116.[57]

And that shift was indeed partly down to the fact that Labour's support collapsed among the occupational groups usually defined as working class (C2DE), falling 14 points, and leaving them (by a 43–36 margin) behind the Conservatives, who were up 4 points among voters in those groups. With Labour falling less in the middle class, the traditional class divide in support, which has (albeit in declining fashion) structured all elections since 1945, was almost completely absent in 2019. In fact, as in 2017, age was again the strongest demographic divide in the electorate: Labour won the under 35s by 56 to 28 percentage points, while the Conservatives won the over 65s by 61 to 21. But luckily for the Tories, there are twice as many over 65s as under 35s in the electorate and they turn out at a much higher rate (77 vs 53 per cent in 2019). Education divides also intensified: Labour narrowly won the graduate vote (by 38 to 36 points) while the Conservatives dominated (by 51 to 29) when it came to those with low or no qualifications. Labour's advantage with ethnic minority voters remained (at 54–24), even if it was sharply down by 18 points on 2017. Indeed, the rise in ethnic minority support for the Conservatives (at 5 points up on 2017) was not that impressive, especially given the prominence of ethnic minority politicians in Johnson's government.[58] It is worth noting, too, that there was a large gender gap in 2019: while the Conservatives enjoyed an 18 point lead among men (47–29), their lead among women was, at 5 points, much lower (i.e. 42–37).

However, it is also vital to recall that people have myriad reasons for voting the way they do at any particular election. For some of those who *switched directly* from Labour to the Tories, for many of those Remainers who may otherwise have been *tempted* to switch from the Tories, and even for some of those Leavers who flirted with the Brexit Party before *voting* for the Tories, dislike and distrust of Labour leader Jeremy Corbyn also played a big part in 2019. Moreover (and every bit as importantly given what all too many people seemed desperate to believe), while Boris Johnson was clearly a big draw for some voters – especially for those who had previously voted for the Brexit Party, for UKIP, and (in much smaller numbers) for the BNP – he was not (compared to, say, David Cameron or Theresa May and absent Brexit) a particularly popular Tory leader, not least with many former Labour voters.[59]

That said, Johnson was, almost uniquely, able to combine relentless message discipline with endearing showmanship – going where he was told to go, doing as he was instructed, but always with pizazz. And all in all, the Conservatives, well organized and with a clear offer for voters who were keen to move on from Brexit, fought an excellent campaign in 2019 – far better than Labour managed and far better than they themselves managed in 2017. However, it remains important to recall that it was in 2017 that the groundwork was laid for Tory candidates to win many, if not most, of the seats in the North and the Midlands that fell to the party in 2019. And an awful lot of them fell mainly because Labour (along with its leader) was so much more unpopular than it had been two years previously. Indeed, had the Brexit Party not stood candidates in Labour-held constituencies, thereby siphoning off some of the votes that might otherwise have gone to the Conservatives, Corbyn would not only have led his party to its biggest defeat since 1935 but would also have won well under 200 seats, gifting the government a landslide majority of around 130. As it was, Farage's decision to stand down candidates in Tory-held seats saved no more than a handful of Conservative incumbents at best, even if it probably allowed high-profile Brexiteers like Iain Duncan Smith and Dominic Raab to make it back to Westminster. It is also worth noting, especially given the subsequent and widespread obsession with the 'Red Wall', that Labour Leave voters there were no more likely to switch away from Labour than Labour Leave voters everywhere else – there were just more of them in those constituencies deemed to constitute it.

In short, what the Conservatives were able to do – helped hugely by the print media and the fact that their support was efficiently distributed, allowing them to pick up many small-town and suburban constituencies that had voted Leave while Labour piled up votes pointlessly in Remain-voting cities – was to 'unite the right' by taking the wind out of the Brexit Party's sails and consolidating some three-quarters of the Leave vote. Equally importantly, neither Labour nor the Lib Dems were able to do the same with the Remain vote – indeed, the Tories were able to hold on to nearly two-thirds of Remain voters who had voted for them in 2017. And while the party lost support in some proverbial 'leafy' (and Remain-voting) constituencies in Berkshire, Buckinghamshire, Cambridgeshire, Oxfordshire, and Surrey, the majorities of their sitting Tory MPs were simply too large for an (often divided) opposition to overcome in one go.

Taken together, this made for an effective electoral coalition which brought together white, relatively affluent, often older, not particularly well-educated, culturally conservative voters in southern England with their (not always quite as affluent but not necessarily 'left-behind') counterparts in the North and the Midlands.[60] But if that constituted a profound electoral realignment, then it had been some years in the making rather than representing a triumph that only Johnson could possibly have pulled off. Nor, sceptics cautioned, should it necessarily be seen as permanent: the impact of Brexit and Corbyn might fade sooner or later; voters were far more inclined to chop and change than they used to be; and a fair number of the Tories' gains had come in seats that Labour had lost before at particularly low points in its political history but had managed to win back when its electoral fortunes improved.[61]

Nor, contrary to the common wisdom, and with the caveat that it contained seven fewer members from Scotland (all of whom lost their seats to the SNP), did the election produce a parliamentary Conservative Party that was so very different to the one which had been elected previously. As one academic expert noted, while there are far more Tory MPs (over half) who were educated at state comprehensive rather than fee-paying independent schools than used to be the case, as well as considerably more women (who would now make up around a quarter of the parliamentary party), this marked no more than a continuation of existing trends. Moreover,

> The 2019 cohort barely differ from previous generations of Conservative MPs in their occupational background. Around one in five worked in 'brokerage' professions such as law or medicine prior to becoming MPs, a further one in five worked in 'instrumental' positions related to politics such as being councillors, special advisers or journalists, and just over two in five worked in business or commerce. These figures are barely different to the pre-Cameron and Cameron cohorts of MPs.[62]

True, in terms of demographics, 'Red Wall' MPs in particular were more likely to be male, white, state-educated, and younger than other Tory MPs. But they were no more likely to be political neophytes. They also had Brexit in common with the majority of their colleagues: indeed, getting on for three-quarters of Tory MPs elected in December 2019 supported Leave in 2016 and almost all of those who did not were now firmly in favour.[63] In fact, after the election, some 80 per cent of Conservatives in the House of Commons represented constituencies that voted Leave in 2016 – not surprising, perhaps, given that over 400 out of 650 constituencies voted Leave, as did the vast majority of the 58 Tory gains. Consequently, Johnson had no hesitation in bringing back to parliament the paused Withdrawal Agreement Bill, now, however, shorn of the concessions offered to Labour Leave MPs in order to ease its passage in the previous session and also containing a new clause making it difficult for ministers, let alone parliament, to extend the transition period due to end on 31 December 2021 – a wise move given reports of many new MPs swelling the ranks of the Brexit-ultras' brotherhood, the ERG.

Whether new Conservative MPs approved of the government's decision to boycott particular news and current affairs shows such as BBC Radio 4's flagship *Today* programme – allegedly to bring them to heel after what the PM's advisers saw as its anti-Tory bias during the election – is less clear.[64] The same could be said for MPs' attitudes to the many pre-Christmas briefings of plans being dreamed up by Johnson's apparently all-powerful Chief Adviser, Dominic Cummings, firstly, to shake up Whitehall and reduce the size of Cabinet and, secondly, to involve himself in the upcoming Defence Review.[65]

There did seem, however, to be widespread support among all Tory MPs for the new Queen's Speech laying out the government's programme, delivered to a packed House of Commons a week after the election.[66] Johnson's commitment to the NHS was symbolized by a bill enshrining in law his government's planned spending increases, while his One Nation credentials were burnished with a bill aimed at outlawing no-fault evictions by landlords. Tougher sentencing and release provisions for terrorists were promised, as well as new legislation to beef up the powers of the security and intelligence services. Meanwhile, trade unions were to be prevented from causing chaos on the country's train network. The speech also flagged up a Constitution, Democracy and Rights Commission, which opponents feared would weaken checks and balances, and a plan to repeal the Fixed-term Parliaments Act, restoring to the Prime Minister the power to call elections whenever he or she believed the time was right rather than every five years. Parliament then adjourned for the Christmas recess the next day. Tory MPs returned home (or in Johnson's case to the Caribbean island of Mustique) to recover from a gruelling winter campaign.[67] Whether, as they recuperated over Christmas and the New Year, many of them even noticed the reports of a mysterious new virus striking down people in the Chinese city of Wuhan, who knows?

7

Pandemonium
(January–December 2020)

As 2019 turned into 2020, one might have been forgiven for thinking that Tory MPs seemed less concerned about the news just beginning to trickle out of China than about the announcement that Big Ben, the bell situated in Westminster's iconic Elizabeth Tower (then undergoing repairs), would not be ringing in Brexit at 11 p.m. on 31 January, the cost of readying it to do so having been judged prohibitive by the parliamentary authorities.[1] Sixty Brexiteers had written to the *Telegraph*, demanding the decision be reversed – not just in the interests 'of many people around the UK who wish to celebrate this momentous event' but also because they believed that 'leaving on January 31 will help to bring a degree of closure, not just in the House but hopefully among the public as a whole. Allowing Big Ben to chime could help to provide some catharsis in this process.' They were not alone: Boris Johnson claimed to be looking into whether the public could 'bung a bob for a Big Ben bong' on Brexit day – a campaign that attracted the support of the party in the media, with the story making the front pages of the *Telegraph* and the *Sun*, and the *Express* going so far as to splash 'BIG BEN <u>MUST</u> BONG FOR BREXIT' and to urge readers to join a crowdfunding campaign to ensure that the bell would indeed be able to 'ring in a new era of freedom'.[2]

The controversy continued, however, when it was revealed that the £272,000 raised by the campaign, spearheaded by the ERG's Mark Francois and the group StandUp4Brexit, could not, according to the House of Commons Commission, be legally used to defray the costs. In the end, the country's loss was charity's gain as the money was eventually donated to Help for Heroes, an organization providing valuable support to UK military veterans. Meanwhile Brexiteers made the best of their tragically bongless bash in Parliament Square. Cabinet ministers may have been conspicuous by their absence, possibly because they'd spent the day in Sunderland, the PM having taken them there in order to hammer home the government's commitment to 'level up' the country and help 'the left behind'. But that didn't dampen the crowd's enthusiasm for Nigel Farage as he took to the stage to the strains of 'The Final Countdown', the 1986 hit from Swedish glam-metal act Europe. The irony was, presumably, unintended, and anyway the song was played as an instrumental by a jazz band, thus sparing the assembled throng its opening refrain: 'We're leavin' together but still it's farewell. And maybe we'll come back to Earth, who can tell?'[3]

None of this, of course, should be taken to suggest that nothing of political significance was going on. In Northern Ireland, for example, where the civil service had essentially been running the government since 2017 in the absence of agreement between unionist and nationalist politicians, the power-sharing Executive was finally able to get up and running. Meanwhile, in the middle of the month, Johnson was writing to Scotland's First Minister, Nicola Sturgeon, rejecting her request for a second independence referendum. Sadly, the largely London-based English media seemed far more interested in what was widely seen as an attempt by Dominic Cummings (now very much back in charge in Number Ten)

'Free at last': Johnson signs the Withdrawal Agreement, January 2020.
Source: 10 Downing Street.

and Lee Cain, Downing Street's Director of Communications, to exert an unprecedented influence over broadcasters' political coverage. There was renewed talk of decriminalizing non-payment of the Beeb's licence fee – long seen by the corporation's fans as the first step towards eventual abolition and therefore as a way of scaring it into taking a less assertive stance. And more immediately there was the government's boycott of BBC radio's flagship *Today* programme, as well as ITV's *Good Morning Britain*. Its attempt to limit supposedly unfriendly journalists' and news organizations' access to the government's lobby briefings, however, proved a bridge too far when, in early February, household names like the BBC's Laura Kuenssberg and ITV's Robert Peston joined the political editors of national newspapers in walking out of a Downing Street briefing from which Cain had reportedly tried to exclude journalists from, among other titles, the *Mirror* and the *Independent*.

In any case, it wasn't long before the lobby had something they could really get their teeth into. Johnson's decision, leaked to the media (some thought by the Treasury), to give the go-ahead to HS2 (a project that was far from universally popular among Tory MPs and newspapers) was not just a story in itself but one which, because Cummings was known to be sceptical, suggested that the supposedly all-powerful adviser was no longer getting everything his own way. This seemed to dovetail with tales of tensions between him and Johnson's fiancée, Carrie Symonds, now firmly ensconced in the PM's Downing Street flat and very much an ally of the Chancellor Sajid Javid, for whom she had once worked. Few could have predicted, however, that, within days, and as the Prime Minister finally began his long-awaited post-election/post-Brexit reshuffle, Javid would be on his way out, having refused to agree to a Cummings-inspired plan to merge the Number Ten and Treasury advisory teams.

Fortunately for Johnson (at least that was the way it seemed at the time), he was able to find a replacement in fairly short order: Chief Secretary to the Treasury Rishi Sunak, a 39-year-old former investment banker and hedge-fund manager, a media-friendly Leaver who had been elected to the Commons in 2015 and who, as a multi-millionaire married to the daughter of a multi-billionaire, was one of the UK's richest members of parliament.[4] Sunak had impressed during the election campaign and was highly thought of by Cummings, who may initially have allowed the Chancellor's evident enthusiasm for Brexit to blind him to the George Osborne-style, small-state fiscal orthodoxy at the heart of the new Chancellor's worldview.[5]

The media made much of the fact that Sunak hailed from an Indian family. However, his promotion did not mean an increase in ethnic minority representation in the Cabinet after the reshuffle was complete; nor, of course, could it disguise the fact that it now contained one woman fewer. It did mean, though, that the proportion of Cabinet ministers who had attended Oxford or Cambridge rose from just over a third to getting on for half. Not that their elite education stopped them from subjecting themselves to the humiliation of an excruciatingly childlike call-and-response Cabinet photo-op – an occasion that only seemed to support accusations that preferment under Johnson depended less on ability than it did on one's willingness to do and say practically anything that the Prime Minister might ask of them.[6]

Accordingly, it was Priti Patel, who, after being reconfirmed as Home Secretary, was able, a few days later, to formally announce the outline of the government's heavily trailed post-Brexit immigration regime. Points-based (in fact, largely salary-based), it was designed to emphasize English language skills, to end any distinction between EU and non-EU applicants, and, much to the consternation of some employers used to hiring relatively cheap labour from abroad, to end (supposedly) low-skilled migration.[7] Patel's claim that any resultant labour shortages could and should be filled by those Brits currently classed as 'economically inactive' may have been swiftly debunked, but those doing the debunking could not deny that the new system had widespread public support, especially among those who saw it as proof positive that Brexit was allowing the UK to 'take back control' of its borders.

Whether the new system would actually deliver the reduction in numbers that so many of them wanted as well remained to be seen. Were it ever to do so, however, one thing, at least, was now certain: Patel would not be celebrating the good news with the most senior civil servant at the Home Office, Sir Philip Rutnam. A couple of weeks after the release of the policy, he resigned in a blaze of publicity, announcing he would be suing for constructive dismissal after what he alleged was an orchestrated campaign of bullying and intimidation by the Home Secretary – an episode some couldn't help linking to the apparent existence of a 'shitlist' of senior civil servants that Number Ten apparently wanted rid of and which also included Cabinet Secretary Mark Sedwill, who, after months of hostile briefing, left in late June, to be rapidly replaced by the supposedly more congenial Simon Case.[8]

Luckily for the government, media coverage of Rutnam's spectacular walk-out had to compete for space with the news that the PM's fiancée was expecting her first (and, it was widely speculated, his seventh) child. This, to some, went part way to explaining why, in spite of the fact that the news out of China about what would soon be routinely referred to as Covid-19 was growing more and more worrying, Johnson had apparently taken a couple of weeks off. In fact, it later transpired (according to Dominic Cummings) that the couple had popped down to Chevening in Kent (one of a number of country residences at the disposal of the Prime Minister) to allow him to make some progress on his book on Shakespeare – one for which he had apparently been paid a half-million-pound advance and the royalties from which he was hoping might help him meet the costs of his divorce and ongoing child support payments.[9] Fortunately, for the Conservative Party's coffers at least, Johnson did nip back to London for its annual Black and White Ball on 23 February, which saw a game of tennis with him auctioned off for £90,000, half of which was stumped up by the Russian millionaire Lubov Chernukhin, who had already given generously to the party in the run-up to the election and whose donations to the Tories were eventually to reach over £2 million.[10] A couple of days later, the PM was back in order to launch the government's official strategy for negotiations with Brussels for a trade agreement which, to no-one's great surprise (probably not even the EU's), effectively junked much of the (admittedly non-binding) Political Declaration signed in December, including, most significantly, the commitment to maintaining a 'Level Playing Field' when it came to regulation. Rather more worrying to some was the strategy document's declaration that 'if it is not possible to negotiate a satisfactory outcome, then the trading relationship with the EU ... will look similar to Australia's' – by now the PM's favourite euphemism for No Deal.

Coronavirus – the crisis begins

But bullying, babies, balls, and even Brexit were very soon to disappear from the headlines as it became clearer and clearer that Covid-19 was going to pose a public health emergency akin to that which was beginning to unfold in Italy – the first European country to be hit broadside by the virus. Johnson at least appeared to recognize the seriousness of the threat, not just by holding a joint Downing Street press conference on 3 March with the government's Chief Medical Officer, Chris Whitty, and its Chief Scientific Adviser, Patrick Vallance, but also by allowing his Health Secretary, Matt Hancock, to include *Today* and *Channel Four News* in his media round – the first time any minister had done so since the Cummings/Cain post-election boycott.

Quite how seriously the Prime Minister himself and, just as importantly, some of those around him were really taking the crisis, however, was questionable.[11] Behind closed doors, he reportedly suggested the whole thing was 'a scare story' and even that Whitty should inject him with the virus on live television to show how mild it was.[12] At the press conference, Johnson had also boasted of shaking hands with everybody during a visit to a hospital, while Rishi Sunak's Budget presented a week later showed little sign (notwithstanding the Chancellor's willingness at that stage to cooperate with Cummings and markedly increase infrastructure spending) of grasping the enormity of the economic dislocation that was to come. Talk of a 'herd immunity' strategy (later denied) inspired little confidence that the government truly was getting a grip on the situation – much to the alarm not just of medics but also of a couple of the politicians Johnson had defeated for the leadership, Rory Stewart (now out of parliament) and Jeremy Hunt, both of whom called very publicly for far more urgency.[13]

By the end of the second week in March, however, Number Ten, and in particular Dominic Cummings, who had been contacted by the data scientist Marc Warner, the brother of one of his key staffers, was persuaded that drastic action had to be taken if the UK were to avoid the NHS being overrun.[14] Yet even then, with Sunak having announced the first of what turned out to be several economic support packages and Isaac Levido (and others from the general election campaign) brought back in to handle messaging and allied opinion research, Johnson – whose libertarian instincts bridled at imposing anything other than voluntary guidance – took at least a week longer than necessary to implement a full lockdown. That delay (along with the discharge of so many untested elderly people from hospital into care homes, many of

STAY AT HOME   PROTECT THE NHS   SAVE LIVES

About time: Johnson gets serious on Covid, March 2020.
Source: 10 Downing Street.

which also relied on agency staff who moved between various homes) almost certainly led to tens of thousands of people dying whose lives might otherwise been spared. And a failure in Downing Street itself to take measures to avoid the spread of the virus among key staff soon saw a number of the Prime Minister's inner circle fall ill, including, most seriously, Johnson himself, leading eventually to his being admitted to hospital in the first week of April and Dominic Raab, as First Secretary of State, chairing key meetings in his absence.

In spite of all this (and partly, perhaps, because of it, voters being naturally inclined to 'rally round the flag' of a leader not only facing a national crisis but also requiring intensive care), and in spite of severe problems with testing and the provision of personal protective equipment (PPE), particularly in care homes, public support for Johnson and his government remained high.[15] Most polls had the Conservatives on around 50 per cent compared to Labour's 30 per cent, with the PM's rating having improved markedly: Ipsos MORI, for instance, reported in mid-April that 'The majority of Britons (51 per cent) now have a favourable opinion of Boris Johnson (up 17 points from early March), with three in ten (31 per cent) saying they have an unfavourable opinion of him (down 16 points).' Predictably enough, Tory and Leave voters (very often the same thing, of course) were most impressed – one reason why Johnson, by then on the mend, felt confident enough to let it be known that the UK would not be bowing to calls on the government, in the light of the pandemic, to extend the Brexit transition period beyond the end of the year, raising once again the possibility of a No-Deal departure from the single market and customs union. In fact, survey research suggested a clear majority of the public would have supported an extension – although there were big differences between, on the one hand, Remain voters and, on the other, the Leave voters whom the PM needed to keep onside.[16]

One thing that did seem to unite Leave and Remain voters was their overwhelming support for both the government's strict public health measures and the financial support it was providing to businesses and households in the form of loans, grants, and furlough payments to the millions prevented from working by the lockdown. By the end of April, however, it was becoming ever clearer that this consensus (never, of course, total even in the electorate) did not stretch to some members of the parliamentary Conservative Party and the party in the media.

For those Tory MPs urging the government to begin easing lockdown (former leader Iain Duncan Smith, former Chief Whip Mark Harper, and the current Chairman of the 1922 Committee, Graham Brady, were the first to publicly voice their concerns, although they were not necessarily speaking for all their colleagues), their desire to see the lockdown eased was in part ideological, feeding off their long-held antipathy to anything smacking of 'the big state'.[17] Indeed, to self-styled 'hardman of Brexit' and 'libertarian' Steve Baker, lockdown was 'absurd, dystopian and tyrannical'.[18] But hostility towards lockdowns among Tory MPs was also practical: they were concerned about how all that financial support was to be paid for (and how businesses in their constituencies were to remain viable) if the economy was shut down for too much longer; they also worried about the inability of the NHS to diagnose and treat non-Covid patients.[19]

As for the party in the media, many right-leaning editors and star columnists – most consistently in the *Telegraph*, the *Spectator*, and the *Sun* – had similar worries, prompting them after just two weeks to question the lockdown and even call for it to be loosened.[20] Added to those worries were presumably even more direct commercial concerns. Admittedly, many readers now consumed their newspapers online, but many titles continued to rely on print sales (and associated advertising). If restrictions continued for much longer, with many people no longer doing anything other than essential shopping and working from home rather than commuting (a practice that was to become a particular bugbear for the party in the media and many MPs), those restrictions risked breaking the print media's business model, even if, as some have noted, it was being given government hand-outs (apparently totalling somewhere between £35 and £100 million) on the quiet.[21] Other businessmen – including high-profile donors to the Conservative Party – also urged the government to open up.[22] Meanwhile, journalists were assiduously briefed that a number of so-called 'hawks' in Cabinet (notably Rishi Sunak and Business Secretary Alok Sharma) were very much on their side and were heroically battling 'doves' like Health Secretary Matt Hancock and Cabinet Office Minister Michael Gove in order to achieve as swift an end to restrictions as possible.[23]

Stories like these were fine, perhaps, as long as they merely enhanced the reputations and leadership ambitions of those involved in the eyes of sympathetic newspapers. But when they risked undermining the government's public health messaging, that was another matter. Quite who was responsible for the briefings in the run-up to the May bank holiday that led to headlines like the *Mail*'s 'HURRAH! LOCKDOWN FREEDOM BECKONS' was difficult to tell. Some suggested they might even have emanated from people around a Prime Minister desperate to show restless backbenchers that he was as much on their side as was his popular Chancellor.[24] Others speculated that they came from colleagues keen to bounce the PM into going further than recommended by his scientific advisers (who were well aware that the country had by then recorded over 30,000 deaths due to Covid).

In the end, however, Johnson's announcement of the government's plans to ease restrictions, when it eventually came a few days later, was not what his self-styled libertarian critics were really hoping for. Still, polls suggested it was given a guarded welcome by the public, even if ConservativeHome's readers' survey suggested Tory members were far less wary than voters when it came to opening up again: whereas YouGov suggested only one in ten voters wanted the government to move faster, as many as one in three of ConHome's members were keen to see it do so.[25] 'Anti-lockdown' Tory MPs, then, could argue that they were supported by a significant proportion of the party's grassroots – one reason (along, perhaps, with Johnson's well-known tendency to curry favour with critics by making promises he couldn't keep) why Ben Gascoigne, the PM's Political Secretary, urged him not to meet with the 'libertarian' Chair of the 1922, Graham Brady, alone.[26]

Barnard Castle and other stories

As spring turned into summer, a number of the post-Brexit policy issues that had inevitably received less attention at the absolute height of the Covid-19 crisis began to receive an airing once again. Some – such as the belated recognition that border checks on certain goods passing between Great Britain and Northern Ireland were inevitable – were highly inconvenient for the government and, as such, quickly passed over. Other policies, however, were very much part of its planned pitch to the electorate and so were given a fanfare – or at least as much of one as continuing Covid-related controversies around test and trace and difficulties around fully reopening schools (all down to 'militant' teaching unions, according to the near-hysterical party in the media) would allow.[27] One such policy was Priti Patel's formal introduction into parliament of her new immigration regime, the outline of which was included in a bill given initial approval in the Commons in the middle of May.

Very few of the votes that pushed that legislation onto its committee stage were cast in person, since the Commons was still operating a hybrid system that allowed MPs to attend (and even contribute) virtually – to the evident frustration of Leader of the House Jacob Rees-Mogg, who believed parliament should be setting an example to the rest of the country by 'getting back to work'. Indeed, so determined was he to get back to an in-person-only chamber (possibly because it was clear that Johnson was finding PMQs trickier without the traditional 'wall of sound' provided by Tory MPs) that he surprised even those on his own side by initially insisting that the temporary arrangements brought in to cope with the pandemic would come to an abrupt end at the beginning of June – a plan to which he was eventually forced by colleagues to make several changes, not least after the sheer absurdity of socially distanced voting was made obvious by shots of MPs wasting their time queuing up, conga-style, in Westminster Hall.[28] Sadly, perhaps, fewer Tory MPs were prepared to criticize the government when it came to a motion proposing that the Commons Liaison Committee, made up of select committee chairs, be henceforth chaired by the Brexiteer Bernard Jenkin, rather than selecting one of its own members to do the job. True, the extent to which the committee's twice-yearly grilling of Prime Ministers really did much to hold them to account could be overstated – and Johnson had so far refused to accept numerous invitations to appear before its members for the best part of a year anyway. But the government picking its own candidate for the job and then whipping MPs to support its nomination was arguably another example of its enthusiasm for eroding the legislature's independence from the executive.

Even those concerned by that trend, however, could hardly be expected to get excited about its latest iteration – especially not when, towards the end of May, one of the biggest political stories of the first year of the pandemic was broken by the *Guardian* and the *Mirror*. Journalists on both papers had discovered that, back in late March, Johnson's Chief Adviser, Dominic Cummings, had apparently broken the government's own lockdown rules by driving hundreds of miles to County Durham with his wife and young son in order to stay in a cottage on his father's estate. Not only that, the family had then taken a 60-mile round trip to nearby Barnard Castle – apparently, Cummings insisted during an extraordinary press conference held in the Rose Garden of Number Ten, so he could test his eyesight before driving back down to London.

Johnson, although hardly delighted, very quickly decided to back Cummings. The Prime Minister had, after all, been in a few scrapes himself and managed to tough things out – indeed, just a day or two previously, the Independent Office for Police Conduct (IOPC) had announced, to his enormous relief, that he would not face a criminal investigation into the financial implications of his relationship with the US businesswoman Jennifer Arcuri while he was Mayor of London.[29] Even better for Cummings, the PM was able to persuade prominent Cabinet ministers, employing a variety of excuses (none of which, if opinion polls were to be believed, really washed with the public – certainly they didn't prompt any of the government's scientific and medical advisers to offer their support), to humiliate themselves and wholeheartedly endorse Johnson's Chief Adviser.[30] Large numbers of Tory MPs, however, looking both at their email inboxes and at the hostile reaction of one or two normally friendly newspapers and a sprinkling of social media wags, clearly felt unable to join their frontbench colleagues, despite a clear steer from the Whips' Office that they should row in behind.[31] Although only 45 of Johnson's MPs were eventually to declare publicly that Cummings should resign or be sacked, another 55 were openly critical of the PM's right-hand man and, off the record, even more than that were unhappy – not entirely surprisingly, perhaps, given that Cummings had never made any secret of the fact that he held most of them in pretty low regard too.

In the end, only one Tory, Douglas Ross (whose seat, perhaps not coincidentally, was one of the most marginal in the House of Commons), ended up resigning from the government frontbench (freeing him, incidentally, to take over as leader of the Scottish Conservatives when the incumbent, Jackson Carlaw, resigned in July). Whether, had Ross been joined by a few more of his colleagues, it would have made much difference to the PM's decision is doubtful. Johnson, after all, depended heavily on Cummings to give him direction, and the latter's 'Vote Leave crew' (not least Director of Communications Lee Cain) occupied a number of key positions in Number Ten. Where would he be if, as seemed perfectly possible, they followed Cummings out of the building? Besides, Johnson's own libertarian instincts made him loath to fire anyone for breaching rules that he himself had only reluctantly agreed to bring in. Nor could he really object to Cummings' refusal to publicly apologize for his behaviour: after all, hadn't that always been his own modus operandi when caught out? Moreover, inasmuch as it was possible to gauge grassroots opinion from ConservativeHome's survey of party members among its readers, the rank and file was – in contrast to the electorate as a whole – remarkably supportive: seven out of ten thought Cummings should stay on.[32]

Yet Johnson's decision to stick with Cummings had severe consequences, both for his own standing with the public and for that of the party as a whole: a YouGov survey splashed by the *Times* on 27 May suggested the Tories' (admittedly very large) lead over Labour had dropped 9 points in just a few short days while Savanta ComRes had

Johnson's personal ratings dropping 20 points, putting him in negative territory once again – falls which poll after poll confirmed over the next few weeks and months. Number Ten was characteristically cock-a-hoop at the BBC reportedly administering something of a telling-off to Emily Maitlis, one of the presenters of its *Newsnight* programme, for hard-hitting comments she'd made about Cummings' trip north. But neither that victory, nor Johnson's announcement that restrictions on outdoor gatherings would be significantly relaxed from 1 June (swiftly christened 'BBQ Monday' by an ecstatic Tory press), could compensate for the lasting damage the affair had done to the government.[33]

Statuesque

Still, at least Conservatives soon had something to distract them while waiting for lockdown restrictions to be eased further – something hawks in the Cabinet (along with Johnson, who shared their concerns about the devastation being wreaked on the country's hospitality sector) made it clear they were desperately keen to accelerate. In early June, a series of Black Lives Matter events were held in cities across the country. One gathering in Bristol resulted in the pulling down of a controversial statue of seventeenth-century slave trader Edward Colston, while a large gathering in Whitehall saw a small minority of protesters attack the police.[34] Tory MPs were quick to join the PM and the Home Secretary in condemnation of lawbreaking, with some particularly exercised by graffiti daubed by a protester on the statue of wartime Prime Minister Winston Churchill in Parliament Square – an act that prompted a Twitter thread from Johnson himself on the need to save statues and the hijacking of protests by 'extremists intent on violence'.[35] A bunch of MPs from the 'Blue Collar Conservatives' group (Matt Vickers, Brendan Clarke-Smith, Gareth Bacon, Lee Anderson, and Peter Gibson) then decided to stage a photo-op of themselves attempting to remove the offending words with nailbrushes and sponges. Although unsuccessful, their efforts opened up a new front in the so-called 'culture wars' carried on by government ministers, by backbenchers, and by the party in the media. The torch was also taken up by right-leaning think tanks like Policy Exchange, which, since David Cameron's departure from Number Ten, had arguably travelled an awfully long way from its origins as a bastion of his kind of liberal conservatism – although it was, of course, possible to maintain, as did its former Director, Neil O'Brien, who used his ConservativeHome column to urge Johnson to 'empower a minister to lay down the law, and wage war on woke', that it was all about defending liberal values rather than simply enraging the left and mobilizing the party's socially conservative voters.[36]

Johnson swiftly followed up his Churchill tweets with an op-ed in the *Telegraph* in which he restated his pro-statue line but also called for the setting up of 'a cross-governmental commission to look at all aspects of inequality – in employment, in health outcomes, in academic and all other walks of life'. Lest anyone get the wrong impression and imagine he might be bowing to political correctness, it turned out that this 'Commission on Race and Ethnic Disparities' would be set up by the Head of the Number Ten Policy Unit and long-time Johnson favourite, Munira Mirza, who, campaigners pointed out, had previously questioned the existence of structural racism, written about 'a culture of grievance', and might even be one of the advisers who had reportedly been urging the PM for some time to declare 'a war on woke'.[37] Meanwhile, the Justice Secretary, Robert Buckland (not really known for being a culture warrior himself), promised in a *Sunday Telegraph* op-ed to respond positively to a call from over one hundred Tory MPs for tougher sentences for those desecrating war memorials.[38]

Lockdown contested

For most Conservative MPs, however, the war on woke remained, at least for the moment, something of a sideshow. Far more important was the need to restore normal life now that the threat from Covid had, many had persuaded themselves, begun to recede. In spite of Rishi Sunak doing his best to assure them he was very much on their side, progress in June had been halting, with some serious disappointments along the way. Predictably enough, those disappointments led to calls – in public and in private – for the Prime Minister to listen to backbenchers and not just a bunch of Number Ten advisers who were, they claimed, too influenced by all the quantitative and qualitative opinion research on which the government was known to be spending a small fortune.[39] The introduction of quarantine for those flying in from abroad, for instance, proved particularly fraught, although, once again, any hysteria in the party in the media (and there was plenty) and in parliament was not reflected in surveys of the public, who (as Number Ten predicted from its own opinion research) were very supportive, even if there was very little scientific evidence behind the policy.[40]

The admission on the part of Education Secretary Gavin Williamson that primary schools would not fully reopen until September had also been a real blow. And Tory MPs had been particularly unimpressed by Number Ten's woefully inept handling of its response to a campaign spearheaded by the Manchester United footballer Marcus Rashford to extend the provision of food vouchers to 1.3 million children throughout the school holidays – a response that, when it looked as if large numbers of worried Conservatives might vote for Labour's motion on the issue, had resulted in a U-turn but had left the government looking heartless. It was therefore with no small relief that the party greeted the announcement towards the end of June that the government would be further easing Covid restrictions: non-essential shops had already been allowed to open, but venues such as pubs, restaurants, hotels, and hairdressers would now be permitted to follow suit from 4 July provided they could maintain 2 metres social distancing; meanwhile two different households would be able to meet together indoors and even stay overnight.

If Downing Street hoped, however, that this announcement would help engender a wave of enthusiasm for what it began to brief the media was its 'New Deal' for the country, post Brexit and post-Covid, it was to be sorely disappointed. Rather than the Rooseveltian shake-up of the UK's political economy that had been hinted at, Johnson's plan was quickly exposed – for all that his 'build, build, build' rhetoric worried some Thatcherite commentators concerned about ushering in the big state – as an unambitious hotchpotch to which few or no new resources had been committed.[41] Nor did the PM do himself any favours by appearing a few days later to try to shift the blame for so many Covid deaths in care homes by suggesting that too many of them 'didn't really follow the procedures'.[42] True, there was a warmer welcome from the parliamentary party and the party in the media for Sunak's mid-July mini-Budget – primarily because it aimed, in traditional Tory fashion, to stimulate the housing market and because his much-hyped 'Eat Out to Help Out' package (sold by a photo-op featuring 'Dishy Rishi' waiting tables at the chain restaurant Wagamama) was one of a number of initiatives designed both to assist the ailing hospitality sector and to convince consumers that it was safe to get out and spend again.[43] Respected independent think tanks like the Institute for Fiscal Studies (IFS) and the Resolution Foundation, however, were far less impressed – calling the Chancellor's announcement inadequate, poorly targeted, and, because of the sleight of hand employed, even 'corrosive to public trust'.

That both the Prime Minister and the Chancellor should want to give the public the impression that they were moving towards a more interventionist, even big-spending, Conservatism than was really the case – or, indeed, than most of their colleagues would have wanted – was understandable given what was needed to hold on to the voters who had switched to the Tories in 2019 at the same time as maintaining the confidence of the party's MPs. Research from the think tank UK in a Changing Europe released in late June had made plain the big difference between the two groups.[44] The bulk of those voters who had 'defected' to the Tories in 2019 had done so because they believed Johnson would get Brexit done and because they were distinctly unimpressed by Jeremy Corbyn and what they saw as the excessive social liberalism and lack of patriotism of his Labour Party, not because they had somehow been converted to Thatcherite Conservatism. Most Tory MPs, on the other hand, were still very much devotees of the latter, willing to countenance a temporary increase in state spending and activity in a national emergency but determined to put an end to it as soon as humanly possible.

Johnson and Sunak – the latter especially – were no different, prepared to take action in order to prevent the economy falling off a cliff but damned if they were going to do more than the minimum required to keep so-called 'Red Wall' voters (and indeed voters in general) onside once the pressure was off. More than that, they, no less than their parliamentary colleagues, wanted to open up the economy as rapidly as possible so as to avoid adding even further to government borrowing. Accordingly, Johnson, in the second week of July, urged people, not least in his 'People's PMQs' where he answered questions on video from members of the public, to 'go back to work if you can'. It was around this time that Dominic Cummings was trying to warn him against 'people running around saying there can't be a second wave, lockdowns don't work' – 'bullshit' that was 'being picked up by editors and by pundits like [the *Mail on Sunday's* Peter] "Bonkers" Hitchens' – to which Johnson apparently replied, 'My heart is with Bonkers. I don't believe in any of this, it's all bullshit. I wish I'd been the mayor in Jaws and kept the beaches open.'[45] Indeed, even the PM's decision to make face coverings compulsory in some public spaces seemed mainly designed to give people confidence to go out, enjoy themselves, and spend – this in spite of the fact that the virus was still circulating widely, as attested by the number of places in the Midlands and the North that had to be placed into local lockdowns a few weeks later.

It was presumably the same blend of optimism, complacency, and ideology that led Number Ten to make a couple of other costly assumptions. The first, that a pliant Chris Grayling could be installed as Chair of parliament's Intelligence and Security Committee, while a deliciously comic failure, was of little importance outside Westminster, although (together with the temporary removal of the Tory whip from Julian Lewis, the MP who got the job instead) it had once again revealed Johnson's thin-skinned abhorrence of scrutiny.[46] The second, equally risible, assumption was that, following the decision to abandon exams earlier in the year, Gavin Williamson could be trusted to ensure that the marking of A-levels (the post-18 qualifications that determine university entry in most parts of the UK) would nevertheless proceed reasonably smoothly. Even so, it was unclear, once the Scottish government had been forced into a humiliating U-turn after thousands of pupils taking Highers (the Scottish equivalent of A-levels) had seen the grades awarded by their teachers arbitrarily lowered by examiners in an attempt to 'maintain credibility', exactly how the UK government had allowed pretty much the same thing to happen south of the border. But allow it it did. And not only that: while two bureaucrats (one of them the Permanent Secretary in the Department for Education) eventually stepped down as a result of the fiasco, Williamson was not sacked, even though he had been warned early on about the problems the algorithm employed to moderate results might cause.

Understandably, this lack of political accountability – increasingly, something of a recurring theme – reinforced the impression that loyalty rather than competence was the main criterion for membership of the

Cabinet: Williamson, it was said, as a former Chief Whip and organizer of Johnson's leadership campaign, simply 'knew too much' for the PM to risk returning him to the backbenches. As for those who normally sat on those benches but who were at that point away from Westminster on summer recess, they could only hope that things might somehow look up in September. Yet, in spite of the opportunity of five days of BBC-bashing afforded to the party's culture warriors by the corporation's decision (later rescinded) to drop allegedly colonialist relics 'Rule Britannia' and 'Land of Hope and Glory' from the Last Night of the Proms, they remained distinctly uneasy.[47]

True, some of the issues that seemed to exercise the party's opponents didn't seem to bother its MPs much. The Intelligence and Security Committee's long-delayed, heavily redacted, and in many ways very worrying 'Russia Report', as well as the government's insouciant response to it, for instance, raised barely an eyebrow on the Conservative benches – possibly because it was now more fashionable (as well as less embarrassing given that a fair few Tory MPs had accepted donations from wealthy individuals linked to Russia) to focus on potential Chinese interference.[48] And the announcement earlier in the summer that the Department for International Development (DfID) was to be folded into the Foreign and Commonwealth Office, thereby bringing an end to UK aid spending being treated, according to the PM, like 'some giant cashpoint in the sky', seemed to upset only those particularly interested in international development – not least former minister Andrew Mitchell, who had supported Johnson for the leadership after being personally assured by him that it wouldn't happen.[49] Nor, interestingly, was there any pushback from Brexiteers to the news that two men who had only recently been hate-figures for them, Ken Clarke and Philip Hammond, had not only been readmitted to the party but were also to be awarded peerages – along with former Scottish leader and unapologetic Remainer Ruth Davidson and the PM's brother Jo (who had twice quit the government over his opposition to a hard Brexit). Brexiteers, in spite of their oft-professed commitment to parliamentary sovereignty, also proved remarkably relaxed about the fact that the government's Trade Bill did not insist on the Lords and Commons ratifying future Free Trade Agreements (FTAs): indeed, fewer than a dozen Conservative MPs supported an amendment to that effect.

Rather more Conservative MPs *were* nervous, though, about the government's attempt, outlined in a White Paper released in early August, to increase housebuilding by easing planning restrictions. Many agreed in principle that this was a vital supply-side reform. But it was also one which, in practice, was bound to upset many of their constituents, especially once it became obvious that what was quickly dubbed the 'mutant algorithm' at its heart would see most new housing built in the proverbially 'leafy' shires and suburbs of southern England, thereby allowing Labour to exploit any consequent disappointment among 'Red Wall voters' in the North and the Midlands while the Lib Dems appealed to NIMBYs in the home counties.[50] Moreover, it was being masterminded (it that was the right word) by Communities Secretary Robert Jenrick – someone who was always willing to go out to bat for Johnson in the media but who had recently got into trouble (without, of course, paying any price), firstly, for apparently breaking the rules by moving between his various pricey properties during lockdown and, secondly, for unlawfully approving a housing development in London by a businessman who had (a) lobbied him about the project at a Conservative Party fundraiser and then (b), once approval was granted (in time to help him avoid paying millions of pounds to the local authority), made a donation to the Tories.[51]

But while planning reform was a concern (so much so that, in the second week of October, just over thirty Tory MPs, among them Theresa May and Jeremy Hunt, successfully supported a Commons motion to pause proposals they claimed risked 'turning the Garden of England into a patio'), it was not yet an urgent one – not compared anyway to the failure so far of the UK and the EU to make significant progress towards a trade agreement, with both Johnson and his chief negotiator David (now Lord) Frost seemingly relaxed about the prospect of a No-Deal exit from transition at the end of the year. While the Brexit-ultras in the ERG would have been more than happy with such an outcome, the majority of their colleagues were far less sanguine. Playing hardball might have been an acceptable negotiating strategy if it had wrung concessions from the EU on fishing and regulatory alignment, but ultimately it was in their constituents' interests that an FTA be done. And even as a negoti-ating strategy, there had to be limits, which was why many in the party – and not just former leaders like John Major, William Hague, Michael

Howard, and, of course, Theresa May herself – were prepared to speak out against the government's proposed Internal Market Bill, which, in seeking to renege on some aspects of the Withdrawal Agreement, would see the UK break international law (albeit, as Northern Ireland Secretary Brandon Lewis famously told parliament, only 'in a very specific and limited way'). In the event, the bill was allowed to progress with only two Tory MPs voting against it at second reading, although some thirty abstained, including two former Attorneys General and two former Northern Ireland Secretaries. Had not most of their colleagues been reassured that the offending clauses would be removed as a result of negotiations or else simply rejected by the Lords, the rebellion would almost certainly have been far more serious.

Covid redux

Most worryingly of all, however, there were clear signs that, inasmuch as it had ever really gone away, Covid was making a comeback – and with a vengeance. By the second week of September, daily cases had reached nearly 3,000 and Health Secretary Matt Hancock was warning young people, who appeared at that point to be the main problem, not to 'kill your gran'. Meanwhile, Johnson was announcing new control measures which included a ban on people meeting indoors or outdoors in groups of more than six – much to the chagrin of the party in the media, the *Mail* having earlier warned him that another lockdown would 'cripple the country'.[52] One or two Conservative donors weren't best pleased either, although those worried that they might even have to cancel their shooting weekends were doubtless relieved to learn that their sport had been granted a last-minute exemption by ministers from the rule of six.[53]

Not for the first time (or the last), sympathetic journalists were briefed that many ministers (most glaringly, Rishi Sunak) shared their editors' doubts about the need for, and economic consequences of, more restrictions.[54] But by the middle of the month it was becoming evident even to them that a second wave was building up steam: the country's testing capacity was overwhelmed and millions of households in the North East of England were now subject to bans on household mixing and a curfew. In the view of the government's scientific advisers, at least, further measures now needed to be brought in across the whole country. Meeting in the Cabinet room on 18 September, Whitty and Vallance, together with Dominic Cummings, tried to persuade the PM to institute a short, sharp national lockdown. And when the Scientific Advisory Group for Emergencies (SAGE) gathered on 21 September, it recommended the government consider the 'immediate introduction' of a list of measures that included a 'circuit-breaker' lockdown: a ban on households mixing; the closure of pubs, restaurants, hairdressers; working from home; and online-only university teaching.[55] Johnson, however, worried about the consequences for the economy and criticism from his MPs, decided to go the next day just with advice to work from home where possible and the imposition of 10 p.m. closing for the hospitality sector.

The PM's decision, which he presented as some kind of middle way, came after he had been encouraged by Sunak to hear personally from academics operating outside the scientific consensus, such as Oxford's Carl Heneghan and Sunetra Gupta, co-author of the consciously heretical 'Great Barrington Declaration', and Sweden's chief epidemiologist, Anders Tegnell, who had become something of a pin-up for anti-lockdown MPs, as well as SAGE's John Edmunds – the only scientist on the call who made the case for a lockdown.[56] Johnson's decision was also made against a background of pressure from Tory MPs, with 1922 Committee Chairman Graham Brady threatening to amend legislation so that a parliamentary vote would be required before any new national restrictions could come into force – a threat which (together with as many as eighty potential rebels) he was eventually persuaded to withdraw after the government conceded that it would allow votes on 'significant national measures ... wherever possible' in the future. Nevertheless, acutely aware that his increasingly ambitious Chancellor had emphasized the need to 'learn to live with [the virus] and live without fear' when he outlined his 'Winter Plan' to replace furlough with a less generous support scheme, Johnson felt obliged, as September turned into October, to couch his own rather more cautious approach in terms of fighting a series of regional outbreaks rather than a single, nationwide threat. This was an approach, he knew, that suited the bulk of his MPs, who sat for constituencies that currently enjoyed low case rates, and one which enjoyed widespread public support even if it made little scientific sense.[57]

Sadly for Johnson, his half-measures weren't doing much to boost ratings with the party's grassroots. Indeed, they were now no more impressed with him than voters as a whole, many of whom were telling pollsters that they thought Labour's leader Keir Starmer, who had been in post half a year by then, might do a better job.[58] ConservativeHome's readers' survey of rank-and-file members, published in the first week of October, suggested nearly two out of three thought Johnson was handling Covid badly. Chancellor Rishi Sunak, by contrast, notwithstanding the pasting he'd got in the party in the media at the end of August when (possibly according to a jealous neighbour) he was said to be considering tax rises to balance the books, continued to top its 'Cabinet League Table' with a net positive rating of 81.5. Meanwhile, the PM had joined Jenrick and Hancock in negative territory, although his -10.3 score was at least still a long way from Gavin Williamson's -43.1.[59]

In a 'normal' year, Johnson might have hoped to quell any discontent by coming up with yet another barnstorming speech at the party conference. This year, however, the whole thing was virtual, and doing it as a piece to camera from a deserted room in Canary Wharf served only to emphasize to his critics how little there was of substance beneath the characteristically upbeat bluster about 'building back better' towards a wind-powered 'New Jerusalem'. Nor could it disguise the contrast between that vision (such as it was) and Sunak's more meaty speech, which talked about 'a sacred responsibility to future generations' to fix the public finances and asked, in true Thatcherite fashion, 'If we argue … there is no limit on what we can spend, that we can simply borrow our way out of any hole, what is the point in us?' No wonder Rupert Murdoch had reportedly been sufficiently impressed with the Chancellor when he'd met him for drinks recently to ensure that his pre-conference interview-and-photoshoot with the *Sun* got top billing.[60]

As it was, conference provided only the briefest hiatus in the government's ongoing battle to bring the second wave of coronavirus under control, not least because its plans to divide England into three tiers leaked to the media. Large parts of the North were about to go into Tier 3, which would involve not just no household mixing but also the closure of the hospitality sector, forcing Sunak to backtrack on his plans to wind down furlough. By the time the tiers were formally announced on 12 October, however, many experts were already throwing their weight behind calls for a two- to three-week national 'circuit-breaker' lockdown – a campaign which Labour leader Keir Starmer (who until then had tended not to get too far out in front of Johnson on Covid) joined after SAGE released minutes of its meeting three weeks previously, thereby making it obvious that it had recommended a far tougher line than the government had decided to take.

In spite of this, forty-two Tory MPs were still prepared to vote against the government when the new regulations were passed in the Commons on the grounds that they inflicted too much damage on the economy and/or constituted an unwarranted attack on civil liberties. The party in the media expressed similar concerns. The *Sun* called on Johnson not to buckle to 'SAGE and Starmer', portrayed as 'scientists covering their backsides and a devious, tribal Opposition hell-bent on deploying a grave national crisis for political advantage'.[61] The *Mail* ('You've defied the boffins, Boris, now stay strong') said pretty much the same. Meanwhile (perhaps most worryingly for Johnson) the *Telegraph* (which, he told Dominic Cummings, was his 'real boss') once again portrayed the Chancellor as the libertarian hero of the hour, its headline reading 'How Rishi Sunak battled scientists, Gove and Hancock in bid to see off circuit breaker lockdown'. Little wonder, perhaps, that Johnson was prepared to clutch at any straw that suggested (at least to him) that further action was unnecessary: after learning that the median age of those dying from the virus was apparently between 81 and 82 for men and 85 for women, the PM messaged his advisers,

> That is above life expectancy. So get Covid and Live longer. Hardly anyone under 60 goes into hospital ... and of those virtually all survive. And I no longer buy all this NHS overwhelmed stuff. Folks I think we may need to recalibrate. ... There are max 3m in this country aged over 80.[62]

Sunak's supposed victory and the PM's Panglossian optimism, however, proved short-lived. As mathematical modelling suggested that the second wave risked killing more people than the first, and as the other nations of the UK moved to impose further restrictions, it became obvious by the end of October that England would have to follow suit lest the NHS be overwhelmed. Johnson, in the face of opposition from the party in parliament and the media (the *Mail* splashed with 'DON'T DO IT, BORIS!' on 29 October), announced a four-week national lockdown starting on 5 November, after which the country would enter a revised tier system that would, he hoped, at least allow families to get together at Christmas.[63] Furlough would now be extended until March, rendering redundant Sunak's various attempts since the summer to make a start on 'balancing the books' by trimming support for businesses and households as he pushed to reopen the economy and by backing the PM's decision to play hardball with 'locked-down' local authorities demanding more support.[64] The government's attempt to avoid a second surrender to Manchester United's Marcus Rashford's campaign to provide meals during the school holidays for kids in receipt of free school meals – a policy which had the support of around a third of grassroots members and a fair few Tory MPs but which also earned some tin-eared brickbats when, in late October, the government had whipped its troops to vote against a Labour motion on the issue – also collapsed in short order.[65]

Throughout, Johnson did his level best to signal publicly that instituting a second lockdown was the last thing he ever wanted to do. And in private, he was even more forthright. Furious – in part because the move went against his instincts, in part because it had been leaked to the media (possibly so as to ensure it went ahead in the face of any last-minute change of heart on his part) – he was said to have shouted 'No more fucking lockdowns – let the bodies pile high in their thousands!' – an outburst that was greeted with horror by bereaved families when it eventually found its way into the newspapers the following spring.[66]

For the moment, however, Johnson and the Whips were preoccupied with minimizing a rebellion, through the usual combination of carrot and stick, when the measures came before parliament a few days later.[67] A number of MPs, given plenty of space by the party in the media on the day after the announcement, had taken the opportunity to express their opposition, with former leader Iain Duncan Smith in the *Sunday Telegraph* labelling it 'a body blow to the British people' and a 'business breaker' rather than a circuit breaker – a move the government had, he claimed, been bounced into by SAGE, whom he accused of 'believing its advice to be more like commandments written on stone'.[68] Sadly, Michael Gove's appearance on television that morning, in which he admitted that there was a possibility that the measures announced might have to last longer than a month, only enraged anti-lockdown MPs further: according to Graham Brady, speaking on Radio 4's *Westminster*

Hour, 'If these kinds of measures were being taken in any totalitarian country around the world we would be denouncing it as a form of evil.'

Predictably enough, Brady's views were echoed over the next few days by the party in the media, which also picked up on the relaunch of Nigel Farage's Brexit Party as (among other things, the anti-lockdown) Reform UK.[69] Given this, it was not altogether surprising that, when the measures were voted on in the Commons, some 34 Conservative MPs voted against them and a further 16 abstained. Nor was it entirely surprising to hear Steve Baker (host of a 'lockdown sceptic' WhatsApp broadcast list that had signed up nearly a hundred colleagues and who had penned an op-ed explaining in the run-up to the vote why he'd rebelled) warning Number Ten on Sky News that any attempt to extend lockdown in December would see an even bigger revolt.[70]

Parliamentary pressure groups and the cancelling of Christmas

Fortunately for Johnson, not all the news that autumn was bad. True, his plans to appoint the *Mail*'s Paul Dacre to chair the media regulator Ofcom and the *Telegraph*'s Charles Moore to chair the BBC would eventually come to nothing. But they won him plenty of applause at the time from the party's culture warriors. True, too, being ridiculed for the fact that his social media graphic congratulating Joe Biden on winning the US presidential election appeared to have been originally intended for his defeated opponent was mortifying – as was a tweet responding to it from a former Democratic staffer that read 'This shapeshifting creep weighs in. We will never forget your racist comments about Obama and slavish devotion to Trump but neat Instagram graphic.'[71] But at least the imminent (if worryingly reluctant) departure of 'the Donald' from the White House undoubtedly removed a serious source of potential (and, all too often, actual) embarrassment and instability from the international scene, even if it may have disappointed the extraordinary 56 per cent of rank-and-file Tories who told ConservativeHome that they wanted him to win.[72]

Moreover, the US election result wasn't the only thing that gave cause for optimism. On the immigration front, with barely anyone noticing, the government had managed to execute a significant relaxation of its new regime, lowering the salary threshold by 30 per cent and making an even more generous offer to people in shortage occupations.[73] And on the Covid front, research was beginning to confirm the utility of relatively cheap lateral flow devices for detecting even asymptomatic infections – a development that was eventually to prove a major leap forward in mass testing. But best of all was the news, released on 9 November, from Pfizer-BioNTech that its Covid-19 vaccine (one of many that the UK's vaccine taskforce set up by the government in May had wisely done a deal for) had proved 90 per cent effective in phase-3 trials. There had been much talk (sometimes too much talk) from ministers about this or that scientific development as a 'game-changer'. This time it really was justified. All the more galling, then, for Johnson and his Cabinet colleagues that the announcement was almost immediately overshadowed by dramatic events much closer to home.

Back in early October, Number Ten had confirmed that it had decided to appoint former journalist Allegra Stratton, who had been working for Rishi Sunak (her husband, the *Spectator*'s Political Editor, James Forsyth, having also been best man at his wedding), to present the presidential-style televised lobby briefings it had decided to introduce in the New Year. Johnson's pick, which had reportedly been influenced by his wife Carrie, had not gone down well with Lee Cain, the Director of Communications, or with Dominic Cummings, making for considerable tension inside Downing Street – with some even suggesting there were now effectively two 'courts' vying for control.[74] Johnson, who was looking for a new Chief of Staff, had hoped to ease the tension by dangling the possibility that Cain could move into that post. When staffers (including, apparently, the Number Ten policy chief Munira Mirza) and some MPs got wind of the idea, however, they made clear their reservations, and Johnson decided not to follow through. His change of heart prompted Cain's resignation on 11 November and, two days later, the departure of Cummings. By then, both men had come under suspicion for leaking to the media the decision to implement a second lockdown – suspicions that were never proven (and were very possibly unfounded) but which were lent an air of plausibility by Cummings' mounting frustration (later vented in public) at Johnson's chronic inability both to take Covid seriously and to act decisively enough to combat it effectively.[75]

Johnson, understandably enough, wanted to signal that the 'Vote Leave gang' era was over, and what better way of doing it publicly than to allow Health Secretary Matt Hancock to talk to Piers Morgan and Susanna Reid on ITV's *Good Morning Britain*, thereby ending the 201-day government boycott of the show? A few days later, he himself was all over the media promoting what he claimed was a serious ten-point plan for a 'green industrial revolution' that would get the UK to net zero by 2050 and create hundreds of thousands of new jobs. He also undertook something of a charm offensive with Tory MPs. Housing Secretary Robert Jenrick – still in post despite being struck by scandal in the summer – was sent out to let them know that planning reforms were to be revised so as to avoid too much development in their constituencies. Meanwhile Johnson himself conducted a series of meetings (perforce online) with the various caucuses in the parliamentary party that, in some cases, had sprung up recently and, in others (the One Nation Group of self-styled 'moderate' Tories being perhaps the best example), could claim a rather longer pedigree.

Among the more recently formed groups there were two or three that were felt to merit particular attention, each of which had nodded to the nomenclature of a caucus – the ERG – which had had an undeniable impact on the politics of the party in recent times. Covid, of course, meant that they mainly met virtually (often simply via WhatsApp messages) rather than physically. Yet the fact that so many MPs were now away from Westminster for so much of the time made it much harder for the Whips to maintain both surveillance and discipline in a parliamentary party which had anyway long since lost the habit of deferring to its leaders and trusting the experts who advised them. That said, the influence of the caucuses in question could easily be overstated in the media. The ease with which MPs were happy to sign up to them went hand-in-hand with a (wholly understandable) temptation on the part of journalists to portray the shifting currents of opinion among an amorphous bunch of backbenchers as more clearly defined (and therefore more intelligible to their readers and listeners) than they may have been in reality. Likewise, even the most random backbencher stood more of a chance of getting quoted (or booked by a broadcaster) if they could be presented as speaking not just for themselves but on behalf of colleagues who'd gone so far as to organize in order to promote a particular viewpoint.

To be fair, one of these caucuses, the China Research Group (CRG), had been set up in April 2020 by two MPs who really did seem to know what they were talking about: Tom Tugendhat and Neil O'Brien. Its aim was to channel the concerns of colleagues about Chinese influence in the UK, initially prompted by what was felt to be the government's complacent attitude to the use of telecoms equipment manufactured by Huawei in key infrastructure projects, most obviously the roll-out of 5G – a decision the government eventually U-turned on. At the very least, its formation suggested that worries about China were no longer the preserve of knee-jerk 'neo-cons' but, in marked contrast to the Cameron years, had now spread to the mainstream of the parliamentary party, with China's delay in alerting the world to the outbreak of Covid-19 and stories of widespread human rights abuses in Xinjiang acting as a wake-up call. Certainly, there was overwhelming support, even among MPs who were normally sceptical about the benefits of mass immigration, for the government's decision in July to make it clear to China, in response to its security crackdown in Hong Kong, that an estimated three million of the territory's citizens would be eligible for fast-track settlement in the UK.

October 2020 saw the founding of the Northern Research Group (NRG) of some fifty or so MPs, many (though not all) of whom had been elected in 2019 in so-called 'Red Wall' seats. Organized by the MP Jake Berry, who had been heavily involved in Johnson's leadership campaign but had been dumped as a minister of state in the February 2020 reshuffle, it had first coalesced around the need to ensure that the region of the country most severely impacted by Covid was receiving sufficient attention (and sufficient funding) from government. After writing an open letter to the PM to that effect, and calling on him to provide a clear 'road map' out of coronavirus restrictions, those involved (including former minister Esther McVey, the face of another caucus, the 'Blue Collar Conservatives') had since broadened their attack.[76] Their key demand was now that, as and when the economy opened up, Number Ten maintain a commitment to infrastructure and other spending designed to 'level up' their constituencies, the needs of which they were perhaps more acutely aware of than ever, having spent so much more time in them than in Westminster because of Covid.

And then there was the newest of the new, the Covid Recovery Group, led by Mark Harper and Steve Baker. This second CRG had developed out of the latter's WhatsApp list and so found itself with a ready-made membership of around seventy MPs (twice the number who had voted against the second lockdown) within a couple of days of going public – an impressive figure given that a caucus like the 'Common Sense Group', set up by veteran MP John Hayes' colleagues who shared his socially conservative, 'anti-woke' views, had slightly fewer than that despite being around for nearly six months longer.[77] Certainly, with a vote on new tiered restrictions due at the beginning of December, numbers like those – sufficient, after all, to force the PM to rely on opposition support – meant that Harper and Baker's demand that the government publish some kind of impact assessment would need to be taken seriously. Moreover, both Number Ten and the Whips' Office could hardly miss the evident crossover between anti-lockdown and anti-EU sentiment: of the 16 MPs who abstained on the second lockdown, only 7 were Leavers, but of the 34 MPs who had actually voted against the government, and who constituted the core of the Covid Recovery Group, some 30 (or 9 out of 10) were Leavers. Moreover, apart from Graham Brady, every one of these Leave-voting MPs had also supported a No-Deal Brexit when given the option in the 'indicative votes' held back in 2019. In short, as with the ERG, this really was a caucus with a degree of ideological coherence (centring on its libertarian aversion to regulation), which was backed by the party in the media, and which (with Farage's formation of Reform UK) was able to play up the risk posed by an insurgent challenger run by a politician with a history of 'stealing votes' from the Tories.[78]

Come mid-November, then, Johnson was far from out of the woods. Indeed, he was very soon under pressure on another front. Following the resignation, back in February, of Philip Rutnam, Permanent Secretary at the Home Office, the Cabinet Office had begun an investigation into accusations of bullying against his former boss, Home Secretary Priti Patel. It had reported to Johnson in June. He, however, was reluctant to criticize, let alone fire, such a loyal supporter. Moreover, her enthusiasm for the 'war on woke' made her a particular favourite in the party in the media, in spite of her ongoing failure to put a stop to migrants crossing the Channel in small boats and to prevent 'activist' and 'lefty' lawyers from continuing to delay deportations. As a result, Johnson had sat on the Cabinet Office report, trying to work out what to do. Now, some five months later, he had made up his mind. Despite the damning findings of the report, he decided that Patel had not breached the Ministerial

Code and could therefore remain in post – a decision that prompted the resignation of his Adviser on Ministers' Interests, Alex Allan.

Johnson's refusal to sack Patel immediately prompted accusations that, Cummings or no Cummings, this was an administration that simply refused to abide by the norms and conventions that, in a country without a codified constitution, had traditionally constrained the executive and promoted at least a modicum of accountability. Indeed, critics noted, it even failed to play by the formal as well as the more informal 'rules of the game', setting up, for instance, a 'clearing house' in the Cabinet Office which was effectively vetting (and doing its best to frustrate) requests for government data and records made, perfectly legitimately, under the Freedom of Information Act.[79] At the same time, fast-track procurement of PPE in the early stages of the pandemic appeared, according to the National Audit Office, to have been open to irregularities that may have wasted millions of pounds of taxpayers' money, some of which, critics suggested, may even have ended up in the pockets of chums of Tory politicians.[80] Not that accusations of government cronyism and even corruption were anything new. Back in August, for instance, a *Times* investigation found that a substantial proportion of appointments to supposedly independent non-executive positions on departmental boards in Whitehall had gone to Conservative sympathizers and former SpAds.[81] A more recent investigation by the same paper found that nearly all the areas selected to receive £25 million each from the new 'Towns Fund' just prior to the 2019 election by Communities Secretary Robert Jenrick and his then junior minister, Jake Berry, were in marginal Conservative-held seats or else in seats on the party's target list.[82]

The government's opponents were similarly outraged when, a few days after it was revealed that Patel was going nowhere, Sunak announced in his Spending Review that, in order to shore up the government's finances, he was reneging (albeit temporarily at this stage) on the UK's commitment (enshrined in legislation) to spend 0.7 per cent of Gross National Income on overseas aid. Still, with only a few outspoken exceptions (Andrew Mitchell told the Commons that the cuts would cause '100,000 preventable deaths, mainly among children', while Liz Sugg resigned from the government frontbench in the Lords), this went down well with Tory MPs, many of whom regarded the promise as a bit of outdated Cameroon nonsense which, polls suggested, enjoyed very little public support.[83] The public sector pay freeze that would guarantee more savings failed to prompt much in the way of protest either: after all, the vast majority of the workforce was in the private sector and nurses and doctors, as well as those earning under £24,0000, were exempt. Nevertheless, combined with a reduction in a planned increase in the minimum wage, and very little for departmental budgets outside the NHS beyond a notional 'levelling up' fund, Sunak's statement (though he had no intention of admitting it, just as he had no intention of admitting the hit to the economy of Brexit flagged up by the Office for Budget Responsibility) effectively rang down the curtain on the so-called 'end of austerity'. Sadly, by declining an invitation to appear before the Treasury Select Committee, he did not give MPs the opportunity to discuss such matters further.

Whether most Tory MPs would have been much interested in hearing further from the Chancellor on the Spending Review is doubtful. Egged on by the Covid Recovery Group, all they really wanted to know, as the end of the four-week lockdown beckoned, was the following. Which of the three Covid tiers were their constituencies going to be placed in? How long were those tiers going to be in existence? Had the government carried out a meaningful impact assessment of its restrictions so it could supply, as Mark Harper put it, 'hard evidence, not hyperbole'? Did it have a convincing approach to lifting them in the medium to long term? And, in the short term, what were its plans for Christmas?

The last question, it turned out, was the first to be answered, Michael Gove having managed to coordinate a UK-wide policy whereby, between 23 and 27 December, people could create a three-household 'bubble' whose members would be able to meet in private homes, outside, and in places of worship, with no restriction on travel between nations and tiers. Soon after, the government announced its answer to the first question. Nearly all of England (including London) would be in Tier 2, thereby banned from indoor mixing between households while venues that did not serve a 'substantial meal' would be closed. Those in the even stricter Tier 3 were once again largely in the North and Midlands – an inevitable source of frustration to Conservative MPs with constituencies in those areas. As one of them, Graham Brady wasted no time in penning an op-ed for the *Mail* pouring scorn on what he saw as the incoherence and illiberalism of the tier system and explaining why he was going to vote against it in a week or so's time.[84]

Johnson, fresh from announcing that he had looked outside the party to appoint his new Chief of Staff, the banker and former Treasury civil servant Dan Rosefield, countered with an upbeat op-ed in the *Mail's* Sunday sister paper pleading for just a few more weeks of caution and patience.[85] In fact, in a tone that contrasted markedly with the unapologetically assertive language employed by Michael Gove in an essay in the *Times*, he had already written to seventy potential rebels the previous evening to assure them that the new regulations would contain a sunset clause that would give MPs the chance to vote on whether to extend them beyond 3 February.[86] He also hinted that mid-December might see some Tier 3 areas moved to the more relaxed Tier 2 – a possibility that stunned many scientific and medical experts, who were already very worried about the planned temporary relaxation over Christmas. A day later, after the government had announced additional subsidies for hospitality venues unable to open, he was writing to potential rebels again, responding to demands by them in the media for greater transparency and better communication, albeit avoiding their call for any vote to extend the 3 February sunset clause to take place as soon as possible after Christmas.[87]

The government also did its best to put out the economic impact assessment that the Covid Recovery Group had been demanding.[88] However, its best (a recycled rush job with very little in the way of analysis) was clearly not good enough, prompting criticism from the party in the media and leading one member of the group to dismiss it to *Politico London Playbook* as 'classic civil service guff that spent 40 pages saying nothing and just fucked everybody off'.[89] That there were 54 Tory MPs who proceeded to vote against bringing in the three tiers, with a further 16 abstaining, therefore came as no surprise, even if, with Labour choosing to abstain, what amounted to the biggest parliamentary rebellion Johnson had so far faced could not prevent the tiers replacing lockdown. But what the vocal opposition of so many of his own colleagues did seem to have influenced (along, perhaps, with the opposition of the party in the media) was feeling at the grassroots: ConservativeHome's readers' survey of party members now found that some 56 per cent of them thought the government should be lifting lockdowns and restrictions 'faster and more widely', while only 11 per cent took the view that it was too soon to open the country back up – quite the contrast with the general public, who remained far more cautious.[90] Still, there was at least one thing everyone could agree on, namely that the approval of the Pfizer/BioNTech by the Medicines and Healthcare Products Regulatory Agency (MHRA) on 2 December meant the country at last had some news on Covid it could really celebrate, although attempts by ministers and the party in the media to suggest (falsely, but it would appear successfully) that it represented some kind of Brexit dividend left, to some at least, a bad taste in the mouth.[91]

Brexit, of course, had never completely disappeared off the agenda and, with time running out to secure a trade deal with the EU, it was now back with a bang. The government had been predictably keen for months to demonstrate to its Brexit-ultras that it was playing hardball with Brussels. This strategy now led it, in the first week of December and with only 3 Tory MPs objecting (and 12 abstaining), to insist on reinserting (albeit, it turned out, only temporarily) in the Commons the clauses in the Internal Market Bill which the Lords had removed on the grounds that they would mean the UK would be breaking international law. There followed daily dire warnings about the imminence of No Deal unless the EU made concessions on fishing and the level playing field – a threat that most trade experts found hard to take too seriously given how unprepared for such an outcome the UK seemed to be and how much harder it would hit the UK than the EU economy.

Perhaps because they were momentarily distracted once again by Brexit, or perhaps because they were beginning to realize that the vaccine programme that had begun in the second week of December might eventually render the debate over lockdowns redundant, Conservative MPs reacted with relative equanimity to the news that rising case rates (possibly due to a new variant) had persuaded the government, on 15 December, to move London and some parts of the home counties that had been in Tier 2 into Tier 3. In spite, however, of those rising rates, pressure from experts (expressed, for instance, in a joint editorial in the *Health Service Journal* and the *British Medical Journal*), and what polls suggested was considerable disquiet among the public, Johnson remained adamant that he would not (as he accused Labour's Keir Starmer of wanting to do) 'cancel Christmas'. It was clear, though, that he was getting nervous. New guidance issued on 16 December strongly suggested people forgo seeing elderly relatives until after they had been vaccinated, that they isolate five days before seeing anyone new at Christmas, that they not travel unless absolutely necessary, and that, ideally, they spend the holidays with their own household or their existing 'support bubble'. Guidance was also changed in Scotland and the law changed in Wales and Northern Ireland, both of which announced they would go into another lockdown after the holiday.

Other developments also suggested things were spinning out of control. School leaders were once again clashing with Gavin Williamson over reopening, and Rishi Sunak announced he was now extending furlough until the end of April – on the same day as a further 4 million people living in the South and South East of England learned they, too, were being moved into Tier 3. In London, already in Tier 3, Liz Truss, who in her role as Trade Secretary had back in October given Brexiteers something to cheer about by negotiating an FTA with Japan, made a combative speech in her role as Equalities Minister that was clearly designed to win her, as an aspiring leadership contender, brownie points from the culture warriors in the party in the media. But, if they were honest, very few people outside Westminster (and probably by then even within it) were paying much attention.[92] For the moment, Covid was virtually all that anyone could think about.

Just a couple of days later, on Saturday, 19 December, Johnson was finally forced to concede defeat. In yet another hastily convened Downing Street press conference, he announced that, in the face of a new, far more transmissible variant, around a third of England's population (most of them living in London and the South East and in eastern counties) was being placed in new 'Tier 4' restrictions, meaning that they would not be able to mix with other households at all over Christmas. A stay-at-home message would be enshrined in law, non-essential shops, indoor leisure, and entertainment venues would close, and no-one in Tier 4 would be allowed to stay overnight away from home. Meanwhile, across the rest of the country, bubbles of up to three households would now be permitted to meet on Christmas Day only.

The immediate reaction in the party in the media was not quite as apoplectic as Johnson feared, with most Sunday papers buying the idea, at least on their front pages, that his hand had been forced by the new 'mutant' strain officially labelled alpha.[93] However, inside, their leader pages were rather less forgiving.[94] The same was true, in spades, for leading lights of the Covid Recovery Group like Steve Baker and Mark Harper, who called (in vain) for the recall of parliament in order to vote on the measures.[95] As usual, however, they were out of step with voters (including Conservative voters), who overwhelmingly supported the new measures, even if, by a large majority, they were critical of the government's handling of the crisis.[96] Still, on the basis that every cloud has a silver lining, at least the furore over Covid and Christmas provided a degree of distraction from the news that Johnson was appointing yet more Tories to the Lords – including a multi-millionaire donor to the party, Peter Cruddas, whose elevation to the peerage went against the recommendation of the House of Lords Appointments Commission and who, three days after he took up his seat in February 2021, gave the party another half a million pounds.[97]

As it turned out, that story was quickly buried anyway by the news that the UK and the EU had, with just days to go and in the midst of chaos at Channel ports due to panic about the new variant, at last agreed a trade deal. In the party in the media, for a few days at least, all was forgiven, with the Christmas Eve edition of the *Mail*, for instance, splashing with 'HALLELUJAH! IT'S A MERRY BREXMAS' and the *Sun*'s front page mocking up a picture of Johnson as Santa Claus pouring presents down the chimney from a Union Jack sack.[98] Even Nigel Farage seemed fairly satisfied, declaring, 'The war is over.' ConservativeHome reported on 27 December that 60 per cent of members who responded to its readers' survey thought that the early signs were that the deal was 'a win for the UK', compared to just 6 per cent who thought it was a win for the EU. And the newspapers that day were full of warm words from high-profile Brexiteers like the *Telegraph*'s Charles Moore, Vote Leave's Matthew Elliot, and former MEP Daniel (now Lord) Hannan. Moroever, the ERG gave the deal the thumbs-up after its 'Star Chamber' of lawyers signalled its approval.[99] As for the public, polls suggested that they, too, backed the deal – some out of genuine enthusiasm, others out of relief.

The Act enshrining the Trade and Cooperation Agreement into law was passed without a single Conservative MP voting against it, gaining Royal Assent in the early hours of the last day of the year. 'Britain begins 2021 as the fully independent country it was always meant to be,' rejoiced the *Sun*. Sadly, Britain was also beginning the year amidst now all-too-familiar chaos and uncertainty as to which schools would be reopening (and when) after the holidays. And as the numbers of Covid cases reached new heights, another 20 million-plus people learned that they, too, would be entering Tier 4, meaning some eight out of ten residents of England were now living once again under virtual lockdown.

8

Coming up for air
(January–October 2021)

A year late, perhaps, but Big Ben did at last 'bong for Brexit' on New Year's Eve 2020, and the next morning Boris Johnson was on the front page of the *Telegraph* pointing to 'a much brighter future' now that vaccines had arrived and the UK had finally escaped the orbit of the European Union.[1] In reality, however, things were still looking pretty grim – particularly for parents of school-aged children and their teachers who had to cope as government suddenly backtracked on its decision to reopen schools. And in a few days' time things got even grimmer when Johnson was forced by rapidly increasing case numbers to implement another national lockdown for England starting on 6 January. Until at least the last week of February, he announced, people should work from home if they could, schools would only be open to the children of key workers, and all hospitality venues and non-essential retail would be closed.

Polls suggested the decision had the support of between seven and eight out of ten people and, although they also suggested that well over half the country thought the government had reacted too slowly, later surveys suggested that twice as many people (and, when it came to Tory voters, nine times as many) reckoned the public rather than the government were most responsible for the recent rise in cases.[2] So steep was that rise that a mere fourteen Conservative MPs voted against the measures when they were laid before parliament, with just nineteen abstaining. Rising infection rates, however, did nothing to discourage the Covid Recovery Group's Mark Harper. Within a week he was telling government that, if people in the top four priority groups were given their first vaccine dose by mid-February, then (presuming protection was conferred after three weeks) there could be no excuse for maintaining the lockdown beyond the first week of March. But with well over a thousand people dying a day and an estimated one in fifty people infected, Tory lockdown sceptics had to be careful not to push things too far – a lesson not lost on Steve Baker after he was obliged to tweet his support for the PM just an hour and a half after the media got hold of a note he'd sent to colleagues advising them to tell the Chief Whip that the 'debate will become about the PM's leadership if the Government does not set out a clear plan for when our full freedoms will be restored'.[3]

To Tory MPs outside the Covid Recovery Group's hard core, Johnson's evident failure to learn from his mistakes in the first phase of the pandemic and to act hard and fast second time around was laid bare in a sobering tweet by Sky News's Nick Stylianou which noted that, while it had taken Covid 251 days (between 2 March and 7 November) to claim its first 50,000 lives, the next 50,000 had occurred in just 79 days (between 8 November and 25 January).[4] In spite of this, the Covid Recovery Group remained absolutely determined to maintain pressure on the PM to reopen schools after the February half term, even if, critics argued, its efforts might have been better directed to getting him to do something about the fact, firstly, that only one in ten schools were confident that their pupils had access to online teaching and, secondly, that (as yet another campaign boosted by the efforts of Marcus Rashford highlighted) some of the country's most deprived kids were being sent scandalously inadequate food parcels in lieu of school lunches.[5] No wonder some of its members' colleagues, not least those in the Northern Research Group (whose constituencies were generally less well off than those of their southern counterparts), were publicly supporting Work and Pensions Secretary Thérèse Coffey in her very public efforts to persuade Chancellor Rishi Sunak not to withdraw the £20 a week uplift to Universal Credit that he had introduced to help poorer people cope in the pandemic. Once again, however, the vast majority of Conservative MPs (in fact, all but six) obeyed what had become their Whips' standard instruction when it came to Opposition motions and abstained when Labour introduced one on the issue in the third week of January.[6]

Fortunately, at least for a Prime Minister who put so much stress on the newspapers' preoccupations, the row was soon overtaken, at least as far as the party in the media was concerned, by a seemingly heaven-sent opportunity to bash Brussels – this time for its call on AstraZeneca to use supplies of its vaccine produced in the UK to fulfil its delivery obligations to member states: 'NO, EU CAN'T HAVE OUR JABS!', thundered the

Mail's front page. Even more usefully for the government, the EU then made two even bigger blunders. First it hinted that it might not allow exports of the Pfizer jab from Belgium to the UK. Then it went so far as to invoke Article 16 of the Northern Ireland Protocol to the Withdrawal Agreement in order to prevent vaccines being exported from the EU to the UK through Ireland. While it backtracked on its decision within a matter of hours, it had huge consequences, making it far easier for Brexiteers in Great Britain (and the DUP in Northern Ireland) to argue for overriding or suspending the Northern Ireland Protocol – something Johnson had already suggested he was prepared to consider.[7] David Frost, whose widely criticized appointment as National Security Adviser never came to fruition and who was instead made the Cabinet minister responsible for Brexit, certainly lost little time (as the UK unilaterally extended the 'grace period' during which full border checks would not take place) in linking the government's desire to renegotiate the Protocol to Brussels' clumsy and counterproductive triggering of Article 16.[8]

Meanwhile, vaccines were also coming in handy in Scotland, with Johnson making a rare foray north of the border to opine, firstly, that there was no need for another independence referendum since the last one had supposedly put the issue to bed 'for a generation' and, secondly, that the ongoing vaccine roll-out in Scotland was a reminder of the benefits of remaining in the UK. Number Ten, however, didn't seem too confident that his message had hit home, announcing a few days later the immediate departure of Johnson's chief adviser on the union, former Tory MP Luke Graham. Graham was immediately replaced by the apparently more confrontational Oliver Lewis, one of the few remaining members of the 'Vote Leave gang' still in Downing Street, only for Lewis to quit within weeks and the work of his supposedly beefed-up 'Union Unit' to be passed to a Cabinet committee – yet another resignation attributed (as were the appointments of Simone Finn and Henry Newman to advisory positions in Number Ten) to the influence of the PM's fiancée, Carrie Symonds.[9]

Polling across Britain as a whole was beginning to suggest that the success of the UK's relatively rapid vaccine roll-out was providing the Conservatives with a much-needed boost.[10] Predictably enough, this, plus the fact that more and more people were presumably protected after getting their jab, only encouraged Tory libertarians to increase the pressure on the Prime Minister to move the country out of lockdown. Indeed, a familiar pattern began to assert itself: the Covid Recovery Group and the party in the media would call on the PM to stop giving so much credence to overly cautious scientists (and/or teaching unions) and to provide a 'roadmap out of lockdown' giving dates for the lifting of restrictions; then these calls would be accompanied by off-the-record briefings claiming that certain ministers (particularly, for some unfathomable reason, those with leadership ambitions like Rishi Sunak and Liz Truss) were pushing him to open up faster too.[11] However, once bitten, twice shy, and seemingly determined for once to avoid overpromising and underdelivering, Johnson struck what was, at least for the lockdown sceptics in the party (although not, polling suggested, for the public), a frustratingly cautious note.[12] At the beginning of the third week of February, he outlined a month-by-month, four-step path out of lockdown with each step dependent on the speed of the vaccination programme, on data showing that vaccines were reducing deaths and hospitalizations, on the NHS not being overwhelmed, and on the absence of worrying new variants.

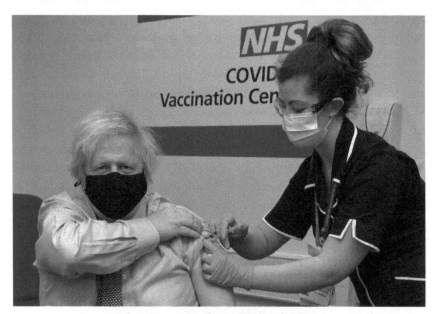

Johnson gets his first jab, March 2021.
Source: 10 Downing Street.

Covid on pause: normal service resumed?

With the roadmap in place, attention turned to the Budget, delivered in the first week of March. Rishi Sunak (who, living up to his reputation as a smooth operator, released a soft-focus, on-brand pre-Budget video covering his first year as Chancellor) had been making it clear to his fellow MPs since January that, as far as he was concerned, the Conservative Party's biggest advantage over Labour was its claim to fiscal responsibility.[13] It was therefore his intention, he'd told them, to repair the public finances and so maintain this 'clear blue water' between government and Opposition, even if that meant raising taxes in the short term in order to cut them again in the run-up to the next general election. It came as no surprise, then, to see him announce a future increase in corporation tax and (following the precedent set by any number of Chancellors in need of additional revenue but hoping to gather most of it by stealth) the freezing of thresholds on income, pensions, and inheritance. Some spending would have to increase, too, largely in order to cushion businesses and individuals during lockdown. Sunak was able, for instance, to reassure worried MPs that the temporary uplift to Universal Credit would be extended into the autumn, although there would, if one looked carefully enough, be cuts to some public services in addition to those already announced in the previous year's Spending Review.

The immediate reaction, helped perhaps by the Chancellor talking a lot about the freeports so beloved of Brexiteers, was relatively positive: the party in the media could hardly ignore the tax rises altogether but the leader pages of Tory papers were fairly complimentary, even if the same couldn't be said for some of their columnists.[14] Nor did the Budget, as occasionally happens, completely unravel once experts dug into the small print in the coming days. That said, there was some understandable criticism of the government after they discovered that forty of the forty-five towns awarded money by its 'Towns Fund' just happened to be represented by Conservatives.[15] There was criticism, too, when it became clear that the government hoped to limit the annual pay award to NHS employees to just 1 per cent – effectively rewarding them with a pay cut after one of the most difficult years any of them had ever had to face. Initial polling, however, suggested that the public were pleased and, importantly (but perhaps illusorily, given only one in five people seemed to think they would be worse off as a result), that they regarded Sunak's programme as fair.[16] That, plus the success of the vaccine roll-out and widespread approval of the cautious roadmap out of lockdown, saw the Conservatives move well above 40 per cent in the polls and once again open up a convincing lead over Labour.

Possibly as a tribute to the extent to which Johnson had managed to present his government as a clean break from the administrations that had run the country for the last decade, whether Tory or Tory-led, the party appeared to suffer little if any immediate damage from revelations about its former leader, David Cameron, personally lobbying his contacts in government on behalf of Greensill – a finance company that was paying him very handsomely as an adviser.[17] Ministers and civil servants, true to Whitehall form, may not have been falling over themselves to hand over texts and emails to those keen to find out what exactly had gone on, but it was noticeable that they made precious little effort to spare Cameron's blushes. In fact, even to those MPs who in some ways owed their career to him, he was now an embarrassment. And many of them, of course, could claim that they had more important things to do than support their former leader. Oliver Dowden, for instance, had been Cameron's Deputy Chief of Staff before being selected for a safe seat in the Commons, but, as Culture Secretary, was far too busy telling museums and the like that they mustn't let themselves be 'pushed around' by left-wingers into changing the way they presented the country's heritage and history.[18]

Home Secretary Priti Patel was another Cabinet minister who had benefited early on in her career from Cameron's patronage. However, as a thoroughgoing Brexiteer, she had long since left him behind and anyway now had more than enough on her plate. Much to her relief, the government had managed to persuade her former Permanent Secretary, Philip Rutnam, to accept a generous financial settlement rather than take his bullying accusations all the way to an employment tribunal. But she was still having to cope, on the one hand, with the fall-out from the Metropolitan Police's widely criticized handling of the vigil held in mid-March in memory of Sarah Everard, who had been kidnapped, raped, and murdered by one of its officers, and, on the other, with the seemingly unprovoked attacks on police during a 'Kill the Bill' protest in Bristol later on that same month. She had other problems to deal with too. One was the need to respond to calls from employers to adjust her new immigration regime to the needs of the labour market – something that she was able to do by quietly adding to the list of shortage occupations that eased entry requirements for those working in them. The other problem was more pressing because it was more political, namely what do about all the asylum seekers who, in their desperation to make it to a country where many of them had family connections and which, they believed, might afford them a chance of a better life, had taken to crossing the English Channel in small boats. Whether the supposedly radical changes to what she called Britain's 'broken' system which she announced in the last week of March would actually achieve much, however, remained to be seen. After all, if the past few years were anything to go by, it wasn't until spring began to turn into summer that crossings would begin in earnest.[19]

For the moment, Covid remained the Conservatives' main preoccupation – not least when it came to the party in the media, with the *Mail* once again devoting page after page (as well as its front page) to protesting against 'draconian' restrictions that it claimed were killing not just the economy but also people unable to access healthcare for other conditions.[20] Anti-lockdown MPs were also back on the warpath, with concern rising about the possible introduction of so-called 'vaccine passports'. Some thirty-five of them (including Charles Walker, who, for a reason no-one could quite understand, then took to touring the TV studios with a pint of milk to highlight his opposition) voted against the extension of coronavirus legislation when it came before the Commons at the end of March.[21] And even when Boris Johnson made use of the Downing Street's new £2.6 million media suite to confirm the government was going ahead as planned with the partial easing of restrictions (lifting the stay-at-home order, allowing six people from two households to meet outside and outdoor sports facilities to reopen), the party in the media the next day was urging him to go further and faster: after all, as Steve Baker told the *Mail*, 'Ministers' monomaniacal focus on Covid cases is leaving us stuck with these road map dates, despite the fact that the vaccine has clearly broken the link between cases, hospitalisations and deaths. It is fiendishly frustrating.'[22]

As Johnson had anticipated, however, the publication of the report of his hand-picked Commission on Race and Ethnic Disparities bought

187

him a bit of a breather, not least because most newspapers were – until very late on – provided only with an advance briefing note which failed to do justice to the rather more nuanced message contained within its 264 pages.[23] Thus the party in the media was able to splash on the fact that, although the commissioners conceded that 'overt and outright racism persists', the country was not institutionally racist and 'should be regarded as a model for other white-majority countries'.[24] It could also highlight the fact that the Commission claimed that 'most of the disparities we examined, which some attribute to racial discrimination, often do not have their origins in racism'. All of this, plus a rather cack-handed discussion of slavery, which some interpreted as the Commission attempting to suggest it had an upside, also led to a fierce backlash against the report from critics. But this was presumably part of the plan since they could then be (and were) caricatured as 'woke warriors' for 'the race relations industry', although it was, admittedly, a little awkward that the day of the report's publication also saw the resignation of Samuel Kasumu, Number Ten's very own special adviser for civil society and communities, who had already been reported as opposed to what he called 'a politics steeped in division'.

Whether, ultimately, much would come of the report was a moot point. After all, Johnson had never committed to implementing any of it twenty-four recommendations, a full two-thirds of which appeared to repeat those made by other official investigations touching on racial inequality and discrimination.[25] And, in any case – and not for the first time – he was soon swept away by the tide of events towards other matters. The third week of April saw him act swiftly, with the help of Culture Secretary Oliver Dowden, to put paid to the idea of a European Super League (not surprisingly, given the overwhelmingly hostile public reaction to the announcement by the big clubs involved).[26] It was therefore more than a little ironic that it was football that, at least in part, then landed him in seriously hot water.

Just before the ESL plan was announced, the *Mail* had run a story suggesting the PM had personally intervened to unblock the purchase of Newcastle United by a Saudi Arabian consortium after coming under pressure from the kingdom's Crown Prince – already notorious for his alleged involvement in the murder of a high-profile journalist and who had, more recently (and rather more trivially), played a minor role in media inquiries into David Cameron's lobbying antics.[27] What caught the eye, aside from the substance of the story, was its sourcing. The indefatigable veteran journalist Simon Walters appeared to have had access to private messages between the Prince and the Prime Minister. Moreover, it soon became apparent, when several outlets revealed conversations between Johnson and the entrepreneur James Dyson about the tax status of his employees, firstly, that Walters wasn't the only one and, secondly, that Downing Street was convinced that the source for both stories was none other than Dominic Cummings.[28] As was his wont, however, Cummings used his blog to hit back hard – not just at Johnson but also at his new Director of Communications, Jack Doyle, recently hired from (where else?) the *Mail*.[29] Some wondered if Number Ten had been seeking to caricature the PM's former adviser as a bitter man out for revenge in order to undermine any testimony he might give to parliamentary and other inquiries into the government's less-than-optimal handling of the pandemic. If so, the plan backfired badly since Cummings, not content with denying the accusations that he was the 'Chatty Rat', breathed new life into what inevitably became known as 'Flatgate' or 'Wallpapergate' ('cash for cushions [or curtains]' never quite caught on) – the mystery surrounding who had paid (and when) for the eye-wateringly expensive refurbishment of Johnson's Downing Street flat, supposedly forced upon him by Carrie Symonds. Cummings, in his blog, wrote that he'd told the PM that 'his plans to have donors secretly pay for the renovation were unethical, foolish, possibly illegal and almost certainly broke the rules on proper disclosure of political donations if conducted in the way he intended'. Cue the Electoral Commission (already an enemy as far as some Tories were concerned for what they regarded as the politically motivated interest it had taken over the years into spending by the party and by Leave campaigners) declaring that it would now look further into the matter, as well as a furious Johnson feeling he had no choice but to allow his new Independent Adviser on Ministers' Interests, Christopher Geidt, to do the same.[30]

Then, as if that wasn't bad enough (ministers appearing on broadcast found they were spending most of their allotted time not talking about what they'd come on for but instead parrying allegations about the flat), the briefing back-and-forth saw the first public airing of Johnson's outburst from back in October.[31] Snap polling suggested that half the country believed he'd made the remark ('No more fucking lockdowns – let the bodies pile high in their thousands!'), although under a third of Tory voters thought so.[32] The only comfort was that, even if it did risk eroding support for the party, there was a long way to go before any drop became seriously worrying: polling commissioned by the *Times* at the end of April suggested that the Conservatives, on 44 per cent, retained an 11-point headline lead over Labour, on 33 per cent. And, as the paper reported, that was 'despite more than half of the respondents agreeing that the Tories are "very sleazy and disreputable" and almost a third saying that they consider Johnson to be less honest than other politicians'.[33] Also, while the party in the media was far from impressed with the Prime Minister's handling of the issue thus far, there was no sense in which they were deserting him. The *Sun*, in its leader column, for instance, thought 'He should come clean' but also reckoned voters weren't that bothered – and anyway, in a none-too-veiled reference to Johnson's predecessor as Tory leader, it was convinced that 'They would rather have a flawed PM who delivers than a morally unimpeachable dud.'[34]

The minority of voters who could be bothered to cast a ballot in elections covering local councils held a week or so later appeared, in the main, to agree. Whether or not Conservative candidates received a bit of a boost from the government's decision just before polling took place to send a couple of armed Royal Navy patrol vessels down to the Channel Islands in a dispute over fishing rights with France, who knows? But it certainly seemed to do them no harm. With the so-called 'progressive' vote splintering between the Lib Dems, the Greens, and Labour, the latter lost control of 8 local authorities in England after losing 327 councillors; the Tories, who did significantly better in Leave-voting than Remain-voting wards, took control of 13 after gaining 235; and the Tory Mayors of the West Midlands (Andy Street) and Tees Valley (poster-boy Ben Houchen) were re-elected with far more comfortable majorities than some had predicted. And any lingering concern that ex-Brexit Party Reform UK might make a mark was put to rest. That said, the Tories – unlike the SNP and Welsh Labour – didn't have much to write home about in Scotland and Wales, which were electing their parliament and Senedd. And, while they did their best to play up a better-than-expected performance in the contest to be London Mayor, in truth Shaun Bailey didn't really come that close to unseating Labour's

Sadiq Khan (although Tory candidates might, it was thought, have more of a chance in years to come if the government went ahead with plans to revert, in mayoralty and Police and Crime Commissioner elections, from the supplementary vote system to first past the post).[35] Nor, although it was admittedly impressive for a governing party, did the Conservative's projected national share of the vote (at 36 per cent to Labour's woeful 29 per cent) come close to matching its current poll rating.

Arguably, however, none of those caveats much mattered because the headlines were grabbed anyway by the Conservatives winning the Hartlepool by-election on a swing of 16 per cent. True, there was an element of hype about the whole thing: after all, Labour's share of the vote had dropped by 15 points at the 2019 general election and it had probably only managed to hold on to the seat as a result of the Brexit Party taking a whopping 26 per cent. With most of that vote always likely to flow to the Conservatives, who had finished a fairly close second a year and a half previously, it was hardly surprising they were able to take the seat this time around. Still, it was a record-breaking achievement: the first time the party had won the seat since its creation in 1974 and the largest increase (23 percentage points) in the share taken by a governing party in all the by-elections held in the post-war era. No wonder Boris Johnson flew straight up to the North East to congratulate his newest MP in the private plane occasionally lent to him by one of the Tories' top donors, JCB chairman Anthony Bamford, where, much to the delight of snappers, he was greeted by a 30-foot inflatable of himself.[36]

Jetting around the country, suggested Johnson's critics, wasn't quite the way to emphasize his green credentials. But that didn't prevent the government carrying over its Environment Bill from the previous session of parliament in the Queen's Speech that took place a few days later. Other measures announced included a bill to repeal the Cameron-era Fixed-term Parliaments Act so as to allow the Prime Minister to call an election at the time of their choosing (and also, presumably, to make certain parliamentary votes matters of confidence in order to force rebels into line, as used to be the case before its introduction). Most controversial, at least for the party's opponents, was the proposed Electoral Integrity Bill. That measure, among other things, aimed to oblige voters to produce certain forms of ID before they could vote. Described as 'total bollocks' by former Scottish Tory leader Ruth Davidson, the plan was a solution to an electoral fraud problem that to all intents and purposes did not exist. As such, it was bound to be seen as a way of making voting difficult for people who would find supplying such ID tricky or just bothersome, most of whom just happened to be more likely, demographically speaking, to vote Labour.[37] There were, by common agreement, some useful ideas in the proposed Skills and Post-16 Education Bill and the Advanced Research and Invention Agency Bill, as well in several bills on animal welfare. Meanwhile there was plenty of red meat for traditional Tories in the Police, Crime, Sentencing and Courts Bill and for those keen to carry forward the so-called 'war on woke' and on 'lefty lawyers' in both the Higher Education (Freedom of Speech) Bill and the Judicial Review and Courts Bill.

Not everyone was satisfied, however. Not only was there no room for a bill on levelling up, but the speech merely promised that the government would level up *opportunities*, as opposed to, say, measurable outcomes. And there was only the merest mention of the plan for social care which Johnson had promised was almost ready to go on the steps of Downing Street back in 2019, provoking the *Mail* (with a keen eye, as ever, on the demographics of its readership) to produce a front-page screamer asking 'WHEN WILL THEY SHOW THEY CARE?'[38]

Conservative MPs, however, seemed far more concerned, predictably enough perhaps, with the proposed Planning Bill, which was intended to implement the government's manifesto promise to massively increase housebuilding by making it easier for developers to obtain consents in areas designated for 'growth' rather than 'protection'. Those representing supposedly 'leafy' southern constituencies that, theoretically anyway, might one day become vulnerable to a Liberal Democrat challenge – constituencies that had begun to be labelled 'the Blue Wall' – were particularly worried about a backlash from voters who approved of providing more housing in the abstract but not if it was going to spoil their views. A few Tory MPs were even reportedly worried that new housing might attract people with less traditional Tory views into their constituencies. Theresa May's own seat of Maidenhead was apparently unlikely to be especially affected by the proposals but, as a former leader sitting as she did for a home counties seat, her warning that it would put the 'wrong homes in the wrong places' garnered a lot of attention.[39] Just as, if not more, worrying was the concern expressed by the *Telegraph*, prompting Housing Secretary Robert Jenrick to try to reassure its readers (and his colleagues) in its pages. He was, he wrote, every bit as concerned with quality as quantity, but wanted to remind them, too, that housebuilding was key to the government's 'levelling up' agenda, as well as the fact that 'The property-owning democracy is one of the foundations of our country and central to our identity as Conservatives. But there is a whole generation that now feels priced out of the dream of homeownership.'[40] Meanwhile, northern MP Simon Clarke, who had been Minister of State for Housing, used a *Times Red Box* article to warn his colleagues even more explicitly that

> Left unaddressed, this situation threatens my party's medium-term prospects. ... There have been some falls in the Conservative vote in the southern shires, which map closely to the areas of greatest housing need, while London remains largely out of reach. For the party of opportunity, delivering good quality, affordable homes lies at the heart of reversing this problem – and stopping it from accelerating.[41]

If few of those worried MPs were convinced on the planning front, they could at least take some comfort from the fact that the easing of Covid restrictions appeared to be progressing according to plan. Johnson was able to announce in the middle of May that groups of up to six people (or people from two households) could meet up indoors, while outdoors they could meet in groups of up to thirty, meaning indoor hospitality and leisure facilities could now reopen. He also warned, however, that the new freedoms should be enjoyed with 'a heavy dose of caution'. This reflected rising concern about the so-called 'Indian variant' (later named Delta), whose entry into the UK was being blamed by the government's critics on delays in adding India to the 'red list' which all but banned passenger air travel between the UK and those countries on it – a delay which appeared to have occurred because Johnson had been so desperate not to have to cancel a planned trip there to promote 'global Britain' in the middle of April.

Dom bites back

But it was not so much the government's current as its past handling of the pandemic that was now causing the biggest political headache. A few days after the new freedoms had come into force, Dominic Cummings, in a Twitter thread backed up by photos taken contemporaneously inside Number Ten and launched in advance of his planned appearance before MPs later in the month, renewed his attack.[42] He focused in particular on those (like Health Secretary Matt Hancock) who denied that the government had ever pursued a 'herd immunity' policy prior to the first lockdown. Number Ten knew from polling that the public had already made up its mind that the government hadn't handled the initial phase too well but was in the main prepared to forgive it, especially now that vaccines had been produced. So it hit back hard with briefings (accompanied by WhatsApp messages) which, it claimed, undermined Cummings' claims. It also took comfort (if that's the right word) from polling which showed that, while only 38 per cent trusted Johnson to tell the truth about the government's handling of the coronavirus outbreak, the proportion that trusted Cummings to do so stood at a mere 14 per cent.[43] Nevertheless, it was bracing itself for the moment Johnson's former adviser actually sat down on 26 May to take questions from members of both the Science and Technology and Health Select Committees.

As it turned out, it was right to try to steel itself, although, in truth, what might otherwise have been a completely devastating assault lost some of its force by its being all-too-easily portrayed by government loyalists as score-settling. During some seven hours of testimony to the assembled MPs, bits of which were replayed on the evening news, Cummings, while noticeably reluctant to criticize politicians he admired like Michael Gove and (notwithstanding the Chancellor's well-deserved reputation as a 'hawk' on Covid) Rishi Sunak, not only comprehensively trashed Hancock's performance as Health Secretary but also painted a picture of Johnson as completely unfit to be Prime Minister – a man obsessed with how he was seen by the media, often distracted by his messy private life, and ultimately so incapable of sticking to a course of action that he was 'like a shopping trolley smashing from one side of the aisle to the other'. At first, the PM had apparently discounted Covid as a 'scare story', calling it 'the new swine flu'. Not only had the PM talked about Chris Whitty injecting him with the virus on TV so as prove it was nothing much to worry about, he'd claimed he preferred 'chaos' to giving Cummings the power to manage a team capable of mounting a sustained response to the crisis since, in his words, 'Chaos isn't that bad – it means that people have to look to me to see who's in charge.' Most seriously of all, Cummings confirmed what many already suspected, namely that Johnson, rather than learning the lessons of the spring, had railed against the first lockdown ('I should have been the mayor of Jaws and kept the beaches open,' he'd cried) and fatally delayed locking down a second time when advised to do so in September. As a result of all this, admitted Cummings, 'Tens of thousands of people died who didn't need to die.'

Snap polling suggested that Cummings' criticisms had some cut-through: even if four out of ten Brits admitted they couldn't tell if they were accurate or not, a third thought that they were compared to a quarter who did not, although there was a marked (and hardly unexpected) reluctance on the part of Conservative voters to believe him.[44] More detailed polling released by Opinium the following weekend, however, suggested rather more damage had been done to Johnson than he'd hoped. People believed the 'herd immunity' accusation by 66 to 20 percentage points. They believed that Johnson had initially seen Covid as a scare story and had described it as the new swine flu by a margin of 60 to 24. They believed he'd taken a break in February 2020 without paying attention to the potential crisis by a 56 to 26 margin. And they believed that he was so distracted by his personal life in March 2020 that he was unable to concentrate on making decisions on Covid by 52 to 34 percentage points. More generally, 33 per cent now saw Johnson as 'best Prime Minister', down from 40 per cent a fortnight before, and his net approval rating had fallen from plus 6 to minus 6. This appeared to have impacted, too, on the party's support, even if the halving of its lead over Labour (from 13 to 6 points) was driven more by a rise in the latter's support than a decline in its own. And while approval of the government's handling of the vaccine roll-out was still phenomenally high (at 71 to 9 points), as many people now disapproved of its handling of the pandemic overall as approved of it, the former rising and the latter falling by 7 points over the fortnight.[45]

Still, Johnson could rely on the backing of ordinary party members, with a ConservativeHome readers' survey suggesting that only one in ten rank-and-file Tories both bought Cummings' critique and thought, as a result, that he should resign the premiership.[46] And because Opinium's depressing poll didn't come out until Sunday, 31 May, at least it didn't put a damper on his wedding on the Saturday – a 'bohemian, festival-style celebration' in the Downing Street garden following a formal ceremony at the Roman Catholic Westminster Cathedral.[47] Moreover, his nuptials weren't the only thing worth celebrating. Earlier in the week, Christopher Geidt, his ethics adviser, had concluded (rather too generously, perhaps) that the Conservative Party, as well as Tory donors, *had* initially stumped up for the costly 'Wallpapergate' refurb of the Downing Street flat, and that Johnson *had* acted 'unwisely' by commissioning the work without 'rigorous regard for how this would be funded'. However, he was persuaded that Johnson was initially unaware that a donor, David Brownlow, and the party had settled the bill, and that when he had realized, he had made a declaration of interests and repaid the money. As a result, Geidt decided, Johnson had not breached his own ministerial code.

In denial on institutional racism?

There was another silver lining to the Cummings cloud, too. His committee appearance had provided a proverbial good day to bury bad news – on this occasion the publication (after months during which it had apparently been sitting on Johnson's desk) of the Independent Inquiry into Alleged Discrimination within the Conservative Party chaired by Professor Swaran Singh, a former commissioner for the Equality and Human Rights Commission (EHRC).[48] Originally a response to Sajid Javid's call, during the 2019 leadership contest, for an investigation into Islamophobia, its remit, when set up, had widened (in order, critics argued, to soften the focus on what they believed was widespread anti-Muslim prejudice within the party's ranks). However, inasmuch as it discovered worrying levels of discrimination, the latter did seem to be mainly directed at Muslims, with two-thirds of complaints alleging discrimination directed at them. And it found failings in the ways those complaints were investigated, although it seemed anxious to excuse high-profile figures (such as Zac Goldsmith and Johnson himself) whom critics had accused of Islamophobia, eschewing harsh criticism in favour of words and phrases like 'insensitive' and 'poor judgement'.

Not everyone, then, agreed with Javid that it represented 'a candid and forthright account of discrimination in our party that doesn't pull its punches and isn't afraid to be blunt' – nor with his reassuring conclusion that 'There's no indication that anti-Muslim sentiment in the party is in any way institutional or systemic.'[49] Certainly, that seemed at odds with some of the evidence presented to the inquiry, most obviously by the anti-racist campaign group HOPE not hate, whose detailed survey of Conservative Party members had found, for instance, that almost half (47 per cent) saw Islam as 'a threat to the British way of life', while over half (58 per cent) believed 'there are no-go areas in Britain where Sharia law dominates and non-Muslims cannot enter'. Perhaps most disturbingly of all, a quarter (24 per cent) of rank-and-file Tories were worried that, because the country's Muslim population was growing faster than its non-Muslim population, Muslims would eventually replace white British people. In spite of all this (or maybe because of it), only one in ten members (9 per cent) thought the party had a problem with Islamophobia, and only one in six party members (17 per cent) felt that the party should be doing more to combat it and other forms of racism within its ranks.[50]

Not surprisingly then, an apology, and a promise to implement the report's recommendations (essentially an action plan, a code of conduct, an improved complaints procedure, and a training programme) that was swiftly issued by Party Co-Chairman Amanda Milling, didn't receive an unqualified welcome from campaigners and some of those affected, a number of whom had already expressed serious concerns about the conduct of the inquiry.[51] Sayeeda Warsi (who had once served as Party Chairman and who was herself Muslim), while welcoming the report, remained convinced that it had shown the party was indeed 'institutionally racist' and hoped (in vain, it turned out) that the EHRC could be persuaded to investigate further.[52]

Brexit, boats, by-elections – and ministers behaving badly

As May turned into June, there was good news and bad news on the health front. And that presented something of a problem. The first day of the month brought with it the announcement that, for the first time since the second week of March 2020, the UK had recorded no fatalities due to Covid, inevitably encouraging the party in the media to insist, as the *Mail* did on its front page, that there was now 'NOTHING TO

FEAR FROM FREEDOM'.[53] Covid Recovery Group luminaries Mark Harper and Graham Brady were also straight out of the gate urging the government to push ahead with reopening – all without mentioning the resignation a day or so before of Kevan Collins, Johnson's so-called 'Catch-up Tsar', in protest at the Treasury offering less than one-tenth of the money he estimated was needed to help children who had missed out on so much education.[54] Yet the speed with which the Delta variant was now spreading was causing serious concern among the government's scientific advisers – so much so that, despite what a hopeful Brady had labelled Johnson's 'instinct ... to move back to a world where people make their own choices and find their own balance of risks', the Prime Minister felt he had no option (even in the face of last-gasp pleas from the party in the media the day before) but to announce on 14 June that the government had decided to move so-called 'Freedom Day' from 21 June back to 19 July.

Tory MPs were, of course, deeply disappointed. Many of them had rather enjoyed the argy-bargy over the Northern Ireland Protocol between Johnson and his fellow EU leaders at the G7 summit in Cornwall a few days earlier – an event graced by David Frost (doubtless much to his own amusement) in Union Jack socks. And even more of them had welcomed the announcement – complete with prime ministerial photo-op in the back garden of Downing Street – of a trade deal with Australia, however infinitesimal the economic benefits that were expected to accrue to the UK as a consequence.[55] But this was a blow, and the usual suspects, including former leader Iain Duncan Smith (who'd only recently presented the PM with a little-noticed report on post-Brexit deregulation), were happy to share their frustration with the party in the media.[56] Fortunately for Johnson, however, the mood amongst most members of the parliamentary party was more-in-sorrow-than-in-anger. Moreover, the government, once again, could be pretty confident, from both private and public polling, that its decision to delay had overwhelming support out there in the country, especially as one moved up the age gradient.[57] Nevertheless, the fact that fifty-one MPs voted against the extension of Covid regulations when they came before parliament a few days later represented a significant shot across the bows, not least because many of those who chose not to rebel made it clear to the Whips that they would not hesitate if, God forbid, there was a next time.

Covid, of course, was not the only thing worrying Tories at Westminster and at the heart of government. With summer, for instance, came a sharp rise in migrants coming across the Channel in small boats, with the nearly 5,000 who had already arrived by the middle of June suggesting the previous year's total of 8,410 would soon be exceeded and making something of a mockery of the party's claim that Brexit would allow the UK to 'take back control' of its borders. This was something that Johnson (who, if he believed anything, believed in ensuring that the Conservative Party must never again risk being outflanked by a Farage-style radical right insurgency) was anxious to avoid at all costs – so much so that, according to one 'government source', he was becoming 'increasingly frustrated at the images of boats arriving day after day' and had asked a colleague, '"What the fuck is the Home Office doing? When is she [Priti Patel] going to sort this out?"'[58]

All that, however, quickly paled into insignificance when, in the early hours of 18 June, the party learned that it had lost the parliamentary by-election in Chesham and Amersham. The constituency, which had been Conservative since its creation in 1974, had been captured by the Liberal Democrats on a huge swing of 25 percentage points – more than sufficient to scare the pants off Tory MPs, especially (but not exclusively) those representing seats in southern England. Their instant analysis, in part driven by what some had heard when sent to campaign in the constituency, put the unexpected defeat down to voters' unhappiness with HS2, which was to run through the constituency, and, most of all, to their concerns (already widely shared by Tory MPs, of course) about the government's proposed relaxation of planning regulations. The upshot? The government needed to junk its legislation or at least go back to the drawing board. And, although only a couple of MPs ignored the Whips' Office (by now standard) advice that they should abstain on an Opposition motion condemning the government's proposals as a 'developers' charter' driven by donations from housebuilders, many used the debate on it to voice their concerns in no uncertain terms.[59] It was, however, a veteran, former leader William Hague, who best expressed the political risks of going ahead, using his weekly newspaper column to draw a worrying parallel with the poll tax in the late 1990s.[60]

The fall-out from a shock by-election defeat for the governing party, especially one that was blamed by its own MPs on one of its flagship policies, can often hog the headlines for a fortnight. Not this time, however. Within just a week, pretty much the whole country (and not just those who normally paid attention to politics) was talking about another political story entirely. The *Sun* had got hold of footage, captured by a hidden camera, of Health Secretary Matt Hancock, who was married with children, in 'a steamy clinch' with Gina Coladangelo, an old friend whom he had appointed as an unpaid adviser and later as a paid non-exec at the Department of Health and Social Care. Said footage wasn't merely embarrassing for Hancock (and presumably very upsetting for his wife, who was said to be suffering from long Covid, having apparently contracted the virus from her errant husband), it also showed he was in breach of the government's own Covid guidelines, which, at the time it was captured, prohibited intimate contact with someone from a different household.

Johnson, as was his wont (he was, after all, the last person wishing to see a politician lose their job as a result of intrusion into their private lives or because they'd broken the rules), initially hoped to hang on to Hancock, accepting his apology and letting it be known that he considered the matter closed. However, it very quickly became obvious, from the reaction both of the public and of his own MPs (including some ministers), that Hancock would have to go, especially when people were reminded how vocal he had been in his criticism of SAGE member Professor Neil Ferguson when the latter had been caught breaking the rules back in May 2020.[61] This was a view shared by some eight out of ten grassroots party members (many of whom, of course, were also inclined to identify Hancock with an overly cautious approach to Covid).[62] In any case, Johnson was able to find a ready replacement as Health Secretary in Sajid Javid, who was offered, and immediately accepted, his sixth Cabinet post in seven years.

Dominic Cummings, while presumably pleased that Hancock, whom he had spent weeks undermining, had finally gone, might not have been impressed that someone he regarded as little more than 'a friend of Carrie' had replaced him.[63] But the anti-lockdown hawks had cause to hope that the balance in Cabinet had now shifted in their favour, especially after Javid's first Commons appearance in his new role. Confirming that he saw 'no reason to go beyond July 19th' and declaring that 'No date we choose comes with zero-risk,' he added that 'We cannot eliminate it, instead we have to learn to live with it.' The fact that he then went on to declare that 'my task is to help return the economic and cultural life that makes this country so great' can only have added to the mounting excitement of the Covid Recovery Group, especially given that his rider – 'while of course protecting life and our NHS' – appeared to have been added almost as an afterthought.[64] Yet they may have been celebrating prematurely. Javid, after all, was one of the few ministers with a genuine affinity for numbers and data. As such, he was probably no more likely than the much-maligned Hancock to ignore whatever the evidence told him, even if he didn't always like it. Nor would he want to start by alienating his top scientific advisers, or the massed ranks of the NHS and its powerful policy community. He was also an elected politician. True, he was bound to fancy another tilt at the leadership someday, so naturally his parliamentary colleagues – including, of course, the lockdown sceptics – mattered. But so too did the voters. And polls showed that they were still cautious: while most people in the summer of 2021 were looking forward to more freedom, they, and especially those who were clinically vulnerable, didn't want it at any price – one reason why, after Javid was roundly criticized at the end of July for tweeting that we shouldn't 'cower' in the face of Covid, he swiftly deleted the tweet and apologized.[65]

All that optimism aside, the beginning of July had brought with it some disappointing news. The by-election in Batley and Spen, which the Tories had hoped, indeed expected, would go the way of Hartlepool, was won by Labour, albeit with a small majority – so small that it inevitably led people in the party to wonder whether Matt Hancock (who, incidentally, retained the support of his constituency association if not all his local councillors) had cost the Tories the seat.[66] Others, however, pointed to rather more prosaic (but in some ways more worrying) explanations: namely shortcomings in the party's ground campaign, with its get out the vote (GOTV) efforts hamstrung by predictive software that, as was often the case in the 2017 general election, proved unable to compensate for the fact that precious little Conservative canvassing had been done in the constituency for years.[67]

Free at last? Not so fast!

Any disappointment, however, soon drained away in the wake of the government's decision to go ahead with ending all Covid restrictions on 19 July, notwithstanding considerable nervousness in the scientific and medical community about doing so when case rates were still relatively high. Johnson, in making the announcement on 5 July, pointed, reasonably enough, to the fact that vaccination appeared to have broken the link between infection, on the one hand, and hospitalization and death, on the other. But his 'if not now, then when' argument was nevertheless somewhat disingenuous, suggesting as it did that the only alternative on offer was to end lockdown in the winter, when the NHS would be at its most vulnerable, rather than the gradual phasing out of measures so the impact of any changes made could be properly assessed. And, in the end, Johnson dared not back out of the decision to go ahead even in the face of continuing concerns about Delta. That said, the run-up to 'Freedom Day' saw him urging caution. It also saw government, much to the chagrin of lockdown sceptics on the backbenches, indicate, firstly, that large venues would be asked to demand proof of vaccination using the NHS app in an apparent change of heart on domestic 'vaccine passports' and, secondly, that rules on self-isolation would stay – a decision that Johnson and Sunak were to fall foul of at the end of the month when, just as the party in the media was obsessing about the so-called 'pingdemic' needlessly preventing millions of healthy Brits going to work, they attempted (until they were forced to reverse course owing to the subsequent outcry) to claim that their participation in an obscure 'pilot project' freed them of the need to obey the rules that they expected the rest of the country to follow.[68]

The Covid Recovery Group was also up in arms about plans to ban unvaccinated workers from entering care homes from the autumn – so much so that thirty of them (including 1922 Chairman Graham Brady, who the week before had survived Number Ten's attempt to replace him in that role with a more biddable alternative) voted against the government on the issue in the middle of the month.[69] For the media, however, this was now such a common occurrence that far more attention was paid to what actually turned out to be a smaller rebellion against the government at around the same time – this one on a vote sprung on Tory MPs opposed to Rishi Sunak's decision to renege (he claimed temporarily) on the UK's Cameron-era commitment to devote 0.7 per cent of gross national income to foreign aid spending, the only alternative to which, apparently, was a huge tax increase. In the end, after a ferocious whipping operation during which threats were allegedly made to withdraw funding allocated to their constituencies, only twenty-four MPs voted against what amounted to a £4 billion cut. For one of the rebels, Theresa May, defying the whip for the first time ever, the measure meant that 'fewer girls will be educated, more girls and boys will become slaves, more children will go hungry and more of the poorest people in the world will die'.[70] These were concerns shared by many of her colleagues who voted with the government, but they were also well aware that the majority of the public (and an overwhelming majority of grassroots Tories) were on the government's side on the issue.[71]

The opposite was almost certainly true when it came to some of the earliest statements made by government ministers on the issue of England's footballers, by then involved in the European Championships, showing solidarity with anti-racist campaigns by 'taking the knee' just before their games kicked off. In the first week of July, Johnson had conspicuously (but, given the government's ongoing 'war on woke', predictably) passed up the opportunity to condemn those fans who booed players for doing so, although a few days later his spokesman, responding to criticism, said he would prefer to see 'everybody getting behind the team to cheer them on, not boo'. Back in June, Skills Minister Gillian Keegan told BBC's *Question Time* that Black Lives Matter was 'really about defunding the police and the overthrow of capitalism', that the England players were 'creating new divisions', and that 'the people who are booing, I'm pretty sure most of them would like to end racism as well'. Home Secretary Priti Patel had likewise refused to condemn booing the players, telling the newly launched GB News channel, 'I just don't support people [i.e. the players] participating in that type of gesture politics.' Once the tournament started, however, she at least affected to be a strong supporter of the England team, even sharing a picture of herself on social media wearing its shirt cheering them on – something that Tory backbencher Lee Anderson, a supposedly archetypal 'Red Waller', could not do on account of his (mercilessly mocked) public promise not to watch the national team while the players continued to take the knee. This did not, however, save Patel from a brutal put-down by one of them when, in the wake of some of his teammates suffering racial abuse after they missed penalties in the final against Italy, she tweeted her support for them: 'You don't get to stoke the fire at the beginning of the tournament', replied Tyrone Mings, 'by labelling our anti-racism message as "Gesture Politics" and then pretend to be disgusted when the very thing we're campaigning against happens.'[72]

Something which *wasn't* happening, but which many Tory MPs, especially those from the so-called 'Red Wall', knew needed to happen – or at least look like it was beginning to happen – was 'levelling up'. A White Paper was supposedly in the works but was months away. Number Ten therefore decided Johnson should make a big speech which would at least set out the vision behind the idea, as well as reassuring people (and especially colleagues representing southern seats) that it was not about hitting up their constituents in order to pay for better infrastructure, services, and opportunities in newly won seats in the North and the Midlands. Unfortunately, his address was so devoid of substance that it was widely dismissed if not panned, leaving many 'Red Wallers' at Westminster (who had earlier in the month learned of the failure of their long-running campaign to persuade the Chancellor to make the £20 per week uplift in Universal Credit permanent) none the wiser and not a little worried.[73] Indeed, the only thing that his MPs were clearer about after Johnson's speech than before it – and only because he answered journalists' questions on it when he'd finished – was that he had next to no intention of implementing any of the suggestions made in the just-published National Food Strategy. In it, the government's 'Food Tsar', Henry Dimbleby, had demanded, among other things, that it take urgent action, not least via taxation, to reduce salt and sugar consumption – an idea which, unsurprisingly, horrified the party in the media, which, in common with many Tory MPs, regarded the imposition of any additional costs and constraints on business as anathema.[74]

Johnson wasn't the only one, however, receiving poor reviews. That Dominic Cummings, who had done a long interview with the BBC's Political Editor, Laura Kuenssberg, was as well doubtless cheered him up. But the fact that Home Secretary Priti Patel was another was more worrying. True, at the beginning of July she had earned plaudits for her Nationality and Borders Bill, which would, among other things, effectively criminalize asylum seekers who entered the UK from other safe countries where they could have claimed first, all in the hope that it would make them easier to deport. However, by the end of the month, her ongoing failure to stop the small boats in which many of them were now arriving was attracting renewed criticism, especially after it was revealed that, by the third week of July, the previous year's total had already been exceeded. And, not surprisingly, there was widespread scepticism, not to say hostility, towards her plan to pay the French tens of millions of pounds to step up the policing of their coastline. She was also in trouble with frontline police officers back at home. The Police Federation even went so far as to pass a vote of no confidence in her over pay, its irritation spilling over into its rejection of the government's much-hyped Beating Crime plan, with its chair arguing in an open letter to Johnson that, 'We don't need old ideas presented as new, we need genuine investment for the whole of the criminal justice system and genuine consultation over new ideas. Without that, this is just another ill-thought-out initiative.'[75]

Criticism of the government's failure to stop migrants crossing the Channel continued into August, not least after records were broken in the first week of the month when getting on for 500 made it over in one day. Patel was naturally quick to join the party in the media in slamming lawyers who made it difficult for the Home Office to deport foreign criminals, but neither that nor her tirades against the French authorities were sufficient to distract from the fact that so many people (nearly 900 on one day in late August) were making it over to the UK from France. And even when a bigger story did blow up – the fall of the Afghan capital Kabul to the Taliban and the subsequent discovery, firstly, that Foreign Secretary Dominic Raab had delayed returning from his beach holiday in Greece and, secondly, that the Prime Minister (and perhaps his wife) had helped a charity to evacuate cats and dogs rather than people – Patel could not escape criticism, and not just from Opposition MPs, for her role in the débâcle.[76] Firstly, the Home Office had not facilitated (and, in some cases, appeared to have actually blocked) the entry of Afghan interpreters who had worked for the government or the armed forces. Then there was the Home Secretary's insistence that the UK would be unable to take more than 5,000 Afghans per year (up to a maximum of just 20,000) on the government's hastily arranged Resettlement Scheme. And it wasn't just Patel and Raab in trouble with disappointed and sometimes furious Tory backbenchers: the Prime Minister himself had a particularly difficult time of it when the Commons (its chamber probably as full now as it had been pre-Covid, albeit with MPs on the Opposition, but not the government, benches wearing face coverings) debated the issue on 18 August.[77]

Tensions – and changes – at the top

Had Johnson otherwise been riding high in his party's, his colleagues', and the public's estimation, the criticism he got might have been all in a day's work. But he wasn't. Tensions had been running high between Number Ten and Number Eleven since the beginning of August, after the *Sunday Times* splashed on a letter from Sunak to Johnson which appeared designed to demonstrate (not for the first time) that the former was keener than the latter on lifting Covid restrictions – a leak which had so enraged the Prime Minister that he'd reportedly even talked about sacking his next-door neighbour.[78] It hadn't helped that ConservativeHome's readers' survey of party members had seen Johnson's net satisfaction rating fall by 36 percentage points in a month, leaving him on only plus 3 per cent, while Sunak's had held steady on plus 74 per cent.[79] The party in the media, now renewing its occasionally hysterical campaign to get people back to the office (and presumably buying more newspapers on their way there), was also stirring the pot, writing up polling which suggested that Sunak (very much a 'back to the office' advocate) was a more popular choice for PM than his boss among voters as a whole – and not that far off when it came to Tory voters either.[80]

Tensions between the two men, however, weren't purely personal. Behind closed doors (and, as usual, via self-interested briefing to the media), they were also in negotiations (along with Sajid Javid) over how, precisely, to fund social care and the Health Service's attempt to clear the massive backlog caused by Covid. Other ministers – especially those desperate to polish their Thatcherite credentials – also talked (or had their 'friends' talk) to journalists, with Liz Truss, Jacob Rees-Mogg, and David Frost (who had clearly begun to see himself as a full-time politician and even, perhaps, as a future Tory leader) most often mentioned as being critical of tax rises. In the end, however, they had little choice but to accept the compromise agreed to by Johnson, Javid, and Sunak: a 1.25 percentage point increase in National Insurance paid by both employees and employers that would eventually show up on people's payslips as a ring-fenced 'Health and Social Care levy' worth about £12 billion a year. Half would go to the NHS in England in the first instance, with the proportion devoted to social care supposedly rising once the Health Service had cleared its backlog, meaning (apparently anyway – it later emerged as rather more complicated than it first appeared) that, from October 2023, no-one would have to pay more than £86,000 for their care. Taxable income from shares would also see a 1.25 per cent rate increase, while, more controversially, the government was suspending its 'triple lock' on pensions since the post-pandemic rise in wages would otherwise have seen it obliged to uprate them by 8 per cent in a year. An increase of that magnitude was not only deemed unaffordable but would also have contrasted rather too sharply with a tax hike that applied only to employees under pensionable age who, irrespective of how well-off they were, were expected to fund a scheme that (in theory if not necessarily in practice) would prevent relatively wealthy old people from having to sell their homes to pay for social care.

As it was, polling suggested voters were either doubtful or else split on the wisdom of the plans, with the biggest divides down to party affiliation (Tory voters being most supportive) and age, with over 65's predictably miffed over the pensions triple lock but more pleased than younger age groups about the National Insurance rise, even though, in reality, the latter was no less of a breach of a promise made by the Conservatives in their 2019 election manifesto.[81] As for the party in the media, it seemed largely pleased that money was going to social care and the NHS but nevertheless extremely concerned about adding to a tax burden it felt was already way too high, with some regulars in the comment pages positively fuming – none more so than the *Telegraph*'s Allister Heath: 'Shame on Boris Johnson,' he declared, 'and shame on the Conservative Party. They have disgraced themselves, lied to their voters, repudiated their principles and treated millions of their supporters with utter contempt.'[82] Fortunately, if the number of MPs who rebelled against the plan was a measure of anything, only 5 Conservative MPs seemed to agree, although another 37 abstained, suggesting they had their doubts too. And when the legislation required to implement the tax rise came before the Commons the following week, it passed all its stages in just one day, with only 10 Tories voting against, albeit 44 abstaining.

Now that he had secured a deal on health and social care, Johnson could at last go ahead with a reshuffle he had been planning for some time but had delayed so as to keep ambitious colleagues in line during what otherwise might have been a fraught fortnight. Long-term liabilities Gavin Williamson and Robert Jenrick left the government altogether while Dominic Raab was given the title of Deputy Prime Minister but demoted from the Foreign Office to the Ministry of Justice, with Robert Buckland (actually a solid performer) making way. Liz Truss replaced Raab as Foreign Secretary, with Anne-Marie Trevelyan taking her place at International Trade. Nadhim Zahawi was promoted to Education Secretary, while Michael Gove (notwithstanding the personal political donations he'd apparently received from developers that year) moved sideways to become Housing Secretary, his mission to salvage something from the wreckage of Jenrick's planning proposals and to take forward levelling up, as well as resolving the all-too-easily forgotten post-Grenfell cladding scandal.[83] The combative culture warrior Oliver Dowden was appointed Party Co-Chairman and tasked with gearing up CCHQ for the next election, while, outside parliament, Ben Elliot continued to raise the money to fight it. Dowden was replaced as Culture Secretary by Nadine Dorries – perhaps Johnson's biggest fan and, as an even more forthright enemy of all things 'woke' and 'Remoaner' than Dowden himself, practically guaranteed to annoy all the right people. Meanwhile, Priti Patel hung on to the Home Office: even if she still couldn't stop those small boats (the previous monthly record for asylum seekers landing in Kent, set in July, was soon to be broken again), she could bang on about migration like no-one else, her heritage helping to insulate her from charges of racism and her hardline rhetoric helping to ensure no space opened up on the Conservatives' flank for a full-blown post-Farage populist party. David Frost likewise stayed in post. So did Rishi Sunak – not just because he was too popular to move, but also because his reputation as a fiscal hawk provided a degree of reassurance to the party's Thatcherite purists that Johnson hadn't led the Tories entirely off the small-state straight and narrow.

More generally, the number of women attending Cabinet increased from six to eight, making up 27 per cent of the whole. Meanwhile, the proportion of attendees who had been privately educated dropped slightly from 65 per cent to 60 per cent, although that was still a greater proportion than the 44 per cent of the parliamentary Conservative Party who had attended fee-paying schools. Accordingly, the number of Cabinet ministers educated at state comprehensives rose from just over quarter to a third. For aficionados of British school sports, however, that didn't seem to impact much on Johnson's 'half-time' pep talk to his newly assembled team: 'This is the moment,' he told them, 'when we spit out the orange peel, we adjust our gum shields and our scrum caps.'

Two of those state-educated ministers, Home Secretary Priti Patel and Transport Secretary Grant Shapps (who, like her, had been reappointed), were pretty soon winning plaudits for the tough stance they were taking on one of the party in the media's *bêtes noires*: the militant environmentalists belonging to Insulate Britain, whose non-violent direct action had become notorious for holding up traffic. Yet it wasn't long before they ran into trouble with colleagues, with the public, and with the party in the media as the ongoing, post-Brexit and post-pandemic shortage of truck drivers – not least tanker drivers who deliver petrol to service stations – became increasingly acute. Not only that but, on this issue, they found themselves on different sides. Shapps may not have been among those ministers keenest to increase the number of visas available to overseas drivers, but he was definitely not as dug in as Patel (and Business Secretary Kwasi Kwarteng), who continued to hold to the idea that UK employers (in all sectors) needed to be weaned off cheaper foreign workers and instead train and properly pay Brits to do the job. Characteristically, Johnson, by now under severe pressure to put an end to the crisis as the party got ready to meet in Manchester for its first face-to-face annual conference since 2019, attempted to have his cake and eat it. On the one hand, he told the BBC's Andrew Marr in his big pre-party conference interview that, in keeping with what people voted for in 2016, the government was calling time on 'the broken model of the UK economy that relied on low wages and low skill and chronic low productivity' and that 'The way forward for our country is not to just pull the big lever marked "uncontrolled immigration".' On the other hand, as well as bringing in the army to help out, he quietly saw to it that an additional 5,000 visas were made available.

As for Johnson's leader's speech to conference, there was, as always, nothing quiet about it. Indeed, it felt to some of those watching more like an after-dinner affair: plenty of patriotism, oodles of optimism, joke after joke, and not much else besides, apart, perhaps, from a brief defence of the government's reluctant decision to tax rather than borrow, a passing plea for folk to get back to the office, a short reprise of his call for a high-wage, low-tax economy, and, of course, some bog-standard Labour-bashing. As such, it did little more than double down on the messages delivered earlier in the week by other ministers. Rishi Sunak, for example, after a casual reminder that (unlike his leadership rival Liz Truss) he had always been a Brexiteer, had condemned excessive borrowing as 'not just economically irresponsible' but actually 'immoral'. And the party's new Co-Chairman, Oliver Dowden, had assured his audience that the government was working tirelessly to keep statues of 'national heroes like Nelson, Gladstone and Churchill in the places of honour they deserve' – in marked contrast to a Labour Party that had 'woke running through it like a stick of Brighton rock'.

But although Johnson's speech went down a storm in the auditorium (which for other speakers had been reconfigured to reduce its capacity so as to ensure it didn't look too empty), it was never going to impress everyone. It didn't, for instance, do much for those business people who were already smarting after 'a source close to a senior Cabinet Minister' had told the *Telegraph* earlier in the week that British firms were 'drunk on cheap labour' from abroad.[84] Indeed, that briefing had prompted one hacked-off entrepreneur, referring to a series of CCHQ videos of the PM drinking beer, buttering toast, and eating fish and chips to promote his 'Build Back Better' slogan via a series of (deliberately?) lame puns, to declare that 'Boris can shove his butter up his backside.'[85] The PM's colleagues might not have gone quite so far, but some of them were nevertheless worried lest the government be seen as anti-business. All in all, however, they had to admit that conference as a whole hadn't gone too badly in the circumstances. Some even left Manchester with their morale boosted. Whether things were genuinely on the up, though, who could really tell?

Things fall apart
(October 2021–April 2022)

Conference may have been over but Covid wasn't. The second week of October saw the long-awaited joint report into the UK's handling of the pandemic by the Commons Science and Health Select Committees.[1] Fortunately for the government, however, its authors chose to balance their pretty sobering criticism of the initial response with plenty of praise for the vaccine programme. And in any case, the current Health Secretary, having been in post for only a month or two, could hardly be blamed for any of the failings identified. Sajid Javid was more inclined anyway to look to the present and to the future. As far as the former was concerned, he responded to complaints from patients and the party in the media (with the *Mail* in the vanguard) by announcing funding (and even, although he soon distanced himself from the suggestion, some sort of league table) to encourage GPs to see as many people as possible face-to-face rather than remotely.[2] As for the future, the fact that the UK seemed to be facing far higher infection rates than comparable countries was beginning to give serious cause for concern, prompting calls by some experts for Javid to implement his so-called 'Plan B' (which might involve measures such as obliging people to wear face coverings in certain areas, a return to rules around social distancing and numbers of people who could meet, and maybe even instructions to work from home).

Javid's response (which had arguably been the government's standard response for most of the pandemic) was to hang fire unless there were clear signs that the NHS risked being overwhelmed and to focus on speeding up the provision of booster shots since the protection conferred by being 'double-jabbed' was now beginning to wane for many, particularly in older age groups. Speaking at his first Downing Street press conference on 20 October, he also urged the public to meet outdoors where possible, to take frequent lateral-flow tests, and to wear face coverings in crowded enclosed spaces. The last of these recommendations obliged him to acknowledge that Conservative MPs (whose dogged refusal to wear masks in the Commons chamber had become something of a badge of honour for lockdown sceptics) should 'set an example'. He was soon contradicted both by the PM's spokesman, who stressed masking up remained a matter of personal choice, and, perhaps most annoyingly, by his Cabinet colleague Leader of the House Jacob Rees-Mogg, who claimed in an interview that the advice on face coverings only covered 'crowded spaces with people that you don't know. We on this side know each other.' In reality, however, Javid's words did seem to have some impact: for a while at least, more Tory MPs seemed to be wearing face coverings, maybe even as a *quid pro quo* for the Treasury and the Cabinet Office finally publishing a cost–benefit analysis of a return to restrictions, which, strategically leaked to the media, suggested that the country and the government would incur astronomical costs for no great health gain.[3]

The public finances were, of course, much in the news as Sunak's autumn Budget and Spending Review approached, in part, at least, because tensions between Chancellor and Prime Minister were still running fairly high. Although the tragic murder of Tory MP David Amess by an Islamist terrorist continued to dominate the media's political coverage, the *Observer* had still found room to run a story based on a leak of Treasury documents that suggested it was seriously worried about the costs of moving to net zero – costs which MPs in the Net Zero Scrutiny Group (NZSG), set up by Steve Baker and Craig Mackinlay, had been warning about for some time, along with the party in the media.[4] Rightly or wrongly, the Treasury's position, and the leak, was interpreted by some as an attempt by Sunak to signal, in the words of one of the paper's sources, that he (like them and a fair few grassroots members) was 'not really down with this green stuff' and wanted 'Boris to own the whole agenda' – and to do so just as the PM was about to unveil the government's plans (immediately criticized by experts as being inadequately resourced) on decarbonizing domestic heating.[5] Johnson was, of course, aware that there were considerable doubts in his own ranks about the affordability of the move to net zero, especially for voters in the fabled 'Red Wall', who, some MPs seemed to assume (despite polling evidence to the contrary), were every bit as sceptical as they were about climate change and the policies needed to tackle it.[6] He therefore took to the pages of the *Sun* to reassure the nation that, 'while we're going to have to make some pretty major changes to the way we heat our homes, the Greenshirts of the Boiler Police are not going to kick in your door with their sandal-clad feet and seize, at carrot-point, your trusty old combi'.[7] Sadly for him, however, the *Sun* was having none of it, its leader the next day (in addition to carrying its now traditional warning to the Chancellor not to raise fuel duty) declaring, 'We fear net zero may become a millstone round our economy's neck while other nations less committed to it thrive.'[8] Nor was it the only organ of the party in the media to express its doubts.[9]

As for the Budget and Spending Review itself, Sunak – urged on by Johnson – affected to loosen the purse strings. The economy had bounced back from the pandemic and given him more money to play with. So, rather than squirrelling all of it away to finance the cuts in personal taxation that he signalled he intended to make towards the end of the parliament, the Chancellor provided a more generous increase in departmental budgets across the piece than many had expected. He also announced additional money for transport projects and the NHS, an increase in the national living wage, the end of the pay-freeze for most public sector employees, and a reduction in the marginal rates paid by those in work but on Universal Credit which would ensure that they (though not the 60 per cent on UC who weren't in employment) would no longer lose out from his decision to end the £20 per week uplift that had applied during the pandemic. And for those sectors that the lockdown had hit particularly hard – retail, hospitality, and leisure – Sunak announced discounts on business rates as well a reform of alcohol duty which would make lower-strength and draught drinks cheaper.

How comfortable the Chancellor (as opposed to the Prime Minister) was with all this was a moot point. Certainly, there seemed to be a mismatch between some of the measures and his rhetoric, most notably, 'Now, we have a choice. Do we want to live in a country where the response to every question is: "What is the government going to do about it?" … Or do we choose to recognise that government has limits. That government *should* have limits.' However, at least Sunak could console himself in the immediate aftermath with the fact that the initial response from the public (as measured by a couple of snap polls) seemed to be broadly positive, even if the Speaker of the House of Commons, Lindsay Hoyle, remained furious that so many of the measures had been 'pre-announced' in the week running up to his speech. He also seemed to have been given the benefit of the doubt when he addressed Tory MPs later in the day at a meeting of the 1922 Committee, especially after assuring them that 'every marginal pound we have should be put into lowering people's taxes'. And the same could be said of the party in the media – judging, at least from the front pages, which (much to the satisfaction of the spinners who had set up a photo-op for Sunak and Johnson in a pub) ran with the cut to alcohol duty.[10]

Sadly, however, things went downhill from there. ConservativeHome's readers' survey of grassroots members showed well over a third of them weren't happy with the Budget and Spending Review and a further fifth were reserving judgement, leaving only just over four in ten who said they were satisfied.[11] And no wonder: digging into the small print, the left-leaning Resolution Foundation calculated that taxes would be £3,000 more per household than when Johnson entered Number Ten, while the Institute for Fiscal Studies and the Office for Budget Responsibility both forecast most people would be no better off and possibly worse off for the foreseeable future. Moreover, not for the first time, a more detailed look at the spending increases outlined in the Budget suggested that many of them weren't all that they seemed either, partly because they didn't actually involve any new money and partly because, even where they did, they couldn't possibly make up for the cuts to departmental budgets over a decade of austerity.[12] For the party in the media, of course, this was not so much the problem: it was far more concerned with what it saw as yet more evidence that the government (indeed, the state as a whole) was moving away from its limited-government, low-tax ideal.[13] Two days of debate in the Commons suggested that those concerns were shared by plenty of Conservative MPs, including Theresa May. Having had time to digest it all, the public (already less taken with Sunak than they had been when he'd been paying the bulk of their wages) weren't quite as enthusiastic as they'd first seemed either, with only 15 per cent telling one pollster that the Budget would help people like them and 54 per cent saying it would not.[14]

A friend in need: Owen Paterson

By then, however, the Westminster caravan had already moved on. Following a hard-hitting report from the Parliamentary Commissioner on Standards, Kathryn Stone, MPs on the cross-party Committee on Standards had unanimously agreed that the veteran Conservative MP, and former Cabinet minister, Owen Paterson should be suspended from the Commons for breaching its rules on paid advocacy, the length of the suspension (thirty days) opening up the possibility of a recall petition and a by-election in his North Shropshire constituency.[15] Paterson insisted, however, that he was blameless and had been denied natural justice. Moreover, as a prominent Brexiteer, he was able to call upon high-profile colleagues and friends in the party in the media to campaign on his behalf.[16] Partly as a result, Johnson, instead of leaving well alone, was persuaded (by, among others, Jacob Rees-Mogg) to take the extraordinary step of throwing the government's weight behind an amendment which halted Paterson's suspension while a new committee, with a Conservative majority, examined changes to the rules.

It was obvious, however, that many Tory MPs (especially those who were relatively new to the Commons and who had not therefore served for years alongside Paterson in the Eurosceptic trenches) were uneasy about the plan. Notwithstanding the three-line whip imposed on them and, some alleged, threats to row back on promises of government funding for improvements in their constituencies, thirteen rebelled and even more abstained. As for the Opposition parties, they immediately announced they would have nothing to do with the new committee. Meanwhile the whole idea got a thumbs-down in the press, not least from true-blue papers like the *Mail*, even if the latter seemed to want to blame MPs in general rather than just those on the Tory benches.[17] As a result, and notwithstanding Business Secretary Kwasi Kwarteng having effectively called on Kathryn Stone to resign just hours earlier on live television, Johnson (who was no fan of Stone, especially after she'd concluded over the summer that he'd broken the rules with regard to declaring who'd paid for his post-election break in Mustique) ordered a climb-down. Paterson, not surprisingly, took this sudden reversal of fortune badly, and announced he was stepping down from parliament.[18]

That Paterson's decision meant a by-election wasn't initially seen as too much of a problem. After all, although opinion polls suggested that, across the nation as a whole, Labour had drawn pretty much level with the Conservatives, Paterson had won two-thirds of the vote in largely rural, Leave-voting North Shropshire at the 2019 general election. As a result, he had won a majority of nearly 23,000, with Labour a very poor second and the Liberal Democrats – the UK's by-election specialists – trailing in third place with just a 10 per cent share of the vote. What worried Conservatives at Westminster more to begin with, then, was the way the Paterson affair had allowed the government's opponents to revive accusations of 'Tory sleaze' that had done the party so much harm back in the 1990s. It had allowed them, too, to bring up the awkward issue of so-called 'second jobs' – jobs which so many Conservative MPs (some of whom now found themselves featuring, with their additional earnings made plain for all to see, in the newspapers) relied upon to keep their families in the style to which they'd become accustomed.[19] Even worse, it meant that Labour's leader, Keir Starmer, who generally speaking hadn't really given them too much to worry about, was, as a former Director of Public Prosecutions, in his element. Throw in a top lawyer on their own side – former Attorney General Geoffrey Cox – who appeared to be earning an absolute fortune outside parliament (and spending an awful lot of time in exotic locations doing it) and the whole thing was threatening to spin out of control.[20] Indeed, polling commissioned by the *Mail* – one of a number of papers whose political allegiances couldn't on this occasion trump their nose for a good story – suggested a good deal of damage had already been done: more than half of respondents (53 per cent) thought the Prime Minister was 'sleazy', with only a fifth (20 per cent) saying the same of the Labour leader. Similarly, nearly half (46 per cent) reckoned the Conservative Party as a whole was 'sleazy', while fewer than one in five (17 per cent) would apply the description to Labour; equally worrying for those Tory MPs relying on the extra cash, six in ten Brits apparently believed MPs should be banned from having second jobs.[21]

Under pressure from the Opposition, Johnson eventually responded, midway through November, by writing to the Speaker proposing what was inevitably labelled 'a crackdown' on second jobs – much to the chagrin of the MPs who might be affected, one of whom complained to the *Mail* that 'He's gone from circling the wagons to handing us over to the Indians.' Ultimately, in fact, they needn't have worried too much: by the spring of 2022, it was agreed that while the rules around roles that blurred the line between consultancy and lobbying were tightened, no limits were imposed on the time or the money involved. At the time, however, Johnson came as near to apologizing to his MPs as he ever did, admitting in a meeting of the 1922 Committee designed to turn a page on the whole sorry business that he'd 'crashed the car into a ditch'.

Saving the planet, social care, and small boats

'Sleaze' wasn't, of course, the only thing Johnson had to deal with that autumn, although it had sometimes bled, very embarrassingly, into other business – most obviously when he was obliged to deny in front of the world's press during COP26 in Glasgow that Britain was a corrupt country. That meeting, taken as a whole, wasn't quite as disappointing as some climate scientists (and its Chair, the Tory MP Alok Sharma) had feared, although whether the promises extracted (after being controversially watered down) from the states that contribute most to the heating of the planet were really worth anything was, as always, a worry. Conservatives at Westminster, however, had more immediate concerns. Some northern MPs, for example, were upset at the government's decision to scale back its ambitions for both Northern Powerhouse Rail and HS2, although others – particularly those in constituencies (Rother Valley, Ashfield, Bolsover, North East Derbyshire, and Penistone and Stocksbridge) which the latter had been due to pass through but not to benefit directly – were pleased. Infrastructure, after all, may sound marvellous but it is also extremely disruptive and extremely expensive to build, and it rarely butters any electoral parsnips in the short term. Northern MPs were also disturbed to learn that, as a result of a change to the way contributions to the costs were measured, their constituents, living as most of them did in regions where housing was relatively affordable, were far less likely to feel the full benefit of the government's social care reform. On this occasion, however, discretion seemed to be the better part of valour. True, nineteen Tory MPs voted against the change when it was brought before the Commons, with nearly seventy absent or abstaining, even obliging ministers to dash away earlier from the Conservatives' fundraiser, the Winter Ball, where an hour's cricket with the Chancellor was auctioned off for £35,000, while dinner with Michael Gove went for £25,000 and karaoke with Liz Truss for £22,000. Yet, in spite of the fact that research suggested that their voters were unhappy about the change, at least when they were alerted to it, they (and, just as significantly, the party in the media) ultimately chose not to prolong the fuss, possibly because the only alternative was said to be additional taxes.[22]

In fact, as autumn began to turn into winter, more concern was expressed about the continued arrival of migrants crossing over from France in small boats. On 11 November, 1,185 made it over, bringing the total to more than 23,000 for the year so far, which was getting on for three times the total for the whole of 2020. This prompted an exasperated Johnson to draft in Cabinet Office Minister Steve Barclay to chair a cross-departmental committee charged with getting a grip on the situation. Undeterred by this tacit criticism (or, indeed, by Albania's denials that it was in negotiations to take asylum seekers off Britain's hands), Priti Patel, journalists were briefed, was considering further toughening up the conditions under which asylum seekers would be held once they reached the UK.[23] She was also supposedly furious, not just with France and other European countries in the Schengen system, but also with Home Office civil servants whom she apparently considered 'not fit for purpose' – briefing which inevitably drew a response from one of them to the effect that 'her suggestions are erratic and outlandish. Any sensible, mature politician would know they are never going to work, but she just comes out with it anyway. Officials come out of the meetings and the texts start flying, describing her as a "moron".'[24] Meanwhile, the party in the media carried hostile, albeit anonymous, briefings against Patel from ministerial colleagues and donors, along with polling that showed 55 per cent of the public and 77 per cent of 2019 Tory voters thought the government's approach to managing Channel crossings was 'too soft', with both Patel and Johnson being rated negatively on the issue by just over half of respondents and only a fifth giving them a positive rating.[25] The news that around thirty people crowded together on an inflatable dinghy had tragically died attempting to make the crossing on 24 November was only likely to upset even more voters, prompting Patel to take to the pages of the country's best-selling red-top to claim (rather ironically, perhaps, given she seemed to have spent most of her time as Home Secretary coming up with schemes that were going to solve the problem once and for all) that, while she understood their frustration, there was 'no magic wand' with which she could wave it away.[26]

Peppa, parties, and 'Plan B'

In fact, 'small boats' wasn't the only issue on which the government and Prime Minister were being given the thumbs-down, and polls were beginning to show Labour at last overtaking the Conservatives. Even Rishi Sunak was now in negative territory, which may or may not have been behind yet another outbreak of anonymous sniping at each other from Numbers Ten and Eleven, especially in the wake of a rambling and confusing speech given by the Prime Minister to the CBI that had seen him lose both his place and his thread. The fact that (much to the bewilderment of his audience but the amusement of journalists for days afterwards) Johnson had also burbled on about children's TV show *Peppa Pig* only increased calls from MPs, and from the party in the media, for him to 'steady the ship' and 'sort out the Downing Street operation' (as if that, rather than the PM himself, were the problem).[27] As was its wont, however, Covid very soon ensured that the party's loudest voices abruptly switched their focus. As reports came in of a new variant – labelled Omicron – that was apparently far more transmissible than its predecessors, they scrambled once again to warn the government (which had already decided, in the words of *Sun* veteran Trevor Kavanagh, to again make 'face-nappies compulsory for shops and public transport') not to heed the advice of 'scaremongering SAGE scientists demanding a new crackdown'.[28] Urged on by the Covid Recovery Group's now familiar cast of characters, some twenty Tory MPs voted against mandating masks when the legislation came before the Commons, and thirty-three voted against new rules making ten-day isolation compulsory for anyone coming into contact with an Omicron case, with Steve Baker declaring during the debate that the country faced 'a fundamental choice between heading towards heaven and heading towards hell'.

The government's response was to promise to accelerate the booster programme and, needless to say, insist that people didn't need to worry about Christmas: there was certainly no need to cancel any parties they had planned, claimed Johnson – a message that provided the perfect hook for a front-page story in the *Mirror* which set off a chain of events that, over time, would help to spell the end of his premiership. In the run-up to Christmas 2020, reported its Political Editor, Pippa Crerar,

Number Ten had hosted a number of parties in clear contravention of Covid regulations in force at the time.[29]

Over the next few days, it quickly became apparent, especially to those ministers tasked with doing broadcast rounds, that parroting the official line that guidelines had been followed at all times was not going to work – not when journalists from other outlets were beginning to dig up more evidence that they most certainly hadn't been. Opinion polls swiftly showed that the story was cutting through with the public, that they were angry about being lied to, and that, as 72 per cent of respondents (including 58 per cent of Tory voters) told Savanta ComRes, there appeared to have been one rule for the government and one rule for everyone else.[30] Things only got worse when ITV News's Paul Brand got hold of a video of a training session for the televised daily press conferences Number Ten had planned but eventually decided not to go ahead with. Shot in December 2020 in the £2.6 million media suite that it had built especially for them, it showed Downing Street staff laughing and joking about the parties, and in short order prompted the tearful resignation of one of those involved, the PM's former Press Secretary, Allegra Stratton.[31] Polling firms across the board were now reporting that the majority of voters wanted Johnson (who claimed, rather implausibly, to have been 'sickened' by the footage and promised the Cabinet Secretary would conduct an internal inquiry) to resign. And any hope that Tory MPs might go in to bat for him evaporated when, simultaneously, the alarming rise in Covid cases prompted by the highly transmissible Omicron variant obliged the government to move, to all intents and purposes, to its 'Plan B'. This meant the renewal of advice to work from home, a move towards face coverings being required in all indoor venues (save, not particularly logically, pubs and restaurants), and 'vaccine passports' being required for entry to large indoor and outdoor gatherings. This practically guaranteed that the party in the media would show no mercy, with the front pages of the top-selling *Mail* ('ONE RULE FOR THEM, NEW RULES FOR THE REST OF US') and *Sun* ('DO AS I SAY … NOT AS I CHRISTMAS DO', featuring Johnson photoshopped as the Grinch) making for particularly brutal reading, while the *Telegraph*'s Allister Heath claimed to have detected 'an overpowering fin-de-regime stench emanating from Downing Street'.[32]

The only crumb of comfort was that, so far, only one MP – Douglas Ross, who, although he was leader of the Scottish Tories, was not a familiar face to voters in other parts of the UK – had suggested Johnson might have to resign should it transpire that, by denying that rule-breaking parties had taken place, he had misled parliament. That said, many Tory MPs were in a murderous mood – and for good reason. Journalists seemed to be uncovering evidence of more and more parties by the day, some of them apparently attended by people, such as the PM's Director of Communications, the former *Daily Mail* journalist Jack Doyle, who had been heavily involved in Number Ten's initial attempt to deny that any such events had taken place, or who, like Cabinet Secretary Simon Case, were supposed to be investigating them.[33] Labour seemed to be opening up a reasonable (although by no means spectacular) opinion poll lead and Starmer (although it wasn't, in truth, much of a contest) was now beating Johnson when people were asked to name who would make 'Best Prime Minister' – not perhaps surprisingly given that the current occupant of Number Ten was apparently convinced that BBC coverage of 'Partygate', rather than his own behaviour, was to blame for his woes.[34] Moreover, the news that the Electoral Commission was fining the Conservative Party for failing to properly declare the donation made to help cover the costs of the PM's flat refurbishment did nothing to help matters, especially when its investigation made it pretty clear that he had known about the source of the cash much earlier than he'd admitted to his ethics adviser, Christopher Geidt. Geidt was – just about – persuaded not to resign in protest, although it was a moot point whether that was fortunate for Johnson or only made matters worse for him by suggesting some sort of establishment whitewash.

Indeed, the only good news for the Prime Minister (the *Mirror* having just published photos of him at the by-then-notorious 'Christmas Quiz') was that, while potential successors like Liz Truss and Rishi Sunak were widely reported to be gearing up for a possible leadership contest, there were no signs that they intended to precipitate one by, for example, resigning in protest at his behaviour. Clearly, in spite of the fact that Johnson himself had proved in 2019 that it was a nonsense, the faux-Shakespearean adage (often attributed to Michael Heseltine) 'He who wields the knife never wears the crown' still seemed to be staying their hands. In any case, under the party's current rules, no-one could directly challenge the Prime Minister. Instead, they had to wait for him to resign or for his MPs to force him out via a vote of no confidence. Such a vote, predicted ConservativeHome's Paul Goodman, might now be 'more likely than not'.[35] Yet it still seemed some way off, even if two MPs who might be instrumental in triggering it – Steve Baker of the ERG, Covid Recovery Group, and now, he announced, a relaunched CWF (the Thatcherite pressure group Conservative Way Forward) and Graham Brady (the 1922 Committee Chairman to whom MPs had to send their letters of no confidence) – were both in the *Sunday Telegraph* making it clear that they and their ilk weren't prepared to accept Plan B's 'disastrous assault on liberty'.[36]

They weren't bluffing either. A few days later, in spite of an alarming spike in Covid cases which even 'libertarians' like Johnson and Javid believed left them no choice but to bring in tougher measures, and in spite of polls showing the public agreed, the government suffered its biggest rebellion so far. Although the measures were approved because Labour voted with the government, some 99 Tory MPs voted against the introduction of vaccine passports, 61 against NHS staff having to be vaccinated, and 38 against the wider mandating of face coverings. If Johnson's notable reluctance, at a Downing Street press conference the following day, to follow Chief Medical Officer Chris Whitty's call on people to scale back their pre-Christmas socializing was anything to go by, the rebellion had the desired impact. With the Chancellor 'letting it be known … that he argued against the introduction of Plan B' and Foreign Secretary Liz Truss 'hosting drinks receptions for potential supporters at a discreet private members' club in Mayfair', it seemed highly unlikely that the Prime Minister would want to (or would even be able to) do anything that could be spun by his critics as 'cancelling Christmas'.[37]

Some relief – but precious little comfort

Whether anyone in Number Ten was feeling particularly festive, however, was debatable – especially after the Lib Dems pulled off another remarkable by-election victory, this time in Owen Paterson's former constituency of North Shropshire, where, coming from third place in 2019, they'd overturned a Tory majority of nearly 23,000 on a massive

34 per cent swing.[38] The mood in Downing Street didn't improve when the *Guardian* published photos of Johnson, Cummings, et al. drinking and chatting (and certainly not socially distancing) in Number Ten's back garden back in May 2020 when the country had been in lockdown. Number Ten also had to suffer the embarrassment of having to hand over the internal investigation into Partygate to the second Permanent Secretary at the Cabinet Office, Sue Gray, after Cabinet Secretary Simon Case was obliged to recuse himself once it became apparent that one of the events in question had taken place in, of all places, his own office. Then, a day or so later, David Frost, presumably disappointed that Johnson once again seemed to be backing away from out-and-out confrontation with the EU over the Northern Ireland Protocol, resigned from the Cabinet, citing 'concerns about the current direction of travel' and claiming he wanted to see faster progress towards 'a lightly regulated, low-tax, entrepreneurial economy' and 'to learn to live with Covid'. His words, as he well knew, came as music to the ears of both ERG and Covid Recovery Group types, to whom he'd become something of an icon, and who were currently up in arms against what they claimed was a deeply damaging tendency on the part of the government's scientific advisers to get hung up on (and, indeed, only to publish modelling based on) worst-case scenarios. Little wonder, perhaps, that, as tales abounded of dozens of MPs getting ready to write to Graham Brady should the Cabinet back further restrictions, it decided against doing so before Christmas unless and until additional evidence suggested there was simply no choice. Leadership hopefuls like Truss and Sunak duly ensured that journalists were briefed (accurately or otherwise) that they had pushed for just such an outcome.[39]

Cue relief on the backbenches, albeit tempered by considerable concern at a YouGov poll suggesting that the party was now on just 30 per cent – its lowest level of support since Johnson took over as leader – with his own ratings now similar to those suffered by Theresa May just before he'd helped to force her out of office.[40] An especially large survey conducted by Focaldata and published by the *Sunday Times* just after Christmas only added to the gloom since, by using the increasingly familiar MRP method, it allowed Tory MPs to see estimated results for their own constituencies and so didn't make for pleasant reading for the 128 of them (including Johnson) who looked like losing their seats if those results were to be replicated at a general election.[41] Work by Survation, using the same method on a different sample, offered only marginally more cheer, suggesting as it did that some 113 Conservative MPs were in danger.[42]

Admittedly, there was some good news – particularly for those MPs whose resistance had probably ensured the Cabinet had decided against further restrictions over Christmas, but also for the country as a whole. Getting a Covid test may have been difficult, and the Office for National Statistics (ONS) survey suggested that over two million people had been infected in the week ending 23 December. But the data coming in from hospitals (at least in terms of mortality if not ambulance and A&E waiting times and cancelled operations) suggested that holding off seemed relatively harmless (a view not shared by experts who continued to be scandalized by daily death tolls in the hundreds), prompting Javid to announce that there would be no new restrictions before the New Year. This – and his insistence (much to the delight of the *Mail*, which carried his op-ed) that 'we must try to live with Covid' – would hopefully maintain his net positive rating in ConservativeHome's readers' poll of grassroots members.[43]

Javid could not, mind, compete with Liz Truss, whose plus 74-point rating put her well ahead of her main rival, Rishi Sunak (on plus 49). Still, events in the Channel meant that Priti Patel was in no position to trouble anyone: her rating was now in negative territory, albeit (at minus 1) only just. But even she had less to worry about than Johnson. He was now on minus 34, although, as ConservativeHome's editors pointed out, 'his score, woeful as it is, is nowhere near as dire as that of Theresa May in the spring of 2019 – when she broke the survey's unpopularity record, coming in at a catastrophic -75 points'. As was so often the case, however, there were some big differences between the Tory rank and file and ordinary voters: an Opinium poll released as the year drew to a close suggested that a Conservative Party led by Sunak would fare far better than one led by Johnson and far, far better than one led by Truss, suggesting her Thatcher tribute act wasn't really doing it for the voters.[44] And while a YouGov survey of party members released by Sky in the second week of January showed, not surprisingly perhaps, that they were rather keener on the Foreign Secretary, it also showed that they were keener still on the Chancellor – indeed, nearly half of them thought he'd do a better job as leader than the Prime Minister, even if 60 per cent still thought Johnson was doing a good job and should remain in post.[45]

Whether that would stay the case now that inflation was running at over 5 per cent, prompting widespread talk of a 'cost of living crisis', remained to be seen. Both Johnson and Sunak were coming under pressure in Cabinet and in the party in the media to act, with the planned rise in National Insurance a particular target of ire. As for the public, they seemed as concerned as ever, and even more angry, about Partygate, as revelation followed revelation – with the leak of an email inviting people to a 'bring your own booze' gathering in the Downing Street garden during lockdown in May 2020, as well as Johnson's claim that he had attended believing 'implicitly' that it was 'a work event', causing particular outrage. Their anger was reflected in snap polling by a number of firms which suggested, first, that around three-quarters of people didn't believe the PM was telling the truth and, second, that two-thirds of voters (and even four in ten Tory voters) thought he should resign.[46] Even Johnson's most loyal supporters in the party in the media now were choosing to reflect rather than dismiss their readers' concerns, emphasizing how much trouble he was in and demanding a show of contrition so he could move on.[47]

More worrying still for the Prime Minister was the painfully belated and pretty lukewarm backing he was receiving from those colleagues who were keenest to succeed him, with both Sunak and Truss failing to post supportive tweets until the evening of 12 January – the day after the 'BYOB' story broke. Johnson didn't help himself either: having just issued what passed for an apology in the Commons, he proceeded to tell Tory MPs in the tearooms that he didn't really deserve the criticism he was getting. And some of his supporters only made things more difficult, with Jacob Rees-Mogg going on television to dismiss Scottish leader Douglas Ross (who'd made it clear, along with many MSPs, he thought Johnson should go), as 'a lightweight'.

True, other Cabinet members, including Michael Gove, were slightly more successful when they backed Johnson (mainly by insisting yet again that he'd 'got all the big calls right') at a tense meeting of the 1922 Committee that evening – but only slightly, as indicated by the fact that the PM's two-faced attempt to deny responsibility in private after supposedly taking it in public was promptly leaked to journalists by a number of his own MPs.[48] By that stage, however, things had gone from bad to worse as even more lurid tales emerged of partying in Downing Street – suitcases full of wine, karaoke machines, a broken swing in the garden – and all on the night before the funeral of Prince Philip, at which the Queen, as per an iconic photo that was duly reprinted again and again, had sat alone in mourning.

Johnson's apology to Her Majesty couldn't, predictably enough, prevent his MPs' inboxes and letterboxes filling with messages from infuriated constituents. Still, he'd at least managed to reach the weekend without any ministers resigning from the Cabinet. And the two who were clearly dying to take over from him – Truss (who was reportedly holding 'Fizz with Liz' meetings with colleagues and 'Biz for Liz' meetings with potential donors) and Sunak (who was seeing groups of backbenchers, but only, of course, to talk about the cost of living) – seemed, at least for the moment, more intent on briefing against each other than against him.[49] Sunak's Treasury was also under fire for quietly writing off £4.3 billion of the £5.8 billion that was estimated to have been stolen by fraud from the government's Covid-19 schemes – a decision that soon resulted in the on-camera resignation (at the despatch box in the Lords) of Treasury Minister Theo Agnew.[50] Moreover, the *Mail* was beginning a concerted campaign to divert attention from Johnson's problems by demanding, along with several Tory MPs, that Durham police reopen an investigation into what the Labour Party insisted (correctly as it turned out) was a legitimate work gathering attended by its leader, Keir Starmer, in the spring of 2021 – 'Beergate' as it soon became known.[51] Number Ten, meanwhile, was briefing what (only half-jokingly) was labelled 'Operation Red Meat': the trailing of policies likely to appeal to the right of the party like the freezing of the BBC's licence fee and greater military involvement in an attempt to stop small boats crossing the Channel, as well as policies with wider appeal aimed at clearing the NHS and courts backlogs, helping voters with rising energy costs, boosting skills training, and (via the long-awaited White Paper) levelling up. Much was also made of the imminent lifting of all Coronavirus rules (barring those on isolation, the length of which had already been shortened) in order to remind MPs (not least those in the CRG) that the Prime Minister had got and was still getting 'the big calls right'.

Not everybody, however, was convinced either by that message, or by Johnson's cringeworthy attempt to simultaneously grovel and deny responsibility during an interview with Sky News's Beth Rigby.[52] A number of newer, younger MPs, taking little care to keep their meeting quiet, got together to discuss their dissatisfaction with their boss and what they might do about it – a gathering that, since it took place under the auspices of Alicia Kearns, the MP for Rutland and Melton (the latter being famous as the home of a traditional English delicacy), was labelled (and ridiculed as such by an outraged party in the media) 'the pork pie plot'.[53] Perhaps prompted by a poll for Channel 4 News that suggested that the government was facing a wipe-out in its 'Red Wall' seats, one of those involved, Christian Wakeford, the Conservative MP for the traditionally Labour seat of Bury South, crossed the floor to join Labour at the beginning of a raucous session of PMQs.[54] Minutes afterwards, David Davis, melodramatically channelling the spirit of the Norway Debate that did for Neville Chamberlain back in 1940, told Johnson, 'In the name of God, go!'

If, as some insisted, the defection of Wakeford (who claimed that Whips had threatened him and other rebels with the loss of government funding for projects in their constituencies unless they fell into line) saw the party suddenly pull together out of some atavistic, tribal instinct, any new-found unity didn't last for long. Some of Johnson's colleagues, along with the party in the media (not least the *Mail*, which began a front-page 'Spike the tax hike' campaign by claiming, a little prematurely perhaps, that 'the entire Cabinet' now backed delaying the National Insurance rise), were clearly hoping to use his weakness to press for policy changes.[55] Meanwhile, a couple of ministers – Education Secretary Nadhim Zahawi and Health Secretary Sajid Javid – demanded (and got) an official investigation into former minister Nus Ghani's allegations that her sacking from the frontbench in early 2020 had come about because she was a Muslim woman.[56] Chief Whip Mark Spencer denied that he'd given that as a reason, but it only added to increasing concerns about the effectiveness of the operation he was running. Those concerns were shared by Johnson himself, who, rather than dealing with them head on, decided to put together a praetorian guard (labelled by journalists as his 'Shadow Whipping Operation') comprised of former Whips Chris Pincher, Chris Heaton Harris, and Nigel Adams, as well as his old friend Conor Burns (shortly to become famous for fifteen minutes for suggesting the PM had been 'ambushed by a cake' rather than being caught attending an unlawful birthday celebration) and Grant Shapps, whose supposedly 'legendary' ability to put together and maintain a spreadsheet covering the whole of the parliamentary party had earned him the breathless admiration of his more technologically challenged colleagues. Meanwhile, Johnson (as well as making whistle-stop appearances in their constituencies) was taking meeting after placatory meeting with backbenchers, reassuring them that he'd stop small boats crossing the Channel, get through what he claimed was a 'Labour/media witch-hunt', and lead them once again to victory – all this, however, without giving in to calls to ditch the planned National Insurance and corporation tax hikes, his resolve not to do so strengthened by his getting together with Sunak to pen a joint article arguing the increases were vital to ensure economic recovery and to clear the NHS backlog.[57]

Sue Gray – and PC Plod

It certainly looked like Johnson needed all the help and protection from colleagues that he could get. At the start of the last week of January, the Metropolitan Police suddenly announced that it was, after all, going to launch an investigation into breaches of Coronavirus rules in Whitehall and in Downing Street itself. This raised the possibility of the Prime Minister being fined for breaking the laws his own government had introduced. It also quickly became apparent that it would delay the publication of Sue Gray's report into Partygate, the production of which many MPs (whether genuinely or because they were simply desperate for an excuse not to act) had told their constituents they would wait for before making up their minds about their leader. Some greeted the news of that delay (and the fact that the Met's investigation could take months to complete) with a degree of relief: obviously, the involvement of the police meant the PM could ultimately be in even more trouble than he already was, but at least it meant they could put off any decision for a little while longer. Johnson loyalists, however, affected outrage that the whole thing was being taken so seriously, especially, they suggested, when Russia's maverick President, Vladimir Putin, looked set to launch an attack on Ukraine – an argument that attracted a good deal of sympathy among the Tory rank and file and was soon being wheeled out to counter virtually any criticism of Johnson.[58] As for those doing the criticizing, they could do little more for the moment than hope that, were he eventually found to have broken the law, even his supporters might finally be forced to recognize his time was up.

Gray's unexpected decision, after the Met made its announcement, to publish an eleven-page *Update* (essentially her interim findings shorn of any details about the events in question) on the last day of January briefly triggered speculation that that moment might have arrived sooner than anyone had imagined.[59] The update's conclusions about Number Ten's drinking culture, about inappropriate gatherings and behaviour, and about a failure of leadership were damning enough in their own right, forcing Johnson, in his parliamentary response, into something that at least resembled an apology, as well as a promise to make formal, structural changes to the way Downing Street had hitherto been run. That didn't, however, spare him from withering criticism from a number of his own MPs. Most wounding was backbencher Aaron Bell's cold fury over his grandmother's funeral ('Does the Prime Minister think I am a fool?') and Theresa May's acidic assertion that her successor either didn't understand the rules or didn't think they applied to him. Indeed, so sustained was the attack from all sides that, having refused to promise during the debate to publish Sue Gray's report in full once the police had completed their investigation, Number Ten decided that evening to U-turn and to commit to doing so.

But it was Johnson's decision to repeat an utterly unfounded slur – one that originated on the far-right fringes of British politics – about Labour leader Keir Starmer, during his time as a top lawyer, supposedly 'prosecuting journalists and failing to prosecute [the infamous sexual predator] Jimmy Savile' that had earned him the greatest contempt that day.[60] Judging by the response of both the media and the public, however, this 'dead cat' didn't even work on its own terms, failing almost completely to distract from Gray's criticisms and his own lack of credibility, which an unusually strong performance from Starmer had helped to underline.[61] Snap polling by Savanta ComRes suggested that between six and seven out of ten voters (and around four out of ten Tories) wanted Johnson out, didn't trust him, and didn't believe he cared about the hurt he'd caused. True, more detailed polling down the line revealed that 29 per cent of respondents (rising to 45 per cent of Tory supporters) believed the Savile smear, while 30 per cent didn't know, but even that research suggested that it had left far more people thinking worse rather than better of Johnson in the aftermath.[62]

Johnson's employment of the Savile smear – and his apparent willingness to double down on it when quizzed by journalists in the days that followed – also had implications closer to home. It proved too much even for his hitherto utterly loyal Head of Policy, Munira Mirza, whose resignation was swiftly followed by that of his Director of Communications, Jack Doyle.[63] By that time, however, it seemed likely that, partly by promising MPs more input into policy by, for example, reanimating backbench policy groups, Johnson had probably managed to achieve his main goal: namely to keep enough of the parliamentary party onside to prevent fifty-four letters going in to demand a vote of confidence.[64] Whether, though, any of them bought the spin that the resignations, and the rushed replacement of Mirza by his Parliamentary Private Secretary, the MP Andrew Griffith, should be seen in the context of Johnson making additional personnel changes in Number Ten (such as the departure of his Chief of Staff, Dan Rosenfield, and his Principal Private Secretary, Martin Reynolds) is highly doubtful.

Johnson had also been hoping that the release of Michael Gove's long-awaited Levelling Up White Paper would both buy him some time and earn him some brownie points, particularly with 'Red Wall' MPs, who were picking up on the doorstep the same loss of enthusiasm that pollsters were observing among voters who'd plumped for the Tories for the first time in 2019.[65] Its reception, however, while by no means hostile, was not hugely enthusiastic. As a number of experts pointed out, its ambitions (mainly centred on boosting R&D, skills training, and transport and digital connectivity) were not necessarily matched by a sense that the government was prepared to sanction either the devolution or the money to realize them – or, indeed, a sense that the White Paper contained the specific policies required to hit its many targets, a number of which seemed very familiar to those who'd taken an interest in the May government's Industrial Strategy.[66] In any case, the whole thing was rather overshadowed by the comings and goings (mainly the goings) among Johnson's staffers and, even more so, by the announcement by Rishi Sunak of an emergency package intended to help people (via an eclectic mix of rebates, benefit increases, and loans) with the huge hike in energy bills triggered by the decision of the independent regulator Ofgem to raise the price cap on gas and electricity. The Chancellor, even his critics acknowledged, had little choice but to act, since the move threatened to push a quarter of households into fuel poverty, some of which were comprised of the nearly 5 million adults who were already struggling to put food on the table as the result of supermarket price rises.[67]

Although he fully supported Sunak's measures, Johnson's mood wasn't improved when, in the Chancellor's brief to journalists on them, he was asked about the Savile slur: 'Being honest,' Sunak replied, 'I wouldn't have said it.' The PM and his closest lieutenants, like his former Political Secretary and now Deputy Chief of Staff, Ben Gascoigne, couldn't have failed to notice media stories that his next-door neighbour's leadership campaign (#Ready4Rishi, apparently) was already at a fairly advanced stage of preparation.[68] It remained to be seen whether the damage done by that remark could really be repaired by the appointment of Sunak's close ally the former Brexit Secretary and now Cabinet Office Minister Steve Barclay MP as Johnson's new Chief of Staff (a highly unusual move since such figures are rarely also serving parliamentarians). Nor was it clear that Johnson's decision to hire the garrulous Guto Harri as his new Director of Communications would do him many favours – especially when, just as he took up his post, Harri (who'd worked for Johnson at City Hall) told a fellow journalist that his arrival in Downing Street had been greeted with a line or two from Gloria Gaynor's 'I will survive' sung by a Prime Minister who, he insisted, 'isn't a complete clown'.[69] That said, Harri at least brought some much-needed energy to Number Ten's attempt to push back against the impression given in Michael Ashcroft's biography of Carrie (then being serialized in the *Mail on Sunday*) that Johnson was 'completely mesmerised' by a supposedly manipulative wife who had installed her friends as his advisers.[70] Tory MPs could also console themselves that the appointment a few weeks later of David Canzini as another deputy Chief of Staff would likely make for a more disciplined Downing Street operation. Although Canzini was most often referred to in the media as a colleague (or even a protégé) of the Australian political consultant Lynton Crosby (whom Johnson still relied on for advice and wise counsel, especially when in a crisis), he had a long association with the party, having started in the 1990s as election agent to Tory MP (and famous diarist) Edwina Currie, and so knew the party inside out and from the ground up. He was also very much a favourite among Brexiteers after taking a leading role, albeit backstage, in their 'Chuck Chequers' campaign during the May years.

A couple of weeks before Canzini came on board, Johnson had also conducted a mini-reshuffle, effectively demoting Jacob Rees-Mogg and Mark Spencer, the two men seen as most responsible for the previous year's Owen Paterson débâcle, but without consigning them to the backbenches, where at least one of them might have constituted a problem. Rees-Mogg was given what many regarded (rightly or wrongly) as a joke job as Minister of State for Brexit Opportunities and Government Efficiency and was replaced as Leader of the House by Spencer. Spencer's role as Chief Whip went to one of the key players in Johnson's so-called 'Shadow Whipping Operation', Chris Heaton-Harris, with Chris Pincher, who'd hoped to get the Chief's job, agreeing to serve as Deputy. Meanwhile, the impression that Johnson was 'circling the wagons' was rather reinforced by his doubling the number of his Parliamentary Private Secretaries to four – all of them very much on the Brexiteer right of the party that he hoped would see him safely through any confidence vote.

What those changes couldn't do, however, was change the policy and electoral fundamentals – all of which was made crystal clear when, in the second week of February, Health Secretary Sajid Javid announced the government's plans to tackle the NHS backlog, which obliged him to admit that, even with the rise in National Insurance designed to help pay for them, waiting lists would actually peak in 2024, while the average waiting time would still be eighteen months well into 2023 – the year the party would normally be expecting to hold the next general election. And if the Prime Minister was hoping for brief respite from Partygate, he was disappointed. As he stood in the chamber for the last PMQs before the recess, MPs' phones began lighting up with another photo of him at the infamous Downing Street Christmas Quiz – only this time it was one that included a tell-tale bottle of Prosecco. To the disappointment of his critics, however, the attention of the party in the media was distracted by the announcement that he wanted to bring forward the ending of virtually all Coronavirus rules by a month to 24 February'.[71]

And meanwhile Number Ten had already begun its efforts to seed the idea, via briefings to journalists, that Johnson would not need to resign were he to be issued with a fixed penalty notice by the police – a course of action that even some of his supporters had initially assumed would be unavoidable.[72]

War – real and imaginary

As the Commons returned after recess, Johnson confirmed – to the obvious delight of his MPs and the party in the media, if not necessarily the rather more cautious general public – that the legal requirement to self-isolate following a positive test was indeed ending, as were isolation support payments.[73] He also announced (more controversially, not least because it resulted from a refusal on the part of Rishi Sunak at the Treasury to provide Sajid Javid at Health with additional funding) that, from the beginning of April, free testing would come to an end – a change supported by fewer than a third of voters and fewer than half of all Tory voters, but not one that seemed to trouble Conservative MPs or the party in the media.[74] In any case, just as all this was happening, Russia began its long-anticipated invasion of Ukraine. This gave Johnson the chance (once widespread criticism of the UK government's initially inadequate response both on sanctions and on refugees had subsided) to set aside his domestic travails and act the statesman – one determined, with all the Churchillian rhetoric at his command, to stand up for Putin's plucky enemy, to the point where, a few weeks later, he drew what even some ardent Brexiteers saw as a distasteful analogy between the Ukrainians' desire to 'choose freedom' and 'the British people's' vote to leave the EU.[75] That said, neither he nor his critics on the Tory benches were able to ignore a new survey which, using MRP to project its findings across the country, pointed to the Conservative Party losing 164 seats, including 70 of the 107 held by those who had entered the Commons for the first time in 2019, as well as the seats of 11 members of the Cabinet, including Johnson himself.[76]

The focus on Russia also inadvertently threw up some familiar questions concerning both the Tories' own funding and their permissive attitude, over years, to 'Londongrad', as well as some awkward questions about Johnson's insistence on granting a peerage to the newspaper owner (and son of a former KGB officer) Evgeny Lebedev in spite of security concerns apparently raised at the highest level.[77] Johnson's determination to override those concerns may, of course, have been down to nothing more than gratitude – in Lebedev's case not because he'd donated millions to the Conservative Party (which is so often the way to secure a peerage) but because of the support that the *Evening Standard* gave Johnson as London Mayor.[78] And the same was presumably true of his decision, in the first week of March, while most observers were preoccupied with the war in Ukraine, to grant a knighthood to Gavin Williamson. While Williamson may have been sacked as Defence Secretary by Theresa May following leaks from the National Security Council and sacked by Johnson himself over his woeful performance as Education Secretary, he still apparently had a place in the latter's heart owing to his role in his 2019 leadership campaign. Whether rumours that Williamson was now hoping to perform a similar role for Liz Truss may also have played a part, who knows? A similar mix of Johnson's gratitude for services rendered and concerns as to the consequences were the politician in question to turn against him may also explain why (in much the same way as her bullying of staff and her failure to grip the 'small boats' crisis had apparently posed no obstacle to her remaining in post) there seemed to be no question of Priti Patel leaving the Home Office, notwithstanding the widespread criticism (both within and without the Cabinet) of her chaotic handling of the country's response to the Ukrainian refugee crisis.[79]

Despite all that, Johnson's ratings during the opening weeks of the Ukraine crisis did seem to be undergoing something of a recovery, albeit from a very low base and not on a scale to suggest that, as some of his most enthusiastic supporters believed, the conflict might be his 'Falklands moment'.[80] Still, it did allow them to persuade at least some of their colleagues at Westminster (250 of whom were prepared to sit through a typically knockabout post-prandial speech by the PM at a 'team bonding dinner' held in the Park Plaza hotel at the end of March) that 'now was not the time' to be trying to get rid of him.

Nor was Johnson the only Tory politician who saw the war in Ukraine as something of an opportunity.[81] For instance, the increasingly vocal Net Zero Security Group of Tory MPs, led by Brexit-ultras Steve Baker and Craig Mackinlay, argued that ensuring the UK's energy security demanded the government now reverse its 2020 ban on fracking, its ongoing concern about 'costly' environmental targets given extra impetus by the news that Nigel Farage was threatening some kind of Brexit-style comeback if Johnson didn't abandon or at least reduce them.[82] Meanwhile, on the other side of the debate – one that was intensifying as the government got ready to publish its long-promised energy strategy – Tory MPs belonging to the Conservative Environment Network (CEN) were pointing to the need to accelerate progress on renewables. Anxious not to alienate anyone, Downing Street's response was to say that it would 'look at all options', obliging Business Secretary Kwasi Kwarteng, who as recently as February had insisted that 'fracking is not the answer to the energy crisis', to tell the Commons that, 'If it can be done in a safe and sustainable way, the government is open to the idea of fracking.' More practically (if hardly environmentally), Johnson flew to Saudi Arabia in the hope he might persuade it to increase oil production – not only, as it turned out, in vain but also somewhat humiliatingly since his assurances that he had raised human rights 'concerns' failed to prevent the authorities there executing a further three people on the day of his visit, thereby adding to the eighty-one it had executed the previous weekend.

Fortunately, Johnson received a rather warmer welcome in Blackpool, where the Tories were holding their spring conference, than he had in Riyadh a few days earlier. If there was an overall theme, it appeared to be – and not for the first time – the continuation of Brexit by other means, namely the so-called 'culture war'. In his speech, the PM declared, 'we don't need to be woke, we just want to be free'. Meanwhile, Foreign Secretary Liz Truss (proclaiming 'Now is the time to end the culture of self-doubt, the constant self-questioning and introspection, the ludicrous debates about language, statues and pronouns') and Party Co-Chairman Oliver Dowden (declaring that 'the privet hedges of suburbia are the privet hedges of a free people' and accusing Keir Starmer of 'kowtowing to the cancel culture brigade') appeared determined to outdo each other on that front. Still, some of their colleagues must have observed, at least they weren't reduced, as Home Secretary Priti Patel was, to defending the lumbering shambles of the government's Ukrainian refugee response by arguing that the bureaucracy that so many were complaining about was vital in order to weed out Russian spies posing as women fleeing the war. Fortunately, however, Patel was on surer ground when talking up her Nationalities and Borders Bill, and could be confident that she would be able to overturn attempts to amend it in the Lords, not least on the part of the sixty-five Tory peers and MPs who'd written an open letter to Johnson suggesting asylum-seekers be permitted to work while they waited for their claims to be processed.[83]

Trouble for Sunak but a let-off for Johnson

Away from Blackpool, Chancellor Rishi Sunak was putting the final touches to a Spring Statement that, he hoped, would go some way to addressing the pleas from Tory MPs that he do more to help their constituents cope with the rising cost of living. Accordingly, he announced a cut in fuel duty and, while he refused to listen to calls (some from Cabinet colleagues) to abandon the National Insurance rises he'd agreed on in order to provide additional funds for the NHS and (eventually) pay for reforms to social care, he nevertheless raised the threshold at which contributions had to be paid. He also announced that income tax would be reduced by a penny in the pound to 19 pence by the end of the parliament. But with the Office for Budget Responsibility (OBR) forecasting the biggest fall in living standards in any single financial year since ONS records began in 1956–7, with inflation predicted to rise to nearly 9 per cent by the end of the year and the energy price cap set to rise even higher in the autumn, and with growth stalling, it simply wasn't enough – at least according to well over two-thirds of the public questioned in one of the first snap polls. Grassroots members, it transpired, weren't any happier: ConservativeHome's survey of readers who were party members suggested that 58 per cent of them were dissatisfied.[84]

Sunak's package didn't convince the party in the media either. The *Telegraph* and its columnists were particularly scathing, while independent think tanks like the Resolution Foundation and the IFS also gave it both barrels, rubbishing his claim to be a tax-cutting Chancellor and forecasting that some 1.3 million people (including half a million children) would be pushed into absolute poverty as a result of his failure to do more for those on benefits.[85] Sunak was even undermined by his own boss, Johnson confessing to journalists that the government would 'need to do more' – this at the same time as the steer from Treasury ministers was now that the government had reached 'the limit of fiscal expansion – the high-water mark of our commitment to honour what we set out in our manifesto, and not a point at which anyone should expect us to go further'.[86] And, as if that weren't bad enough, the Chancellor's morning after the night before turned into a broadcast nightmare. He was noticeably thin-skinned and defensive when asked about his fabulously wealthy wife's finances. His throw-away comment, when asked the predictable question about the cost of a loaf of bread, that 'We all have different breads in my house' only served, to some anyway, as a reminder of his family's multi-millionaire lifestyle. And his petrol station photo-op only ended in further embarrassment: firstly, it transpired that Sunak had needed to borrow a supermarket employee's modest hatchback to show him filling up at the pump; secondly, journalists found that, in addition to the fairly ordinary car he claimed to drive, his family owned a number of rather swisher vehicles (kept apparently in his country manor and his pad in Santa Monica); and, thirdly, he didn't seem to know quite how to make the kind of contactless payment that had long since become an everyday experience for most ordinary people.

It was little wonder after all that, perhaps, that in ConservativeHome's monthly Cabinet league table, Sunak fell from 11th out of 32 the previous month to 30th, with a net rating from readers of just 8 points – a long way off leadership rival Liz Truss, up there in 4th place on 61.[87] It was little wonder either that his standing with the public fell just as precipitately: before the Spring Statement, his favourability rating stood at minus 5 (a long way from the plus 49 it had reached in March 2020 but still relatively decent); two weeks after the Spring Statement, it had dropped to minus 15. This was still not as low as Johnson's minus 42, admittedly, but (more worryingly for his leadership ambitions perhaps) the two were now only neck and neck (on plus 6 and plus 7) with Tory supporters, and Sunak was, for the very first time, regarded even less favourably by the public than Labour's leader Keir Starmer.[88] Worse, however, was soon to come.

At the beginning of April, journalists revealed that Sunak's wife, Akshata Murthy, whose personal fortune was far greater even than his (and even, it was reported, the Queen's), had been claiming 'non-dom' status for years, presumably in order to save millions of pounds of tax which otherwise would have been due on her huge overseas earnings from, among other things, her shares in her father's firm Infosys. In the scramble to cope with the fall-out, the couple only dug a deeper hole for themselves by suggesting that it had been incumbent on her, as an Indian citizen, to do so – a defence that, as journalists quickly discovered, had no basis in fact, thus leaving her little alternative but to say that she would, while resident in the UK, pay tax on her overseas earnings there, albeit without apparently relinquishing her non-domiciled status. It was then revealed that Sunak, like her, had held a green card, granting him permanent residence in the US, and had done so for six years while he had been an MP, nineteen months of which he had spent as Chancellor, allowing opponents to suggest he had little more long-term commitment to the UK than had his wife. No laws, nor even the ministerial code, had been broken. But the blow to Sunak's reputation by what he'd initially tried to pass off as a 'smear' (thereby prompting the *Sun* to go with the gloriously unlikely front-page screamer 'RISHI: LAY OFF MY MISSUS') was undoubtedly huge. And the Opposition's script (one no doubt appreciated by his internal rivals, too) practically wrote itself: the super-rich guy who'd put up taxes for the rest of us had a mega-rich foreign wife who'd chosen not to pay her full whack in the UK; how could he possibly understand or care about the plight of ordinary people; in fact, did he even intend to stay in this country once he'd finished trying to run it?

For Sunak himself, there was one more nagging question. It was more than possible that the information on which all these damaging stories were based had come from a government rather than an Opposition source. Could it really, as some of his allies suggested to journalists, have come from Number Ten itself, revenge for his less than full-throated support for Johnson over the last few months?[89] He could at least reassure himself that Johnson's surprise visit to Ukraine that weekend was presumably some time in the planning. Even so, it undoubtedly drew what, for the PM anyway, wasn't just a stark but also a very welcome contrast between, on the one hand, an international statesman flanked by heavily armed soldiers touring the streets of Kyiv with the hero of the hour, President Zelensky, and, on the other, a much-diminished colleague back at home.

The furore over Sunak's personal finances and the hype surrounding the trip to Kyiv had another upside for Johnson too, distracting Westminster and Whitehall, and those who reported on them, from what really should have been a much bigger story in terms of its long-term impact, namely the adequacy or otherwise of the Energy Security Strategy that the government had finally been able to publish. Not for the first or the last time – and not necessarily inappropriately in a parliamentary democracy, of course – it bore the imprint of the pressure Johnson was under to keep as many of his colleagues on board. So while nuclear power and offshore wind featured heavily, and while new oil and gas licences were also in the mix, there was no significant expenditure earmarked to promote better insulation – and mooted changes to planning regulations in order to encourage onshore wind farms (still a particular bugbear for Conservative MPs worried about constituency opposition) had been unceremoniously dropped.[90] Naturally, the supposedly 'selfish, fanatical and frankly dangerous so-called activists' and 'eco-mobs' (as Priti Patel was quick to label them) who were currently blocking roads, fuel depots, and a couple of bridges in central London weren't impressed, but, then again, Extinction Rebellion weren't the ones in a position to send in letters to the Chairman of the 1922 in order to trigger a vote of confidence in Boris Johnson.[91]

As it turned out, Johnson's determination to offend as few of his colleagues as possible paid dividends sooner than even he had imagined. Just a day or two after his Ukraine visit, both he and Rishi Sunak were issued with fixed penalty notices for having attended an illegal gathering in Downing Street. The PM, predictably enough, had absolutely no intention of resigning. Less sure was the Chancellor (who arguably had far more reason to feel aggrieved than almost anyone else present since he was only there having arrived early for a scheduled meeting). However, after consulting his advisers (and presumably his conscience), he decided not to quit. Tempting as it might have been to do so (especially after the pasting he'd had to put up with over the past fortnight) and thus put pressure on Johnson to do the same, Sunak knew that resignation on his part would have been tantamount to admitting that ministers who make the laws cannot be allowed to break them, in so doing, perhaps, disqualifying himself from holding high office ever again.

His decision allowed Number Ten, once the PM had issued a carefully worded on-camera apology filmed at Chequers, to press 'go' on a patently coordinated campaign of support from ministers and MPs on Twitter.[92]

Meanwhile, the party in the media did its level best – its task made easier by the gathering which triggered the fine being one of the more trivial occasions under investigation – to minimize and even ridicule the whole thing.[93] Snap polls also provided some crumbs of comfort: while they suggested around six in ten voters thought Johnson and Sunak should resign, a similar proportion of *Conservative* voters thought they should stay on; they also suggested that the vast majority of voters, including those who wanted them to go, assumed (cynically yet helpfully) that they wouldn't. The only cloud on the horizon, were Johnson ever to face a charge of misleading parliament, was that three-quarters of those asked (including just over half of all Tory supporters!) reckoned he'd 'knowingly lied' about breaking lockdown rules.[94] But that was for the future. Right now, no more than a handful of Tory MPs, plus the party's high-profile former leader in Scotland, Ruth Davidson, were suggesting he resign. It looked, then, as if 'the greased piglet' was going to escape the clutches of his pursuers once again.

End of the road?
(April–September 2022)

Had Boris Johnson been on the look-out for something simply to distract everyone from his Partygate fixed penalty notice, he could not have been more fortunate. On 14 April, he was able to travel down to Kent to announce that the UK had agreed a deal with Rwanda which would see it take large numbers of supposedly 'illegal' asylum seekers off the government's hands, albeit in return for hundreds of millions of pounds of British taxpayers' money. Human rights groups and refugee charities were outraged, convinced (in common, it turned out, with the Archbishop of Canterbury, Prince Charles, civil servants, and even one or two of Johnson's own MPs) that the move was not only morally but also legally and financially questionable, while Labour's Shadow Home Secretary, Yvette Cooper, immediately branded it 'unworkable, unethical and extortionate'.[1]

Their criticisms, of course, were completely predictable. Indeed, they were just what Number Ten, with one eye on the local elections due to take place in a month's time and the other on the general election to come, was hoping for. Not only did the storm of protest help publicize the plan to an electorate that was historically hardline on immigration, it also drew a dividing line that, once again, pitched the government against a Labour Opposition unable to proffer any alternative and supposedly in cahoots with 'lefty lawyers' and 'activists' determined to appeal to the idea of 'human rights' in order to prevent Johnson fulfilling his Brexit-based promise to take back control of the country's borders.[2] Moreover, Number Ten could defend the agreement on the grounds that it would supposedly deter migrants from crossing the Channel in small boats provided by cruel and exploitative 'people smugglers' – a rationale which a predictably thrilled party in the media unsurprisingly bought into.[3] Its reporters, some of whom had flown to Kigali with Priti Patel to witness the signing ceremony, then got on with supporting what the government's critics saw as its next attempt at misdirection (this time one that dovetailed directly with a business model which relied in part on commuting): namely the campaign (backed by Jacob Rees-Mogg and the Covid Recovery Group) to get the civil service back to the office.[4]

Trouble upon trouble

None of this, of course, could spare Johnson completely – nor could it prevent him from being, not for the first or last time, his own worst enemy. Having spent his first appearance in parliament after being fined for breaking lockdown issuing what, for him, were unusually grovelling and repeated apologies, he proceeded (again not for the first or the last time) to adopt a markedly less contrite and more bullish tone when he addressed the 1922 Committee behind closed doors not long afterwards. The public, he assured them, wanted him to get on with more important matters. He also claimed, only half-jokingly, that the BBC and the Archbishop of Canterbury had been more critical of the government's Rwanda scheme than they had been of Putin's invasion of Ukraine. His remarks, however, didn't remain private for long, reinforcing the already widespread impression among the general public that any contrition expressed on his part was always less than sincere. They also suggested to his MPs that Johnson didn't really appreciate quite how much trouble he and they were in. The polls showed Labour overtaking the Tories on managing the economy, while both the Prime Minister's and the Chancellor's favourability ratings had crashed to minus 45 and minus 44 respectively.[5] Moreover, Tory members, as both men were about to find out, seemed, if anything, even less inclined to give them the benefit of the doubt, with Sunak bottom of ConservativeHome's monthly 'Cabinet league table' on minus 6 and Johnson (albeit in positive territory on plus 7) only a couple of places above him.[6]

The only good news for Johnson from polling (apart from the fact that Sunak's ratings had fallen even faster than his and that 'only' 35 per cent of ConservativeHome's respondents thought he should resign, as opposed to 58 per cent who thought he should stay) was that the Rwanda plan was popular with Tory voters. Some 59 per cent approved of it, compared to just 35 per cent of voters as a whole.[7] Even more encouragingly, it seemed to attract more support over time, a survey two months later, in the middle of June, suggesting more voters approved than disapproved of the plan (by 44 to 40 per cent), with Tory supporters (at 74 to 16 per cent) even more enthusiastic than they had been initially.[8] Tory members, at least according to ConservativeHome's readers' survey, were, predictably, the keenest of all, with eight out of ten expressing their support when asked towards the end of April.[9]

Even that, however, could provide little consolation for the fact that, in the week after the Rwanda announcement, the Commons Speaker, Lindsay Hoyle, had agreed to the House debating a Labour motion referring Johnson to the Privileges Committee on the grounds that he had misled parliament on Partygate – and not only that but, on the motion itself, MPs would be permitted to use the normally 'unparliamentary' term 'liar' to describe the conduct of the PM. Moreover, the government's response, far from fitting the prevailing narrative that the new whipping operation and Number Ten staffers had brought some much-needed professionalism and discipline to Downing Street, was as chaotic as it had always been. Initially the plan was to try to persuade Tory MPs to oppose Labour's motion, suggesting instead that any vote should be held after Sue Gray reported. But this had to be dropped when it became obvious that many of them (including some frontbenchers) would at the very least abstain to avoid being portrayed by Opposition candidates at a future election (and indeed at the upcoming local elections) as voting against an investigation. That left the government with little choice but to allow its MPs a free vote on a one-line whip, letting them know that Johnson was apparently 'happy' to leave the whole thing up to the Commons since, as he later put it speaking on a trip to India, he had 'absolutely nothing, frankly, to hide'. The motion, accordingly, was passed unopposed, but not before Steve Baker (he of the European Research Group, the Covid Recovery Group, and the Net Zero Scrutiny Group) suggested 'the Prime Minister should just know the gig's up'. Clearly he'd changed his mind about forgiving Johnson after his behind-closed-doors performance at the 1922 Committee a week or so before made a mockery of his apparently 'heartfelt' apology to the Commons earlier the same day.

But if the PM couldn't count on each and every MP sticking with him, he could still rely on some of the biggest beasts in the party in the media to come to his aid, not least the *Mail*, which – with the help of the

Durham MP, Richard Holden, and, of course, Johnson uber-fan Nadine Dorries – renewed what would now become a relentless campaign to persuade the county's police to investigate Keir Starmer (and eventually his deputy Angela Rayner) over 'Beergate' on the grounds (specious, as it transpired) that new evidence (including a video) had emerged that all was not what it seemed.[10] Sadly for Johnson, however, the story simply couldn't compete with one that even the normally supportive *Sun* felt was too good to pass up. Apparently, a number of (mainly female) Tory MPs had had the temerity to complain about sexist and inappropriate behaviour on the part of their colleagues at a meeting attended by the Chief Whip, during which it was alleged that one of them – soon to be named as the member for Tiverton and Honiton, Neil Parish – had even been using his phone to watch pornography in the Commons chamber.[11]

Number Ten would have much preferred the complaints to have been made more discreetly. But once Parish was named, and once he'd admitted what he'd been up to (albeit with the comical explanation that on the first occasion he had been looking to buy a tractor and had accidentally landed on the porn site in question), his resignation from the Commons was inevitable. That meant the government was now facing two by-elections: one in Parish's Devon seat, with a majority of just over 24,000, and, following the recent conviction of Ahmad Khan MP for sexual assault, one in Wakefield, where Khan had won a majority over Labour of just under 3,500 in 2019. In the meantime, however, there were local elections to think about. Johnson could do little, then, but press on with a programme of activities designed to boost his reputation as an international statesman (such as addressing Ukraine's parliament) and to show he was listening to people's concerns, which, as polling showed, were now dominated, in the vast majority of constituencies, by the cost of living.[12] He even agreed to speak to the famously combative Susanna Reid, the co-host of ITV's flagship *Good Morning Britain* – his first interview appearance on the show in years and one he quickly regretted when he proved embarrassingly unable to come up with a convincing answer as to how the government could do more to help people struggling with the steeply rising cost of utilities and other basics.[13]

In this context – one in which, according to one charity, more than two million adults had gone without food for a whole day over the past month because they were unable to afford to eat – the best the Conservatives could aspire to in the local elections held on 5 May was to sell their overall result as better than they could possibly have hoped for and, if they were lucky, perform against the trend in places where they'd done well at the 2019 general election.[14] And, in fact, they pretty much achieved both aims. The 'expectations management' efforts of CCHQ's comms team under Alex Wild meant that ministers going out to bat on broadcast could argue that things really hadn't gone that badly for a government in mid-term, while they could point to reasonable results in local authorities in the Midlands and the North containing marginal seats recently won from Labour – proof, apparently, that the wedge issues favoured by the likes of Number Ten's 'properly Conservative' Deputy Chief of Staff, David Canzini (Rwanda being the most obvious example), were playing well there.

But in the end, whatever the wags like to say, perception is not reality. True, there was never much chance that the Tories would do well in Scotland (where Labour overtook them for the first time since 2017) and Wales (where they lost control of their only council and won just 6 per cent of the seats). But the results in England were far from encouraging either. Even with some councillors labelling themselves 'Local Conservatives' on the ballot paper, the party lost control of 13 councils (including London 'flagships' like Westminster and Wandsworth as well as rural West Oxfordshire) and, at 24 per cent, won its lowest proportion of seats up for grabs in the last ten years, losing nearly 350 English council seats in the process – a fair few (worryingly for MPs sitting in 'Blue Wall' seats in southern England) to the Liberal Democrats.[15] Moreover, when it came to the National Equivalent Share of the Vote (the NEV projection calculated by political scientists Colin Rallings and Michael Thrasher), the Conservatives dropped from 40 per cent in 2021 to 33 per cent, the only consolation being that, although Labour picked up 5 points on the previous year, its share was still only 35 per cent – hardly a ringing endorsement for a party hoping to win a general election in 2023/4, although, as a couple of more thorough analyses noted, not quite as disappointing as many relieved Tories had initially assumed.[16] The Lib Dems on 17 per cent (and, indeed, 19 per cent in the BBC's projection), however, looked like they were gaining in strength and seemed at last to have been forgiven by centre-left voters for going into the coalition while being either rewarded or else forgiven for their ultra-Remain stance by voters on the centre right.

The results from elections to the Northern Ireland Assembly also brought little joy for Johnson. Sinn Féin ended up as the largest party, having won 27 of the 90 seats – 2 more than the DUP). And the majority of those elected to Stormont were clearly content that the Northern Ireland Protocol the PM now disowned be made to work rather than wanting to see it overridden or even scrapped. The latter, however, now seemed to be the price the government might have to pay in order, firstly, to persuade the DUP to restore power-sharing and, secondly, to shore up support for Johnson among Westminster's Brexit-ultras – a group that the tough stance on the Protocol taken by leadership aspirant Liz Truss was clearly designed to impress.

Johnson, of course, was equally keen to please – one reason why the Queen's Speech (read in her absence due to ill-health by her son Charles) was spun by him, initially in an interview with the *Sunday Express*, as part of a 'relentless drive to deliver on the promise of Brexit', or what he obviously wanted people to think of as a 'super seven' set of bills designed to help Britain 'thrive as a modern, dynamic and independent country'.[17] In fact, the government's programme (with its commitment, for instance, to cracking down on public protest, permitting more gene editing, and making it easier to replace law inherited from the EU) included thirty-eight bills in total.[18] But even then, what was not included (for instance, a bill banning the import of fur, foie gras, and the products of trophy hunting, as well as a bill to upgrade audit and corporate governance, a bill banning trans conversion therapy, and a bill to boost employee rights and make flexible working a default option) received almost more attention than what was actually in the Speech – partly because whatever was dropped apparently reflected the increasing influence over Johnson of David Canzini. It was therefore doubly disappointing to find that, with the odd exception (the *Mail*'s front-page screamer 'DEATH KNELL FOR WORK FROM HOME'), the speech received a fairly lukewarm welcome from some of the PM's most ardent backers, not least his 'real boss', the *Telegraph* – a kick in the teeth that not even Johnson's launch of Downing Street's first foray into TikTok could make up for.[19]

That said, it wasn't all bad news. Former Cabinet minister Robert Jenrick may have warned that the government looked likely to miss its

2019 manifesto pledge to build 300,000 homes a year by 2025 'by a country mile'. But the vast majority of his colleagues (especially those representing proverbially 'leafy' constituencies) were happy to see the bold planning reforms he'd tried to push through diluted to positively homeopathic levels in Michael Gove's proposed 'Levelling Up and Regeneration Bill'. Moreover, while it wasn't in the Queen's Speech, Johnson's announcement a few days later that the government was aiming to cut 91,000 civil service jobs in order to save money that could one day be returned to voters as tax cuts went down a storm as well. So, too – in spite of the angry criticism the move attracted from former leader William Hague – did the government's decision to drop plans (drawn up as part of its anti-obesity strategy) to ban supermarkets' 'Buy One Get One Free' deals and to impose a 9 p.m. watershed on junk food advertising on TV, supposedly on the grounds of its desire to help people with the cost of living.[20] And Johnson himself was still capable of getting the party in the media (and at least some of his colleagues) excited by, among other things, ridiculing working from home and laying into 'lefty lawyers', as he did in a characteristically 'irrepressible' post-Queen's Speech interview with the *Mail*'s Political Editor, Jason Groves.[21]

The camera doesn't lie: Gray releases the photos, May 2022.
Source: No. 10 Official Photographer / Sue Gray report.

No surprise, then, that it was that title which cheered loudest when the Met, having issued 126 fines (but only one to the PM), announced the end of its Partygate investigation, apparently leaving 'the massed ranks of Boris-haters' to discover 'that months of hysteria, hyperbole and confected rage had come to nothing'.[22] Nor that the *Mail* did the same (its front-page screamer asking 'IS THAT IT?') upon the publication, a few days later, of Sue Gray's full report, with all its damning detail on the culture of boozy impunity which those in charge had allowed to persist and which was laid bare by a hard-hitting BBC documentary the evening before.[23] Voters weren't quite so forgiving. Snap polling (published in the wake of the report and Johnson's carefully crafted statement to the Commons taking 'full responsibility' but simultaneously asserting that he'd done nothing wrong, at least *knowingly*) suggested two-thirds thought that the PM hadn't learned his lesson and that he should resign, while three-quarters believed he'd misled the House of Commons over what he knew.[24] However, the rest of the party in the media – the *Sun*, the *Express*, and the *Telegraph* – were similarly keen (albeit with one or two reservations on the part of the latter) to move on, urging Johnson to just get on with helping people with the cost of living and trailing a package from the Chancellor intended to do just that.[25]

Fortunately for Sunak, his announcement was much better received than his damp-squib Spring Statement. It proposed over £15 billion worth of subsidies for households, paid for mainly out of unexpectedly robust revenues and partly by a windfall tax (cutely labelled a 'temporary targeted energy profits levy') on oil and gas firms' profits – a wildly popular measure for which Labour had been calling for months and about which ministers had been arguing with each other for almost as long. Think tanks like the IFS and the Resolution Foundation were much happier that it would provide help where it was most needed. Conservative MPs were, in the main, relieved that something was at last being done to help their struggling constituents, if peeved that, yet again, they'd initially been expected to defend the government doing something (or, in the case of the windfall tax, *not* doing something) only for it to U-turn soon afterwards. Not everyone was cheering, however. A number of MPs had made it plain that they, like a handful of ministers (and, as it was alleged, Johnson's latest 'Wizard of Oz', David Canzini), were opposed to the idea both on ideological grounds (it was 'anti-' or 'un-Conservative') and because they believed it would frighten off investors.[26] But only a few wanted to go as far as the right-winger Richard Drax, who, when the Commons discussed the measures, accused Sunak of throwing 'red meat to socialists'. The party in the media had its doubts too: help was badly needed, but shouldn't a Tory government be limiting spending and cutting, not raising, taxes?[27] The grassroots were less disappointed than they'd been with the Spring Statement but they were hardly ecstatic: ConservativeHome's readers' survey suggested 51 per cent were satisfied with Sunak's package, although that still left 43 per cent who weren't.[28]

Yet while things might have been looking up – if only a little – for the Chancellor, that didn't seem to be the case for the Prime Minister. Whether it was the tax increases, or the fact that Johnson, with what some regarded as breathtaking complacency, had decided to issue an updated version of the Ministerial Code shorn both of its reference to Lord Nolan's 'principles of public life' and of the expectation that breaches would lead to dismissal or resignation, or whether it was simply that post-Gray opinion polls were giving Labour double-digit leads, more and more Tory MPs were beginning to suggest, both publicly and – in letters to Graham Brady calling for a vote of confidence – privately, that the PM's time might be up.[29]

Some of those who were wavering may have responded positively to personal phone calls from the Prime Minister. Some may have taken heart from the announcement that the first flight of asylum seekers bound for Rwanda would take place in a couple of weeks' time. Some may even have been convinced by newspaper briefings from the PM's allies that those seeking to get rid of him were 'rebels without a clue', not least with regard to who (Sunak having supposedly imploded) should take over what, even after a confidence vote, let alone a leadership contest, would be a badly divided party.[30] In reality, however, it was pretty clear that there would be no shortage of candidates willing to try. Foreign Secretary Liz Truss could rely on her role in the government's move to unilaterally rewrite the Northern Ireland Protocol to keep her in the spotlight, especially because, journalists were very helpfully briefed, she was battling in Cabinet to toughen up the bill in question with the assistance of the ERG and in the face of reservations expressed by her rival, Rishi Sunak. Trade Minister Penny Mordaunt was busy hyping her memorandum of understanding not with India but with Indiana, while the Chairman of the Foreign Affairs Committee, Tom Tugendhat, made sure he was one of the first to slap down fellow army veteran and Chair of the Defence Committee, Tobias Ellwood, for daring to suggest that it might be better if the UK decided to become part of the EU's single market again, perhaps on the same basis as Norway.[31] Even Defence Secretary Ben Wallace, who didn't really seem that interested in taking over from Johnson but was continually being touted as a contender because of his pole position in ConservativeHome's Cabinet league table, was making it pretty clear he wanted more spending on the armed forces than the PM (and the Chancellor) seemed prepared to sanction. Moreover, none of those potential pretenders were being booed and jeered by upstanding members of the public, as Boris and Carrie Johnson were as they made their way into St Paul's Cathedral for the Platinum Jubilee service of thanksgiving.

Indeed, it was that incident, plus polling (carried out for the *Sunday Times* by James Johnson, Theresa May's former pollster) that pointed to a heavy defeat in the Wakefield by-election scheduled (along with the contest in Tiverton and Honiton) for 23 June, which for some MPs proved the final straw.[32] Any hesitation they may have felt owing to the belief (a misleading one, it was now pointed out) that a Johnson victory in a vote of confidence would preclude another vote for a year was set aside.[33] Even before a CCHQ-style briefing note that had been circulated to Tory MPs by Johnson's critics was leaked to journalists on the afternoon of Sunday, 5 June, Graham Brady, in his role as Chairman of the 1922 Committee, had received enough letters (some of them, in fact, written a few days before the Jubilee and simply post-dated) to trigger a contest.[34] Rather than wait until after the weekend, he rang the PM to tell him that a vote would now have to be held.

Zebra with a gammy leg

Like Theresa May before him, Johnson was persuaded that it would be best to hold the vote as quickly as possible in order to afford his critics (who, in marked contrast to hers, were far from an organized cabal) as little time as possible to canvass support. It was therefore agreed that Brady would make the announcement the very next morning with the vote taking place that evening. Johnson then got together with some close advisers – in this case, Steve Barclay, his Chief of Staff, Chief Whip Chris Heaton-Harris, Cabinet Office Minister Nigel Adams, Communications Director Guto Harri, CCHQ Political Director Ross Kempsell, and his old friend Lynton Crosby. Rather than remaining neutral, the Whips' Office, it was agreed, would send Tory MPs a CCHQ-style briefing note reminding them of the PM's achievements and noting that a leadership contest would be 'distracting, divisive and destructive'.[35] Meanwhile, his supporters (including his Cabinet ministers, all of whom, judging their boss was very likely to win more than the 50 per cent of MPs voting required to survive, chose to stay on) would take to mainstream and social media, as well as (more or less privately) to WhatsApp, to support him as soon as Brady announced. Johnson himself would address a meeting of the parliamentary party in the afternoon, before which he would (as he had on several other occasions on which he was in deep trouble at home) have an officially publicized conversation with President Zelensky of Ukraine.[36]

In the event, however, none of this – except perhaps the typically hyperbolic Twitter attack on leadership hopeful (and former contender) Jeremy Hunt by Nadine Dorries – came close to matching the splash created in Westminster and beyond by former frontbencher (and long-term Boris supporter) Jesse Norman.[37] Before Brady had even had time to make his formal announcement, Norman released a copy of the letter he had sent to his old friend not only urging him to go but also outlining, clearly and concisely, exactly why he must do so.[38] To many (perhaps even to some of those reluctantly determined to stick with Johnson), his missive was more persuasive, and certainly more cogently argued, than Johnson's own (individually signed) letter to his 358 parliamentary colleagues asking for their support.[39] A powerful op-ed in the *Telegraph* from Theresa May's former Chief of Staff, Nick Timothy, contrasting 'the selfless service of Her Majesty with the casual corrosion of ethical standards and pursuit of purposeless power by her prime minister' didn't help either.[40] Nor did a snap poll by YouGov: although it suggested that 59 per cent of those who'd voted Conservative in 2019 thought the party's MPs should vote to keep Johnson in office, it nevertheless found that 32 per cent thought the opposite, while among voters as a whole, the figures were 60 per cent for removal and 27 per cent for keeping him.[41] YouGov also managed to pull together a relatively small (and so heavily weighted) sample of party members, which provided slightly more encouragement: although they appeared to approve of a vote being held by a 50 to 44 margin, they also believed by a margin of 53 to 42 that MPs should vote confidence in Johnson, and their responses when asked who they'd like to take over showed an utterly split field with only three possible runners even getting into double figures – and then only by the skin of their teeth.[42] Tory MPs getting ready to vote could also glance at the ConservativeHome readers' poll of party members, which made rather less encouraging reading for Johnson since it suggested 55 per cent of the rank and file wanted them to vote Johnson out while only 42 per cent wanted him kept on – and this from a panel which according to the site's editor was largely composed of the same people who had given the PM a 93 per cent net approval rating just after the 2019 election.[43]

In the event, 211 of the party's MPs expressed confidence in their leader, as against 148 who did not – a 59–41 per cent margin that was far tighter than many had expected and Johnson had hoped for. But just as John Major's and Theresa May's teams had done in 1995 and 2018 respectively, his supporters immediately went out that evening and the following morning to declare to anyone who would listen that the result had settled the matter – including, to much hilarity, Jacob Rees-Mogg, who'd not hesitated, back when he'd played assassin rather than bodyguard, to declare that May's (effectively larger) margin of victory had been 'a very bad result … a third of the parliamentary party, the overwhelming majority of backbenchers have voted against her'. Speaking for himself, Johnson noted that more MPs had voted for him than had done so in the leadership contest three years before. It was, he claimed, 'a convincing result, a decisive result and what it means is that as a government we can move on and focus on the stuff I think really matters to people'.

To many Tory MPs, however, it now seemed obvious that, as one of them memorably put it to the *i* newspaper's chief political commentator, Paul Waugh, 'It's like a lion chasing a zebra. The zebra may escape but with a gammy leg that will get infected. And he'll be down in the end.'[44] Just as damagingly, any hope that said zebra might have had that he could still rely on absolutely unquestioning support from the party in the media swiftly began to evaporate: the *Mail* ('BORIS VOWS: I'LL BASH

ON') and the *Express* ('DEFIANT AND UNBOWED') thankfully held firm, but the *Sun*, despite talking about a stab in the back, was upfront about the narrowness of Johnson's win; and most painfully (and in some ways most worryingly) of all, the *Telegraph*'s front page declared 'Hollow victory tears Tories apart – Johnson's authority crushed'.[45] Over at the *Times* (not part of the party in the media but by no means inherently hostile to the Tories), their star columnist, former Conservative leader William Hague, wasn't prepared to dissimulate:

> Words have been said that cannot be retracted, reports published that cannot be erased, and votes have been cast that show a greater level of rejection than any Tory leader has ever endured and survived. Deep inside, he should recognise that, and turn his mind to getting out in a way that spares party and country such agonies and uncertainties.[46]

ConservativeHome's Paul Goodman, always one of the most astute voices in Tory politics, said pretty much the same thing, calling on Cabinet ministers (albeit with no great confidence that they would listen) to persuade Johnson to 'leave office undefeated sooner rather than lose a ballot later – or have no option but to quit before it (thus gaining nothing other than more agonising months or weeks in office but not in power)'.[47]

Johnson, of course, had absolutely no intention of quitting of his own accord. As was his wont, he again invited cameras into the Cabinet room in a rather desperate attempt to demonstrate that he and his ministers were getting on with the job. He then travelled north to deliver a speech (though not a particularly coherent one, even by his standards) whose main purpose seemed to be to project confidence and to showcase one or two eye-catching new policies – the main one being the extension of right-to-buy to housing association tenants and those on benefits. He also made it clear, via briefings, that, in order to prevent the 'wage-price spiral' he'd talked about in his speech, he wouldn't 'roll over and surrender' to railway unions which were about to go on strike and, at least according to some Tory MPs and the party in the media, were thereby threatening a 'summer of discontent' that would 'take Britain back to the seventies' – a fate ministers hoped to avoid by preparing legislation to make it legally possible for employers to hire temporary employees to

Unconvinced: Cabinet after the confidence vote, June 2022.
Source: Ian Vogler / Reuters / Alamy.

replace striking employees. And, in a sign of just how prepared Johnson was to flout Cabinet collective responsibility in order to stay in office, journalists were also briefed by 'allies of the Prime Minister' that he was 'determined to stop' the planned rise in corporation tax (which the *Times*'s headline chose to label a '£15bn tax raid on business') signalled by Rishi Sunak, his Chancellor, back in 2021.[48]

All this – together with the rather tougher than expected Northern Ireland Protocol Bill and the fact that the government's new food strategy junked key recommendations (e.g. the introduction of levies for sugar and salt and the expansion of free school meal provision) made by its 'Food Tsar', Henry Dimbleby – was patently intended to shore up support on the right of the parliamentary party, as well as the party in the media. So, too, was the oblique hint Johnson gave, in the wake of the first flight carrying (in the end just seven) asylum seekers to Rwanda being grounded following a last-minute ruling from Strasbourg, that the UK might need to leave the European Convention on Human Rights – something that furious Tory MPs were demanding both publicly and (supposedly) privately in their various WhatsApp groups.[49]

Embarrassment after embarrassment

But as much as Johnson could hint, could bluster, and could dangle all sorts of possibilities in front of his backbenchers, he couldn't control everything and everybody. He'd barely finished with the failure of the Rwanda flight to take off when news broke that his second ethics adviser in a row was departing with immediate effect. Christopher Geidt, who had been subject to a humiliating grilling by members of the Commons Public Administration and Constitutional Affairs Committee the day before, had finally (some would say belatedly) decided that enough was enough and that he was resigning – a move that, when he'd taken the job just over a year before, he had said would be a 'last resort' designed to send 'a critical signal into the public domain'. Johnson's response – much to the irritation of MPs from the Northern Research Group, who, as well as calling for cuts to green levies, VAT on energy, and fuel duty now that inflation was forecast to reach 11 per cent, were expecting him to speak at their inaugural conference in Doncaster – was to make another flying visit to Kyiv and to pen an op-ed for the *Sunday Times* on why (as if there were the slightest risk that the UK would do so) 'we must never turn our backs on valiant Ukraine'.[50] For the Westminster bubble if not the country as a whole, however, even that wasn't enough to draw attention away from the sudden disappearance from the pages of its sister paper the previous morning of a story, written by veteran reporter Simon Walters, detailing how Johnson, when Foreign Secretary, had apparently tried to hire Carrie Symonds (as she then was) as his Chief of Staff – an illustration some said of 'the Streisand effect', where an attempt (in this case, it was alleged, on the part of Downing Street) to remove something from the internet only creates more interest in it.[51] Still, the controversy couldn't be allowed to put a dampener on the party's Summer Ball fundraiser held a couple of days later at London's Victoria and Albert Museum, where, following the traditional auction, donors reportedly went home with an African safari (£65,000), a shooting weekend (£37,000), a wine tasting (£30,000), and, best of all, dinner with Johnson, May, and Cameron (together in the same room apparently), which reportedly went for around £120,000.

To get into the bash via the front entrance, guests, including ministers, had to cross a picket line run by the Public and Commercial

Services Union, but it was not in fact the PCS that was the union on everyone's mind. That was the National Union of Rail, Maritime and Transport Workers, the RMT, which had just begun a series of strikes which crippled the rail network for much of that week but which, to the disappointment of the government, elicited (if polling was to be believed) a fair degree of public sympathy, notwithstanding the efforts of Transport Secretary Grant Shapps and the party in the media.[52] That it did so wasn't altogether surprising given that the vast majority of people in work were well aware that their own salaries weren't keeping pace with inflation any more than were the railway workers'. That was also true, of course, of those in receipt of welfare benefits and/or the state pension. But for them, the government had some good news: from 2023, at a cost of £20 billion, benefits and pensions would rise in line with inflation, the latter because the triple lock (by which pensions increase annually by the rate of inflation, wage growth, or 2.5 per cent, whichever is the highest) was being reinstated.

The announcement was made on the eve of crucial by-elections being held in Wakefield and in Tiverton and Honiton, prompting some to suggest that it was more than coincidence: after all, people aged 60 and over were normally the most reliable source of support for the Conservatives. But if that was the case, the move clearly had no more success in mobilizing Tory voters in Yorkshire and in Devon than did hints of a return to grammar schools or, indeed, the publication on the same day of Dominic Raab's 'Bill of Rights Bill', which would, as well as protecting free speech from the threat posed to it by 'cancel culture', impose new limits on interventions by the European Court of Human Rights in UK affairs of the type that had prevented the Rwanda flight taking off.[53] In Wakefield, Labour finished 18 points ahead of the Conservatives, winning with an 8.6 point swing – which, were it to be repeated at a general election, would be easily enough to deprive many 'Red Wall' Tory MPs of their seats. Meanwhile, down in Tiverton and Honiton, the Lib Dems pulled off yet another spectacular by-election victory, overturning a 24,000 Conservative majority with a 29.9 point swing – a result which left the twenty to thirty Tory MPs facing a realistic threat from Lib Dem opponents at the next general election seriously worried.[54] True, CCHQ could take some share of the blame for not ensuring that the local associations concerned selected more able candidates. But it was hard to believe that that would have made much difference given the nature of the scandals that had obliged the sitting MPs to resign in the first place – and given the unpopularity of the government and, of course, the Prime Minister himself.

As it happened, Johnson was in Kigali for the Commonwealth Heads of Government meeting and was apparently taking an early morning dip in his hotel's pool when he was alerted to the news that, on top of the bad results from the by-elections themselves, the Co-Chairman of the Conservative Party – the previously ultra-loyal culture warrior Oliver Dowden – was resigning, and was doing so in what had now become the traditional manner, namely a letter to the PM posted on Twitter. In it Dowden argued that 'We cannot carry on with business as usual' and made it pretty obvious to anyone reading between the lines (not least by pledging his continued loyalty to the Conservative Party without mentioning Johnson in the same breath) that he believed he was not the only one who needed to 'take responsibility'.[55] It therefore came as some relief to the PM's team in Rwanda that they were able to establish fairly quickly that Dowden's departure was not the first move in a coordinated sequence of Cabinet resignations. And the party in the media's reaction, although worrying in its talk of renewed hopes on the parts of the PM's critics that he could be removed sooner rather than later, was not as brutal as it might have been, the *Mail's* front page going with the rather bizarre call by some Tories that Labour and the Lib Dems should 'come clean' about their (shock, horror!) tacit encouragement of tactical voting, while the *Express* went with the slightly desperate-sounding 'BORIS VOWS TO FIGHT NEXT ELECTION ... AND WIN!'[56]

Once again, however, Johnson (facing further embarrassment back home as it was revealed he and Carrie had tried and failed to get approval for a £150,000 treehouse for their son in the garden of Chequers) proved his own worst enemy. Speaking from Rwanda, he told the BBC's Mishal Husain in a rare appearance on its flagship *Today* programme that 'As a leader, you have to try to distinguish between the criticism that really matters and the criticism that doesn't.' He also assured her that he wasn't about to undergo some kind of 'psychological transformation', thereby reminding all too many of his MPs that not only did he fail to appreciate how much all this was his fault but also that he was simply incapable of change.[57] He then compounded matters by trying too hard to convey a measure of confidence, telling reporters that he was 'thinking actively about the third term and what could happen then' – words which, as far as his worried colleagues were concerned, couldn't help but bring to mind Margaret Thatcher's imperious 'I hope to go on and on' and her doomed and delusional 'I shall fight on. I shall fight to win.'[58]

Not surprisingly, then, whispers that the PM's critics would use the upcoming elections to the Executive of the 1922 Committee to secure a rule change enabling a second vote of confidence to take place in, say, the autumn grew louder and louder.[59] And the fact that not a single Tory MP voted against Liz Truss's Northern Ireland Protocol Bill on second reading, despite some of them speaking out against it in no uncertain terms ('a muscle flex for a future leadership bid' by Truss [Simon Hoare] that 'brazenly breaks a solemn international treaty' [Andrew Mitchell] and would 'diminish the standing of the United Kingdom in the eyes of the world' [Theresa May]), was far from an unalloyed triumph for the Whips. Over seventy Conservative MPs abstained (at least forty on principle) – a fair few of them (along with others, who voted with the government) choosing to do so because they wanted (a) to ensure that they didn't lose the whip for voting with the Opposition and therefore find themselves unable to participate in another vote of confidence and any subsequent leadership contest, and (b) to avoid losing out on a promotion if and when a new leader (who would of course be a Brexiteer) was putting together their new frontbench. Whether any of them were just keeping their heads down so as not to identify themselves as one of the (some said three, some six) MPs who, the rumour mill had it, were supposedly close to crossing the floor to join Labour, who knows?[60] Still, it looked like Johnson would at least make it to the summer recess, during which some of the bad blood that had built up while he was away on his diplomatic travels might drain away.

But it was not to be. On the evening of the last day of the month, the *Sun* broke the story that Chris Pincher, appointed Deputy Chief Whip in February after helping Johnson to fend off his critics at the height of Partygate, had resigned after drunkenly groping two men at the Carlton Club the evening before.[61] Rather than taking immediate action to suspend him from the parliamentary party, Johnson decided that, since Pincher had supposedly 'done the decent thing' by resigning from the Whips' Office, no further action needed to be taken. It soon became clear, however, that the Prime Minister had (just as he had with Hancock and Paterson) not only completely misread the mood of his colleagues but, just as seriously (and despite sending out ministers to effectively deny that it was the case), had also been no less aware than the rest of them of Pincher's reputation and, indeed, record as a sex pest before he'd appointed him – a fact attested to by Dominic Cummings and, then, in even more damaging detail, by former Permanent Secretary at the Foreign Office Simon McDonald.[62] For once, Johnson had not only been caught out lying, it could be proved beyond all doubt that he'd done so. Pincher's suspension pending an investigation came too late to make a difference, while efforts by the rapidly dwindling band of government ministers still prepared to try to defend Johnson by suggesting that he'd simply forgotten that he'd been informed of specific complaints against Pincher were greeted with the incredulous ridicule they deserved. The party in the media had initially backed him, but in the case of the *Telegraph* and the *Sun*, if not the uber-loyal *Mail*, not perhaps as enthusiastically as the PM might have hoped.[63] Meanwhile, the publication of two very depressing polls had done nothing to improve the mood of his parliamentary colleagues, far too many of whom looked destined, according to one of them, to lose their seats.[64] Johnson's desperate attempt to seize the initiative by talking about tax cuts and, yet again, inviting cameras into the Cabinet room to convey unity of purpose backfired badly, the funereal expressions on the faces of those around the table telling a totally different story.[65]

That said, it nevertheless came as a bombshell when, shortly after 6 p.m. on Tuesday, 5 July, just as viewers of the BBC's evening news were watching an interview with the Prime Minister in which he finally admitted he'd made a mistake in appointing Pincher, Health Secretary Sajid Javid and then Chancellor Rishi Sunak announced on Twitter that they were resigning from the Cabinet with immediate effect, setting in train what, for once, can truly be described as mass resignations from the government frontbench over the course of the next thirty-six hours.[66] Johnson's rapid replacement of Javid (by Steve Barclay) and Sunak (by Nadhim Zahawi), and his attempt to laugh off the departure of his Chancellor by suggesting to loyal MPs that it would make 'cutting taxes now somewhat easier', failed to stem the bleeding. Snap polling suggested that even a majority of 2019 Tory voters now wanted him gone, and by the Wednesday morning even the party in the media, with the predictable exception of the *Express*, appeared none too convinced that he could (or even should) stay on.[67] PMQs on Wednesday lunchtime was a car crash: Starmer was on good form, noting that 'the sinking ships [were] fleeing the rat' and calling the rejigged Cabinet 'the charge of the lightweight brigade', but, if anything, it was the calls for him to go (some heartfelt, others dripping with sarcasm) from his own backbenchers that were the most wounding. Johnson then had to sit through Javid's prosaic but nonetheless brutal resignation statement before going on to appear before the Commons Liaison Committee in a pathetic attempt to simultaneously pretend that everything was hunky-dory and yet to hint that he might call an election if anyone tried to force him out – a threat that, given the consensus view of expert commentators was that the Queen would be well within her rights to refuse him a dissolution, even the most gullible of his colleagues no longer took seriously.[68] He returned to Downing Street to meet with a number of different delegations telling him his time was up – a message for which he'd decided to sack Michael Gove (later called 'a snake' by allies of the PM) for delivering on his own account earlier in the day. The *coup de grâce*, however, was delivered by Nadhim Zahawi on Thursday morning when he tweeted an open letter, penned on Treasury notepaper, telling the PM he had to 'go now'.

Knowing that elections to the 1922 Committee in a few days' time would produce an Executive that would be willing, if necessary, to enable the holding of a second vote of confidence, and having spoken to the Queen the previous evening, Johnson finally bowed to reality. Having obtained a degree of reassurance that he would be allowed to stay on in Number Ten in what amounted to a caretaker capacity until a successor could be appointed, he stepped out into Downing Street on Thursday lunchtime to make what will surely rank as one of the most graceless resignation speeches ever made by a British Prime Minister, framing his departure as the betrayal of a political colossus by faint-hearted, lesser creatures who simply couldn't see what a huge mistake they were all making.[69]

And they're off! Choosing a new leader

Predictably enough, however, Tory MPs wasted little time in turning their thoughts as to who they wanted to take over. Indeed, one of those who hoped to do so, Suella Braverman, who'd called on Johnson to quit but insisted she needed to stay on as Attorney General, even declared she was running before he announced he was going. Others soon followed over the course of the next two or three days, including a couple of Cabinet ministers (or at least former Cabinet ministers!), Sajid Javid and Grant Shapps, who subsequently decided they lacked sufficient support and withdrew before voting got underway. The only notable absentee was Defence Secretary Ben Wallace, who, despite being hotly tipped because of his standing in ConservativeHome's regular reader surveys, declined the opportunity to stand, claiming he wanted to focus on 'keeping this great country safe'.

Just as it had done in 2019, the 1922 Committee again tweaked the rules for the contest, raising the thresholds for progression still further in order to discourage no-hopers and to ensure MPs that they could come up with a final two before parliament went into recess on 21 July, after which members would put them through their paces in a series of hustings before voting closed on 2 September, with the winner announced on Monday the 5th. This time around, candidates would need to be nominated by 20 MPs (i.e. 5.6 per cent of the total parliamentary party, up from 2.6 per cent in 2019). In order to qualify for subsequent rounds, they would have to secure more than 30 votes (8.4 per cent of the total number of MPs, up from 5.4 per cent in 2019) in the first round, which would take place on 13 July. Then, from, the second round onwards, the last-placed candidate would be eliminated.

The higher hurdle imposed on candidates in round one was sufficient to see two of them knocked out in short order (see Table 2). Jeremy Hunt, the runner-up in 2019, faced pretty much the same fate as Andrea Leadsom had back then: in his case, any delusions of grandeur he'd been harbouring were dashed after he won the support of just 18 MPs, his pitch as the party's experienced moderate rather undermined by his counter-intuitive (not to say bizarre) choice of 'running mate', Esther McVey – a colleague very much on the populist right who had, back in 2019, been eliminated in the first round of parliamentary voting after securing a mere 9 votes. Nadhim Zahawi (Johnson's Chancellor but also, in some ways, his executioner) did slightly better, but the 25 votes he garnered still weren't enough to see him advance beyond the first round either. Suella Braverman, standing on a predictably Eurosceptic

Table 2. The 2022 leadership contest: parliamentary stage

Candidate	First ballot: 13 July		Second ballot: 14 July		Third ballot: 18 July (preceded by two TV debates)		Fourth ballot: 19 July		Fifth ballot: 20 July	
	Votes	%	Votes	%	Votes	%	Votes	%	Votes	%
Rishi Sunak	**88**	**24.6**	**101**	**28.2**	**115**	**32.1**	**118**	**33.0**	**137**	**38.3**
Liz Truss	**50**	**14.0**	**64**	**17.9**	**71**	**19.8**	**86**	**24.0**	**113**	**31.6**
Penny Mordaunt	67	18.7	83	23.2	82	22.9	92	25.7	105	29.3
Kemi Badenoch	40	11.2	49	13.7	58	16.2	59	16.5	Eliminated	
Tom Tugendhat	37	10.3	32	8.9	31	8.7	Eliminated			
Suella Braverman	32	8.9	27	7.5	Eliminated					
Nadhim Zahawi	25	7.0	Eliminated							
Jeremy Hunt	18	5.0	Eliminated							

and tax-cutting platform, just made it over the line with 32 votes, only to be eliminated in the second round the next day, having gone backwards on 27 votes, after which she endorsed Liz Truss, in return for a promise she would be made Home Secretary.[70] Tom Tugendhat, Chair of the Commons Foreign Affairs Select Committee, who pitched himself as a combination of One Nation Conservative, China hawk, and (having served in the military but not in government) clean skin, also lost support in spite of the polling which suggested he'd done pretty well in the first televised debate. It therefore came as no surprise to see him eliminated in round three. The next round saw the elimination of Kemi Badenoch, who, unlike Tugendhat, had served in government (albeit only in a relatively junior capacity) and, having made a name for herself as something of a culture warrior, won support on the right of the party for her no-nonsense small-state views and her concerns about the government's net zero target.

And then there were five: leadership debate, July 2022.
Source: Jonathan Hordle / ITV / Shutterstock.

Both Tugendhat and Badenoch (who had also performed pretty well in the televised debates she'd featured in) could console themselves with the thought that they had probably done enough to earn themselves a decent job in Cabinet. The question was where would their supporters go now in the final ballot? Rishi Sunak may not have been wildly popular, and was already being sniped at by 'Number Ten sources' and 'friends' of Johnson, but he seemed almost certain to finish top, having garnered endorsements from 47 colleagues by the close of nominations. Liz Truss (who'd secured just 22 by that stage), however, was by no means sure of second place: true, the way she carried herself in the second televised debate represented a marked improvement on her halting performance in the first, but polling suggested that the public (who, to be fair, weren't madly enthusiastic about any of the candidates) didn't warm to her. That said, among Tory MPs and members, as an instinctive small-state Conservative who had spent her time in Johnson's government (a) negotiating and celebrating post-Brexit trade deals, (b) bashing the EU as well as China and Russia, and (c) banging on about 'woke', Truss was still in some ways the logical choice to 'unite the right' against 'Rishi'

– especially because, in addition to having extensive Cabinet experience, she'd chosen, unlike Sunak, not to resign and so wasn't open to the accusation, now routinely levelled at him by those who found it difficult to reconcile themselves to Johnson's departure, that she'd somehow 'stabbed him in the back'. However, she had struggled to match the showmanship displayed by Penny Mordaunt, another supposedly no-nonsense Brexiteer from a relatively ordinary background.

Mordaunt, like Badenoch, came over well on television – at least in the view of grassroots members – and, unlike Badenoch, could point to Cabinet experience as Secretary of State for International Development and for Defence. Despite the fact that she wasn't close to Johnson, having paid the price for backing Jeremy Hunt in 2019, and despite some controversy over her campaign video and attempts by allies of her opponents to portray her as 'woke' on transgender issues, she had garnered considerable support among her colleagues, beating Truss in all of the first four ballots. However, thanks, perhaps, to the efforts of Truss's fans in the party in the media to undermine Mordaunt, the gap between them had narrowed considerably in rounds three and four, suggesting that Badenoch's supporters had (predictably enough perhaps) broken more strongly for Truss, as had (perhaps more surprisingly) some of Tugendhat's.[71] By the final round, Truss had, indeed, managed to 'unite the right' to finish as runner-up, almost certainly helped by the fact that polling of Conservative members, although it wasn't so overwhelming that it could get a bandwagon rolling yet, suggested to those opposed to Sunak that she now stood as good a chance of beating him as Mordaunt, which hadn't initially been the case.[72]

But while the exhaustive ballot system had, in the end, done its job, it had also exposed the reality that neither of the two candidates who would now face the membership were that popular with their colleagues. Both Theresa May (fairly easily) and Boris Johnson (albeit only just) had finished the parliamentary stage of their contests with a majority of MPs voting for them, and even David Cameron had come fairly close in 2005. But neither Sunak (who – in a sign that Gavin Williamson, supposed master of 'the dark arts', had lost his touch – managed to secure the support of only four in ten of his colleagues) nor Truss (who cobbled up the votes of just three in ten) had managed that. A survey of party members conducted by YouGov just after Sunak and Truss were confirmed as the final two suggested that the grassroots – overwhelmingly white, generally comfortably off, average age just under 60, and the majority of whom lived in southern England – weren't too impressed either.[73] With respondents given the choice of all those who had stood, they garnered just 11 and 13 per cent respectively, behind Badenoch (on 24) and Mordaunt (on 20).[74] The same survey suggested, however, that, far from this meaning that, for both Sunak and Truss, there was now all to play for, the contest was actually the latter's to lose. Forced now to choose between the two of them, some 49 per cent said Truss and only 31 per cent said Sunak – a margin, when the don't knows and won't votes were excluded, of 62 to 38. What seemed to give Truss her initial edge was the fact that some 40 per cent of members didn't feel Sunak could be trusted (compared to just 18 per cent who said the same of her), suggesting, perhaps, that a combination of anger over his resignation from Johnson's Cabinet and the earlier non-dom/green card scandal was going to make it very hard for the former Chancellor to turn things around. Moreover, any hopes that he might be able to persuade some of those members who had already voted for Truss to change their minds and switch to him – something CCHQ (rather bizarrely) was going to allow people to do by letting them override their first vote by going online and changing it – was snatched away after the UK's National Cyber Security Centre recommended (surely unsurprisingly) that the idea should be junked since it would render the process open to manipulation. Given the party was already vulnerable to the accusation that non-citizens who had joined Conservatives Abroad could vote in the contest, even if they were not on the electoral register in the UK, discretion proved the better part of valour and members were instructed that they could vote only once – either by post or online.[75]

Truss's lead was confirmed by a YouGov survey of members conducted in mid-August, although it also suggested, rather embarrassingly, that both she and Sunak would have lost to Johnson if he had been on the ballot; it suggested, too, that some 55 per cent of members thought MPs were 'effectively wrong to force Boris Johnson to resign'.[76] Just as interestingly, when respondents were asked whether it was more important for the next Prime Minister to 'get inflation under control' or 'reduce people's taxes', they plumped 63 to 33 for controlling inflation (Sunak's priority) over tax cuts (which were Truss's). For all the twists and turns of the contest in the country, then – the twelve hustings that were held; the sometimes bitchy and bitter exchanges between the candidates and their campaign teams; the talk of Truss emerging as the 'change' or 'anti-establishment' candidate whose offer to cut taxation was too tempting to resist vs Sunak the highly polished but occasionally tetchy technocrat determined to bring down borrowing; and the tweets about her £4.50 earrings vs his £450 Prada shoes – it would appear that, ultimately, many members weren't ever going to vote for the man who'd not only insisted on raising their taxes while his wife didn't pay all she might have done but who also, worse than that, had helped to bring down their hero.[77]

Perhaps if Sunak had been able to argue, as many initially thought he would, that he was seen as a far better pick for Prime Minister by the electorate as a whole, they might have set aside their desire for revenge. Academic research, however, suggests that when governing parties in the UK are choosing a leader, they tend to prioritize perceived competence (often measured by how long a candidate has been in Cabinet) over electability.[78] And in any case, Sunak's clear advantage over Truss in respect of the latter had, by the end of July, dwindled to virtually nothing.[79] So, too, by the end of August had his advantage among MPs. Since she was by no means the frontrunner in the parliamentary stage, Truss's bandwagon had taken longer to start rolling than Johnson's had in 2019. But as membership polling made it more and more obvious that she was going to win, more and more MPs joined former candidates Suella Braverman, Nadhim Zahawi, Tom Tugendhat, and Penny Mordaunt by jumping on that bandwagon – one which picked up even more momentum as endorsement after endorsement came in from the party in the media and as it became patently obvious that Johnson (who seemed to have decided that Sunak was the main author of his downfall) was backing her, albeit not in so many words. By the end of the contest, Truss, who ultimately managed to raise nearly as much as her rival in donations to her campaign, had been endorsed by 158 of her colleagues.[80] Sunak, by contrast, had just 138 backers, and gained no others after 12 August, whereas Truss accrued a further 33 – including nearly all the government's Whips. Interestingly, only 3 MPs who'd earlier declared for Sunak actually felt able to confess publicly that they were switching, but by no means all of those who'd previously backed him were, by the end, doing so very vocally.

Given the final result of the contest, they were right not to do so. Although Truss's margin of victory might not have been quite as resounding as some predicted or as impressive as Johnson's 66–34 in 2019, it was still reasonably convincing, even if some nay-sayers insisted on pointing out that she hadn't secured a majority of those grassroots members entitled to vote in the contest. As it turned out, some 83 per cent of a total membership of 172,437 (up from just 160,000 three years previously) took part – not far off the 87 per cent who did so in 2019, with Truss winning 57 per cent to Sunak's 43 per cent. The public, however, were sceptical. Snap polling suggested as many as 50 per cent of voters were disappointed that she'd been chosen as the country's next Prime Minister compared to 22 per cent who were pleased. Even 34 per cent of Tory voters confessed to being disappointed (the same proportion, incidentally, who thought she'd be a worse Prime Minister than Johnson), although 41 per cent were pleased. The fact that in both cases a quarter or more replied 'don't know', however – plus the fact that it is always easier to exceed low expectations than to meet high hopes – meant there was at least something to play for, especially given that Johnson had been the source of many of the Conservatives' problems and Keir Starmer had yet to convince the electorate he could do much better.[81] Truss was also able to count on an enthusiastic welcome from most of the party in the media, with both the *Sun*'s and the *Express*'s front pages choosing to greet her on first-name terms and the *Mail* splashing with 'Cometh the hour, cometh the woman'. The only slight cause for concern was the *Telegraph*, which, while not unsympathetic, was rather more lukewarm, its leader column concluding only that Truss 'deserves a chance to show what she and her new government are capable of delivering before judgment is passed'.[82]

11

Two last bites at the cherry
(September–November 2022)

Conservative MPs – including the six-in-ten who hadn't endorsed Liz Truss in the leadership contest in spite of the fact that she had, for weeks, looked certain to win it – had little option other than to give her the benefit of the doubt. That, and hope that she could put together a package to deal with increases in the cost of energy which would be sufficient to convince voters that she was, after all, on their side rather than a true-believer in 'trickle-down economics', convinced (as she put it in an interview) that it was wrong 'to look at everything through the lens of redistribution'. However much that package might go beyond (or even completely contradict) her promises on the campaign trail and offend their small-state sensibilities, all that mattered at the outset was that she not sink herself (and therefore their chances of hanging onto their seats) before she'd effectively left port. As former leader (and Rishi Sunak backer) William Hague put it in his *Times* column the day after she was elected, 'The Conservative Party cannot change its leader again before a general election due in two years' time, unless it is to be the laughing stock of the country and the world.'[1] But Hague also urged her to show 'just how different' she was going to be from Johnson, especially when it came to 'high standards of conduct, truthfulness and fair dealing', which, in particular, meant that 'the inquiry into Johnson's own conduct should be left to the House of Commons' – something that those MPs most loyal to the outgoing Prime Minister (along with much of the party in the media) had spent weeks campaigning against.

The high priestess of the cult of Johnson, Nadine Dorries, announced – doubtless to the relief of some of her colleagues after one or two interventions she'd made in the leadership contest – that she was resigning from Cabinet (presumably on a promise of a peerage), but whether this portended a degree of acceptance on her part, no-one could be quite sure.[2] The same went for the departure of Home Secretary Priti Patel,

268

who was widely rumoured to be facing the sack or, at the very least, demotion. It soon became obvious, however, that their leaving did not prefigure a determination on Truss's part to sweep away some of the detritus of the Johnson years. Nor, in appointing her new ministerial team, did she signal a desire to reach across the party rather than tribally reward colleagues who had backed her and, in most cases therefore, had likewise remained uncritical of her predecessor's behaviour to the bitter end.

In the event, of the 31 people appointed to or allowed to attend Cabinet, some 25 openly supported Truss, while 5 did not declare for anyone. Moreover, the only Cabinet loyalists from the Johnson era to be effectively sacked had also been prominent Sunak supporters: Dominic Raab, Grant Shapps, Steve Barclay, and George Eustice. And there was seemingly no attempt to persuade Sunak himself to come on board. True, Sajid Javid was offered something (widely thought to be Northern Ireland), but he turned it down. True, too, Michael Ellis was made Attorney General and therefore the only out-and-out Sunak supporter to attend Cabinet, but then he had made a name for himself over the

Truss takes over, September 2022.
Source: 10 Downing Street.

spring and summer as the man most prepared to go in to bat for Johnson in the Commons. Ultimately, then, neither Ellis's appointment, nor the fact that a smattering of MPs who'd backed Sunak (such as former Cabinet minister Robert Jenrick) were given jobs as junior ministers, could disguise the fact that Truss, following in Johnson's rather than in May's footsteps, had clearly decided to burn rather than build bridges.

Keeping many of the same faces, just sitting them in different seats around the Cabinet table, had its advantages, of course. Very few of those concerned looked capable of posing any kind of threat to her, and some (most obviously Kwasi Kwarteng, her pick for Chancellor, and Suella Braverman, her pick for Home Secretary) were of a similar cast of mind. They were keen to see lower taxes and less regulation and at the same time more than happy to bang the drum on culture war issues, crime, immigration, and Europe if it helped 'Red Wall' MPs hang on to their seats and to persuade Brexit-ultras that the government wasn't going to make concessions to the EU, especially over Northern Ireland – a message positively sledge-hammered home with the appointment to the latter brief of both Chris Heaton-Harris and Steve Baker. Moreover, the ideological affinity at the very top meant there was at least a chance that government policy might achieve a degree of coherence and a sense of direction that were often lacking under Johnson – something that might have been trickier to achieve if, in the words of one anonymous Cabinet minister, she ended up 'appointing people who didn't support her – people who very publicly said her ideas were shit and she's incompetent'.[3]

But there were downsides to not reaching out, too. Was there really enough talent on the Tory benches among the four in ten MPs who had endorsed her in the leadership contest to make it worthwhile taking what Hague rightly called the 'calculated risk' of excluding from all of the top jobs many of those who hadn't, even if a few of them were forgiven and rewarded with less prestigious government posts? Certainly, a number of 'Red Wall' MPs (indeed, all those colleagues elected in 2019 in marginal seats in the North and the Midlands) were worried that, after Gove's departure, there didn't seem to be an awful lot of room for advocates of 'levelling up' in Truss's Cabinet. And then, of course, there would be the predictable welter of resentment among those who had been let go or left out, especially when Truss had brought back into government (albeit in a junior role) someone like Mark Spencer, who, as Chief

Whip under Johnson, had been heavily involved in the doomed and damaging effort to oblige colleagues to rescue Owen Paterson. Indeed, even some of those MPs for whom room *had* been found were entitled to feel a little hard done by, not least former leadership contenders Penny Mordaunt, who'd been given a non-departmental role as Leader of the House, and Kemi Badenoch, made Trade Secretary – a role that would presumably give her less visibility than she might have liked, especially when Michelle Donelan, the new Culture Secretary, could be relied upon to do the heavy lifting on the anti-woke agenda in her stead. Still, any disappointment felt by Mordaunt may at least have been eased by the knowledge that David Frost, who had attacked her at a key point in the parliamentary stage of the leadership contest, thus doing Truss a huge favour, hadn't been offered a place in the new administration – or at least not one he felt was commensurate with what he regarded anyway as his considerable talents.[4]

As for the demographic composition of the Cabinet, much was (quite rightly) made in the media of the fact that, for the first time in history, none of the four 'great offices of state' – Prime Minister, Chancellor, Home Secretary, and Foreign Secretary – was occupied by a white man. However, only a third of the Cabinet were women, although that meant they were overrepresented in terms of a parliamentary party which was still three-quarters male. Some observers also noted that, of the eight female Cabinet ministers appointed by Truss, six had previously chosen not to join seventy-two of their Conservative colleagues who, on a free vote on the issue in March 2022, had ensured that women would continue to get home abortion medication following a telemedicine consultation with a doctor – including (presumably on religious grounds in her case) the new Health Secretary and Deputy PM, Thérèse Coffey.[5] As for the class composition of the Cabinet (using educational background as a proxy), some 68 per cent of its attendees went to fee-paying schools. This was around seven times the number of children who were privately educated in the country as a whole and one-and-a-half times the proportion of Tory MPs in the Commons who'd been to fee-paying schools. Moreover, it was more than twice the proportion in May's first Cabinet (30 per cent) and more than the proportion in Johnson's and Cameron's 2019 and 2015 Cabinets (64 and 50 per cent respectively).[6] In short, some welcome diversity, yes, but all too easily exaggerated.

Having flown up to Balmoral to 'kiss hands' with the Queen (Johnson having already paid her a visit to tender his resignation, although not until after he'd given yet another painfully self-pitying/self-aggrandizing farewell speech earlier that morning), Truss returned to London to give her first Downing Street address as Prime Minister.[7] What it lacked in rhetorical graces and, indeed, originality (borrowing as it did from both Churchill ['action this day'] and Cameron ['aspiration nation']), it made up for in clarity.[8] Her aim (although, perhaps significantly, there was no mention of 'levelling up') was to inject growth into the economy by simultaneously lowering taxes and investing in infrastructure, to sort out the ongoing crisis in the NHS, and to cap energy prices in order to avoid high bills driving millions into poverty. It was, of course, the latter aim – neatly encapsulated in Truss's insistence that 'Together, we can ride out the storm' (which the *Times*, *Metro*, *Mail*, *Telegraph*, and *Express* all used as their front-page headline) – that had to take priority. Accordingly, a couple of days later – albeit via a Commons debate rather than a Commons statement (which made it easier for the government to avoid having to answer detailed questions) – the cap was confirmed. Significantly, it was to be financed by long-term borrowing rather than (as Labour insisted should happen) an additional windfall tax on the astronomical profits gas and oil companies were making.

Whether or not this was sensible, it served a number of purposes. Firstly, although most Conservative MPs suddenly seemed prepared to countenance adding an eye-watering one-off amount to the national debt in order to hang on to their seats at the next election (testament, perhaps, to Anthony Trollope's assurance that 'no innovation ... stinks so foully in the nostrils of an English Tory politician as to be absolutely irreconcilable to him. When taken in the refreshing waters of office any such pill can be swallowed'), they nevertheless expected Truss to live up to her campaign promise not to introduce new taxes.[9] Her insistence that energy producers should not be expected to foot the bill lest it discourage them from investing in the UK suggested not only that she would keep her word but also that she really did believe in the 'enterprise economy'. Secondly, loading the costs onto debt rather than worrying about 'balancing the books' in the short term suggested she meant what she'd said about challenging what she called the 'abacus economics' of 'Treasury orthodoxy'. And that impression was only reinforced when

Kwasi Kwarteng (seen, since the publication of *Britannia Unchained* ten years previously, as her 'ideological soulmate') announced the immediate departure of the Treasury's experienced Permanent Secretary, Tom Scholar – a move greeted with raised eyebrows by, among others, former Chancellor Sajid Javid and Scholar's predecessor Nick Macpherson.[10]

Early indications, to the obvious relief of the party in the media, were that Truss's rescue package, by helping out everyone rather than trying somehow to target assistance to less well-off households, had gone down well with the public, while the markets, having already heavily discounted sterling, remained, so far at least, reasonably calm.[11] How long this initially positive response would last, however, remained to be seen: after all, if gas prices should rise higher than the already dizzying heights that experts were predicting, then borrowing would automatically balloon even further. Moreover, the cap meant that the need to save energy was now less pressing and yet, given shortages in supply, blackouts were still a serious possibility – something that, from the summer onwards, had prompted other European governments (but not the UK's) to ask their populations to cut back where they could. Finally, there was the distinct chance that the 'fiscal loosening' required to finance the energy package, as well as any negative impact on the value of sterling, would oblige the Bank of England to raise interest rates even further and faster than it already intended to do in order to counter any consequent inflation – a move that would not only slow any growth that might be generated by Truss's cherished tax cuts but also raise the cost of mortgages (and quite possibly, therefore, rents) for millions of households across the country.

Whether those households were quite as enthusiastic about the other part of Truss's plan to deal with the energy crisis – namely to end the moratorium on fracking – was unclear. Certainly, it was bound to concern those Tory MPs sitting in constituencies where exploratory drilling might begin. Likewise the 130 or so associated with the Conservative Environment Network (CEN) set up to promote the move to net zero within the party – some of whom were worried enough already by the appointment as Business Secretary of Jacob Rees-Mogg (who'd previously talked about 'climate alarmism') and were not entirely convinced that it would be offset by the appointment of 'green Tories' Graham Stuart as the junior minister responsible for 'Climate' and Chris Skidmore as the MP in charge of a new net zero review. Moreover, few if any of the staff appointments to Number Ten – made as part of an internal reorganization that, by moving the Policy and Delivery Units, as well as Legislative Affairs, over to the Cabinet Office (under Nadhim Zahawi), would leave it with fewer (but therefore arguably more powerful) advisers – gave them much confidence either. As was the case with Truss's new Head of Strategy, Ian Carter, the choice of Mark Fulbrook as her new Chief of Staff had more to do with his deep roots in the Conservative Party than with his firm views on climate change or his work as a lobbyist. However, her new economic adviser, Matthew Sinclair, certainly could be labelled something of a sceptic: as a former chief executive of the Taxpayers' Alliance, he had, a decade previously, written a book exposing 'the myths perpetuated by the burgeoning climate change industry' and examining 'the potentially disastrous targets being put into place by ambitious politicians'.[12] And some of the other advisers brought in by Truss, like Sophie Jarvis and Ruth Porter (of the free market think tanks the Adam Smith Institute and the Institute for Economic Affairs respectively), weren't exactly known for their enthusiasm for green government.

Truss self-immolates: hubris begets nemesis in just forty-four days

Discussion of the energy measures, however, was swiftly swept aside when the news broke that Queen Elizabeth, who had reigned for seventy years and who only a day or two earlier had appointed the new Prime Minister, had died, plunging the nation into nearly a fortnight of national mourning.[13] But while politics was formally supposed to be on hold, speculation – much of it suspiciously well informed – continued as to the policy changes Truss was planning to introduce, not least when it came to a lifting of the cap on bankers' bonuses originally brought in by the EU, as well as the rolling back of restrictions imposed on the food, drinks, and retail sectors as part of the UK's anti-obesity strategy. Certainly, the contents of the 'fiscal event' (a mini-Budget without the tiresome need for an official, and potentially awkward, forecast from the OBR) held a few days after the state funeral came as no great shock to anyone who'd being paying attention: the increases in corporation tax and National Insurance announced by Rishi Sunak were abandoned, while his one penny cut in income tax was brought forward to April

2023; stamp duty paid by those buying properties was reduced; the cap on bankers' bonuses was lifted; and welfare benefit rules were tightened. Indeed, the only real surprise was the abolition of the 45 per cent top rate of tax paid by those earning over £150,000 per year. The financial markets, independent think tanks like the IFS – and indeed a fair few Conservative MPs – may have been sceptical about this 'Growth Plan', to say the least.[14] But, although the pound's subsequent plunge on the currency markets gave them pause for thought a few days later, the initial reaction of the party in the media was predictably ecstatic, with the *Mail* leading the cheering by splashing with 'AT LAST! A TRUE TORY BUDGET'.

All this, in addition to the deregulatory, market-friendly, and 'pro-growth' mood music coming out of Downing Street, suggested – superficially at least – a significant break with the more cautious and in some ways more state-centric approach signalled (albeit not necessarily actually followed) by May and Johnson. In its seemingly relaxed attitude to borrowing (dubbed more Reaganite than Thatcherite by some commentators), that approach was also the mirror image of Cameron's combination of tight fiscal policy and loose monetary policy, even if many economists predicted that Truss would eventually have to cut government spending even more sharply than he did if she were to retain (or, given their initial thumbs-down, regain) the confidence of the financial markets and bear down on inflation.

Just as importantly, the reorientation of policy announced by Truss and Kwarteng amounted to a reinterpretation of both the meaning and the implications of Brexit. True, it was still, in essence, about the UK regaining its sovereignty. But the primary purpose of so doing was no longer about taking back control of Britain's borders, as it had been for May. Nor was it about the government levelling up the country, as it had been for Johnson (or at least for some of those advising him). Now, under Truss, Brexit was all about allowing government to finally rid the country of the EU-inspired rules and regulations that had supposedly been holding it back for decades. Truss's elevation to the premiership, then, represented the triumph of the so-called 'hyperglobalist' strand within British Conservatism.[15]

But while that may have been the case, the immediate, highly negative reaction on international finance markets to the mini-Budget also made a mockery of the idea that Brexit, by 'restoring Britain's sovereignty', would henceforth allow the country's governments the freedom to do pretty much what they wanted. A less 'Brexity' (and, frankly, less intellectually arrogant) Chancellor of the Exchequer might have appreciated that there were bound to be some limits on that freedom and that the package he'd introduced on the Friday was about as far as they could sensibly be stretched. But not Kwasi Kwarteng. Instead, he told Laura Kuenssberg on the BBC's new Sunday morning politics show that there was 'more to come'.[16]

Downfall

The party in the media was delighted – 'KWART'S NOT TO LIKE?', asked the *Sun*, although it was noticeable from the polling that accompanied the story that 'Delighted Brits' were not quite so delighted by the bungs to higher-rate taxpayers and corporations as they were by the reductions in the basic rate, in National Insurance, and in stamp duty.[17] But as soon as the markets opened after the weekend it was obvious that the Chancellor had only made a bad situation worse. Bond traders were now responding, their evident lack of confidence in the mini-Budget significantly pushing up not just the cost of government borrowing but also what ordinary people could expect to pay on their mortgages. Pension funds also came under pressure to sell their stocks of government bonds (known as 'gilts') to meet their short-term obligations, all but forcing the Bank of England (which had, ironically, been about to start selling its own stock) to start buying them in order to protect the stability of the country's financial system. The Bank, however, made it clear that this could not continue for more than a few days, thereby throwing the responsibility for reassuring the markets back on to the government.

The only way that Truss could offer that reassurance was to begin to reverse some of the unfunded tax cuts that Kwarteng had promised. She had ended the week on a spectacularly low note after a series of local radio interviews had once again cruelly exposed her limitations as a communicator.[18] But humiliation was piled on humiliation when, after meeting with 1922 Committee Chairman Graham Brady as the Conservative Party conference got under way in Birmingham, she instructed Kwarteng to announce that the 45p cut would not now go ahead – less than twenty-four hours after she had appeared on Kuensberg's Sunday show to confirm that it would. Worse, at least in terms of her authority as party leader, was that her decision to do so had obviously been driven by it being made abundantly clear to her (not least by Michael Gove, who had been sitting across from her in the same BBC studio) that Conservative MPs were prepared to veto the measure when the legislation implementing it came before the House.

Not surprisingly, the conference then descended into something approaching chaos, with Tory MPs who were dissatisfied with Truss briefing against her while her supporters briefed back. Kwarteng's speech, during which he attempted to shrug off the U-turn, predictably went down like the proverbial lead balloon. Truss's own contribution, interrupted by Greenpeace protesters wielding a banner asking 'Who voted for this?', didn't bomb quite so badly, although one section in particular was later widely ridiculed for the transparently populist caricature it presented of the government's critics:

> Labour, the Lib Dems and the SNP, the militant unions, the vested interests dressed up as think-tanks, the talking heads, the Brexit deniers and Extinction Rebellion and some of the people we had in the hall earlier. The fact is they prefer protesting to doing. They prefer talking on Twitter to taking tough decisions. They taxi from north London townhouses to the BBC studio to dismiss anyone challenging the status quo. From broadcast to podcast, they peddle the same old answers. It's always more taxes, more regulation and more meddling. Wrong, wrong, wrong.

Tory MPs – especially those who'd left Birmingham early to avoid a train strike or, like Rishi Sunak, hadn't bothered going in the first place – were already beginning to talk in terms of when, not if, Truss would have to be replaced. Grant Shapps (who was apparently firing up his famous spreadsheet containing the views of his fellow MPs) told the popular new politics podcast *The News Agents* that she had just days to turn things around.[19] The chatter only grew louder as opinion poll after opinion poll suggested that Labour's lead over the Conservatives was getting bigger and bigger as Truss's personal approval ratings (and the government's reputation for competence) continued to plunge.[20] News that the government was thinking of filling the hole in the public finances created by Kwarteng's mini-Budget by uprating welfare benefits according to the rise in average earnings rather than by the rate of inflation only served to increase anxiety on the backbenches still further – so much so that Tory MPs were openly (if, for the most part, anonymously) telling journalists that they would not vote to support the measure. Others were equally concerned about the government's decision to end the moratorium on fracking, particularly those representing constituencies that might be directly affected. All were adamant that if things didn't begin to look up very soon, then pressure would be brought to bear on the 1922 Committee's Executive to change the rules so that a confidence vote could be held in a matter of weeks, even days, rather than in a year's time.

Commentators such as the contemporary historian Dominic Sandbrook were already wondering whether Truss might be the worst Prime Minister the country had ever seen, and more and more of her parliamentary colleagues seemed to be thinking the same.[21] Anonymous briefings to Sunday newspapers from Number Ten – including the suggestion that Michael Gove was some sort of 'troubled' sadist – just made matters worse.[22] So did the desperate pleas for unity and time in newspaper op-eds penned by no fewer than four Cabinet ministers, among them the supposedly-loyal-but-hyper-ambitious leadership aspirants Penny Mordaunt and Suella Braverman.[23] Indeed, it was an open secret that, behind the scenes, the latter was already causing her boss multiple headaches. Banging on about immigration was very much part of Braverman's brand (she'd told a fringe event in Birmingham, for instance, that 'I would love to have a front page of the *Telegraph* with a plane taking off to Rwanda. That's my dream, it's my obsession'). But banging on about immigration didn't really dovetail with Truss's growth agenda or her hopes of signing a trade deal with India, especially after New Delhi had apparently taken umbrage at the Home Secretary's remarks about its citizens overstaying their UK visas.

Truss attempted to ease some of the pressure on herself and her Chancellor by bringing forward what would effectively be an Autumn Statement from the Treasury, which had decided to appoint an old hand rather than an outsider to replace Tom Scholar as Permanent Secretary and which, this time around, was planning on releasing an accompanying OBR forecast. Truss also changed her mind and attended the inaugural gathering of the new 'European Political Community' in Prague, though only after ensuring that no EU flags would be flown outside the venue so as not to spoil any suitably prime ministerial photo-opportunities. But few of her colleagues back at home were convinced, especially after she struggled badly at PMQs on Wednesday, 12 October, and then put in a similarly poor performance in front of restive Tory MPs at a meeting of the 1922 Committee later in the day.

In fact, behind her back, but not particularly discreetly, those MPs (when they weren't busy texting grateful journalists with poisonous and often profane off-the-record quotes about Truss) were already discussing how exactly she could be removed and replaced. Most were convinced that the 1922 Executive would, if pressed, change the rules to allow a vote of confidence, the threat of which might well persuade her (as it did Johnson) to stand down so as not to face a humiliating defeat. What they were less sure about was how they could subsequently avoid holding a leadership contest – or, at the very least, avoid a prolonged contest in which the entire membership would be offered a vote. Ultimately, three options stood out: a so-called 'coronation', perhaps by way of 'a joint ticket' between, say, Rishi Sunak and Penny Mordaunt; a contest, with whoever emerged as the runner-up in the parliamentary stage being persuaded to step down, leaving the winner as the sole candidate and so negating the need for a membership vote; or the Executive setting the threshold for nominations high enough to ensure that only one candidate was likely to be able to cross it.

Number Ten's initial response to the chatter (which, somewhat ominously, had finally hit the front page of the previously supportive *Mail* and, more comically, the *Daily Star*) was to signal that another U-turn – the reversal of the decision to keep corporation tax at 19 per cent – was imminent.[24] But it was Truss's next move (urged upon her by both the Chairman of the 1922 Committee and the Chief Whip as well as her Deputy Prime Minister, Thérèse Coffey) that really hit the headlines.[25] Having ordered Kwarteng to fly home early from the IMF meeting in Washington, she promptly sacked him on his return, replacing him with Jeremy Hunt – the former Health Secretary whose second bid for the party leadership had, just a couple of months previously, not ended in humiliation as such but rather gone largely unnoticed.

If Truss thought Kwarteng's departure might save her, however, she was mistaken. For one thing, snap polling suggested that, although just over half of voters agreed with her decision, only 15 per cent said that it had left them with more confidence in her premiership while 44 per cent said it had left them with less. For another, she had not only sacrificed one of her oldest allies, in so doing losing a useful lightning rod, but she was now the prisoner of a virtually unsackable Chancellor. Perhaps if Truss had possessed the communication skills and chutzpah to talk her way out of such a tight spot, there might have been some hope for her. But the hastily convened press conference she gave in the afternoon of Friday, 14 October, in which she admitted that parts of the mini-Budget had gone 'further and faster than markets were expecting', only served to demonstrate once again that both were badly lacking – in marked contrast, many noted, to Penny Mordaunt, who'd impressed Tory MPs in the Commons just the day before.[26] Some who until then had held off writing to Graham Brady to demand a vote of confidence now did so, and the Sunday papers were replete with rumours that Rishi Sunak was readying himself to take over. But, fresh from an event held to thank the team who'd organized his leadership bid over the summer (and which had already begun re-contacting potential supporters on his behalf), the man himself had clearly decided, now it was obvious to everyone that he'd been proved right about Truss, that his best bet was to maintain a dignified silence rather than 'wield the dagger' and so fail to 'win the crown' at the second as well as the first time of asking.

Sajid Javid, who'd quit Johnson's Cabinet along with Sunak, however, had no plans to stand for the leadership again and therefore had no such hesitation. He had been understandably livid on reading that weekend that a 'Number 10 source' had dismissed rumours that he might be the one to replace Kwarteng by assuring the *Sunday Times* that 'The prime minister laughed out loud at the suggestion. … She has sat in the cabinet with Javid for ten years and she knows who is good and who is shit.'[27] Moreover, once he believed he'd discovered the culprit, he apparently told Downing Street that, unless it took action, he would be asking Truss about the incident at PMQs. In the event, just as the session began at Wednesday lunchtime, Number Ten announced that her special adviser, Jason Stein, had been temporarily suspended. Its decision appeared to have satisfied Javid. But by then, as far as many of his fellow MPs were concerned, the damage had already been done.

The weekend's toxic briefings (along with several scoops concerning the unorthodox salary arrangements and lobbying activities of Truss's Chief of Staff, Mark Fulbrook) served to confirm the widespread impression that the Number Ten operation was no less a shambles now than it had been under Johnson.[28] Meanwhile, a new mega-poll from Opinium suggested that the Tories would, on current form, end up with fewer than 150 seats at a general election, its impact on the parliamentary party amplified by the fact that it was done using MRP and therefore allowed every worried Tory MP to check out the projected result in their own constituency.[29] Not surprisingly, there were rumours of yet more letters going in to Brady in an attempt to force the Prime Minister's resignation. It came as no surprise then, on the morning of Monday, 17 October, to find the Mail's front-page screamer predicting 'PLOT TO TOPPLE TRUSS THIS WEEK' and the Telegraph's leader column suggesting that it was 'debatable whether she any longer has the authority to withstand this assault'.[30]

Whatever authority Truss did have left was further shredded when later that same morning, Jeremy Hunt made it clear in a live televised address that (with the exception of the National Insurance and stamp duty reductions) not only was he reversing virtually all the mini-Budget's tax-cutting measures and looking for significant reductions in public spending, but he would also be reviewing Truss's flagship energy price guarantee so as to lower its cost to the Treasury. It didn't help either that Penny Mordaunt, in her role as Leader of the House, felt obliged to tell MPs that Truss, who hadn't yet appeared in the Commons, was not (as Labour's Stella Creasy suggested) hiding under a desk somewhere, afraid to come out. The Prime Minister did, however, find time in her diary to meet with Graham Brady, who made the scale of opposition to her within the parliamentary party very clear. She also found time – but probably wished she hadn't, given how poorly she came out of it – for a sit-down interview with the BBC's Political Editor, Chris Mason.[31] Evidently, a phone call from Theresa May (she of the leather trousers and 'Nothing has changed') in which the former PM had apparently dispensed fashion tips and advice that Truss should be more up front about her mistakes hadn't helped that much.[32]

By the Tuesday morning, it was equally evident that Truss had lost the backing of the party in the media, the Mail having decided on its front page to go with that 1990s classic 'IN OFFICE BUT NOT IN POWER' while the *Sun* went with 'THE GHOST PM'.[33] To add insult to injury, the *Sun* also carried a Redfield and Wilton poll putting Labour on 56 per cent and the Tories on just 20, with 71 per cent wanting Truss to resign, although the accompanying headline 'READY FOR RISHI' was something of a stretch, given the former Chancellor won the support of just 21 per cent of respondents, followed, on 16 per cent, by Boris Johnson. Still, a YouGov poll of 530 Conservative Party members published later that same day found that, were they given the chance to re-run the summer's leadership contest, they would split 55:25 in favour of Sunak rather than Truss, who was judged to be doing badly as PM by eight out ten of them (including seven out of ten of those who had voted for her).[34]

Ben Wallace, the Defence Secretary (who had ruled himself out of the leadership contest in the summer yet was still seen as a possible replacement by some MPs) did not feature in the *Sun's* reporting of the Redfield and Wilton poll, but he did add to Truss's misery by making it clear that any attempt by her to renege on her pledge to raise defence spending to 3 per cent of GDP would prompt his resignation. Wallace, however, was less of an immediate headache than his Cabinet colleague, Home Secretary Suella Braverman.

In a meeting with Truss on the Tuesday evening, she had expressed (in no uncertain terms) her reluctance to publish a ministerial statement endorsing the idea of a new 'growth visa' designed to attract more high-skilled migrants to the UK, not least because it would contradict the rousing anti-immigration speech she had given to the party conference a fortnight before. Rather than accept the situation, Braverman decided to consult – not for the first time – John Hayes (Chair of the backbench, anti-woke Common Sense Group and a hardliner on immigration), sending him a copy of the draft statement from her personal email account on the Wednesday morning, thus breaking the ministerial code twice over. Unfortunately for the Home Secretary, she had accidentally copied the email to an assistant working for another MP, who (quite correctly) reported the breach to Number Ten, resulting in her immediate dismissal. However, instead of bowing to the inevitable by agreeing to the traditional, mutual exchange of anodyne letters with the PM, Braverman published a version that was all her own and which effectively suggested Truss should consider her position too.[35]

As if that weren't enough drama for one day, the parliamentary party, reeling from the news of the Home Secretary's resignation, was then thrown into further confusion just a few hours later. Number Ten, clearly believing that Chief Whip Wendy Morton's decision to treat a vote on fracking as a confidence issue might end in disaster, decided at the last minute to downgrade the vote to a three-line whip. Cue chaos in the chamber of the Commons and the sight of Morton being pursued by Truss though the corridors of parliament in order to persuade her not to resign. This proved to be the last straw for most Tory MPs. Truss might have claimed earlier in the day at yet another excruciating PMQs that she was 'a fighter not a quitter', but she had now turned them into a complete laughing stock and she simply had to go.

It was left to Graham Brady to slip (though not unnoticed) into Number Ten on the morning of Thursday, 20 October, to confirm what the Prime Minister and her aides already knew, namely that she had no option but to resign or else be forced out in a vote of confidence.[36] At 1.30 p.m., Truss stepped out into Downing Street to concede, in a brief address – one remarkable both for its brevity and for its matter-of-factness – that, 'given the situation, I cannot deliver the mandate on which I was elected by the Conservative Party'. In so doing, she became – by far – the shortest-serving premier and shortest-serving leader of the Conservative Party in modern British political history.[37]

Least said, soonest mended

In her address, Truss noted that she and Graham Brady had agreed there would be 'a leadership election to be completed in the next week'. Not long afterwards, Brady and Truss's Party Chairman, Jake Berry, stood outside the Palace of Westminster to explain to reporters the process that the 1922 Executive and the Party Board had agreed on. Nominations would close at 2 p.m. the following Monday, 24 October, after which hustings would be held. To progress to the parliamentary round of voting, leadership hopefuls would require one hundred nominations – 'a high threshold', Brady admitted, 'but one that should be achievable by any serious candidate'. Should voting in the parliamentary party produce two final candidates for the grassroots to choose between, there would be an indicative ballot of MPs held so that rank-and-file members taking part in what Berry called 'an expedited, binding, online vote' would know who had the support of the majority of their parliamentary colleagues – a device that would hopefully avoid a repeat of what had happened in the summer when Truss was elected by the membership with the votes of fewer than a third of her parliamentary colleagues. The whole thing would therefore be wrapped up by Friday week at the latest.

The process chosen contained obvious flaws in that any online vote would be far from secure and would potentially exclude the thousands of members who lacked verified email addresses.[38] Fortunately (and as those who came up with it must have hoped would turn out to be the case), those flaws were never exposed since, in the end, one candidate garnered enough support to ensure that nobody else entered the race proper.

That outcome was by no means certain to begin with. Boris Johnson proved willing to suffer the apparently unfamiliar indignity of flying home economy class in order to return early from the Caribbean holiday he'd been enjoying while the rest of his colleagues were busy working at Westminster. And he was clearly hoping that a 'shock and awe' campaign, boosted by the inevitable media interest in his candidacy, would convince even those Tory MPs who had deserted him in the summer that he had sufficient momentum to get over the initial hurdle, after which (he hoped they would presume) he would romp home in any membership vote. But despite his best efforts, and those of all-too-familiar superfans like Nadine Dorries, to suggest that only he had the star quality to turn the party's fortunes around, memories were simply not that short, particularly since the former Prime Minister was still under investigation for misleading parliament – an offence that, for anyone judged to have committed it, can, in the worst-case scenario, lead to a suspension from the Commons and even a recall petition triggering a by-election.

This did not prevent fifty-eight Conservative MPs declaring publicly for Johnson, nor did it put off even more of them (sufficient, it later transpired, to meet the threshold for nomination) from doing so privately.[39] But the remaining two-thirds or more of his colleagues were simply tired of the psychodrama; indeed, one or two went so far as to tell journalists they would actually quit parliament should Johnson return to lead the party. And besides, the dire economic situation required a steady, credible, and competent hand on the tiller, not a one-man moral minefield with no discernible interest in the business of governing and whom nobody outside his charmed circle trusted anymore. For most Tories at Westminster, then, the spell had been broken. Johnson's insistence that this wasn't the case (summed up for many by his ludicrous attempt to strong-arm his rivals into standing aside for him and by his even more ludicrous statement rationalizing his withdrawal from the contest on the Sunday evening) was more than faintly tragicomic.[40] It also, incidentally, ran counter to a ConservativeHome readers' poll (albeit one conducted after he had pulled out) suggesting he would have won the support of fewer than a third of rank-and-file members.[41]

In the event, Johnson was one of two candidates to withdraw. Unlike him, however, Penny Mordaunt, really did take it to the wire, tweeting to announce she was quitting just two minutes before the close of nominations.[42] Her team claimed that, in spite of the fact that only twenty-six MPs had backed her publicly, she actually had the support of nearly ninety, presumably as a result of colleagues switching from Johnson to her after his withdrawal – an implicit acknowledgement, at least, that she hadn't quite made it over the line.

Rishi Sunak, who managed to reach the nomination threshold before he had even officially declared his candidacy on the Sunday, enjoyed more support from Tory MPs than the other two candidates put together, eventually gaining the endorsement of 193 of his colleagues – nearly 60 more than the number who had voted for him in the summer and well over the 179 who constituted a majority of the parliamentary party. This was not entirely surprising: his warnings as to the consequences of Trussonomics had proved prescient; he was *not* Boris Johnson; he had proven financial and economic experience; he looked likely to keep Jeremy Hunt, who seemed to have calmed the markets, as Chancellor; and his remarkable decision to say virtually nothing in public from the moment Truss resigned to the moment he was officially declared as her successor minimized risk. Moreover, in all the snap polling of the general public carried out in the few days following Truss's resignation as leader, he had the beating of both Johnson and Mordaunt, while the argument that Johnson was the favourite among *Conservative* voters cut far less ice than it might have done had there been rather more of them in the electorate as a whole.[43] All this (not for the first time, as we have seen) contributed to a bandwagon effect and, having seen which way the wind was blowing, many of those hoping for frontbench jobs scurried to add themselves to his list of supporters.

One of the most high-profile and (at first glance anyway) unlikely converts to Sunak's cause was none other than Suella Braverman. Most MPs assumed that she had given the frontrunner her backing in return for a promise that he would reappoint her as Home Secretary once he'd won – a promise made in the belief that her endorsement would limit the number of ERG/Common Sense Group types who might otherwise flock to Johnson. The extent to which it did so will always be a moot point. A glance through the list of Sunak's supporters reveals that it included only seven of the twenty-eight original ERG 'Spartans' who voted against Theresa May's Brexit deal on all three occasions it came before the Commons, as well as just ten of the thirty or so MPs most commonly associated with John Hayes' anti-woke ginger group – not enough to stop Johnson getting over a hundred nominations but enough perhaps to halt his momentum and to have given him pause for thought before entering the parliamentary lists. The assumption that a deal had been done, however, seemed to be borne out. When Sunak announced his new Cabinet, Grant Shapps, who had been drafted in as Home Secretary by Truss, was made Business Secretary (admittedly a step up from his role as Transport Secretary under Johnson) while Braverman returned to the Home Office.

Those appointments, like so many of Sunak's picks, reflected the reality that his administration was far from the fresh start he pretended to represent. Indeed, it saw the return of some very familiar (possibly all-too-familiar) faces. True, only a bare majority (twelve out of twenty-three) of Truss's outgoing Cabinet continued to sit around Sunak's table (albeit not all of them representing the same department). But a number of those who joined them – Steve Barclay, Oliver Dowden, Michael Gove, and Dominic Raab – were veterans of the May and/ or Johnson Cabinets. And among those MPs who weren't formally members but were allowed to attend, there were two (Robert Jenrick and Gavin Williamson) who (like Raab) hadn't exactly covered themselves in glory in their previous posts.[44] All of this suggested, as did Braverman's reappointment, that Sunak's claim in his speech on the steps of Downing

Second time lucky – Sunak becomes PM, October 2022.
Source: Simon Walker / 10 Downing Street.

Street that he would be bringing 'integrity, professionalism and account-ability' back into government was contestable, to say the least.[45] The claim that a Cabinet appointed by the UK's first Prime Minister of South Asian heritage also struck a blow for diversity rang no less hollow. While it was, of course, encouraging to see five Cabinet ministers from ethnic minority backgrounds, Truss had originally appointed seven. Moreover, over half of the Cabinet had been privately educated – admittedly fewer than the getting on for three-quarters who'd gone to fee-paying schools in Truss's original Cabinet, but hardly a shining example of social mobility given that fewer than one in ten British children attend such schools.[46] Braverman's presence did at least mean that there was one more woman in Sunak's Cabinet than there might have been otherwise, but since that meant that only six out of the twenty-three members were female (compared to eight under Truss), the new administration couldn't really be said to be particularly representative on that score either.

Turn-around and transformation?

None of the above, of course, mattered to most Conservatives. Notwithstanding the obvious pleasure they routinely take in the fact that the party has produced no fewer than three female and two ethnic minority Prime Ministers whereas Labour has produced none), they (equally routinely) insist that promotion should be a matter of rewarding merit rather than a matter of 'identity politics'. What did matter, however, was whether ditching Truss and switching to Sunak might help them climb out of the electoral hole she'd dug for them in just a few short weeks. And on that score there was some room for optimism. Not only did early polling suggest that Sunak was regarded much more favourably than Truss, it also suggested that his approval ratings matched and in some cases bettered those that voters accorded to Keir Starmer.[47] It also looked as if his appointment to the premiership might be helping the Tories close the gap on Labour. So what if, for the moment, Sunak was still outpolling the party? His relative popularity might in time pull its ratings up even further – especially if he and Hunt could demonstrate a degree of competence that might help the economy come through any recession relatively unscathed.[48] Sure, the combination of tax rises and public spending cuts that they insisted on in their November 2022 Autumn Statement were hardly likely to get the warmest of warm welcomes. But if they went some way to re-establishing the party's economic credibility and re-emphasizing one of its remaining brand strengths – namely, its willingness to take 'tough decisions' – then that was probably a trade-off worth making. And while Sunak's early 'flip-flopping' – for example, on whether or not to attend the COP27 meeting in Egypt in early November 2022 – may have attracted lots of media comment, it wasn't the kind of thing that most voters paid much attention to or, frankly, really cared about.[49]

Overly optimistic? Maybe. While some of those representing less affluent Red Wall seats expressed concerns about what the Opposition immediately characterized as 'austerity 2.0', the bulk of Tory MPs appeared to have no more objections to it than they had to austerity 1.0 under George Osborne – in spite of the fact that the economic and social consequences of retrenchment in a recession were likely to be dire.[50] Voters, however, were another matter. Research on underlying values suggests that they (including some of those voters the party badly needed to keep onside) are far less enthusiastic about shrinking the state, particularly if core public services like health and education are visibly falling apart and their workforces are taking strike action.[51] Moreover, there is also every reason to believe that double-digit inflation and the falling real wages that are triggering those strikes, combined with the hammer-blow dealt to perceptions of government competence and cheap mortgages by the markets' negative reaction to the 'mini-Budget', may already be sowing the seeds of a vote-switching 'electoral shock' by increasing the salience of economic issues and altering opinion as to which party is best equipped to handle them.[52]

In addition, we know that while the bitter debate about the UK's departure from the EU helped give rise to profound and polarizing 'Remain' and 'Leave' political identities, we may be starting to see their electoral influence waning – even, perhaps, to the extent that Brexit may turn out to have been 'a fling, a marriage of convenience for people of widely differing life experiences who wanted something different and are now going their separate ways'.[53] The chances that 'levelling up' might prevent that happening seem to be receding as well – in part because there is precious little evidence (or indeed belief) that it has actually happened, in part because most of the people surrounding Sunak (Deputy Chief of Staff Will Tanner excepted, perhaps) are every bit as sceptical as those who surrounded Truss about what Theresa May (Tanner's former boss), back in 2016, referred to as 'the good that government can do'.[54] Nor should anyone bet on their enthusiasm for improving the 'supply side' of the economy granting Sunak any more luck than Johnson enjoyed in overriding the interests of developers and the objections of Tory MPs so as to allow Britain to build the houses that its recent manifestos have promised but never really delivered.[55]

Given all this, the temptation for Conservative politicians to pursue their 'war on woke' against 'lefty lawyers', universities, the civil service 'blob', the BBC, the 'Remoaner elite', or, indeed, any of the other shadowy forces determined to deny 'the people' the 'common-sense' policies they supposedly long for and deserve is likely to prove overwhelming. Certainly, anyone expecting Rishi Sunak to eschew such an approach is deluding themselves. Just because he is a super-rich, super-educated member of the global elite (exactly the kind of green card-holding, Atlantic-hopping hedge fund manager whom Theresa May might have labelled 'a citizen of nowhere' back in 2016) doesn't mean he espouses (out loud anyway) the kind of socially liberal values with which that elite is commonly (if not always accurately) associated. Sunak may have refused in the summer 2022 leadership race to simply tell Tory members what they wanted to hear when it came to tax and spending. But when it came to culture war issues and immigration, that is *exactly* what he did, claiming, for instance, that 'I want to stand up to that lefty woke culture that seems to want to cancel our history, our values and our women!', as well as reassuring them he had 'a radical plan to finally get to grips with illegal migration' that would 'stop the boats, restore trust, and take back control of our borders!'[56]

Seen from this perspective, Sunak's decision to appoint Suella Braverman as Home Secretary (and Kemi Badenoch as Minister for Women and Equalities and Michelle Donelan as Culture Secretary) made perfect sense. This is not, of course, to suggest that such a strategy is bound to work: for instance, by rekindling the values divides that were both triggered and amplified by Brexit.[57] After all, immigration – very much a staple for radical right populist parties everywhere – can be a double-edged sword for any government. The controversy over small boats crossing the Channel and the Rwanda scheme designed to deter them could be the gift that keeps on giving for the government. On the other hand, the evident failure to prevent what Braverman controversially called 'the invasion on our southern coast', as well as the fact that the numbers entering legally from outside Europe are rising rather than falling, could just as easily become a growing source of embarrassment.

In the wake of Brexit, voters appeared to be becoming markedly less concerned about immigration than they once were.[58] This prompted speculation that attempts to mobilize ill-feeling on the issue might turn out to be less of a vote-winner for the Tories than they used to be – especially perhaps in the so-called 'Blue Wall' seats in the home counties, whose affluent residents are increasingly likely to have been to university and to exhibit the liberal social attitudes associated with higher education.[59] But it is as well to recall that while that drop in salience and the growth of liberal attitudes in the population as a whole could change the game in the long term, in the short term, many of the constituencies the party needs to retain in the North and the Midlands still seem to contain 'anti-immigration majorities', plenty of whom (if polling and focus groups are correct) agree with Braverman and believe that Brexit hasn't actually led to the UK 'taking back control' of its borders, especially when it comes to Channel crossings.[60] Remember, too, that Nigel Farage hasn't gone away, and the latent fear that he might be able to piggyback onto the latest in a long, long line of media-fuelled moral-cum-migration panics in order to turn Reform UK into another UKIP/Brexit Party undoubtedly still haunts many Tories.[61] Thus anyone hoping that, under Sunak, they will downplay the culture war strategy so evident under Boris Johnson is likely to be sorely disappointed. Indeed, rather than the installation of a supposedly more 'technocratic' Cabinet halting and even reversing any transformation on the part of the Conservative Party from a mainstream centre-right formation into an ersatz radical right-wing populist outfit, it could (on the grounds that said Cabinet needs, now more than ever, to show that it's in touch with 'the people') just as easily accelerate and accentuate it.

Of course, radical right-wing populist parties are about more than migration and, indeed, culture wars more generally. Typically, they also put a premium on charismatic leadership and, if in office, on the rights of the executive over other branches of government and any intermediate institutions. And this is exactly what we have seen from the Conservative Party since 2019, whether we are talking about what amounted (indeed, for some Tories, still amounts) to the cult of Boris Johnson or else the blatant attempts to sideline parliament, pack its upper house, rein in the judiciary, and reduce the independence of the Electoral Commission. Rishi Sunak never once expressed any concerns over any of this. Nor, by the same token, did he raise any objection to a policy that should, perhaps, have outraged any true Tory: the insistence that Brits must now provide state-approved photo-ID in order to vote. It therefore seems fair to presume that he will, in this respect at least, carry on regardless. Moreover, since he, like so many of his colleagues, effectively enabled the sheer dysfunction and dishonesty that characterized Johnson's conduct of government for three years, it is difficult to believe that his administration is that much more likely than Johnson's to adhere to the seven 'Nolan Principles' of public life: selflessness, integrity, objectivity, accountability, openness, honesty, and leadership.

But if the Conservatives post-Brexit really have slipped their moorings as a mainstream centre-right party, that need not mean they are doomed to go down to defeat – either in the short or the long term. Yes, 'the liaison between property and discontent' that this 'amalgam of populists and libertarians' has sought to establish may seem increasingly, even inherently, unstable.[62] Yet we shouldn't forget that many British people remain deeply uncomfortable with social change – particularly if they're older, didn't go to university, and live in towns rather than cities. Nor should we ignore the fact that research suggests that their attitudes towards those who make and spend lots of money remain relatively positive, meaning that Sunak's immense personal fortune and his privileged background (both of which have registered with the public – far more so than his backing Leave, for instance) may not constitute as much of a problem as some on the left assume, not least because the wealthy are often assumed to be good at managing money.[63]

Neither is it a racing certainty that the party management problems Sunak will face will be quite as acute as those faced by his predecessors. Admittedly, some of those problems are inevitable. Deference towards their leaders has been declining among Tory MPs for decades, but that decline has undoubtedly accelerated in recent years – firstly, via the rise of social media and 24/7 rolling news, both of which have facilitated the kind of celebrity that few could have dreamed of in more innocent times, and, secondly, by a pandemic that made it far more difficult to build parliamentary fellow-feeling than it might have been had, say, the 2019 entry been able to spend more time at Westminster at the beginning of their first term. Yet Sunak nevertheless has some advantages over his predecessors. His essentially Thatcherite instincts, after all, are pretty much in line with those of most of his colleagues. And, given how hard it would be for the Conservatives to change leaders again without calls for a general election becoming overwhelming, the conviction that it is 'Rishi or bust' may stay the hand of even the most rebellious Tory MP – particularly if the polls improve and the Prime Minister can hold his own at PMQs (although the Labour leader won't be short of ammunition given some of the glaring gaffes and mistakes Sunak made during his time at the Treasury and in the summer 2022 leadership contest).[64] Moreover, while there is still plenty of ill-will towards Sunak for the role he played in the defenestration of Boris Johnson, the way the latter mobilized his long-suffering supporters for a crack at the leadership after Truss resigned, only for them to find out via Twitter that he was pulling out of the contest at the last minute, ensured that many of them will hesitate before rallying to his cause again – confirmation, some would say, of what Johnson's biographer notes is a long-held suspicion among his fellow MPs 'that he did not regard most of them as his equals, and thought of them as minor figures'.[65] In short, while there are bound to be bitter rows over particular policies, and while parliamentary caucuses like the ERG, NRG, and NZSG haven't melted away, the Conservative Party may not be as irredeemably 'ungovernable' as many commentators have understandably come to assume.

More generally, in spite of the hit the Conservatives' reputation for economic competence took in the wake of Truss and Kwarteng's ill-judged mini-Budget in September 2022, as long as the cost of living doesn't spin completely out of control, the NHS isn't completely overwhelmed, pensioners continue to be spared any great hardship, and the economy begins to grow again, many of those people will still give Sunak and his colleagues the benefit of the doubt, allowing them, if not necessarily to win, then at least to limit the damage. The bulk of the party in the media will probably stay the course too. Certainly, it will do its level best to encourage voters to draw a line under the chaos of the Johnson years and the brief nightmare that was Truss's premiership in the hope that they can be persuaded to embrace the idea that the 'grown-ups are back in charge' under the hard-working, clean-living, more professional, and more 'market-literate' Sunak. The wider media's tendency to portray the government's finances as if they were a household's is also likely to prove helpful to Jeremy Hunt – just as it was to George Osborne.[66] That said, it will be up to Sunak himself to make a better fist than, say, Gordon Brown did of swapping Number Eleven Downing Street for Number Ten. The model, at least in this respect, would be former Chancellor John Major, who, in the autumn of 1990, took over a deeply unpopular and badly divided party and an economy in the doldrums and, having junked one or two of his predecessor's signature policies, managed to steer the Conservatives to a bombshell election victory less than two years later. It's often said that voters have long memories, but sometimes they can be surprisingly short.

Support for the Tories in their current incarnation, then, might just prove more resilient than many of their opponents imagine, especially when we recall, as Enoch Powell (perhaps the ultimate neoliberal populist) once put it, that 'There is one thing you can be sure of with the Conservative Party, before anything else – they have a grand sense of where the votes are.'[67] That was certainly true in 2019, which is why, despite the constraints implied by their determination to 'balance the books', they seem determined to do their best to recreate the electoral coalition that won them such a big majority back then. Occasionally, however, that sense deserts them – just as it did, spectacularly so, in the mid-1940s, the mid-1960s, and the mid-1990s. After getting on for fifteen long and often chaotic years in office, and with virtually all the economic fundamentals currently pointing in the wrong direction, the mid-2020s looks odds-on to produce another of those heavy, albeit rare, defeats. But, with the Opposition needing a huge, thirteen-point swing simply to win the narrowest of narrow majorities at Westminster, don't bank or bet the (wind) farm on it just yet.

Postscript

British politics may have calmed down a little since Rishi Sunak took over as Prime Minister. But it's all relative. Although the frenetic pace of events under Boris Johnson and Liz Truss has sometimes been dubbed 'the new normal', it was bound to slow somewhat once a more conventional politician moved into Number Ten. Sunak may share the Thatcherite, low-tax, low-spend, light-regulation instincts of his immediate predecessor, but he is far more fiscally conservative than Truss. And, while he may share Johnson's (and indeed Truss's) willingness to engage in populist politics, particularly on immigration, he is far less likely to bend or break the rules. Moreover, his pitch to his party and to the electorate revolves around competence rather than zealotry or charisma – partly through inclination, partly because the latter is not something with which he is particularly blessed.

Indeed, while Sunak is clearly very bright and very hard-working, as well as very rich, he can hardly be said to exude authority. This, plus the range of 'pop-up' or 'whack-a-mole' parliamentary rebellions (on planning and on onshore wind, for instance) he has faced, encouraged the Labour Party to portray him as 'weak' from the get-go – an impression reinforced by some of his Cabinet appointments and arguably highlighted rather than contradicted by promise after promise that he is about to 'get tough' and 'crack down' on folk devils like public sector strikers, asylum seekers, and 'eco-zealots.'

Then again, Sunak's measured response to the 'little local difficulties' caused by restive (and, when it comes to one or two Truss and Johnson supporters, just plain resentful) backbenchers has arguably been relatively sensible. He is by no means unique among Tory leaders since 2010 in beating a tactical retreat on housing targets in the face of MPs convinced that their constituents simply won't wear them, no matter what the long-term consequences for the party of it failing to offer young people affordable homes. And, whatever he said to win over sceptical party members in the summer of 2022, he knows full well (and probably always did) that the economic and environmental case for onshore wind is overwhelming, as is support for it among the general public, particularly if it remains subject to local consent.

'Small boats' and strikes, of course, are rather harder nuts to crack but are just as likely to exercise Tory MPs, and even more likely to generate hysteria bordering on moral panic in the party in the media, thereby only encouraging those self-same MPs to 'demand action', especially when, on immigration and asylum, Nigel Farage is said to be pondering 'a return to frontline politics'.

On public sector strikes, the Conservative Party faces a difficult choice. It may well be that the electorate's patience with them isn't infinite. Some voters may even have bought the government's argument (one straight out of the Vote Leave playbook, in that those trying to correct its fake figures end up repeating them) that settling with the unions would cost every household £1,000. And there are undoubtedly some Tory MPs who believe that a relative (as well as an absolute) decline in public sector wages will prompt more workers to move into what they see as the 'productive' side of the economy. Many more are convinced – as is the party in the media – that strikes inevitably spell trouble for a Labour Party supposedly 'in hock to its union paymasters'. A handful may even thrill to the idea of 'bringing the army in' to help minimize disruption and introducing 'tough new laws' to make it much harder for transport and emergency service personnel to go on strike.

On the other hand, the idea that, in 'backlog Britain', 'nothing works' is not one that Sunak and his colleagues can afford to allow to take hold and become common wisdom: after all, voters are ultimately more likely to blame them than the unions, or at least to conclude that an alternative government might do a better job of managing the situation. And, even if the public buys the idea that government finances are tight, that the offers made to unions are the product of 'independent review bodies', and that doing more could fuel an (imaginary) inflationary 'wage-price spiral', in the end they just want trains to run on time, ambulances and A&E departments to save lives, nurses to be on the ward, teachers to be in the classroom, and border staff to be there to check their passports when they return home from holiday.

The arrival of tens of thousands of asylum seekers on the Kent coast, after which local authorities are obliged to house them at huge expense to the public purse, is likewise a double-edged sword for Sunak. On the one hand, there are some Conservatives who are convinced that, although there are votes to be had by them painting Labour as 'soft on immigration', unless they can 'stop the boats', then the Tories are toast at the next election. On the other, there is also the risk (some would say the certainty) that the myriad magic bullet solutions they routinely tout (Rwanda, criminalization, increased police and intelligence cooperation with the French, etc.) will prove neither workable nor effective at the very same time as they (and their friends in the media) make the issue more and more salient, helping to ensure that voters lose faith in the government's ability to control the UK's borders – which, as we have seen, is precisely what happened to the party between 2010 and 2016 (with truly historic consequences). Official figures that show big increases in numbers coming to the UK from outside the EU (many of them making up for a post-Brexit decline in migration from Europe) worry many Conservatives, but their calls for a 'clamp-down' on overseas students (who are a big revenue raiser for the UK) only smacks of panic. True, the idea that demand for foreign labour might be lower if domestic employers could be persuaded to train Brits to do the jobs migrants currently do might not be quite so economically illiterate. But it does seem slightly fantastical – at least in the short to medium term. Nor is it easy to square with, say, a trade deal with India that might make it easier for citizens of that country to gain entry to the UK.

Whatever happens on this front, the idea that the UK could compensate for the increasingly tangible loss of trade with the EU by signing comprehensive FTAs with the world's biggest economies looks like something of a pipe-dream. Sunak may call for 'robust pragmatism' in dealing with China, for instance, but a lucrative trade deal is clearly not on the cards for years, even decades, to come. Nor is there much sign of talks even starting with a friendly power like the USA. It is hard to believe that the Prime Minister, notwithstanding his support for Brexit back in 2016, doesn't know this, at least in his heart of hearts. He must know, too, that for all the easing of the restrictions imposed on Britain's financial services sector after the global financial crisis of 2007/8, forecasts of the long-term hit to UK GDP from leaving the EU now look eminently reasonable, virtually ensuring slower growth and therefore the need for higher taxes in order to prevent public services falling even further into disrepair. Notwithstanding any deal reached with the EU to settle the situation in Northern Ireland, however, neither Sunak nor any of those hoping to climb further up the Conservatives' greasy pole (some of whom never shared his enthusiasm for leaving in the first place, of course) can ever admit this publicly – and, given the emotional and ideological sunk costs involved, perhaps even to themselves.

The same goes for their attitude to those colleagues who have patently let themselves, the party, and indeed the country down – either by breaking the law, breaching the ministerial code, or contravening parliamentary standards, or by simply behaving in ways that fall below commonly accepted workplace norms. The ability to forgive and forget is admirable – but not when it is motivated by fear or the desire for a quiet life. Those Tories, some at the grassroots, some at Westminster, who remain obsessed with the idea, for instance, that the leadership was somehow stolen from Boris Johnson and must be restored to him, or, failing that, that it should pass to someone willing to carry on his populist, supposedly 'Red Wall-friendly' legacy, will never be satisfied. Nor will those MPs for whom sticking it to the leadership for the sake of it has become a pleasurable pastime and a great way to get on TV. It would be better, so much better, for the Conservative Party if Sunak and co. were to stop trying to appease them. But they won't – and, as some of their colleagues who have announced they will be quitting the Commons seem to have concluded already, it's probably too late now anyway.

Notes

Chapter 1 Going with the flow

1 See Tim Bale, *Brexit: An Accident Waiting to Happen? Why David Cameron Called the 2016 Referendum – and Why He Lost It* (KDP, 2022).

2 Dominic Cummings, 'On the referendum #21: Branching histories of the 2016 referendum and "the frogs before the storm"', https://dominiccummings .com/2017/01/09/on-the-referendum-21-branching-histories-of-the-2016 -referendum-and-the-frogs-before-the-storm-2/. For a more sceptical take on three 'what-ifs', see Stephen Bush, 'Was there a way Brexit could have been stopped? David Lidington's three hypotheticals', *New Statesman*, 3 August 2021. For a brilliant essay on the tension between contingency and the ability of analysts to explain (and predict) outcomes using Brexit as a case study, see Colin Hay, 'Brexistential Angst and the paradoxes of populism: On the contingency, predictability and intelligibility of seismic shifts', *Political Studies*, 68 (1), 2020, pp. 187–206.

3 See, for example, William Cross, Richard Katz, and Scott Pruysers (eds), *The Personalization of Democratic Politics and the Challenge for Political Parties* (ECPR Press, 2018), and Paul Webb, Thomas Poguntke, and Robin Kolodny, 'The presidentialization of party leadership?', in Ludger Helms (ed.), *Comparative Political Leadership* (Palgrave, 2012), pp. 77–98. For a scintillating analysis of government as a court, see R.A.W. Rhodes, 'Court politics in an age of austerity: David Cameron's court, 2010–2016', in Kristoffer Kolltveit and Richard Shaw (eds), *Core Executives in Comparative Perspective* (Palgrave, 2022), pp. 79–122.

4 See Simon Kuper, *Chums* (Profile, 2022).

5 Tim Bale, *The Conservative Party from Thatcher to Cameron*, 2nd Edition (Polity, 2016)

6 See Tanya Gold, 'The man trying to take down Boris Johnson', *New York Magazine*, 30 January 2022, and https://dominiccummings.substack.com/i/63528762 /a-few-random-thoughts-on-the-tory-race. Cummings is not wrong: interview-based academic research on MPs also suggests they are 'generally media obsessed': see Aeron Davis, *Political Communication: A New Introduction for Crisis Times* (Polity, 2019), p. 98.

7 The latest circulation figures we have are as follows (data for print from ABC, June 2022, and for online from Statista, September 2021): *Sun* (print 1.2m [March 2020]; online 3.7m) *Daily Mail* (print 860k; online 4.1m): *Daily Telegraph* (print 318k [December 2019]; online 1.1m); *Daily Express* (print 205k; online 1.6m); and the *Spectator* (print 107k). According to survey research in 2017 by the ESRC-funded Party Members Project, the *Daily Telegraph* is read by 33 per cent of Conservative Party members, the *Daily Mail* by 17 per cent, the *Sun* by 3 per cent, and the *Daily Express* by 2 per cent.

8 Those 'other books' include, most recently, Tim Bale, Paul Webb, and Monica Poletti, *Footsoldiers: Political Party Membership in the 21st Century* (Routledge, 2019) and Paul Webb and Tim Bale, *The Modern British Party System* (Oxford University Press, 2021).

9 In what follows, tweets are referenced by their URLs. Should access to the site prove difficult in the future, they should be locatable via their URLs using the 'wayback machine' (https://archive.org/web/). Generally, however, citations from websites refer to the author, title, source, and date on the basis that these can easily be searched for, negating the risk of the URL changing or disappearing. Note that, despite my best efforts, dates of newspaper articles may occasionally be out by one day owing to them being published earlier (or sometimes exclusively) on the paper's website. Citations for interviews are only given where they are on the record and/or publicly available.

Chapter 2 May in her pomp (July 2016–April 2017)

1 David Cameron, *For the Record* (William Collins, 2019), p. 681. See also Craig Oliver, *Unleashing Demons* (Hodder & Stoughton, 2016), pp. 363–4, Kate Fall, *The Gatekeeper* (HQ, 2020), pp. 296–7, and (from the only person in the inner circle who argued forcefully for staying on) Oliver Letwin, *Hearts and Minds* (Biteback, 2017), pp. 1–3. For what it's worth, Andrea Leadsom, who in short order declared herself a candidate to replace him, claims that the idea that Cameron would quit had only occurred to her in 'the final few days leading up to the referendum' and records that she and some of her Vote Leave colleagues wrote to him 'setting out the reasons he should remain in office'. Accordingly, she came to believe that 'he let his country down', his leaving 'a dereliction of duty at the worst possible time'. See Leadsom, *Snakes and Ladders* (Biteback, 2022), pp. 60, 77–8.

2 YouGov/*Times* Survey Results, June 2016, https://d25d2506sfb94s.cloudfront .net/cumulus_uploads/document/sp4prmurxb/TimesResults_160629 _ConMembers.pdf.

3 Tom Newton Dunn, 'Why should I do the hard s**t?', *Sun*, 25 June 2016.

4 Janan Ganesh, 'Let the Leavers govern as best they can', *Financial Times*, 27 June 2016.

5 Letwin, *Hearts*, p. 27.

6 Survation, 'Post-Brexit poll', *Mail on Sunday*, 25 June 2016. https://survation.com/wp-content/uploads/2016/06/Final-MoS-Post-Brexit-Tables-240616SWCH-1c0d3h3.pdf.

7 YouGov/*Times* Survey Results, June 2016.

8 For more detail on the demographics, values and activity levels of Conservative Party members (and the members of other British parties) see Tim Bale, Paul Webb, and Monica Poletti, *Footsoldiers: Political Party Membership in the 21st Century* (Routledge, 2019).

9 YouGov/*Times* Survey Results, June 2016 and YouGov Survey Results, February 2016, https://d25d2506sfb94s.cloudfront.net/cumulus_uploads/document/681loa3q0n/InternalResults_ToryPoll1_W.pdf.

10 Thomas Quinn, 'The Conservative Party's leadership election of 2016: Choosing a leader in government', *British Politics*, 14, 2019, pp. 63–85.

11 See, for example, Harry Mount, *Summer Madness* (Biteback, 2017), p. 146.

12 This is based on an interview with someone at the meeting. See also Tim Shipman, *All Out War* (William Collins, 2017), pp. 540–1, 544–5.

13 Owen Bennett, *Michael Gove: A Man in a Hurry* (Biteback, 2019), pp. 340, 344–5 and Shipman, *All Out War*, pp. 534–7.

14 Anthony Seldon with Raymond Newell, *May at 10* (Biteback, 2019), p. 30.

15 'A party in flames and why it must be Theresa for leader', *Daily Mail*, 30 June 2016.

16 YouGov/*Times* Survey Results, June 2016.

17 Shipman, *All Out War*, pp. 556–9.

18 See Rosa Prince, *Theresa May: The Path to Power* (Biteback, 2017), pp. 347–8. For a blow-by-blow account of the Johnson–Gove–Leadsom mix-up, see Shipman, *All Out War*, pp. 522–32, and for a first-hand account of it, see Leadsom, *Snakes and Ladders*, Chapter 6, which, along with Chapter 7, also gives her take on the 2016 leadership contest as a whole – not least on her decision to quit before the membership stage began.

19 David Jeffery, Tim Heppell, Richard Hayton, and Andrew Crines, 'The Conservative Party leadership election of 2016: An analysis of the voting motivations of Conservative parliamentarians', *Parliamentary Affairs*, 71 (2), 2018, pp. 263–82.

20 For the record, MPs gave the following mandates to her predecessors: Heath 49 per cent; Thatcher 53; Major 50; Hague 56; Duncan Smith 32; and Cameron 45. See Jeffery et al., 'The Conservative Party leadership election', p. 264.

21 On the dismissals, and the pleasure some of them may have given the new PM, see Prince, *Theresa May*, pp. 355–61.

22 On Osborne's sacking, see Seldon with Newell, *May at 10*, pp. 76–7.

23 Prince, *Theresa May*, pp. 362–3. Over the years, PMs taking over between elections have tended to make more changes than used to be the case: see Nicholas Allen, 'Brexit, butchery and Boris: Theresa May and her first cabinet', *Parliamentary Affairs*, 70 (3), 2017, pp. 633–44.

24 Chris Grayling, UKICE Brexit Witness Archive, 21 October 2020, p. 9.

25 Theresa May, 'I can be a bloody difficult woman . . . as EU chiefs are about to find out', *Sun*, 10 July 2016.

26 Ivan Rogers, UKICE Brexit Witness Archive, 27 November 2020, p. 39.

27 For a transcript, see 'Britain after Brexit. A vision of Global Britain. May's conference speech: full text', ConservativeHome, 2 October 2016, and for background, see Chris Wilkins, UKICE Brexit Witness Archive, 22 June 2020, p. 8.

28 See Wilkins, UKICE Brexit Witness Archive, p. 7.

29 Rogers, UKICE Brexit Witness Archive, p. 39.

30 Philip Hammond, UKICE Brexit Witness Archive, 13 and 20 November 2020, pp. 14–15.

31 For the speech, see 'Theresa May's keynote speech at Tory conference in full', *Independent*, 5 October 2016.

32 To read the speech, see 'Full text: Amber Rudd's conference speech', *Spectator*, 4 October 2016. See also Amber Rudd, UKICE Brexit Witness Archive, 19 March 2021.

33 Oliver Letwin, UKICE Brexit Witness Archive, 11 December 2020, pp. 11–12 and 14–15.

34 On this 'affective polarization', see Sara B. Hobolt, Thomas J. Leeper, and James Tilley, 'Divided by the vote: Affective polarization in the wake of the Brexit referendum', *British Journal of Political Science*, 51 (4), 2021, pp. 1476–93. See also Maria Sobolewska and Robert Ford, *Brexitland* (Cambridge University Press, 2020), pp. 237–49.

35 See Tim Bale, *The Conservative Party from Thatcher to Cameron*, 2nd Edition (Polity, 2016).

36 Like St Peter, she thrice denied it in public (and did so even more often in private): see Philip Cowley and Dennis Kavanagh, *The British General Election of 2017* (Palgrave Macmillan, 2018), pp. 1–2.

37 In fact, Truss had been under pressure from 'the Chiefs' (Timothy and Hill) not to comment at all. Tim Shipman, *Fall Out* (William Collins, 2018), pp. 51–2.

38 As ever, a full flavour of the media and political reaction can be best gleaned by

going to ConservativeHome: see 'Newslinks for Friday 4th November 2016', ConservativeHome, 4 November 2016. There is even a Wikipedia page devoted solely to the Mail's front page: https://en.wikipedia.org/wiki/Enemies_of_the _People_(headline).

39 For the most comprehensive guide to the history, tactics and strategy of the ERG, see C.R.G. Murray and Megan A. Armstrong, 'A mobile phone in one hand and Erskine May in the other: The European Research Group's parliamentary revolution', *Parliamentary Affairs*, 75 (3), 2022, pp. 536–57.

40 For a transcript, see Prime Minister's Office, 10 Downing Street, Department for Exiting the European Union, and the Rt Hon Theresa May MP, 'The government's negotiating objectives for exiting the EU: PM speech', GOV.uk, 17 January 2017. See also Wilkins, UKICE Brexit Witness Archive, pp. 11–13.

41 Rogers, UKICE Brexit Witness Archive, pp. 47–51.

42 David Gauke, UKICE Brexit Witness Archive, 26 June 2020, pp. 9–10.

43 YouGov/*Times* Survey Results, July 2016, https://d25d2506sfb94s.cloudfront .net/cumulus_uploads/document/dgak27s1eh/TimesResults_160704 _ConservativeMembers.pdf .

44 For some idea of the vitriol involved, see Shipman, *Fall Out*, pp. 140–6. See also Seldon with Newell, *May at 10*, pp. 171 and 173. Whether the briefing, apparently from Number Eleven, that described the occupants of Number Ten as 'economically illiterate' equates to the allegedly frequent use of the c-word to describe the Chancellor by May's advisers is best left to the reader to judge.

45 Hammond, UKICE Brexit Witness Archive, p. 17.

46 Seldon with Newell, *May at 10*, p. 169.

47 Hammond, UKICE Brexit Witness Archive, p. 18.

48 Joanna Penn, UKICE Brexit Witness Archive, 16 October and 17 November 2020, p. 6.

49 Alan Duncan, *In the Thick of It* (William Collins, 2021), p. 179.

50 On the details of the deal done in Downing Street to avert defeat, see Shipman, *Fall Out*, pp. 118–19.

51 Penn, UKICE Brexit Witness Archive, p. 6.

52 Denzil Davidson, UKICE Brexit Witness Archive, 14 September 2020, p. 16.

53 See Cowley and Kavanagh, *British General Election*, pp. 56–9.

54 See Shipman, *Fall Out*, p. 189.

55 See Wilkins, UKICE Brexit Witness Archive, p. 15.

56 See Tim Ross and Tom McTague, *Betting the House* (Biteback, 2017), pp. 85–6.

57 George Eaton, 'Exclusive: Conservative poll showed party would "lose seats" to the Liberal Democrats', *New Statesman*, 5 April 2017.

58 Ross and McTague, *Betting the House*, p. 80 and Shipman, *Fall Out*, p. 186.

59 Seldon with Newell, *May at 10*, p. 203.

60 William Hague, 'The case for an early general election', *Daily Telegraph*, 6 March 2017.

61 The following is taken from CTF's private polling (fieldwork 7–11 April 2017) and its memo sent to Stephen Gilbert on 12 April 2017.

62 Seldon with Newell, *May at 10*, p. 204.

Chapter 3 Hubris to nemesis (April–June 2017)

1 Tim Shipman, *Fall Out* (William Collins, 2018), pp. 194–5.

2 See Andrea Leadsom, *Snakes and Ladders* (Biteback, 2022), pp. 145–6.

3 See Philip Cowley and Dennis Kavanagh, *The British General Election of 2017* (Palgrave, 2018), pp. 8–10 and 58–9.

4 Cowley and Kavanagh, *British General Election*, pp. 58–9. See also Tim Ross and Tom McTague, *Betting the House* (Biteback, 2017), p. 183 and Shipman, *Fall Out*, p. 184.

5 The following is taken from a 'Strategic Note' prepared for Stephen Gilbert by Lynton Crosby and Mark Textor on 16 April 2017.

6 For more detail, see Cowley and Kavanagh, *British General Election*, p. 205 and Ross and McTague, *Betting the House*, pp. 321–8.

7 Anthony Seldon with Raymond Newell, *May at 10* (Biteback, 2019), pp. 225–7.

8 Shipman, *Fall Out*, p. 316.

9 For a discussion, see Emily Harmer and Rosalynd Southern, 'More stable than strong: Women's representation, voters and issues', in Jonathan Tonge, Cristina Leston-Bandeira, and Stuart Wilks-Heeg (eds), *Britain Votes 2017* (Hansard Society and Oxford University Press, 2018), pp. 237–54, especially pp. 238–9.

10 For the gruesome detail, see Seldon with Newell, *May at 10*, pp. 214–21. On this, and on focus group testing, and arguments about what it did and didn't reveal, see also the interviews in Ross and McTague, *Betting the House*, pp. 255–7 and 278–9.

11 Cowley and Kavanagh, *British General Election*, pp. 166–7.

12 See Leadsom, *Snakes and Ladders*, p. 152.

13 See the Conservative Party's 2017 manifesto: *Forward, Together*. See especially, pp. 6–10. See also the interview excerpts in Seldon with Newell, *May at 10*, pp. 210–12.

14 Cowley and Kavanagh, *British General Election*, p. 169.

15 See David Thackeray and Richard Toye, 'An age of promises: British election manifestos and addresses 1900–97', *Twentieth Century British History*, 31 (1), 2020, pp. 1–26.

16 See Shipman, *Fall Out*, pp. 237–9 and 274–7.

17 Shipman, *Fall Out*, p. 400.

18 For the detail, see Katharine Dommett and Luke Temple, 'Digital campaigning: The rise of Facebook and satellite campaigns' and Stephen Ward and Dominic Wring, 'Out with the old, in with the new? The media campaign' – both chapters in Tonge et al. (eds), *Britain Votes 2017*, pp. 189–202 and 203–21 respectively. See also Stephen Cushion and Charlie Beckett, 'Campaign coverage and editorial judgements: Broadcasting' and Dominic Wring and David Deacon, 'A bad press: Newspapers' – both chapters in Cowley and Kavanagh, *British General Election*, pp. 323–46 and 347–84 respectively. And see the discussion of digital in Ross and McTague, *Betting the House*, pp. 158–65.

19 For all the details – and a discussion of the trends in getting and spending – see Justin Fisher, 'Party finance', in Tonge et al. (eds), *Britain Votes 2017*, pp. 171–88.

20 For the figures (and a comparison with 2015, when the Tory grassroots seem to have done rather more for their party than they did in 2017), see Tim Bale and Paul Webb, '"We didn't see it coming": The Conservatives', in Tonge et al. (eds), *Britain Votes 2017*, pp. 46–58, especially pp. 48–50.

21 For an excellent discussion of all this, see Mark Wallace, 'Our CCHQ election audit: The rusty machine, part one. Why the operation that succeeded in 2015 failed in 2017', ConservativeHome, 5 September 2017, and, in particular, Mark Wallace, 'Our CCHQ election audit: The rusty machine, part two. How and why the ground campaign failed', ConservativeHome, 6 September 2017.

22 May visited 43 seats not held by the Conservatives, only 6 of which (3 Labour; 3 SNP) fell to them at the election, and there was no appreciable difference in vote share between the seats she visited and those she did not. On this, and on targeting more generally, see Cowley and Kavanagh, *British General Election*, Chapter 12. See also Ross and McTague, *Betting the House*, pp. 138–41.

23 CTF Track 1 Report, 26 April 2017.

24 On the Tories' internal polling as election day approached, see Shipman, *Fall Out*, pp. 403–5. Afterwards there were arguments about who saw what and when, although it is hard to imagine, even if everyone had seen everything, exactly what could have been done at that late stage that would have made any material difference to the final result.

25 The following paragraphs make extensive use of the absolutely invaluable (mainly quantitative) analysis provided by Cowley and Kavanagh, *British General Election*, Chapter 16, plus the Appendix written by John Curtice, Stephen Fisher, Robert Ford, and Patrick English, as well as Tonge et al. (eds), *Britain Votes 2017*. See also Maria Sobolewska and Robert Ford, *Brexitland*

(Cambridge University Press, 2020), especially Chapter 10, and Ed Fieldhouse and Chris Prosser, 'The Brexit election? The 2017 General Election in ten charts', *British Election Study*, 1 August 2017.

26 'Identity conservatives' are people who, among other things, are uncomfortable with increasing diversity – particularly ethnic diversity. See Sobolewska and Ford, *Brexitland*, Chapter 3.

Chapter 4 A bad hand played badly (June 2017–May 2019)

1 Nick Timothy, *Remaking One Nation: Conservatism in an Age of Crisis* (Polity, 2020), p. 13.

2 On Crosby, see Timothy, *Remaking One Nation*, p. 13: 'Lynton showed me a text message he had received from Theresa. "She's fucking blaming me!" he complained.'

3 See Anthony Seldon with Raymond Newell, *May at 10* (Biteback, 2019), pp. 246–8, 314–16. See also Andrea Leadsom, *Snakes and Ladders* (Biteback, 2022): 156.

4 Will Tanner, interview, 17 July 2020.

5 For details of the Cabinet meeting, see Tim Shipman, *Fall Out* (William Collins, 2018), pp. 458–9, and for the 1922, see Seldon with Newell, *May at 10*, pp. 284–7.

6 See Theresa May, 'I made mistakes but one year on I'm going Green for Grenfell', *Evening Standard*, 11 June 2018.

7 The ESRC-funded Party Members Project run out of Queen Mary University of London and the University of Sussex surveyed 1,002 Conservative Party members between 21 June and 13 July 2017. For more details on the project, see https://esrcpartymembersproject.org/ as well as Tim Bale, Paul Webb, and Monica Poletti, *Footsoldiers: Political Party Membership in the 21st Century* (Routledge, 2019).

8 See those interviewed in Seldon with Newell, *May at 10*, pp. 299–302.

9 Philip Hammond, UKICE Brexit Witness Archive, 13 and 20 November 2020, p. 29.

10 Tom Newton Dunn, 'BREXY BEAST Boris Johnson reveals his four Brexit "red lines" for Theresa May', *Sun*, 29 September 2017.

11 See Gavin Barwell, *Chief of Staff: Notes from Downing Street* (Atlantic, 2021), pp. 146–9.

12 The Conservative Party does tend to remove even quite important documents from its website fairly swiftly, but there is a copy stored (for the moment) here: https://esrcpartymembersprojectorg.files.wordpress.com/2016/07/tory2017_ge -review-document.pdf.

13 For more on the differences between attitudes to membership in the Conservative Party and other parties, see Bale et al., *Footsoldiers*, Chapter 9.

14 Timothy Edward Hallam Smith, 'Incumbency advantage of UK members of parliament 1959–2010', University of Nottingham PhD thesis, 2019.

15 James Johnson, interview, 2 July 2020.

16 On all this – and how it fitted into Number Ten's analysis of the 2017 result and how to move on from it – see Barwell, *Chief of Staff*, pp. 83–96. On MPs' support for greater NHS spending, see also p. 141, where Barwell notes that 239 out of 255 who responded to a request from the Chief Whip in early 2019 agreed that the NHS should be the top priority for additional spending.

17 For a ringside seat, see Barwell, *Chief of Staff*, pp. 161–7.

18 See Sebastian Whale, 'Karen Bradley: "I'm not here for the headlines. I'm here to get the best thing for the country"', Politics Home – The House, 6 September 2018.

19 For a detailed and harrowing account of the Windrush Scandal by the journalist who broke the story, see Amelia Gentleman, *The Windrush Betrayal: Exposing the Hostile Environment* (Guardian Faber, 2020).

20 Davis told his ministerial team a day or two before Chequers that he would be resigning. See Mark Francois, *Spartan Victory* (KDP, 2021), p. 176.

21 Leadsom, *Snakes and Ladders*, p. 211. This was not quite true of Davis (if his own account is to be believed), who, although he thought his resignation would ultimately end in May going because she couldn't deliver the Brexit he (and the ERG) wanted, resigned principally in order to try to kill what he regarded as a bad deal. For that account, which is particularly interesting when it comes to how he choreographed his resignation and on Boris Johnson following him, see David Davis, UKICE Brexit Witness Archive, 8 July 2021, pp. 28–36.

22 See Barwell, *Chief of Staff*, p. 269.

23 For the details see John Curtice, 'Why Chequers has gone wrong for Theresa May', What UK Thinks, 17 July 2018.

24 See Mark Francois, *Spartan Victory*, p. 177 and European Research Group, 'The border between Northern Ireland and the Republic of Ireland post-Brexit', 12 September 2018, https://www.scribd.com/document/388422435/European -Research-Group-plans-for-Irish-border-and-Brexit.

25 Boris Johnson and Jeremy Hunt, '"It is a humiliation. We look like a seven-stone weakling being comically bent out of shape by a 500 lb gorilla": BORIS JOHNSON'S blistering denunciation of our Brexit strategy . . . and his successor JEREMY HUNT'S trenchant defence', *Daily Mail*, 9 September 2018.

26 Boris Johnson, 'We are heading for a car crash Brexit under Theresa May's Chequers plan', *Daily Telegraph*, 16 September 2018.

27 Alix Culbertson, 'Nigel Farage back in politics to challenge Theresa May's Brexit', Sky News, 18 August 2018.

28 Benjamin Butterworth, 'Full text of Boris Johnson's "alternative leader's speech"', *inews*, 2 October 2018.

29 https://www.youtube.com/watch?v=tbCDFNRA-Wo. This unusual but disarmingly effective piece of self-mockery sprung from earlier, cruelly amusing footage of the PM dancing awkwardly on an overseas trip that had gone viral on social media: https://www.theguardian.com/politics/video/2018/aug/28/theresa-may-dances-at-south-african-secondary-school-video.

30 See Prime Minister's Office, 10 Downing Street, and the Rt Hon Theresa May MP, 'PM Brexit negotiations statement', GOV.uk, 21 September 2018.

31 Barwell, *Chief of Staff*, p. 138.

32 Hammond, UKICE Brexit Witness Archive, p. 32.

33 Tim Shipman and Caroline Wheeler, 'Four meetings and a political funeral', *Sunday Times*, 21 October 2018.

34 For a sense of the poisonous post-conference atmosphere, see Seldon with Newell, *May at 10*, pp. 466–9.

35 Barwell, *Chief of Staff*, pp. 169 and 302.

36 Hunt, quoted in Seldon with Newell, *May at 10*, p. 489.

37 Francois, *Spartan Victory*, p. 191.

38 See Tom Newton Dunn, 'Michael Gove leads Cabinet "Pizza Club" to salvage Brexit Withdrawal Agreement in a 7-day race against time – instead of toppling Theresa May', *Sun*, 16 November 2018. See also Leadsom, *Snakes and Ladders*, pp. 213ff.

39 For a detailed analysis, which makes it clear that opposition to May in the vote was heavily correlated with opposition to her deal, see Andrew Roe-Crines, Tim Heppell, and David Jeffery, 'Theresa May and the Conservative Party leadership confidence motion of 2018: Analysing the voting behaviour of Conservative parliamentarians', *British Politics*, 16 (3), 2021, pp. 317–35.

40 See Leadsom, *Snakes and Ladders*, p. 215.

41 See Seldon with Newell, *May at 10,* p. 542.

42 For full details, see ESRC Party Members Project, 'No deal is better than May's deal', Party Members Project, 4 January 2019.

43 See 'New survey of MPs shows a Commons more divided on Brexit than ever before', UK in a Changing Europe, 2020.

44 The cleft stick Smith continually found himself in is neatly summarized by Gavin Barwell, *Chief of Staff*, p. 135. See also Seldon with Newell, *May at 10*, p. 498.

45 For more about the Buddies, see Francois, *Spartan Victory*, pp. 193–9.

46 Seldon with Newell, *May at 10*, p. 542.

47 See Philip Lee, UKICE Brexit Witness Archive, 9 April 2021, pp. 10–21.

48 It is clear that (in Number Ten at least) Party Chairman Graham Brady and Housing Minister Kit Malthouse were both seen as attempting to be helpful rather than wanting to create mischief. See Hammond, UKICE Brexit Witness Archive, Gavin Barwell, UKICE Brexit Witness Archive, 1 and 25 September 2020, and Joanna (JoJo) Penn, UKICE Brexit Witness Archive, 16 October and 17 November 2020.

49 Amber Rudd, Greg Clark, and David Gauke, 'If we don't get a deal next week we MUST delay Brexit', *Daily Mail*, 23 February 2019.

50 Chief Whip Julian Lewis quoted in Seldon with Newell, *May at 10*, pp. 558 and 561.

51 Seldon with Newell, *May at 10*, pp. 551–4.

52 Prime Minister's Office, 10 Downing Street, and the Rt Hon Theresa May MP, 'PM speech in Grimsby', GOV.uk, 8 March 2019.

53 For details of the 'bloodbath' in Cabinet that followed the second Meaningful Vote, see Seldon with Newell, *May at 10*, pp. 573–4.

54 Gavin Barwell, *Chief of Staff*, pp. 345–6: 'politically it was nuts'.

55 Prime Minister's Office, 10 Downing Street, and the Rt Hon Theresa May MP, 'PM statement on Brexit', GOV.uk, 20 March 2019. See also the UKICE Brexit Witness Archive interviews with Barwell and Penn.

56 Tim Shipman, 'Cabinet coup to ditch Theresa May for emergency PM', *Sunday Times*, 24 March 2019. On the parliamentary reaction to May's address, see Francois, *Spartan Victory*, p. 279.

57 See Francois, *Spartan Victory*, pp. 285ff., 396.

58 On the bypasses and infrastructure spending that were supposedly on offer to persuade Tory MPs to back the government, see Francois, *Spartan Victory*, p. 290.

59 The ERG hardcore took their nickname from the film *300*, based on the comic book version of the battle of Thermopylae in 480 BC when a few hundred Spartan soldiers attempted to hold out against a Persian army that massively outnumbered them. Some pointed out that the Brexiteers' choice of moniker might be a little ironic since all the Spartans had died, although, to be fair, Sparta, together with other Greek city-states, eventually won the war of which the battle was just one part. As to how the nickname came about, see Francois, *Spartan Victory*, pp. 281–2.

60 See Paul Goodman, 'Our survey. How Party members would cast indicative votes. They are overwhelmingly for No Deal', ConservativeHome, 1 April 2019.

61 Barwell, *Chief of Staff*, pp. 173, 182, and 184.

62 James Johnson, interview, 2 July 2020.

63 For details, see Christopher Howarth, 'Mrs May: My part in her downfall', *The Critic*, July 2021, and Michael Spicer and Archie Hamilton, 'If Tory MPs wish to change the 1922 committee no confidence vote rules there is nothing standing in their way', *Daily Telegraph*, 13 April 2019.

64 On the Conservative side, see the UKICE Brexit Witness Archive interviews with Barwell, Hammond, and Penn.

65 Leadsom, *Snakes and Ladders*, pp. 217–21 and 225–9.

Chapter 5 Over before it began (June–July 2019)

1 See Lord Ashcroft, 'My Euro-election post-vote poll: Most Tory switchers say they will stay with their new party', Lord Ashcroft Polls, 27 May 2019, and Chris Curtis, 'If everyone revealed how they voted last week Labour would have to kick out four in ten members', YouGov, 30 May 2019.

2 There may have been little or no activism on the part of its footsoldiers but, as figures released by the Electoral Commission later revealed, the Conservative Party nevertheless managed to spend £2.6 million on the campaign – interestingly, almost the same amount as the Brexit Party spent. That worked out at £1.72 for each Tory vote and just 50p for each Brexit Party vote. Information kindly provided by David Cowling.

3 Chris Curtis, 'If everyone revealed how they voted last week Labour would have to kick out four in ten members', YouGov, 30 May 2019.

4 For a running report on the numbers collected by each candidate, see John Rentoul's periodically updated Twitter thread: John Rentoul, Tweet, 26 May 2019, 9.35 a.m., https://twitter.com/JohnRentoul/status/1132565829181235200. For a full spreadsheet from Guido Fawkes, see 'Tory leadership MP backers', https://docs.google.com/spreadsheets/d/1hLVVTLnTTPIO43qTM7GsGs5G qvQ1UVGKmd_n1B51s5M/edit#gid=0.

5 For an excellent guide to research to date as well as the history, see Andrew Denham, Andrew S. Roe-Crines, and Peter Dorey, *Choosing Party Leaders: Britain's Conservatives and Labour Compared* (Manchester University Press, 2020).

6 Steven Swinford and Camilla Tominey, 'Boris Johnson is best placed Tory candidate to beat Farage and Corbyn in a "Brexit election", poll finds', *Daily Telegraph*, 7 June 2019.

7 Matthew Smith, 'Boris Johnson holds commanding lead among Tory members', YouGov, 17 May 2019.

8 ESRC Party Members Project, 'No deal is better than May's deal', Party Members Project, 4 January 2019.

9 Glen Owen, 'Jeremy Hunt's wife Lucia reveals her pet name for him is "Mr Big Rice" as he dubs himself the "insurgent" Conservative leadership candidate after Boris Johnson storms ahead', *Mail on Sunday*, 16 June 2019.

10 Marina Hyde, 'Opium-pipers, bluffers and no-dealers impress in this Tory battle of nonentities', *Guardian*, 31 May 2019.

11 See Andrea Leadsom, *Snakes and Ladders* (Biteback, 2022), pp. 229–35.

12 Hancock's request to be promoted to Number Eleven only provoked ridicule (once he had left the room) from the man who was set to move into Number Ten. See Andrew Gimson, *Boris Johnson: The Rise and Fall of a Troublemaker at Number Ten* (Simon & Schuster, 2022), p. 135.

13 Owen Bennett, *Michael Gove: A Man in a Hurry* (Biteback, 2019), pp. 394–7.

14 Mark Francois, *Spartan Victory* (KDP, 2021), pp. 324–7.

15 Matthew Smith, 'Most Conservative members would see party destroyed to achieve Brexit', YouGov, 18 June 2019.

16 Jeremy Hunt, 'Forget your private life Boris, but man up and face me', *Sunday Times*, 23 June 2019.

17 Jim Waterson, 'Boris Johnson: Police called to loud altercation at potential PM's home', *Guardian*, 21 June 2019.

18 Watch https://www.youtube.com/watch?v=AqIG9NPKHVw.

19 Francis Elliott, Rachel Sylvester, and Alice Thomson, 'Boris Johnson set for landslide in battle to reach No. 10', *Times*, 6 July 2019.

20 For details, see Gavin Barwell, *Chief of Staff: Notes from Downing Street* (Atlantic, 2021), Chapter 22.

21 James Johnson, interview, 2 July 2020. For a sense of the frosty relations between the two at this stage, see Anthony Seldon with Raymond Newell, *May at 10* (Biteback, 2019), pp. 635–6. See also Philip Hammond, UKICE Brexit Witness Archive, 13 and 20 November 2020.

22 Seldon with Newell, *May at 10*, p. 634. Whether, in view of her much-criticized resignation honours list, she had quite as much right to claim the moral high ground is for others to judge: see Alex Wickham, 'Theresa May has been accused of "foul play" after giving honours to her aides and donors', Buzzfeed News, 10 September 2019.

Chapter 6 Brexit achieved; Boris rampant (July–December 2019)

1 John Major, 'Statement on the new Prime Minister', John Major Archive, 22 July 2019.

2 Boles deleted this account but the tweet is preserved for posterity by the invaluable Wayback Machine: just go to https://web.archive.org/web/20190802024600/https://twitter.com/NickBoles/status/1154093304327356416.

3 Full transcript available at 'Full text: Boris Johnson's victory speech', *Spectator*, 23 July 2019.

4 For details, see this excellent Twitter thread: https://twitter.com/rowlsmanthorpe /status/1154153775541751810.

5 Chris Hanretty, 'The pork barrel politics of the Towns Fund', *Political Quarterly*, 92 (1), 2021, pp. 7–13.

6 Alex Wickham, 'Insiders say Dominic Cummings has instilled a culture of fear in Boris Johnson's new government', Buzzfeed News, 5 August 2019.

7 Isaac Levido, interview, 13 July 2020. The following quotes from Levido come from the same interview.

8 Sajid Javid, 'Next week's Spending Round will clear decks to let us focus on Brexit', *Daily Telegraph*, 27 August 2019.

9 Tim Shipman, 'Climb aboard for Boris Johnson's white-knuckle general election ride', *Sunday Times*, 25 August 2019.

10 See Will Tanner and James O' Shaughnessy, *The Politics of Belonging*, Onward, October 2019.

11 https://twitter.com/Steven_Swinford/status/1161383461095129090.

12 See Harry Cole, 'Boris Johnson savages the saboteurs', *Mail on Sunday*, 18 August 2019, and Rosamund Urwin and Caroline Wheeler, 'Operation Chaos', *Sunday Times*, 18 August 2019.

13 Camilla Tominey, Christopher Hope, and Harry Yorke, 'Boris Johnson has public's support to shut down parliament to get Brexit over line, exclusive poll suggests', *Daily Telegraph*, 12 August 2019.

14 For the (embarrassing) details, see Simon Murphy, 'Then and now: What senior Tories say about proroguing parliament', *Guardian*, 29 August 2019.

15 See Jack Doyle and Jason Groves, '"We are going to PURGE you": What Boris Johnson's enforcer Dominic Cummings "warned a former cabinet minister in foul-mouthed rant ahead of the crucial Brexit vote"', *Daily Mail*, 5 September 2019. See also Jack Doyle, 'Explosion of loathing at No10: Inside the incendiary row between ex-Chancellor Philip Hammond and table-thumping Boris Johnson that led to Tory defeat', *Daily Mail*, 3 September 2019.

16 Abigail Axe-Browne, 'Public attitude towards Boris Johnson has improved since move into Number 10', YouGov, 2 September 2019.

17 Chris Curtis, 'Everything we know about what the public think of Boris Johnson', YouGov, 23 July 2019.

18 See James Tapsfield and Jason Groves, 'Backlash as Business Minister Kwasi Kwarteng accuses Scottish judges of "interfering in politics" after they ruled Boris Johnson broke the law by suspending parliament', *Daily Mail*, 12 September 2019.

19 See Rowena Mason and Heather Stewart, 'Tory Brexiters rally around Johnson after Supreme Court defeat', *Guardian*, 25 September 2019, and https://twitter .com/jackwdoyle/status/1176590566173401089.

20 Matthew Smith, 'By 49 per cent to 30 per cent, Britons agree with the Supreme Court's ruling that proroguing parliament was unlawful', YouGov, 24 September 2019.

21 Glen Owen, 'No. 10 probes Remain MPs' "foreign collusion"', *Mail on Sunday*, 29 September 2019. For hard-hitting critiques of what some see as 'client journalism' and the spinners who take advantage of it, see both Peter Oborne, 'British journalists have become part of Johnson's fake news machine', open-Democracy, 22 October 2019, and Nick Cohen, 'Meet Dominic Slack-Oxley: The biggest source of fake news in Britain', *Spectator*, 22 October 2019.

22 Matthew Smith, 'Only a quarter of Britons now think PM will meet Brexit deadline', YouGov, 4 October 2019. For ComRes, see Camilla Tominey, Anna Mikhailova, and Christopher Hope, 'Parliament and Remain MPs will be blamed more than Boris Johnson for Brexit delay, poll reveals', *Daily Telegraph*, 7 October 2019.

23 Macer Hall, 'Priti Patel vows crackdown on crime blighting Britain: "Criminals we're coming after you!"', *Daily Express*, 1 October 2019.

24 '8 in 10 dissatisfied with how the government is running the country', Ipsos MORI, 30 September 2019.

25 Steven Swinford and Francis Elliott, '"Many" Tory MPs to quit if it comes to No-Deal Brexit', *Times*, 9 October 2019.

26 On the economics of the deal, which, significantly, barely got a look in during the debate on it within the Conservative Party, see Anand Menon and Jonathan Portes, 'Boris Johnson's Brexit deal would make people worse off than Theresa May's', *Guardian*, 13 October 2019.

27 See Camilla Tominey, 'New allegiance of Brexit Spartans could yet win the war for Boris Johnson', *Daily Telegraph*, 19 October 2019. See also Jonathan Isaby, 'How Steve Baker exhorted the ERG to back the Johnson deal', BrexitCentral, 20 October 2019, https://web.archive.org/web/20200130170729/https:// brexitcentral.com/exclusive-how-steve-baker-exhorted-the-erg-to-back-the -johnson-deal/.

28 For a summary of the polling, see John Curtice, 'Leave supporters back a harder Brexit', *Times*, 21 October 2019.

29 For a flavour, see Kate Lyons, '"How dare they!": What the papers say about the battle over Johnson's Brexit deal', *Guardian*, 21 October 2019.

30 For details, see Henry Hill, 'The full list of 22 Bills from today's Queen's Speech', ConservativeHome, 14 October 2019.

31 See Richard Partington, 'No-Deal Brexit would "push national debt to levels last seen in 60s"', *Guardian*, 8 October 2019.

32 https://twitter.com/rowenamason/status/1171833547407187968.

33 See Chapter 11, 'Political recruitment under pressure, again: MPs and candidates in the 2019 general election' (written by Chris Butler, Rosie Campbell, and Jennifer Hudson) of Robert Ford, Tim Bale, Will Jennings, and Paula Surridge, *The British General Election of 2019* (Palgrave, 2021), pp. 390–1.

34 See Paul Goodman, 'Selections. How activists find themselves crushed by the attritional, grinding juggernaut of the party machine', ConservativeHome, 20 November 2019.

35 See, for example, Edward Malnick and Tony Diver, 'Revealed: Nigel Farage's election pact offer to Tories to defeat Corbyn and deliver Brexit', *Sunday Telegraph*, 7 September 2019.

36 Brendan Carlin, 'Conservatives "try to buy off Nigel Farage with a peerage" amid fears over the threat he poses in an election', *Mail on Sunday*, 19 October 2019. Tice subsequently wrote that 'The Conservatives never had any intention of negotiating any form of deal, not even for a single seat.' See Richard Tice, 'After a momentous 2019, it's time to feast on the delicious opportunities afforded by Brexit', 6 January 2020, https://richardtice.com/2020/01/after-a-momentous-2019-its-time-to-feast-on-the-delicious-opportunities-afforded-by-brexit/.

37 Iain Duncan Smith, 'The Tory Party is now the Brexit party: Leavers must unite or let a Remainer into No. 10', *Daily Telegraph*, 31 October 2019.

38 Tim Shipman, 'Nigel Farage: The Tories have offered to make me a peer twice', *Sunday Times*, 3 November 2019.

39 Harry Yorke and Christopher Hope, 'Nigel Farage risks becoming the "man who threw away Brexit", warns senior Tory backbencher', *Daily Telegraph*, 3 November 2019.

40 https://twitter.com/JamesKanag/status/1161639282450321409.

41 For details, see 'Grenfell Tower: Second apology over Jacob Rees-Mogg comments', BBC News, 6 November 2019.

42 See Rosie Carter, 'Brexit is not Labour Leavers' number one priority', HOPE not hate, 13 November 2019.

43 Matthew Smith, 'YouGov snap poll finds viewers split on who won ITV general election debate', YouGov, 19 November 2019.

44 Matthew Smith, Nicola Wildash, Tanya Abraham, Adam McDonnell, and Chris Curtis, 'The key findings from our MRP', YouGov, 27 November 2019.

45 All four (Annunziata Rees-Mogg, Lance Forman, Lucy Harris, and John Longworth) later joined the Conservative Party.

46 Dominic Cummings, 'On the referendum #34: BATSIGNAL!! DON'T LET CORBYN-STURGEON CHEAT A SECOND REFERENDUM WITH MILLIONS OF FOREIGN VOTES', 27 November 2019, https:// dominiccummings.com/2019/11/27/on-the-referendum-34-batsignal-dont-let -corbyn-sturgeon-cheat-a-second-referendum-with-millions-of-foreign-votes/.

47 Elaine McCahill, 'Donald Trump says he "wouldn't take NHS if it was offered on a silver platter"', *Daily Mirror*, 3 December 2019.

48 Steven Swinford and Kate Devlin, 'Election 2019: Boris Johnson to blitz seats in Labour heartlands', *Times*, 9 December 2019.

49 See Priti Patel, 'The Tories will do what it takes to keep Britain safe', *Daily Telegraph*, 8 December 2019, and Kate Ferguson, 'Labour's soft stance on stop and search could lead to extra killing a week, Tories warn', *Sun*, 8 December 2019.

50 Gordon Rayner, 'Tactical voting could hand Jeremy Corbyn keys to No. 10', *Daily Telegraph*, 10 December 2019.

51 See Chris Smyth and Oliver Wright, 'Voters lose interest in "get Brexit done" pledge', *Times*, 11 December 2019.

52 Conservatives, 'Boris Johnson's funny Love Actually parody', YouTube, 9 December 2019, https://youtu.be/nj-YK3JJCIU.

53 Conservatives, 'End the argument. Get Brexit done. Vote Conservative.', YouTube, 7 December 2019, https://youtu.be/FPjkTCQh3RM.

54 Rory Cellan-Jones, 'General election 2019: Do social media ads work, are they fair?', BBC News, 11 December 2019.

55 https://twitter.com/BorisJohnson/status/1204454731193688065.

56 For the record, see Timothy Heppell and Thomas McMeeking, 'The Conservative Party leadership transition from Theresa May to Boris Johnson: Party popularity and leadership satisfaction', *Representation*, 57 (1), 2021, pp. 59–73.

57 Neil O'Brien, 'Policies for a new Britain – in which the central point for new Tory MPs is the moors on the edge of Sheffield', ConservativeHome, 16 December 2019.

58 Six ethnic minority MPs attended Johnson's first post-election Cabinets: Sajid Javid (Chancellor), Priti Patel (Home Secretary), Alok Sharma (International Development Secretary), Rishi Sunak (Chief Secretary to the Treasury), James Cleverly (Party Chair), and Kwasi Kwarteng (Business, Energy and Industrial Strategy).

59 See these very useful (and concise) Twitter threads: the first from Will Jennings (https://twitter.com/drjennings/status/1488489166275059712) and the second from Marios Richards (https://twitter.com/MariosRichards/status /1488831306905628673).

60 For two useful correctives to the assumption that all the party's northern voters and the places they live in are dirt poor and stuffed full of old people because the youngsters have all fled, see Torsten Bell, 'The Tories can't help "blue wall" voters unless they understand them', *Guardian*, 12 February 2020, and 'The truth behind the Tories' northern strongholds', *Economist*, 31 March 2021.

61 On increased voter volatility over time, see Edward Fieldhouse, *Electoral Shocks: The Volatile Voter in a Turbulent World* (Oxford University Press, 2020) and Paul Webb and Tim Bale, *The Modern British Party System* (Oxford University Press, 2021).

62 Chris Butler, 'Are the new Conservative MPs really so different?', UK in a Changing Europe, 28 January 2022. In fact, transparency campaigners even suggested that a fifth of new Tory MPs had worked as lobbyists: see Philip Cowley and Matthew Bailey, 'Labour's history of highs and lows – and what it reveals', *Times*, 12 February 2020, and Adam Ramsay, Caroline Molloy, and Tamasin Cave, 'Revealed: A fifth of new Tory MPs have worked as lobbyists', open-Democracy, 12 December 2019. The website ConservativeHome concurred: see its detailed analysis (complete with pen portraits) by Henry Hill, 'Boris' Boys and Girls: The Conservative Commons intake of 2019', ConservativeHome, 21 January 2020. See also Daniel Bond, 'Class of 2019: Meet the new MPs', Politics Home – The House, 16 December 2019.

63 See Tim Bale and Hovik Minasyan, 'Does Boris Johnson have the Conservative Party's permission to extend transition?', UK in a Changing Europe, 30 April 2020.

64 Matthew Taylor and Jim Waterson, 'Boris Johnson threatens BBC with two-pronged attack', *Guardian*, 15 December 2019.

65 See, for example, Steven Swinford, 'Dominic Cummings: Whitehall in fear of "Valentine's massacre"', *Times*, 21 December 2019 and Helen Warrell, 'UK's military seeks new place in world after Brexit', *Financial Times*, 23 December 2019.

66 Taylor and Waterson, 'Boris Johnson threatens BBC'.

67 On the subsequent controversy over who paid for the holiday, see 'Boris Johnson criticised over Mustique trip explanation', BBC News, 8 July 2021.

Chapter 7 Pandemonium (January–December 2020)

1 The whole heart-breaking tale is told in detail by Mark Francois, *Spartan Victory* (KDP, 2021), pp. 371–3.

2 On what Dominic Cummings (understandably perhaps) saw as Johnson's obsession with the question, see Tanya Gold, 'The man trying to take down Boris Johnson', *New York Magazine*, 30 January 2022.

3 For a glimpse at the rapturous reception with which Brexit Day was greeted by the Leave-supporting press and the dolorous reception accorded to it by Remain-supporting titles, see Martin Farrer, '"Leap into the unknown": What the papers say about Brexit Day', *Guardian*, 21 January 2020.

4 On just how media-friendly Sunak would turn out to be, see Isabel Hardman, 'The rise of Brand Rishi', *Spectator*, 9 July 2020.

5 See the interview Sunak gave to the *Spectator* at the end of his first year in Number Eleven: Katy Balls and Fraser Nelson, '"It's not morally right to keep borrowing at these levels": Rishi Sunak's plan to fix the UK economy', *Spectator*, 19 December 2020. Certainly, there wasn't much to distinguish him ideologically or in economic policy terms from Javid, who penned the following for the *Daily Telegraph* later in the year: Sajid Javid, 'We can grow our way out of this economic crisis', *Daily Telegraph*, 22 June 2020.

6 For the full horror, see the clip here https://twitter.com/Haggis_UK/status /1228263906277253121.

7 For details, see Home Office and UK Visas and Immigration, 'UK points-based immigration system: Policy statement', GOV.uk, 19 February 2020.

8 See Edward Malnick, 'Top civil servants on Tories' "hit list"', *Sunday Telegraph*, 22 February 2020. Sedwill had reportedly clashed with Cummings and Johnson over Covid, and had earlier blotted his copy book when, just prior to the 2019 election, he had blocked a plan to use Treasury civil servants to publish costings of the Labour Party's fiscal policies.

9 Alix Culbertson, 'Dominic Cummings claims Boris Johnson was writing Shakespeare book instead of dealing with COVID', Sky News, 12 November 2021.

10 For more on Mrs Chernukhin, see James Oliver, Steve Swann, and Nassos Stylianou, 'Tory donor's "link" to sanctioned oligarch's secret London property', BBC News, 21 April 2022.

11 See Laura Kuenssberg, 'Covid: The inside story of the government's battle against the virus', BBC News, 15 March 2021.

12 Dominic Cummings gave evidence to that effect at his appearance before the Science and Technology and Health Select Committees on 26 May 2021 (see Chapter 8).

13 As to whether herd immunity was the initial strategy, see Secunder Kermani, 'Coronavirus: Whitty and Vallance faced "herd immunity" backlash, emails show', BBC News, 23 September 2020 and Lawrence Freedman, 'The real reason the UK government pursued "herd immunity" – and why it was abandoned', *New Statesman*, 1 April 2020. See also https://twitter.com/Dominic2306/status /1396415862618435584.

14 On the key role played by Warner, see Matthew Syed, 'The genius who finally persuaded Boris Johnson to lock down', *Sunday Times*, 17 October 2021.

15 On the public's dissatisfaction with testing and PPE provision, see *The Political Report*, Opinium/Observer polling series, 5 May 2020, https://www.opinium .com/wp-content/uploads/2020/05/Opinium-Political-Report-5th-May-2020 .pdf. Presumably it was this that led Business Secretary Alok Sharma, on a Sunday TV show on 12 April, to issue a classic 'non-apology apology' to health and social care workers – namely 'I'm incredibly sorry that people feel they're not able to get this equipment.'

16 John Curtice, 'How do voters feel about delaying the end of the transition?', What UK Thinks: EU, 15 April 2020.

17 Opinion on the backbenches at that stage was mixed. See Paul Goodman, 'What Conservative MPs told us about the lockdown's future. The consensus is for a gradual easing', ConservativeHome, 24 April 2020.

18 See Steve Baker, 'Boris Johnson must end the absurd, dystopian and tyrannical lockdown', *Daily Telegraph*, 3 May 2020.

19 See, for one of the earliest examples, Mark Harper, 'We can't continue the current lockdown while waiting for a vaccine – and need a recovery plan to get out of it', ConservativeHome, 22 April 2020.

20 Early examples include *Spectator* Editor Fraser Nelson, 'Boris is worried lockdown has gone too far, but only he can end it', *Daily Telegraph*, 9 April 2020, fellow *Daily Telegraph* columnist Dan Hannan, 'It's time to start loosening the lockdown', *Daily Telegraph*, 11 April 2020, and *Sun* veteran Trevor Kavanagh, 'Let's get back to work before Britain goes under because of this coronavirus lockdown', *Sun*, 14 April 2020.

21 On subsidies, see Brian Cathcart, 'From cronyism to corruption: Giving away public money to newspaper friends', in John Mair (ed.), *Boris Johnson: Media Creation, Media Clown, Media Casualty?* (Mair Golden Moments, 2022), pp. 55–60. See also https://twitter.com/Dominic2306 /status/1524394482938093571 and https://twitter.com/Dominic2306/status /1526836612990177280. On working from home, see, for example, Ross Clark, 'Workshy Whitehall is wrecking the recovery', *Daily Mail*, 4 August 2020, and https://twitter.com/hendopolis/status/1299087662255681538. Note that, whatever their motivation, those critical of working from home could point to evidence that Brits had not returned to the office in anywhere near the same numbers as workers in large continental European countries: Sascha O'Sullivan, 'More Brits continuing to work from home than any other major European country', *Sun*, 5 August 2020.

22 Caroline Wheeler, Oliver Shah, Tom Harper, and Tom Calver, 'Tory grandees

tell PM: It's time to ease the coronavirus lockdown', *Sunday Times*, 26 April 2020.

23 See Glen Owen, 'Cabinet splits over coronavirus lockdown: Chancellor Rishi Sunak warns Britain faces irreparable damage if restrictions aren't lifted soon – while Health Secretary Matt Hancock favours extending the measures to protect NHS workers', *Mail on Sunday*, 11 April 2020.

24 For an example of the briefing that set Sunak up as someone keen to reopen while the PM was less gung-ho, see George Parker, Daniel Thomas, and Jim Pickard, 'Sunak at odds with Johnson over speed of UK lockdown exit', *Financial Times*, 22 May 2020.

25 Compare the survey results from YouGov/*Good Morning Britain*, 10 May 2020, https://docs.cdn.yougov.com/h6nwhcsrrv/GMBResults_200511.pdf and Paul Goodman, 'Our snap survey. Over half of our Conservative member panel backs Johnson's plan. A third want a Sweden-style looser lockdown', ConservativeHome, 12 May 2020.

26 Lucy Fisher, 'Don't meet backbench leader Sir Graham Brady alone, Boris Johnson told in memo slip', *Times*, 14 May 2020.

27 On school reopening and unions, see, for example, Jason Groves and Josh White, 'Let teachers teach! Education Secretary Gavin Williamson demands unions "do their duty"', *Daily Mail*, 15 May 2020, Allister Heath, 'Boris can't afford to surrender to contemptible teaching unions', *Daily Telegraph*, 20 May 2020, and 'You would think teachers' unions would want to heed science and re-open schools', *Sun*, 19 May 2020.

28 See 'Coronavirus: Discrimination row over MPs queuing up to vote', BBC News, 2 June 2020.

29 For details, see Matthew Weaver, 'Boris Johnson will not face criminal inquiry over Jennifer Arcuri', *Guardian*, 21 May 2020.

30 For the public's scepticism, see the YouGov survey results, 26 May 2020, https://yougov.co.uk/topics/politics/survey-results/daily/2020/05/26/3fb8f/1. On quite how much one particular minister compromised herself, see David Allen Green, 'Why the Attorney General should resign', Law and Policy Blog, 5 June 2020, https://davidallengreen.com/2020/06/why-the-attorney-general-should-resign/.

31 The *Daily Mail*, in particular, was outraged, although the *Daily Telegraph* (as was its wont) was rather more sympathetic to the PM, as were the *Sun* and the *Daily Express*. See Clea Skopeliti, '"What planet are they on?": The papers on the PM's defence of Dominic Cummings', *Guardian*, 24 May 2020 and Alison Rourke, '"Stay elite": What the papers say about Dominic Cummings' refusal to quit', *Guardian*, 26 May 2020. For one of the most popular social media takes, see https://twitter.com/paddymcguinness/status/1265314862491631617.

32 Paul Goodman, 'Our survey. Seven out of ten Tory members back Cummings', ConservativeHome, 31 May 2020.

33 For what Maitlis said, and the BBC's reaction, see 'Newsnight "breached BBC impartiality guidelines" with Cummings remarks', BBC News, 27 May 2020. For BBQ Monday headlines, see '"Happy Monday": Easing of lockdown restrictions dominates papers', ITV News, 29 May 2020.

34 For an overview with pictures, see James Hockaday, 'Black Lives Matter protesters spray "racist" on Winston Churchill statue', *Metro*, 8 June 2020.

35 https://twitter.com/BorisJohnson/status/1271388180193914880.

36 See Policy Exchange, 'History Matters Project', https://policyexchange.org.uk/history-matters-project/ and Neil O'Brien, 'Johnson should instruct a team of ministers to wage war on woke', ConservativeHome, 21 September 2020.

37 For a sympathetic portrait of her, see Andrew Gimson, 'Munira Mirza, the Muslim from Oldham who leads Johnson's Policy Unit', ConservativeHome, 21 May 2020.

38 Robert Buckland, 'Vandalising memorials is truly beyond the pale', *Daily Telegraph*, 20 June 2020.

39 See Harry Yorke and Gordon Rayner, 'Pull down "iron curtain" at Number 10, MPs urge Prime Minister', *Daily Telegraph*, 17 June 2020. For an example of Sunak's ongoing attempt to ingratiate himself with backbenchers keen to see the country get back to work, see Steven Swinford and Andrew Ellson, 'Coronavirus: Rishi Sunak targets two-metre rule and calls for a spending spree', *Times*, 11 June 2020. As for opinion research, the government commissioned YouGov and Hanbury (some of whose analysts had helped the Tories during the election campaign) to carry out frequent (sometimes even daily) polling on Covid and other issues, while the qualitative work went to Public First, the firm founded by James Frayne, a ConservativeHome columnist, and Rachel Wolf, one of the co-authors of the Tories' 2019 manifesto. For details, see Tim Shipman, 'Coronavirus: Boris Johnson spends millions to keep the crowd onside', *Sunday Times*, 21 June 2020.

40 Contrast https://twitter.com/bbcnews/status/1267934578418823174 with Matthew Smith, 'Most Britons back government plans to quarantine travellers to UK', YouGov, 8 June 2020.

41 See 'Boris Johnson: Economy speech fact-checked', BBC News, 30 June 2020, and Richard Partington, 'How does Boris Johnson's "new deal" compare with Franklin D. Roosevelt's?', *Guardian*, 30 June 2020.

42 'Coronavirus: Boris Johnson criticised over "cowardly" care home comments', BBC News, 7 July 2020. Johnson, as per, refused to apologize for the remark but didn't repeat it, preferring instead to suggest (just as falsely) that the

NOTES TO PP. 160–4

government didn't know that 'Covid could be transmitted asymptomatically in the way that it was' when deciding to discharge patients in order to protect the NHS – a policy later ruled by the High Court to have been unlawful: see Jane Merrick, 'All 20 warnings the government had over asymptomatic Covid before patients were sent to care homes', *The i*, 28 April 2022.

43 See Beth Hale, 'Dinner's on Dishy Rishi! Everything you need to know to get up to £10 off your meal per head when chancellor's Eat Out To Help Out scheme launches on Monday', *Daily Mail*, 31 July 2020. See also Theresa Villiers, 'City centres need our help – it's our patriotic duty to eat, drink & shop', *Sun*, 12 July 2020.

44 Tim Bale, Aron Cheung, Philip Cowley, Anand Menon, and Alan Wager, 'Mind the values gap: The social and economic values of MPs, party members and voters', UK in a Changing Europe, June 2020.

45 Cummings, quoted in Jeremy Farrar and Anjana Ahuja, 'Out of control: The moment Boris Johnson let Covid run rampant', *Sunday Times*, 18 July 2021.

46 For the best account of the affair, see Paul Waugh, 'How Julian Lewis pulled off a very British coup to chair the Intelligence and Security Committee', *Huffington Post*, 15 July 2020.

47 Harry Cole and Simon Boyle, 'Rule Britannia ban: Laurence Fox urges BBC viewers to cancel licence fee after lyrics ditched from Proms songs', *Sun*, 24 August 2020.

48 Simon Murphy, 'UK report on Russian interference: Key points explained', *Guardian*, 21 July 2020, and George Greenwood, Emanuele Midolo, Sean O'Neill, and Lucy Fisher, 'Conservative Party ministers bankrolled by donors linked to Russia', *Times*, 23 July 2020.

49 See Andrew Mitchell, *Beyond a Fringe: Tales from a Reformed Establishment Lackey* (London: Biteback, 2021), p. 260.

50 See Christopher Hope and Dominic Penna, 'Tory heartlands will have to find space for 1.5m new homes', *Daily Telegraph*, 27 September 2020.

51 See David Churchill, Andy Dolan, and Jim Norton, '"Codswallop": Fury at "lockdown busting" Cabinet minister Robert Jenrick grows', *Daily Mail*, 10 April 2020, and Peter Geoghegan and Jenna Corderoy, 'Property tycoons gave Tories more than £11m in less than a year', openDemocracy, 26 June 2020.

52 Sophie Borland, Hugo Duncan, and Claire Ellicott, '"We can't lock the UK down again": Scientists, MPs and industry leaders warn Boris another coronavirus shutdown could cripple the country', *Daily Mail*, 8 September 2020.

53 See Anna Mikhailova and Glen Owen, 'Stop strangling the economy – and get people back to work! Tory donors tell PM his Covid rules will wreck Britain and put the NHS in danger', *Daily Mail*, 12 September 2020, and Paul Waugh,

'Grouse shooting and hunting exempt from Johnson's "Rule of Six" Covid curbs', *Huffington Post*, 14 September 2020.

54 Jason Groves, 'Cabinet at war over the rule of six: Almost every minister on Boris Johnson's Covid committee argued against the stringent limit – and even the PM himself was "cautious" – but Matt Hancock got his way', *Daily Mail*, 10 September 2020.

55 See Scientific Advisory Group for Emergencies, 'Fifty-eighth SAGE meeting on Covid-19', 21 September 2020.

56 For the origins of, and debate over, the Great Barrington Declaration, see https://en.wikipedia.org/wiki/Great_Barrington_Declaration.

57 On low case rates in Tory as opposed to Labour constituencies, see https://twitter.com/ChristabelCoops/status/1321078956519555075. Ipsos MORI reported on 22 September that 'local lockdowns' in regions where coronavirus cases were rising had the support of 76 per cent with only 9 per cent opposed.

58 Lord Ashcroft, *A New Political Landscape?*, October 2020, https://lordashcroftpolls.com/wp-content/uploads/2020/10/A-NEW-POLITICAL-LANDSCAPE-Oct-2020.pdf.

59 See Paul Goodman, 'Our Cabinet League Table. The Prime Minister falls into negative territory', ConservativeHome, 3 October 2020, and Paul Goodman, 'Our survey. Under one in three Party members think Johnson is dealing well with the Coronavirus as Prime Minister', ConservativeHome, 2 October 2020.

60 See Harry Cole and Matt Dathan, 'Rishi Sunak insists Eat Out scheme did NOT fuel Covid spike as he vows to fight second lockdown', *Sun*, 4 October 2020.

61 'Boris Johnson must take time to make the right call after refusing to surrender control to erratic Sage scientists', *Sun*, 13 October 2020.

62 'Covid: Boris Johnson resisted autumn lockdown as only over-80s dying – Dominic Cummings', BBC News, 20 July 2021.

63 For the *Daily Mail*'s front-page plea, see https://twitter.com/hendopolis/status/1321579392989016069.

64 On the row with Greater Manchester, see James Robinson, 'Mayor Andy Burnham blames Chancellor Rishi Sunak for being "the problem" in row over financial support for Manchester', *Daily Mail*, 18 October 2020.

65 Hannah Richardson, 'Marcus Rashford welcomes school holiday support climbdown', BBC News, 8 November 2020. See also Amy Walker, 'Ben Bradley urged to apologise over free school meals tweets', *Guardian*, 24 October 2020. Some thirty-eight Tory MPs abstained rather than vote with the government, while five voted with Labour. ConservativeHome's readers' survey of party members found that 38 per cent thought the government should extend free

school meals to eligible children over the Christmas holidays, although that still left 56 per cent who thought it should not: see Henry Hill, 'Our survey. More than half of members back the Government over extending free school meals', ConservativeHome, 3 November 2020.

66 For the original story, see Simon Walters, 'Boris Johnson: "Let the bodies pile high in their thousands". PM's incendiary remark during fight over lockdowns is latest claim in No. 10 drama – amid spectacular row with Cummings', *Daily Mail*, 25 April 2021.

67 See Jessica Elgot, Simon Murphy, and Peter Walker, 'How a full-scale lockdown rebellion by Tory MPs was called off', *Guardian*, 6 November 2020.

68 Iain Duncan Smith, 'SAGE believes its advice to be more like commandments written on stone', *Daily Telegraph*, 1 November 2020.

69 For two prime examples, see Steven Glover, 'A calamitous, hurried U-turn and why I now have an inkling of what it must be like to live in a dictatorship', *Daily Mail*, 1 November 2020, and Trevor Kavanagh, 'Forget about Christmas – brace yourselves for a miserable, jobless & bankrupt New Year', *Sun*, 1 November 2020. On Reform UK, see Nigel Farage and Richard Tice, 'We're relaunching the Brexit Party to fight this cruel and unnecessary lockdown', *Daily Telegraph*, 1 November 2020.

70 For Baker's contribution, see Steve Baker, 'I cannot support this second lockdown', *Daily Telegraph*, 3 November 2020. See also Mark Harper, 'Lockdown 1) Why I will vote against it today', ConservativeHome, 4 November 2020.

71 See Alex Hern, 'Johnson's Biden win tweet contains hidden Trump congratulations', *Guardian*, 10 November 2020.

72 See Henry Hill, 'Our survey: More than half of Tory members want Trump to win next week', ConservativeHome, 31 October 2020. Only 22 per cent went for Biden!

73 Charles Hymas, 'Net migration targets abandoned as £38,500 salary threshold to settle in UK ditched', *Daily Telegraph*, 23 October 2020.

74 One well-sourced investigation into the supposed power of the PM's wife is Michael Ashcroft, *First Lady: Intrigue at the Court of Carrie and Boris Johnson* (Biteback, 2022).

75 For detailed accounts of the dramatic events, see Tim Shipman, 'There were three in this marriage: Boris, Carrie and Dominic Cummings', *Sunday Times*, 14 November 2020, and Glen Owen, Dan Hodges, and Katie Hind, 'What a way to run a country! The hatreds, tears and tantrums behind the ousting of Dominic Cummings revealed – and the "victory party" thrown by Carrie Symonds to celebrate his humiliating departure', *Daily Mail*, 14 November 2020. According to Cummings, Johnson was told that the evidence pointed to

Cabinet Office SpAd Henry Newman (later made an adviser to Johnson himself) and others in his office, to which his response was, 'If Newman is confirmed as the leaker then I will have to fire him, and this will cause me very serious problems with Carrie as they're best friends ... [pause] perhaps we could get the Cabinet Secretary to stop the leak inquiry?' Dominic Cummings, 'Statement regarding No. 10 claims today', 23 April 2021, https://dominiccummings.com/2021/04/23/statement-regarding-no10-claims-today/. Naturally, Number Ten disputed this account, claiming that MI5 evidence pointed to Cummings.

76 See Helen Pidd, 'Over 50 Tory MPs in northern England press PM for roadmap out of lockdown', *Guardian*, 26 October 2020.

77 For an idea of its preoccupations, see Glen Owen and Brendan Carlin, 'Tory MPs urge Boris to go to war on BBC and National Trust wokery: PM told to speak out for Britain's patriotic silent majority against "elitist bourgeois liberals" at institutions', *Daily Mail*, 21 November 2020.

78 The big difference between the Brexit Party and Reform UK, however, was that the former was tapping into widespread Euroscepticism, whereas support for the anti-lockdown cause was much more limited – particularly amongst older voters who formed the core vote for the Conservatives. See Tim Bale, 'The United Kingdom: The pandemic and the tale of two populist parties', in Nils Ringe and Lucio Rennó (eds), *Populists and the Pandemic: How Populists around the World Responded to COVID-19* (Routledge, 2023), pp. 68–78.

79 See 'Michael Gove smeared us. Now we have been vindicated by an official inquiry', openDemocracy, 29 April 2022.

80 See National Audit Office, 'Investigation into government procurement during the COVID-19 pandemic', 18 November 2020; see also Robert Barrington, 'Britain's PPE procurement: Chumocracy, cronyism, corruption', UK in a Changing Europe, 3 December 2020.

81 See George Grylls and Oliver Wright, 'Tories make donors and friends directors of civil service boards', *Times*, 5 August 2020.

82 See George Grylls and Esther Webber, 'Robert Jenrick ignored civil servants to spend Towns Fund millions on Tory marginals', *Times*, 24 September 2020. For a detailed academic analysis showing beyond reasonable doubt that the allocation decisions were biased, see Chris Hanretty, 'The pork barrel politics of the Towns Fund', *Politics Quarterly*, 92 (1), 2021, pp. 7–13.

83 A snap poll by Savanta ComRes found that 61 per cent supported the cut to foreign aid while 13 per cent opposed it and that 44 per cent supported freezing public sector pay while 30 per cent were opposed. In both cases, older voters were significantly more supportive of the proposals.

84 Graham Brady, 'Chairman of the 1922 committee of Tory MPs SIR GRAHAM

BRADY says the Tier system is destroying Britain . . . so he'll be voting AGAINST', *Daily Mail*, 27 November 2020.

85 Boris Johnson, 'We are so nearly out of our captivity, we can see the sunlit upland pastures ahead . . . but if we try to jump the fence now, we will tangle ourselves in the last barbed wire', *Mail on Sunday*, 28 November 2020.

86 See Michael Gove, 'Lockdown was the only way to stop the NHS being broken', *Times*, 28 November 2020.

87 See, for example, Tobias Ellwood, 'The tiered system is crushing constituencies like mine. We must do better', *Daily Telegraph*, 29 November 2020, and Jonathan Reilly, 'Only 732 pubs out of 38,277 in England will be able to open in Tier 1 as brewers warn of Christmas beer shortage', *Sun*, 29 November 2020.

88 See HM Government, 'Analysis of the health, economic and social effects of COVID-19 and the approach to tiering', 30 November 2020.

89 Alex Wickham, 'Baker's dozens – Warner brothers – one month to go', *Politico London Playbook*, 1 December 2020.

90 Henry Hill, 'Our survey. Members strongly back faster liberalisation of Covid-19 restrictions', ConservativeHome, 1 December 2020.

91 See Arj Singh, 'No, Brexit hasn't made Covid vaccine approval quicker in the UK', *Huffington Post*, 2 December 2020, and, on the long-term effect on public opinion, see https://twitter.com/RedfieldWilton/status/1525113930540097536.

92 See, for example, Fraser Nelson, 'The new Tory equality agenda is far more than a victory over wokeness', *Daily Telegraph*, 17 December 2020 and, for the speech, see Liz Truss, 'The new fight for fairness', 17 December 2020, https://cps.org.uk/events/post/2020/speech-by-the-rt-hon-elizabeth-truss-mp-the-new-fight-for-fairness/.

93 For the front-page coverage, see Warren Murray, '"Christmas cancelled": What the papers say as UK Covid bubbles burst', *Guardian*, 20 December 2020.

94 For a selection, see 'This is a monumental U-turn that devastates us all', *Daily Telegraph*, 19 December 2020 and 'How many more times must we suffer this dimming of the light with Covid-19 restrictions?', *Daily Mail*, 20 December 2020.

95 See Mark Harper and Steve Baker, 'Chair and Deputy Chair of the Covid Recovery Group MARK HARPER and STEVE BAKER: We need to know how many lives lockdown is destroying', *Daily Mail*, 19 December 2020.

96 See Matthew Smith, 'Strong support for Tier 4 introduction and Christmas rules changes', YouGov, 20 December 2020. Anti-lockdown MPs dismissed such polling as 'flawed rubbish'. See Isabel Hardman, 'Today's Tier 4 extension will spark another clash between Boris Johnson and his MPs', *Guardian*, 23 December 2020.

97 Henry Dyer, 'A disgraced Lord gave the Conservatives £500,000 days after his peerage was forced through by Boris Johnson', *Business Insider*, 3 June 2021.

98 https://twitter.com/bbchelena/status/1341884081102008321 and https://twitter.com/MrHarryCole/status/1341869025991733248.

99 Francois, *Spartan Victory*, pp. 379–80. See also Craig Mackinlay and Andrea Jenkyns, 'The first step in a new relationship with our continental neighbours – and with the wider world', ConservativeHome, 30 December 2020, and Andrew Bridgen, 'I see no traps . . . that's why I'll seize our day of destiny, writes ANDREW BRIDGEN, Tory MP for North West Leicestershire', *Daily Mail*, 29 December 2020.

Chapter 8 Coming up for air (January–October 2021)

1 *Daily Telegraph* front page, 1 January 2021, https://twitter.com/AllieHBNews/status/1344766349273419779.

2 See YouGov, 11 January 2021, https://yougov.co.uk/topics/politics/survey-results/daily/2021/01/11/02042/3.

3 Harry Cole, 'BO WOE: Boris Johnson given bombshell warning to lift lockdown soon or face leadership threat', *Sun*, 14 January 2021.

4 https://twitter.com/nmsonline/status/1354109873936601089.

5 See Harry Cole, 'VACC TO SCHOOL: Boris Johnson must get kids back to school next month or risk "lost generation", warn MPs and parents', *Sun*, 25 January 2021, as well as Sutton Trust, *Remote Learning: The Digital Divide*, 11 January 2021, and Sally Weale and Patrick Butler, 'Ministers urged to change "food parcel first" policy', *Guardian*, 12 January 2021.

6 'Universal Credit: MPs urge PM to keep £20 benefit "lifeline"', BBC News, 18 January 2021.

7 See, for example, Oliver Wright, 'Britain will protect trade with Northern Ireland, EU warned', *Times*, 14 January 2021.

8 David Frost, 'Brussels needs to shake off its remaining ill-will and treat Brexit Britain as an equal', *Sunday Telegraph*, 6 March 2021.

9 On Carrie Johnson's alleged influence on appointments (and much else), see Michael Ashcroft, *First Lady: Intrigue at the Court of Carrie and Boris Johnson* (Biteback, 2022).

10 See, for instance, 'Strong approval for government's vaccine programme as Johnson preferred to lead pandemic response', Ipsos, 8 February 2021.

11 See, for example, Connor Boyd, '"Do the maths, Boris!" 70 Tory MPs demand a route out of lockdown amid fears Boris is being "beaten up by the scientists", despite multiple signs Covid is on the run', *Daily Mail*, 4 February 2021. See also Trevor Kavanagh, 'Boris Johnson wants to free the long-suffering British

public ... SAGE won't let him', *Sun*, 8 February 2021, and, for an arche-typal front-page screamer, *Daily Mail*, 18 February 2021, https://twitter.com /hendopolis/status/1362165956768894979.

12 For the distinctly unimpressed reaction of the party in the media, see the front pages of the *Daily Mail*, 23 February 2021, https://twitter.com/hendopolis /status/1363975510112555015, and the *Sun*, 23 February 2021, https:// twitter.com/hendopolis/status/1363974862868533249. Meanwhile, the Covid Recovery Group's Mark Harper took to Twitter to criticize modelling which he believed failed to take account of more encouraging real-world data on vaccine roll-out and efficacy: https://twitter.com/Mark_J_Harper/status /1364294661469335557.

13 To watch this video (clocking in at just under six minutes!), go to https://twitter .com/RishiSunak/status/1366376006462881810.

14 See, in particular, Allister Heath, 'The Tories have trashed Thatcherism and embraced Europe's politics of decline', *Daily Telegraph*, 4 March 2021.

15 On how Towns Fund grants were allocated, see Anthony Reuben, 'Towns Fund: How were the winners chosen?', BBC News, 4 March 2021.

16 Anthony Wells, 'Budget 2021 measures prove popular with Britons', YouGov, 4 March 2021.

17 The complicated affair is concisely explained here: 'Greensill: What is the David Cameron lobbying row about?', BBC News, 9 August 2021.

18 Mark Bridge, 'Don't be bullied by left on statues, Oliver Dowden tells museums', *Times*, 3 March 2021. See also Oliver Dowden, 'We won't allow Britain's history to be cancelled', *Daily Telegraph*, 15 May 2021.

19 Harry Cole and Jonathan Reilly, 'PRITI TOUGH: Priti Patel vows illegal immigrants landing on UK beaches face deportation in as little as 24 HOURS', *Sun*, 24 March 2021.

20 See *Daily Mail* front page, 22 March 2021, https://twitter.com/AllieHBNews /status/1373758437876711429.

21 John Crace, 'Tory milkman delivers speech surreal even by Commons' standards', *Guardian*, 25 March 2021.

22 Jason Groves, Eleanor Hayward, and Tom Witherow, 'What are we waiting for?', *Daily Mail*, 30 March 2021.

23 On the highly unusual release strategy, see Peter Walker, '"Brazen" government media strategy muddies detail of UK race report', *Guardian*, 31 March 2021. On the nuances, see Sunder Katwala, 'Is Britain racist? This binary question is unhelpful and obstructs real progress', *Independent*, 31 March 2021.

24 *Daily Mail* front page, 31 March 2021, https://twitter.com/AllieHBNews /status/1377008002448900099.

25 See Anoosh Chakelian, 'Sixteen of the race report's 24 recommendations have been made before', *New Statesman*, 7 April 2021.

26 Even the PM's critics had to admit he played a blinder. For an example of his pitch-perfect performance, see Boris Johnson, 'Ludicrous . . . I'll give it a red card', *Sun*, 20 April 2021. Whether, right at the start of the affair, Johnson had been as opposed to the idea, however, is highly questionable: see Pippa Crerar, 'Johnson gave green light to Super League, then railed against it', *Daily Mirror*, 26 May 2021.

27 Simon Walters, 'Boris Johnson was lobbied by killer Saudi prince', *Daily Mail*, 15 April 2021.

28 Harry Cole, 'BORIS: DOM'S A TEXT MANIAC', *Sun*, 23 April 2021.

29 Dominic Cummings, 'Statement regarding No. 10 claims today', 23 April 2021, https://dominiccummings.com/2021/04/23/statement-regarding-no10-claims-today/.

30 See 'Newspaper headlines: "Boris painted into corner" and how to get "fancy wallpaper"', BBC News, 29 April 2021.

31 Simon Walters, 'Boris Johnson: "Let the bodies pile high in their thousands"', *Daily Mail*, 26 April 2021. See also Brendan Carlin, 'Abolish "incompetent and biased" electoral watchdog investigating Boris Johnson's flat makeover, say Tory MPs', *Mail on Sunday*, 2 May 2021.

32 Connor Ibbetson, 'Do Britons believe Boris Johnson made the "let the bodies pile high" remark?', YouGov, 30 April 2021.

33 Steven Swinford and Oliver Wright, 'Tories increase lead over Labour despite Boris Johnson flat row', *Times*, 30 April 2021. Note that headline leads routinely exclude those who respond 'don't know', who say they wouldn't vote, and who refuse to answer. If these are counted, the Conservatives were on just 31 per cent to Labour's 23 per cent.

34 'Boris Johnson must end this saga and come clean about his flat refurbishment', *Sun*, 27 April 2021.

35 See Stephen Fisher, 'Reverse electoral reform', *Prospect*, 18 May 2021.

36 See Tom Wilkinson, 'Boris Johnson meets 30ft inflatable doppelganger on visit to Hartlepool', *Evening Standard*, 7 May 2021.

37 See https://twitter.com/itvpeston/status/1392588377971740674. For a more technical take which effectively arrives at a similar conclusion, see Toby S. James and Alistair Clark, 'Electoral integrity, voter fraud and voter ID in polling stations: Lessons from English local elections', *Policy Studies*, 41 (2–3), 2020, pp. 190–209.

38 *Daily Mail* front page, 13 May 2021, https://twitter.com/alliehbnews/status/1392228038377627653.

39 See also an article by an MP with a much smaller majority (albeit one vulnerable to Labour): Theresa Villiers, 'The public must not be pushed out of the planning process', *Times Red Box*, 12 May 2021.

40 See Harry Yorke, 'Britain's planning system is "not fit for purpose"', says Robert Jenrick', *Daily Telegraph*, 17 May 2021.

41 Simon Clarke, 'Why Tory MPs must back Boris on planning', *Times Red Box*, 18 May 2021.

42 https://twitter.com/Dominic2306/status/1396116963827634183.

43 https://twitter.com/yougov/status/1397479385171701760.

44 Connor Ibbetson, 'Dominic Cummings: What do Britons make of his accusations against the government?', YouGov, 27 May 2021.

45 Opinium, *The Political Report*, 27 May 2021.

46 Charlotte Gill, 'Our survey. Over 50 per cent of respondents think Cummings' critique of the government was wrong', ConservativeHome, 1 June 2021.

47 See (if you can bear it) Hayley Dixon, Tony Diver, Ben Riley-Smith, and Lizzie Roberts, 'Boris and his barefoot bride: Inside the bohemian wedding party that no one saw coming', *Daily Telegraph*, 30 May 2021.

48 The Singh Investigation, *Independent Investigation into Alleged Discrimination*, 25 May 2021, https://singhinvestigation.co.uk/.

49 Sajid Javid, 'Following society is not enough: Tories have to lead Britain against racism', *Times*, 26 May 2021.

50 HOPE not hate, 'The cultural problem of Islamophobia in the Conservative Party', 30 September 2020. The ESRC-funded Party Members Project found in 2019 that a quarter of grassroots Tories wanted to see fewer Muslim MPs (who at the time made up 2.5 per cent of all MPs when Muslims made up an estimated 5 per cent of the population) – twice as many, incidentally, as said the same about ethnic minority MPs as a whole: see Tim Bale, 'Is the Conservative Party full of Islamophobes?', *Independent*, 12 April 2019.

51 Basit Mamhood and Peter Oborne, '"Junk idea of Islamophobia" says adviser to Conservative racism inquiry', *Middle East Eye*, 31 March 2021, and Lucy Fisher, 'Boris Johnson's Islamophobia inquiry accused of whitewash', *Daily Telegraph*, 6 April 2021.

52 See https://twitter.com/SayeedaWarsi/status/1397286600724320257 and Alix Culbertson, 'Tory Islamophobia inquiry: Former Conservative chair says report shows party "institutionally racist"', Sky News, 25 May 2021.

53 For a summary of the coverage and a look at the front pages that day, see Graham Russell, '"Zero": How the UK papers covered a day without a single reported Covid death', *Guardian*, 2 June 2021.

54 See interview with Mark Harper in Emilio Casalicchio, 'Unlockdown wars

– Last Porto call – Taxing the Rishi', *Politico London Playbook*, 4 June 2021, and Graham Brady, 'Don't be fooled: Keeping restrictions in place beyond June 21 comes with a hefty price tag', *Daily Telegraph*, 3 June 2021.

55 Katy Balls, 'The political advantages of the UK–Australia trade deal', *Spectator*, 15 June 2021.

56 See John Stevens, 'Now it's Tory civil war: Boris Johnson's own MPs accuse him of panicking and "lockdown without end" after he postpones Freedom Day', *Daily Mail*, 15 June 2021. See also Iain Duncan Smith, Theresa Villiers, and George Freeman, *Taskforce on Innovation, Growth and Regulatory Reform Independent Report*, GOV.uk, 16 June 2021.

57 Camilla Walden, 'Seven in ten English people support delaying the 21 June lockdown lifting by four weeks', YouGov, 14 June 2021.

58 Matt Dathan, 'Boris Johnson furious at Priti Patel over migrant Channel crossings', *Times*, 11 June 2021.

59 See Aubrey Allegretti, 'Property developers gave Tories £891,000 in first quarter of 2021', *Guardian*, 11 June 2021.

60 William Hague, 'Planning reform could be Boris Johnson's poll tax', *Times*, 21 June 2021.

61 https://twitter.com/Haggis_UK/status/1408320963196985345.

62 Paul Goodman, 'Hancock's resignation. It is now open season on every Cabinet minister who may have broken the Covid rules – in any circumstance', ConservativeHome, 27 June 2021.

63 https://twitter.com/Dominic2306/status/1408866176323706891.

64 See also Sajid Javid, 'The economic arguments for opening up Britain are well known. But, for me, the health case is equally compelling', *Mail on Sunday*, 4 July 2021.

65 'Sajid Javid apologises for "cower" Covid remark', BBC News, 25 July 2021.

66 Jack Elsom, 'ON HANS AND KNEES: Matt Hancock makes grovelling apology to local party bosses as he fights to cling on as an MP', *Sun*, 1 July 2021, and Kate Ferguson, 'MATT'S YER LOT: Shamed ex Health Sec Matt Hancock told to quit by local councillors who blast "hypocrisy and hubris" of lockdown affair', *Sun*, 28 July 2021.

67 Mark Wallace, 'Tory arrogance has cost the party yet again', *Sunday Telegraph*, 4 July 2021, and Paul Goodman and Harry Phibbs, 'Is the Tory machine still rusty? Five lessons from the three recent by-elections', ConservativeHome, 14 July 2021.

68 *Daily Mail* front page, 19 July 2021, https://twitter.com/AllieHBNews/status/1416864518874017798.

69 Paul Goodman, 'Brady's re-election will make any future Covid lockdowns more difficult to achieve', ConservativeHome, 7 July 2021.

70 Esther Webber, 'Boris Johnson's Partygate troubles put parliament whips in the spotlight', *Politico*, 27 January 2022.

71 See Matthew Smith, 'Two thirds of Britons support cutting the foreign aid budget', YouGov, 25 November 2020, and Paul Goodman, 'The campaign to oppose the 0.7 per cent aid cut will gain very little support from party members', ConservativeHome, 10 January 2021.

72 https://twitter.com/TyroneMings/status/1414655312074784785. At least Patel didn't go quite as far as Dover MP Natalie Elphicke, who messaged colleagues just after the defeat to say '*They* lost [italics mine] – would it be ungenerous to suggest Rashford should have spent more time perfecting his game and less time playing politics,' earning her a reply from her fellow Tory MP Simon Hoare, 'Would it be ungenerous? Yes. Unwarranted? Yes. Wrong? Yes' (https://twitter.com/simon4ndorset/status/1414535697441214467), as well as a world of unwanted publicity which obliged her to issue a grovelling (yet wholly unconvincing) public apology. Elphicke was one of a handful of MPs sanctioned by the Commons Standards Committee later that month for attempting to bring their influence to bear in the case of her then husband, Charlie Elphicke, the former MP for her constituency, who was subsequently jailed for sexual offences.

73 See, for example, Madeline Grant, 'Is Boris Johnson off his shopping trolley when it comes to levelling up?' *Daily Telegraph*, 16 July 2021.

74 See, for example, Kate Ferguson, 'BASKET CASES: Bonkers sugar and salt tax to cost each household £172 extra a year', *Sun*, 16 July 2021.

75 On the plan, see Priti Patel, 'The public want to see justice done . . . and offenders pay for crimes', *Daily Mail*, 26 July 2021.

76 See Alix Culbertson, 'Afghanistan: What happened with Pen Farthing and the animal evacuation – and did Boris Johnson intervene?', Sky News, 27 January 2022.

77 Esther Webber, '5 tough questions for Boris Johnson on Afghanistan', *Politico*, 18 August 2021. On face coverings, see 'Covid: Most Conservative MPs ditch masks as Commons returns', BBC News, 18 August 2021.

78 Tim Shipman and Gabriel Pogrund, 'Together alone, embattled Boris Johnson and Keir Starmer wish they weren't here', *Sunday Times*, 8 August 2021.

79 Henry Hill, 'From self-isolation to score annihilation', ConservativeHome, 1 August 2021.

80 Jack Elsom, 'RISH YOU WERE HERE: Brits want Rishi Sunak to replace Boris Johnson in No. 10 in wake of rift between PM and Chancellor, shock poll shows', *Sun*, 11 August 2021. See also Britta Zeltman, 'BACK TO WORK: Rishi Sunak warns home working will harm your career', *Sun*, 3 August 2021.

81 Matthew Smith, 'Snap poll: Britons split 44 per cent to 43 per cent on increasing National Insurance increase', YouGov, 7 September 2021.

82 See Helen Sullivan, '"Boris plays catch-up": What the papers say about Johnson's tax plan', *Guardian*, 8 September 2021. Allister Heath, 'Boris's shameful Tory betrayal guarantees the total victory of socialism in Britain', *Daily Telegraph*, 9 September 2021.

83 Bethany Dawson and Henry Dyer, 'Michael Gove, the UK's new Housing Secretary, has received £120,000 from property developers in 2021 alone', *Business Insider*, 16 September 2021.

84 Gordon Rayner, Ben Riley-Smith, and Harry Yorke, 'Businesses have become "drunk on cheap labour", say Tories', *Daily Telegraph*, 5 October 2021.

85 James Tapsfield and Mark Duell, '"It's easier for Boris to make a video stuffing his face with chips than solve problems"', *Daily Mail*, 5 October 2021.

Chapter 9 *Things fall apart (October 2021–April 2022)*

1 House of Commons Health and Social Care and Science and Technology Committees, *Coronavirus: Lessons Learned to Date*, UK Parliament, October 2021.

2 Contrast the *Daily Mail*'s front-page splash on 14 October 2021, https://twitter .com/hendopolis/status/1448400188666785796 with this follow up from the GP's trade paper: Caitlin Tilley, 'Health Secretary denies there was ever a plan for GP face-to-face "league tables"', *Pulse*, 2 November 2021.

3 Alex Wickham, 'Coronavirus "Plan B" would cost UK up to £18B, documents warn', *Politico*, 26 October 2021.

4 On the NZSG's ongoing links with climate change 'sceptics', see 'Net Zero Scrutiny Group', *DeSmog*, https://www.desmog.com/net-zero-scrutiny-group/ and https://twitter.com/leohickman/status/1477562398307405831.

5 On members' views, see, for example, Henry Hill, 'Our survey. On the environment, Tory members support action but not hysterics about an "emergency"', ConservativeHome, 2 June 2021.

6 See, for instance, Gabriel Milland, 'Ignore the climate change sceptics. They speak only for themselves – not the mass of centre right and Red Wall voters', ConservativeHome, 1 November 2021, and James Blagden, Alex Luke, and Will Tanner, 'Thin ice? Understanding voters' support for net zero', *Onward*, 8 November 2021.

7 Boris Johnson, 'GREEN PM: Boris Johnson tells Sun readers "Boiler Police are not going to kick your door in & seize your trusty combi"', *Sun*, 19 October 2021.

8 'We fear PM's "net zero" plans may become a millstone round our economy's neck', *Sun*, 20 October 2021.

9 See, for example, Philip Johnston, 'Boris is courting political disaster by trying to guilt us into going green', *Daily Telegraph*, 20 October 2021 and Alex Brummer, 'No wonder Rishi Sunak is on red alert for Boris Johnson's new green nirvana', *Daily Mail*, 20 October 2021.

10 Samantha Lock, '"Hey, big spenders": What the papers say about Sunak's 2021 autumn Budget', *Guardian*, 28 October 2021.

11 Henry Hill, 'Our survey. Party members are marginally in favour of Sunak's tax and spending plans', ConservativeHome, 29 October 2021.

12 See, for example, Anoosh Chakelian and Katharine Swindells, 'How generous was Rishi Sunak's 2021 Budget and spending review really?', *New Statesman*, 27 October 2021.

13 Three paradigmatic examples will have to suffice: Ruth Sutherland, 'How YOU are funding the bill for Rishi Sunak's big spend', *Daily Mail*, 29 October 2021; Fraser Nelson, 'Tories have taken taxes to a 71-year high, and this could be just the start', *Daily Telegraph*, 29 October 2021; and Robert Colvile, 'The Budget is more proof that Britain is turning into an elderly care system with a state attached', *Sunday Times*, 31 October 2021.

14 James Johnson, 'Boris Johnson risks overlooking voters he needs', *Politico*, 2 November 2021. See also Matthew Smith, 'Autumn Budget 2021: The public's verdict', YouGov, 29 October 2021.

15 House of Commons Committee on Standards, *Mr Owen Paterson*, UK Parliament, 26 October 2021.

16 For example, Charles Moore, 'The hounding of Owen Paterson sets a dangerous precedent in parliament', *Daily Telegraph*, 30 October 2021, and David Davis, 'Owen Paterson, a good man, has lost his wife and faces political ruin because of an absurdly flawed Commons investigation', *Mail on Sunday*, 31 October 2021.

17 *Daily Mail* front page, 4 November 2021, https://twitter.com/bbcnews/status /1456035462737444876.

18 Kwarteng later issued a formal apology. See 'Minister Kwasi Kwarteng sorry for upset caused by Standards Commissioner remarks', BBC News, 15 November 2021.

19 See, for example, Harry Cole, '12 MPs coining £3.5m', *Sun*, 9 November 2021 and, for a personal favourite, Poppy Wood and Richard Vaughan, 'Tory MP who said Marcus Rashford should stick to the day job … has second job', *The i*, 11 November 2021. For a longer list, see Jessica Murray, '30 MPs who could be affected by proposed consultancy ban', *Guardian*, 8 November 2021. Note that twenty-eight of the thirty were Tories.

20 See Jason Groves, Harriet Line, and Glen Keogh, 'New Cox bombshell', *Daily Mail*, 10 November 2021.

21 Simon Walters, 'Clean up your act, Boris!' *Daily Mail*, 5 November 2021. Tory Party members were apparently far more relaxed about the issue: see Paul Goodman, 'Three quarters of party activists believe that MPs should have outside interests. Our survey', ConservativeHome, 29 November 2021.

22 Jessica Elgot, 'Tory voters in north of England view social care reforms as "toxic" – research', *Guardian*, 29 November 2021.

23 Chris Kitching, Geraldine Scott, Gavin Cordon, and Flora Thompson, 'Priti Patel plans "Greek-style clampdown" on migrants with strict new rules', *Daily Mirror*, 20 November 2021.

24 Glen Owen and Jake Ryan, 'Whitehall row erupts as Home Secretary Priti Patel denounces her own officials', *Mail on Sunday*, 21 November 2021.

25 Edward Malnick and Lucy Fisher, 'Migrant crisis puts Tories in peril', *Sunday Telegraph*, 21 November 2021.

26 Priti Patel, 'I understand your frustrations but there is no magic wand to solve migrant crisis', *Sun*, 28 November 2021.

27 See Jason Groves, 'No. 10 fury over Chatty Pig leak', *Daily Mail*, 24 November 2021.

28 Trevor Kavanagh, 'It was all going so well … don't let Omicron wreck it', *Sun*, 29 November 2021.

29 Pippa Crerar, 'Boris Johnson "broke Covid lockdown rules" with Downing Street parties at Xmas', *Daily Mirror*, 1 December 2021.

30 Savanta ComRes 'NO. 10 CHRISTMAS PARTY SNAP POLL', ComRes Global, 8 December 2021.

31 'Boris Johnson's former Press Secretary Allegra Stratton resigns amid No. 10 party row', ITV News, 8 December 2021.

32 See, for the *Daily Mail* front-page, 9 December 2021, https://twitter.com/hendopolis/status/1468710662721388553 and for the *Sun* front page, 9 December 2021, https://twitter.com/hendopolis/status/1468706481331712002. See also Allister Heath, 'Boris Johnson may not recover from this double Covid catastrophe', *Daily Telegraph*, 9 December 2021.

33 See Tim Shipman, 'Boris Johnson faces rebellion from 60 Tories as Omi-shambles rolls on', *Sunday Times*, 12 December 2021.

34 Glen Owen, 'Boris Johnson's blast at BBC over Partygate', *Mail on Sunday*, 12 December 2021.

35 Paul Goodman, 'A vote of no confidence in Johnson has suddenly become more likely than not', ConservativeHome, 9 December 2021.

36 Graham Brady, 'We must end this disastrous assault on liberty', *Sunday Telegraph*, 12 December 2021, and Steve Baker, 'Boris Johnson's overreaction

to Omicron variant is squandering the goodwill and trust of voters', *Sunday Telegraph*, 12 December 2021.

37 Jason Groves, 'What Boris MUST now do to see off Liz and other ambitious rivals after bruising 100 MP rebellion', *Daily Mail*, 16 December 2021.

38 Note that the Tories had hung on in a by-election in Old Bexley and Sidcup (prompted by the death of its sitting MP) earlier in the month, albeit with a 10-point swing to Labour.

39 Chris Smyth and Matt Dathan, 'Libertarian Tory leadership rivals just look pathetic, say Boris Johnson's allies', *Times*, 22 December 2021. Self-promoting briefing by the supposedly heroic 'hawks' carried on, retrospectively, into the New Year: see Glen Owen, 'How Cabinet coup stopped Boris' "insane" plan to cancel Christmas', *Mail on Sunday*, 30 January 2022. Fast forward to the summer 2022 leadership contest and Sunak was still doing his best (albeit in vain) to leverage his opposition to a Christmas lockdown (and, indeed, his scepticism about lockdowns more generally) to his advantage – much to the irritation of some who had worked with him earlier on in the pandemic and were understandably resentful at what they saw as a wider attempt to effectively rewrite history by suggesting that lockdowns were rushed into and may have done more harm than good. See Fraser Nelson, 'Why it's still worth asking questions on lockdown', *Spectator*, 3 September 2022.

40 YouGov/*Times* survey results, December 2021, https://docs.cdn.yougov.com /7za8e4puku/TheTimes_VI_211220_W.pdf.

41 See https://twitter.com/focaldatahq/status/1475061773401300996.

42 See https://twitter.com/Survation/status/1475381060326367236.

43 Sajid Javid, 'I'm acutely aware of the cost of curbs – we must try to live with Covid', *Daily Mail*, 1 January 2022.

44 Jamie Grierson, 'Boris Johnson a drag on Tories and Sunak would do better, poll shows', *Guardian*, 28 December 2021. See also Liz Truss, 'Russia will pay the price if it invades Ukraine', *Daily Mail*, 30 November 2021. In this case, to see the pictures, the online version is definitely the one to go for.

45 Sam Coates, 'Nearly half of Conservative members think Rishi Sunak would make better party leader', Sky News, 9 January 2022. See also, for another survey with similar findings, https://twitter.com/OpiniumResearch/status /1483153525442064387.

46 Newspapers and news websites regularly updated the list of apparent breaches. See, for example, Andrew McDonald, 'All the times Boris Johnson's Tories are accused of lockdown partying', *Politico*, 12 January 2022.

47 See for example, the *Daily Mail's* front page on 12 January, https://twitter.com /hendopolis/status/1481029561047564294.

48 Steven Swinford, Henry Zeffman, Oliver Wright, Chris Smyth, and George Grylls, 'Contrite? Boris Johnson doesn't believe he did anything wrong, say Tories', *Times*, 13 January 2022.

49 Brendan Carlin, 'War of words breaks out between rival camps for potential leadership successors Rishi Sunak and Liz Truss as Boris battles Partygate storm', *Mail on Sunday*, 16 January 2022.

50 Watch https://www.youtube.com/watch?v=IeCRYqVu0Pw.

51 The campaign, which would eventually produce nearly a fortnight of front pages in the spring, started on the Sunday and continued into Monday, 17 January, with that day's front page reproduced here: https://twitter.com /AllieHBNews/status/1482842484002721793.

52 A video clip is available here: Alix Culbertson, 'Boris Johnson says "nobody told me" Number 10 lockdown garden party was against the rules', Sky News, 19 January 2022.

53 'Pork pie plotters will pay for foolish putsch', *Daily Mail*, 19 January 2022. See also, for a wry take on one of the red-tops' weirdest ever front-page splashes, Martin Belam, 'PM-supporting pork pie front page puzzles Sun pundits', *Guardian*, 20 January 2022.

54 For the poll, see https://twitter.com/jamesjohnson252/status/1483742661999 837187.

55 See https://twitter.com/hendopolis/status/1485378439771267075.

56 Nus Ghani, 'Why I'm speaking out against my own party's Islamophobia', *Times Red Box*, 24 January 2022.

57 For details of these face-to-face and WhatsApp meetings, see Anushka Asthana, 'Boris Johnson starts meetings to win over backbenchers who tell him: "Be more Conservative"', ITV News, 26 January 2022. See also Boris Johnson and Rishi Sunak, 'We must stick to our recovery plan – tax will rise to pay for it', *Sunday Times*, 30 January 2022.

58 Paul Goodman, 'A majority of our party member panel now believes that "Partygate" is overblown', ConservativeHome, 30 January 2022.

59 *Investigation into Alleged Gatherings on Government Premises during Covid Restrictions: Update*, Cabinet Office, 31 January 2022.

60 By way of background, see Reality Check, 'No evidence for Boris Johnson's claim about Keir Starmer and Jimmy Savile', BBC News, 3 February 2022, and Arj Singh, 'How Boris Johnson's false claim about Jimmy Savile gained traction as a far-right conspiracy theory', *i-paper*, 1 February 2022.

61 Virginia Harrison, '"Zero shame": How the papers covered anger at Boris Johnson over Sue Gray report', *Guardian*, 1 February 2022.

62 See https://twitter.com/OpiniumResearch/status/1492601905947631618.

63 Mirza's forthright resignation letter appeared first here: James Forsyth, 'Exclusive: No. 10 policy chief quits over Boris's Jimmy Savile slur', *Spectator*, 3 February 2022.

64 On the policy groups, see 'Tories' new policy chiefs', *Guido Fawkes*, 3 March 2022.

65 See Adam McDonnell, 'The Conservatives are losing their recent converts', YouGov, 3 February 2022.

66 See, for example, Dave Richards, Diane Coyle, Martin Smith, and Sam Warner, 'Whitehall's centralised system can't deliver Boris Johnson's promises to "level" up', and Jack Newman, Nigel Driffield, Nigel Gilbert, and Simon Collinson, 'Levelling up: Four problems with Boris Johnson's flagship project', both in *The Conversation*, 4 February 2022. See also Rachel Wolf, 'My verdict on Levelling Up? Very good in parts. But even Gove cannot paper over the cracks', ConservativeHome, 4 February 2022, and Anoosh Chakelian, 'Michael Gove's Levelling Up plan looks suspiciously familiar', *New Statesman*, 2 February 2022.

67 Bethan Staton, 'Rising cost of living leaves 4.7mn Britons struggling to feed themselves', *Financial Times*, 6 February 2022.

68 Anna Isaac, 'Rishi Sunak puts final touches to leadership bid and says Partygate could be "unsurvivable" for Boris Johnson', *Independent*, 29 January 2022.

69 Rowena Mason and Aubrey Allegretti, 'Boris Johnson "not a complete clown", says his new press chief', *Guardian*, 7 February 2022.

70 Michael Ashcroft, *First Lady: Intrigue at the Court of Carrie and Boris Johnson* (Biteback, 2022). See also Glen Owen, 'Bombshell biography', *Mail on Sunday*, 6 February 2022.

71 For the *Daily Mail*'s front-page celebration, see https://twitter.com/AllieHBNews/status/1491539717518729223.

72 Steven Swinford, Henry Zeffman, and Oliver Wright, 'Boris Johnson accused of dodging the big question in his "menshuffle"', *Times*, 9 February 2022.

73 One survey found that only 17 per cent of voters (and only 20 per cent of Conservative voters) agreed with scrapping the requirement. See 'Do you think people should or should not be legally required to self-isolate if they test positive for Covid-19?', YouGov, 9 February 2022. This didn't seem to be reflected in the *Daily Mail*'s front-page screamer ('BORIS THROWS OFF SHACKLES'): https://twitter.com/AllieHBNews/status/1495885468495405062.

74 See 'Nearly half of Britons think UK Government is relaxing COVID rules too quickly', Ipsos, 24 February.

75 See https://twitter.com/JuliaHB1/status/1505199026446163971.

76 See https://twitter.com/jamesjohnson252/status/1497928002637762567 for details.

77 See 'Boris Johnson was warned of Lebedev security concerns, says Cummings', BBC News, 16 March 2022. On funding, the sources and examples are legion. For a contemporary instance, see Peter Walker, 'Party funding linked to Russia – how much have Tories benefited?', *Guardian*, 23 February 2022. For Londongrad, listen to *Tortoise Media*'s eponymous podcast (https://www.tortoisemedia.com/listen/londongrad/) and read Oliver Bullough, *Butler to the World* (Profile, 2022).

78 As a recent authoritative study notes, the odds of the correlation between giving money to a party and being nominated for a seat in the Lords being purely coincidental are 'approximately equivalent to entering the National Lottery and winning the jackpot 5 times in a row'. See Simon Radford, Andrew Mell, and Seth Alexander Thevoz, '"Lordy Me!" Can donations buy you a British peerage? A study in the link between party political funding and peerage nominations, 2005–2014', *British Politics*, 15, 2020, pp. 135–59 (p. 153).

79 On the Cabinet, see Matt Dathan and Henry Zeffman, 'MPs attack Priti Patel's "ineptitude" on Ukrainian refugees', *Times*, 9 March 2022. And for the fury among Tory MPs, watch https://youtu.be/-Neabd958aw.

80 Jonathan Gullis MP quoted by Steven Fielding, 'Ukraine isn't Boris's "Falklands moment"', *Spectator*, 8 March 2022.

81 'Ipsos poll shows public views towards Boris Johnson recovering but half still unfavourable', Ipsos, 11 March 2022.

82 Nigel Farage, 'The Net Zero zealots are the same elitists who sneered at Brexit and don't have to worry about paying their gas bills', *Mail on Sunday*, 6 March 2022. On the links between Brexiteers and net zero sceptics, see Esther Webber and Karl Mathiesen, 'Britain's net zero skeptics reach for the Brexit playbook', *Politico*, 17 March 2022.

83 See https://twitter.com/JimBethell/status/1505877844379025416.

84 Paul Goodman, 'Our survey. It's a thumbs down to Sunak's Spring Statement, and a thumbs up to Johnson's war handling', ConservativeHome, 3 April 2022.

85 See Martin Farrer, '"The forgotten millions": How the papers covered Rishi Sunak's Spring Statement', *Guardian*, 24 March 2022. See also 'Lack of support for low-income families will see 1.3 million people pushed into absolute poverty next year', Resolution Foundation, 24 March 2022.

86 Speech by the Chief Secretary to the Treasury to the Institute for Economic Affairs: Simon Clarke, 'The quiet revolution: Redefining the "how" of government spending', GOV.uk, 29 March 2022.

87 Paul Goodman and Henry Hill, 'Our Cabinet League Table. Sunak plunges to third from bottom', ConservativeHome, 4 April 2022.

88 Connor Ibbetson 'Rishi Sunak's favourability drops to new low following Spring Statement', YouGov, 25 March 2022.

89 Ben Riley-Smith, 'Rishi Sunak says he is the victim of a "smear" campaign', *Daily Telegraph*, 8 April 2022. For a detailed account, which suggests that, if Number Ten wasn't the source, some of its occupants nonetheless found it difficult to conceal their schadenfreude, see Matthew d'Ancona, 'Downfall: Twenty days that did for Rishi Sunak', *Tortoise*, 9 May 2022.

90 On the internal opposition to onshore wind, see Rowena Mason, Rob Davies, and Helena Horton, 'Boris Johnson blows cold on onshore wind faced with 100-plus rebel MPs', *Guardian*, 5 April 2022. On the Strategy itself, and the reaction to it, see Becky Mawhood, Paul Bolton, and Suzanna Hinson, *British Energy Security Strategy*, House of Commons Library, 4 July 2022.

91 See David Churchill and Jason Groves, 'Priti Patel blasts "selfish" petrol protests', *Daily Mail*, 11 April 2022.

92 For the line-to-take Twitter messages of support, see https://twitter.com/_johnbye/status/1514008753586282498. And for the PM's apology, watch https://www.youtube.com/watch?v=Ubapijzpgz8.

93 For the front pages, see Warren Murray, '"Liars and lawbreakers": What the papers say about Johnson's Partygate fine', *Guardian*, 13 April 2022. And for the ultimate example of exculpation by trivialization, see Daniel Martin, 'Nine minutes, no cake . . . and unopened beer', *Daily Mail*, 13 April 2022. There were, of course, (literally) honourable exceptions among Conservative columnists, the best example being Daniel Finkelstein, 'Lawmaker can't be lawbreaker so Boris Johnson must resign', *Times*, 13 April 2022.

94 See Connor Ibbetson and Isabelle Kirk, 'Snap poll: Following lockdown fines, most say Boris Johnson should resign', YouGov, 12 April 2022 and 'SNAP POLL – PARTYGATE & PM RECEIVES A FINE', Savanta ComRes, 12 April 2022.

Chapter 10 End of the road? (April–September 2022)

1 On the internal civil service reaction, see, for example, 'Patel personally approved Rwanda plan launch after civil servant concerns', BBC News, 16 April 2022, and Lizzie Dearden, 'Government officials told Priti Patel not to do asylum deal with Rwanda, court hears', *Independent*, 19 July 2022. Tory MPs generally either celebrated the policy or kept their doubts to themselves. For a couple of (in one case very!) notable exceptions who proved the rule, see Andrew Mitchell, 'The Government's Rwanda plan will be impractical,

ineffective – and expensive', ConservativeHome, 19 April 2022, and 'Rwanda asylum seeker policy: Ex-PM Theresa May criticises government plan', BBC, 19 April 2022.

2 See https://twitter.com/BBCHelena/status/1514714696447889408.

3 See https://twitter.com/AllieHBNews/status/1514356072622010372.

4 See, for example, Graham Brady, 'All those government staff who STILL insist on working from home are ruining this country', *Mail on Sunday*, 17 April 2022, and the leader column 'Bone-idle bureaucrats must get off their sofas', *Daily Mail*, 19 April 2022.

5 Matthew Smith, 'Labour have caught up with Tories on best government to manage the economy' and Isabelle Kirk, 'Non-dom scandal and COVID fines send Johnson and Sunak favourability scores tumbling', both at YouGov, 19 April 2022.

6 Paul Goodman and Henry Hill, 'Our Cabinet league table', ConservativeHome, 25 April 2022. See also Goodman, 'Our survey. Over a third of Tory members think that Johnson should resign. And over half don't', ConservativeHome, 24 April 2022.

7 https://yougov.co.uk/topics/travel/survey-results/daily/2022/04/14/8bb29/1.

8 https://yougov.co.uk/topics/politics/survey-results/daily/2022/06/13/c8bf1/1.

9 Paul Goodman, 'Our survey. Eight in ten Tory activists line up behind the Government's new asylum seekers' scheme', ConservativeHome, 25 April 2022.

10 See Daniel Martin, 'Police review over Keir Starmer's lockdown drinks', *Daily Mail*, 27 April 2022.

11 Kate Ferguson and Jack Elsom, 'PORN MP: Tory MP caught watching PORN in Commons chamber by disgusted colleagues', *Sun*, 27 April 2022.

12 See https://www.royalholloway.ac.uk/about-us/news/royal-holloway-and -survation-launch-new-tracker-revealing-important-issues-across-great-britain -s-parliamentary-constituencies/.

13 'Boris Johnson's "mind-blowing" response to case of struggling pensioner Elsie', ITV News, 3 May 2022.

14 Patrick Butler, 'More than 2m adults in UK cannot afford to eat every day, survey finds', *Guardian*, 9 May 2022. See also 'Food banks provide more than 2.1 million food parcels to people across the UK in past year', Trussell Trust, 27 April 2022.

15 See Richard Tunnicliffe, 'Local Elections 2022: Results and analysis', House of Commons Library, 13 May 2022. See also Sophia Sleigh, 'Ex-Tory councillor tells voters to back Labour in local elections', *Huffpost*, 4 May 2022.

16 Stephen Fisher, 'Local elections 2022: The media got it wrong. Labour did

make real progress', *Prospect*, 10 May 2022, and Paul Whiteley, 'Boris Johnson should be very worried about what 2022 local council results mean for the next general election', *The Conversation*, 11 May 2022.

17 David Williamson and Jonathan Walker, 'PM to unleash SEVEN Brexit freedom bills and SLASH hated EU red tape', *Sunday Express*, 8 May 2022.

18 See 'Queen's Speech 2022: Full list of bills', politics.co.uk, 11 May 2022.

19 See https://twitter.com/BBCHelena/status/1524140200221417472 for the *Daily Mail*'s front page and the *Telegraph*'s leader column, 'A Queen's Speech lacking in direction', 11 May 2022. The latter seemed disappointed, for instance, with the greater protections offered to renters in one of the bills proposed. For the TikTok launch, see https://www.tiktok.com/@10downingstreet/video /7096051570969726214.

20 William Hague, 'Obesity U-turn is weak, shallow and immoral', *Times*, 17 May 2022.

21 Jason Groves, 'WFH? You spend all your time walking to the fridge, hacking off cheese and then forgetting what you're doing: Boris Johnson on "war criminal" Putin, battles with "leftie lawyers", kick-starting the economy and the perils of home working', *Daily Mail*, 14 May 2022.

22 'If there's one lesson from this pitiful farrago, it's that such a sweeping affront to our liberties must never happen again', *Mail on Sunday*, 20 May 2022.

23 For the final report, which included photographs but which did not, for reasons that many found hard to understand, investigate all the alleged gatherings, and in particular one (the so-called 'ABBA party') in the PM's Downing Street flat, see *Findings of the Second Permanent Secretary's Investigation into Alleged Gatherings on Government Premises during Covid Restrictions*, Cabinet Office, 25 May 2022. See also Laura Kuenssberg, 'Partygate: Insiders tell of packed No. 10 lockdown parties', BBC News, 24 May 2022.

24 Chris Hopkins, 'Pollwatch: Two thirds say PM should resign given Gray Report's findings', Savanta ComRes, 30 May 2022. On Johnson's statement, see David Allen Green, 'The lawyering-up of Boris Johnson', *The Law and Policy Blog*, 26 May 2022.

25 See Martin Farrer, '"Failure of leadership": What the papers say about Johnson and the Sue Gray Partygate report', *Guardian*, 26 May 2022.

26 For example, David Davis, 'Windfall taxes are a betrayal of Conservatism', *Daily Telegraph*, 23 May 2022.

27 See https://twitter.com/AllieHBNews/status/1529930376847757312 and https://twitter.com/AllieHBNews/status/1529933161727246350. The *Daily Telegraph*'s leader column was particularly portentous: see 'Conservatism is in a dark place', 27 May 2022.

28 Paul Goodman, 'Our survey. Sunak's latest package lands better than his Spring Statement', ConservativeHome, 31 May 2022.

29 See *Revisions to the Ministerial Code and the Role of the Independent Adviser on Ministers' Interests*, Cabinet Office, 27 May 2022.

30 See https://twitter.com/TmorrowsPapers/status/1531752507202207744.

31 On Mordaunt's 'deal', see Peter Ungphakorn 'Milestone or inchpebble', *Trade β Blog*, 29 May 2022, and for Tugendhat's take-down, see https://twitter.com/tomtugendhat/status/1532445501563469824.

32 For the polling, see https://twitter.com/jamesjohnson252/status/153314754033502464.

33 On the 'no vote for another year' myth, see Tim Bale, 'Tories should take a tip from Macbeth and be bold', *Observer*, 5 June 2022.

34 The briefing note can be read in full here: https://twitter.com/adampayne26/status/1533476836860170250.

35 For the text, see https://twitter.com/tomhfh/status/1533713550929276928.

36 For a full list of the coincidences, see Jane Merrick, 'How Boris Johnson's calls with President Zelensky have been announced just after the PM's biggest crises', *i-news*, 17 June 2022.

37 https://twitter.com/NadineDorries/status/1533763405844185088.

38 https://twitter.com/jesse_norman/status/1533699235417403393.

39 For the full text of Johnson's letter, see '"I am asking you for your support": Boris Johnson's letter to MPs in full', CNN, 6 June 2022.

40 Nick Timothy, 'There is both an ethical and political vacuum at the top of government', *Daily Telegraph*, 6 June 2022.

41 Connor Ibbetson, 'Snap poll: 60 per cent of Britons and 32 per cent of Tory voters say MPs should vote to remove Boris Johnson', YouGov, 6 June 2021.

42 See https://docs.cdn.yougov.com/kl6i0gpr2q/Internal_ConservativeParty Members_VoteOfNoConfidence_220606_w.pdf.

43 Paul Goodman, 'Our snap survey. Fifty-five per cent of ConHome's party member panel say Tory MPs should remove the Prime Minister', Conservative-Home, 6 June 2022.

44 https://link.news.inews.co.uk/view/6154b3e44f1a9e0dee1b7fabgnfdt.i43/59d467f4.

45 Martin Farrer, '"Out in a year": What the papers say about Tory vote on Boris Johnson', *Guardian*, 7 June 2022.

46 William Hague, 'Boris Johnson should look for an honourable exit', *Times*, 7 June 2022.

47 Paul Goodman, 'The Cabinet should act. (Though doubtless it won't.)', ConservativeHome, 7 June 2022.

48 Oliver Wright, 'Boris Johnson determined to reverse £15bn tax raid on business', *Times*, 15 June 2022.

49 For a taste of their messages in response to the news that the deportation flight had been grounded, see https://twitter.com/patrickkmaguire/status /1536840268074426368.

50 Boris Johnson, 'We will never be secure if we turn our backs on valiant Ukraine', *Sunday Times*, 19 June 2022. See also Kate Ferguson, 'ECO-TAX PLEA: Red Wall Tories call on Boris Johnson to ditch eco levies and cut taxes', *Sun*, 18 June 2022.

51 For an account of what happened, see Mandrake [Tim Walker] 'The extraordinary detail of how Downing Street tried to bury that Carrie Johnson story', *New European*, 21 June 2022.

52 See, for example, the *Daily Express*'s front page, https://twitter.com /TmorrowsPapers/status/1538635680133308421. On public opinion, which was divided rather than uniformly hostile, see, for example, Chris Hopkins, 'Pollwatch: Majority of public say rail strikes "justified"', Savanta ComRes, 22 June 2022.

53 For a succinct summary of the government's case, see Christopher Bellamy, 'The Bill of Rights, introduced today, builds on the long tradition of British justice', ConservativeHome, 22 June 2022. For a detailed critique, see Mark Elliott, 'The UK's (new) Bill of Rights', Public Law for Everyone, 22 June 2022. On the (in practice fairly remote) possibility Downing Street might be about to 'usher in a new generation of grammar schools', see Henry Zeffman and Nicola Woolcock, 'Grammars could level up country, MPs tell Johnson', *Times*, 20 June 2022.

54 Estimates, of course, varied, depending on boundary changes and the potential for tactical voting. See Tim Bale, Alan Wager, and Aron Cheung, 'Where next for the Liberal Democrats?', UK in a Changing Europe, 29 July 2020, and Alan Wager, Aron Cheung, and Tim Bale, 'Breaching the Blue Wall', UK in a Changing Europe, 16 September 2021.

55 https://twitter.com/oliverdowden/status/1540191893258207232.

56 See Martin Farrer, '"Go now": What the papers say about Tories' double byelection defeats', *Guardian*, 25 June 2022.

57 Joseph Lee, 'PM: I will not undergo psychological transformation after poll defeat', BBC News, 25 June 2022.

58 Alex Forsyth, 'Boris Johnson "actively thinking about" third term as PM', BBC News, 26 June 2022.

59 See, for example, Aubrey Allegretti, '"Ruthlessly organised" Tory rebels plot 1922 takeover to oust Boris Johnson', *Guardian*, 29 June 2022.

60 Numbers given varied: the *Times* said six, the *Telegraph* three, and the *Guardian* only one. In reality, no-one defected, strengthening the suspicion that it was only ever Labour spin designed to unnerve the Tories.

61 Noa Hoffman and Kate Ferguson, '"EMBARRASSED MYSELF": Tory whip Chris Pincher RESIGNS after "groping 2 men" & claims he "drank too much" – but will remain as an MP', *Sun*, 1 July 2022.

62 For an excruciating example of a minister being hung out to dry after being sent out on the broadcast round, see https://twitter.com/RidgeOnSunday/status /1543503625636483072. For the confirmation provided by Cummings and, a couple of days later, by McDonald, see https://twitter.com/Dominic2306 /status/1543208854325977088 and https://twitter.com/simonmcdonalduk /status/1544206976820854784.

63 See the leader columns of all three on Monday, 4 July: 'Boris must be firm on misbehaviour', *Daily Telegraph;* 'The problem for Boris Johnson is the public wants and expects better from his government', *Sun*; and 'Boris Johnson is still the best man to lead Britain', *Daily Mail.*

64 See 'Conservative Party image weakens with lowest score since 2011 on being seen as "fit to govern"', Ipsos, 1 July 2022, and Patrick English, 'Conservatives set to lose 26 of their 64 Lib Dem battleground seats', YouGov, 2 July 2022.

65 Steerpike, 'Watch: Johnson's awkward Cabinet meeting', *Spectator*, 5 July 2022.

66 See https://twitter.com/sajidjavid/status/1544366218789937152 and https:// twitter.com/RishiSunak/status/1544368323625947137.

67 See their respective leader columns for 6 July: 'With Sunak out the way we might finally see some Conservative policies', *Daily Express*; 'Whatever lies ahead, Tories must get back to real issues', *Daily Mail*; 'Time is running out for Boris Johnson – unless he delivers for the British people', *Sun*; and 'This political crisis must be resolved', *Daily Telegraph*. For the poll, see Matthew Smith, 'Snap poll: Most Conservative voters now want Boris Johnson to resign', YouGov, 5 July 2022.

68 For a concise summary of the constitutional position, see Stephen Bush, 'Boris Johnson had to resign', *Financial Times*, 7 July 2022.

69 Watch the speech at https://www.youtube.com/watch?v=5mYDyxMDwaw. For an amusing but nonetheless accurate analysis, see John Rentoul, 'What Boris Johnson said in his resignation speech – and what he really meant', *Independent*, 7 July 2022.

70 Harry Cole and James Heale, *Out of the Blue: The Inside Story of the Unexpected Rise and Rapid Fall of Liz Truss* (HarperCollins, 2022), p. 245.

71 On the *Daily Mail's* pro-Truss, anti-Mordaunt campaign, see Jim Waterson and Jessica Elgot, 'Press attacks take toll as Penny Mordaunt misses out in PM race', *Guardian*, 20 July 2022.

72 Compare the YouGov polling conducted on 12 and 13 July (https://docs.cdn
.yougov.com/6shnrhfen6/ConservativePartyMembers_LeadershipContenders
_220713_w.pdf) with that conducted on 18 and 19 July (https://docs.cdn
.yougov.com/wue1nfg0b7/ConMembers_July19th_head_to_heads_w.pdf).

73 For portraits of the grassroots derived from the ESRC Party Members Project,
see Brian Wheeler, 'Tory leadership: Who gets to choose the UK's next Prime
Minister?', BBC News, 14 July 2022, and (for a neat comparison with the
demographics of the population as a whole) Jennifer Williams, 'Who are the
Tory Party members picking the next UK Prime Minister?', *Financial Times*, 21
July 2022.

74 Patrick English, 'Liz Truss leads Rishi Sunak by 62% to 38% among Tory
members', YouGov, 21 July 2022.

75 This did not satisfy critics, some of whom, under the umbrella of Tortoise
Media, went so far as to try to get a judicial review of the process, on the
grounds that a contest which was effectively going to allow a tiny proportion
of the voting public to elect the country's Prime Minister should be transparent
and totally above board. See https://www.tortoisemedia.com/democracy-in
-britain-who-decides-the-next-pm/.

76 This feeling was shared by Tory donor Peter Cruddas (whose appointment to
the Lords by Johnson had once upon a time caused so much controversy), who
promptly set about organizing a petition to try (in vain) to force Johnson's name
onto the ballot. On Cruddas (much of it in his own words), see Paul Caruana
Galizia and Lewis Vickers, 'Thank the Lord', *Tortoise*, 30 August 2022.

77 See, for perhaps the ultimate example, https://twitter.com/NadineDorries/status
/1551459390502440960. There are some who argue that Sunak's ethnicity may
have played a part in his defeat. This cannot be discounted: in 2017, the Party
Members Project found that 13 per cent of Tory members (around 97 per cent
are White British) would like to see fewer ethnic minority MPs in parliament,
which perhaps suggests a hard core of racists does exist. But attitudes on this
issue are very difficult to measure directly. For a characteristically thoughtful
discussion, see this thread by Sunder Katwala: https://twitter.com/sundersays
/status/1554604376160976897.

78 See Thomas Quinn, 'The Conservative Party's leadership election of 2016:
Choosing a leader in government', *British Politics*, 14(1), 2019, pp. 63–85.

79 'Rishi Sunak losing "electability" advantage over Liz Truss according to public',
Ipsos, 10 August 2022.

80 The candidates could spend a maximum of £300,000 – a sum comfortably
raised by both Sunak (who raked in nearly £460,000) and Truss (who managed
close to £425,000, including a small donation from the Bamford family, who,

it turned out, had gifted nearly £24,000 to Johnson for his wedding party over the summer).

81 Camilla Walden, 'By 50% to 22% Britons are disappointed that Liz Truss will be the next PM', YouGov, 5 September 2022. See also James Johnson, 'Voters may like Liz Truss more than you think', *Politico*, 6 September 2022. For an insight into ordinary voters' willingness to give someone who few of them knew much about a hearing, not least because her straightforward, unvarnished style contrasted with that of her predecessor, listen to the focus group convened for Times Radio: https://play.acast.com/s/timesredbox/times-radio-focus-group-liz-truss.

82 For the front pages, see Martin Farrer, '"Straight to business": What the papers said about Liz Truss's victory', *Guardian*, 6 September 2022.

Chapter 11 *Two last bites at the cherry (September–November 2022)*

1 William Hague, 'Like Truss or not, we all need her to succeed', *Times*, 6 September 2022.

2 On those interventions, see, for example, Dan Bloom, 'Nadine Dorries shares image of Rishi Sunak stabbing Boris Johnson in back with a knife', *Daily Mirror*, 31 July 2022.

3 https://twitter.com/PippaCrerar/status/1567103200125149184.

4 For Frost's attack, watch https://www.youtube.com/watch?v=tzMVV1Axssc. As for his fate, one can't help but recall Oscar Wilde's famous quip: 'One must have a heart of stone to read the death of little Nell without laughing.'

5 See https://twitter.com/globalhlthtwit/status/1568941894188634112.

6 See *Sutton Trust Cabinet Analysis 2022*.

7 Johnson's speech in all its (vain)glory can be watched here: https://www.youtube.com/watch?v=9Gf5X1BC7tY. Or readers can save themselves the time and trouble and read Robert Hutton, 'Expulsion from Borisland', *The Critic*, 6 September 2022.

8 To watch the speech, go to https://www.youtube.com/watch?v=o5Wm_N3R0yo. It was widely seen as an improvement on her acceptance speech the day before, which not only contained one or two awkward moments, but also managed to be derivative, although on that occasion of Tony Blair rather than her Conservative predecessors: she said, for example, that 'I campaigned as a Conservative and I will govern as a Conservative' and used the epizeuxis 'We will deliver, we will deliver, and we will deliver.' See https://www.youtube.com/watch?v=w69QaK8NpZI.

9 Anthony Trollope, *The Bertrams: A Novel, Volume 2* (Chapman & Hall, 1859), p. 4.

10 See https://twitter.com/sajidjavid/status/1567916952378654722 and (rather

less implicitly!) https://twitter.com/nickmacpherson2/status/1567907661584 236545. Other civil servants and one or two Tory politicians also criticized the move: see 'Tom Scholar: Former top civil servants hit out at Treasury boss sacking', BBC News, 12 September 2022.

11 Harriet Line, 'Boost for Liz Truss as new poll shows nine in 10 voters BACK her plan to freeze energy bills to help families through cost of living crisis', *Daily Mail*, 11 September 2022.

12 See Matthew Sinclair, *Let Them Eat Carbon* (Biteback, 2011).

13 Whether it was really true that Elizabeth II had as low an opinion of Boris Johnson as some suggested we may never know, but see Tim Shipman, 'She was a PM's best confidante, but what did the Queen really think of them?', *Sunday Times*, 11 September 2022.

14 Aubrey Allegretti and Rowena Mason, 'Tory backbenchers despair at "toxic" mini-Budget', *Guardian*, 23 September 2022.

15 David Baker, Andrew Gamble, and David Seawright, 'Sovereign nations and global markets: Modern British Conservatism and hyperglobalism', *British Journal of Politics and International Relations*, 4 (3), 2002, pp. 399–428. See also Ben Rosamond, 'Brexit and the politics of UK growth models', *New Political Economy*, 24 (3), 2019, pp. 408–21.

16 Tom Espiner, 'Kwasi Kwarteng: I want to keep cutting taxes', BBC News, 25 September 2022.

17 Kate Ferguson and Jonathan Reilly, 'KWART'S NOT TO LIKE? Delighted Brits back Kwasi Kwarteng's key income tax and stamp duty cuts, poll shows', *Sun*, 25 September 2025.

18 For readers who can bring themselves to listen, the highlights (if that is the right word) are available here: https://www.youtube.com/watch?v=_q0rlT-5oxE.

19 https://www.globalplayer.com/podcasts/episodes/7DreVQu/.

20 For a useful summary, go to https://mailchi.mp/redfieldandwiltonstrategies /issue-52.

21 Dominic Sandbrook, 'Is Truss the worst PM in history?', *Unherd*, 7 December 2022.

22 For an example of the briefing, see Tim Shipman, 'The rebels' smartphone spreadsheet that means Liz Truss is still in deep trouble', *Sunday Times*, 9 October 2022.

23 See Penny Mordaunt, 'We have to unite behind the Prime Minister and fight – or the anti-enterprise coalition will win', *Sunday Telegraph*, 9 October 2022, and Suella Braverman, 'Home Secretary tells Tory rebels they must stop attacking the PM or they will end up with a Labour government', *Sun on Sunday*, 9 October 2022.

24 For the Mail's claim that Truss had just seventeen days to save her premiership, see https://twitter.com/hendopolis/status/1580674121209303040. The same morning saw the first appearance of the *Daily Star*'s match-up between a lettuce and Liz Truss that, in asking which would last longer, went on to become not just a meme but also a livestream: see https://twitter.com/hendopolis/status/1580660036581265408 and https://www.youtube.com/watch?v=6xno8tGBKlA.

25 See Harry Cole and James Heale, *Out of the Blue: The Inside Story of the Unexpected Rise and Rapid Fall of Liz Truss* (HarperCollins, 2022), p. 298.

26 To watch the press conference in full, see https://www.youtube.com/watch?v=GZv9CYhppdY.

27 Caroline Wheeler and Harry Yorke, 'Truss is the latest victim of a never-ending Tory death cult', *Sunday Times*, 16 October 2022.

28 On the state of the Number Ten operation, see, for example, Cole and Heale, *Out of the Blue*, pp. 289 and 301.

29 https://www.opinium.com/wp-content/uploads/2022/10/MRP_Tables_2022.pdf.

30 For the *Daily Mail*'s front page, see https://twitter.com/hendopolis/status/1581754519964495872. See also 'This is a crunch week for Liz Truss and her party', *Daily Telegraph*, 17 October 2022.

31 To watch the interview, go to https://www.youtube.com/watch?v=nMDzkCzV3I8.

32 Theresa May's call features in Cole and Heale, *Out of the Blue*, p. 302.

33 See Samantha Lock, '"The ghost PM": What the papers say about Liz Truss's hold on power', *Guardian*, 18 October 2022.

34 Patrick English, 'Conservative members have buyer's remorse', YouGov, 18 October 2022.

35 See https://twitter.com/suellabraverman/status/1582762282626736128.

36 For details of their conversation, see Annabel Tiffin and Paul Seddon, 'Boris Johnson had backing to challenge Rishi Sunak, Sir Graham Brady confirms', BBC News, 4 November 2022

37 https://www.youtube.com/watch?v=sxT9gOS6_j0.

38 Anthony Reuben, 'Tory leadership: How secure is the online vote?', BBC Reality Check, 21 October 2022.

39 The figures given here are those recorded by the BBC. See 'How many backers do Rishi Sunak and Penny Mordaunt have?', BBC News, 24 October. Other sources gave each candidate between one and four more endorsements than the BBC did: see https://en.wikipedia.org/wiki/Endorsements_in_the_October_2022_Conservative_Party_leadership_election. For confirmation that Johnson did

have sufficient nominations, see Tiffin and Seddon, 'Boris Johnson had backing to challenge Rishi Sunak'.

40 'Boris Johnson's full statement withdrawing from No. 10 race', *Guardian*, 23 October 2022.

41 See William Atkinson, 'Our survey. More than half of our panel would have voted for Sunak – and only three in ten wanted Johnson', ConservativeHome, 2 November 2022. The precise figures were 30 per cent for Johnson and 52 per cent for Sunak.

42 https://twitter.com/PennyMordaunt/status/1584529702466686977.

43 For a summary of the polling (with links), see https://en.wikipedia.org/wiki /October_2022_Conservative_Party_leadership_election#Polling.

44 Sunak's ill-judged appointment of Williamson, predictably enough, caused him a huge headache less than a week after he became PM: see Gabriel Pogrund, 'No. 10 refuses to endorse Gavin Williamson as threatening texts revealed', *Sunday Times*, 5 November 2022.

45 For Sunak's first speech as Prime Minister, watch https://www.youtube.com /watch?v=sEFAzNc3P3Y, and for an astute piece of decoding, see John Rentoul, 'Rishi Sunak's speech in Downing Street: What he said – and what he really meant', *Independent*, 25 October 2022. Liz Truss's farewell speech (in which she insisted she was 'more convinced than ever we need to be bold') suggested that, as Talleyrand is said to have remarked about France's Bourbon dynasty, she had learned nothing and forgotten nothing. It can be watched here: https://www .youtube.com/watch?v=ScWVAbifOOQ.

46 For the Sunak Cabinet, see https://www.suttontrust.com/wp-content/uploads /2022/10/Sutton-Trust-Cabinet-Analysis-Oct-2022.pdf.

47 See, for example, https://redfieldandwiltonstrategies.com/latest-gb-voting -intention-30-october-2022/ and Matthew Smith, 'Rishi Sunak's greater popularity has yet to rub off on the wider government', YouGov, 1 November 2022.

48 Research suggests that Prime Ministers can (at least marginally) improve their party's chances, although, as one veteran political analyst reminds us, there is no guarantee that this will happen: see Peter Kellner, '1945, 2022: Respected PM, shame about his party', *The Politics Counter,* 2 November 2022.

49 See Laura Kuenssberg, 'Climate change: Where does Rishi Sunak stand ahead of COP27?', BBC News, 5 November 2022.

50 See Larry Elliott, 'The UK economy is about to be thrown into a black hole – by its own government', *Guardian*, 3 November 2022.

51 See Tim Bale, Aron Cheung, Philip Cowley, Anand Menon, and Alan Wager, 'Mind the values gap: The social and economic values of MPs, party members and voters', UK in a Changing Europe, June 2020.

52 Edward Fieldhouse et al., *Electoral Shocks: The Volatile Voter in a Turbulent World* (Oxford University Press, 2021), p. 190. See also James Tilley, Anja Neundorf, and Sara Hobolt, 'When the pound in people's pocket matters: How changes to personal financial circumstances affect party choice', *Journal of Politics*, 80 (2), 2018, pp. 555–69.

53 Alain Catzeflis, 'The slow death of Tory England', *The Article*, 29 June 2022. On Brexit identities, see Sara Hobolt, Thomas Leeper, and James Tilley, 'Divided by the vote: Affective polarization in the wake of the Brexit referendum', *British Journal of Political Science*, 51 (4), 2021, pp. 1476–93, and on their potentially waning power, see Alan Wager and Anand Menon, 'Can Liz Truss win?', UK in a Changing Europe, 8 September 2022.

54 See Andy Westwood, 'The Johnson legacy: Levelling up', UK in a Changing Europe, 2 September 2022, and Suzanne Hall et al., 'Levelling up: What England thinks', UK in a Changing Europe, October 2022.

55 Developers happen to be a major source of donations to the Tories: see Transparency International UK, *House of Cards* (April 2021). For the others, see Chris Mason, 'Conservatives: Who funds them, and what's in it for them?', BBC News, 2 October 2021.

56 Watch, for example, https://twitter.com/talktv/status/1557072775902289920.

57 See John Curtice, 'Could "culture wars" rekindle the Brexit divide?', What UK Thinks, 22 September 2022.

58 Cassilde Schwartz, Miranda Simon, David Hudson, and Jennifer van-Heerde-Hudson, 'A populist paradox? How Brexit softened anti-immigrant attitudes', *British Journal of Political Science*, 51 (3), 2021, pp. 1160–80.

59 See, for example, https://twitter.com/robfordmancs/status/1450031386191073283.

60 See John Burn-Murdoch, 'Britain and America's electoral geographies are broken', *Financial Times*, 28 October 2022, and, for more detail, James Blagden and Will Tanner *After the Fall: Where the Conservatives Went Wrong … and How They Can Win Again* (Onward, 24 October 2022). For polling, see https://yougov.co.uk/topics/politics/survey-results/daily/2022/11/01/5c45d/1 and, for focus groups, see https://twitter.com/jamesjohnson252/status/1588462874070257665. See also Michael Savage, 'Most Britons think country has lost control of its border since Brexit: Poll', *Observer*, 6 November 2022.

61 See, for example, Christopher Hope and Louisa Wells, 'New Ukip-style party could form to "nick" Tory votes over migrant crisis', *Daily Telegraph*, 4 November 2022.

62 Edmund Fawcett, *Conservatism: The Fight for a Tradition* (Princeton University

Press, 2020), pp. 345, 416. See also Noam Gidron and Daniel Ziblatt, 'Center-right political parties in advanced democracies', *Annual Review of Political Science*, 22, 2019, pp. 17–35 (p. 28).

63 On Brits' relatively sanguine and benign attitudes to the wealthy compared to those exhibited in some other countries, see Rainer Zitelmann, *The Rich in Public Opinion* (Cato Institute, 2020), Chapter 13. See also https://twitter .com/robfordmancs/status/1573275330562981889 and Philip Cowley, 'What voters already know about Rishi Sunak – and what they don't', *Times Red Box*, 4 November 2022.

64 Any list would include his insistence, detailed in earlier chapters, on opening up the economy too early and simultaneously failing to prevent billions of pounds' worth of fraud during the pandemic. For a selection of some of his more amusing (but possibly just as damaging because eminently memeable) gaffes, see Lisa O'Carroll, 'Coke, car trouble and class: Some awkward Rishi Sunak moments', *Guardian*, 25 October 2022.

65 See Andrew Gimson, *Boris Johnson: The Rise and Fall of a Troublemaker at Number Ten* (Simon & Schuster, 2022), p. 94. There must surely be some doubt now as to whether Johnson can ever make a comeback as leader – especially if the party takes the advice of the man who gave members the final say on the leadership in the first place and somehow manages to take it away again (as Michael Howard failed to do in 2005). See William Hague, 'Tory members must not pick next leader', *Times*, 1 November 2022.

66 On this tendency, see Anoosh Chakelian, 'Inside the BBC reckoning over its economic coverage', *New Statesman*, 1 November 2022.

67 Enoch Powell, '"I am a loner by nature"', *The Listener*, 28 May 1981.

Index

Illustrations are denoted by *italic* page numbers, tables by **bold** ones.